COMPUTERIZED ACCOUNTING WITH PEACHTREE COMPLETE ACCOUNTING
VERSION 6.0

Second Edition

Roger H. Hermanson
Georgia State University

Rosanne Walker
Kennesaw College

Linda Plunkett
College of Charleston

Deborah Turner
Georgia Institute of Technology

IRWIN
Burr Ridge, Illinois
Boston, Massachusetts
Sydney, Australia

Printed in the United States of America.

ISBN 0-256-11191-X

2 3 4 5 6 7 8 9 0 ML 0 9 8 7 6 5 4 3

PREFACE

This text is based on Version 6 of one of the most successful commercial microcomputer accounting packages now in use. Unlike similar textbooks, this one uses a real accounting software package—Peachtree Complete Accounting by Peachtree Software—not a simulation of one. Understanding the content of this text will enable you to use Peachtree Complete Accounting in a job situation. Since many of the features of the package are similar to other commercial microcomputer accounting packages, you should be able to use other accounting packages in a job situation with a minimum of additional training.

Before using this text it would be helpful to have taken at least one course in accounting principles.

The organization of the text is as follows. Chapter 1 provides an introduction to Peachtree Complete Accounting and gives helpful information for working with the package. Chapters 2 through 13 cover seven different modules included in the package. These seven modules are: General Ledger, Accounts Payable, Accounts Receivable and Invoicing (covered together), Inventory, Payroll, and Fixed Assets. Chapter 14 covers financial statement analysis (including the Statement of Cash Flows). There are four appendices at the end of the text that give an overview of the Job Cost, Purchase Order, and Data Query modules and describe certain DOS fundamentals that may be helpful in working with Peachtree Complete Accounting. Throughout the text you will work with an imaginary company, W. D. Peachtree, to learn the features of Peachtree Complete Accounting.

Each module presented is covered in two chapters. The first chapter on a given module is an overview of that module and is in programmed learning format. (Chapters 1 and 14 also use this programmed learning format.) The programmed learning format means that you are periodically asked questions as you read the chapter. You are then referred to the correct answers. Thus, you receive immediate re-enforcement of correct understanding and immediate correction of misinterpretations. This method of learning has been used successfully for many years in various situations to enhance the effectiveness of learning. At the end of each overview chapter, there are sample reports for that module. These are examples of the reports that you will learn to produce in the chapters following the overview chapters. Finally, there are questions and matching problems that your instructor may want to assign and have you turn in for credit.

The second chapter on each module is a practice chapter. When working through a practice chapter, you work at the computer and follow the simple, clear instructions provided. As you work through the chapter, the computer will print out various reports. Your instructor will probably ask you to turn these in so that your successful progress through the chapter can be confirmed. System error messages could be encountered when working the practice chapters. You probably will not encounter any of these system errors, but if you do please see your instructor and do not try to correct the error yourself. At the end of each of the practice chapters there is a problem that your instructor may ask you to work and turn in for credit. Before working this problem, you will be asked to restore your data files for that module back to the condition they were in before you worked through the chapter. This procedure is easy to perform and is described in detail in Chapter 1.

Any suggestions for improvement in the text should be sent to one of the authors in care of:

> Richard D. Irwin, Inc.
> 1818 Ridge Road
> Homewood, IL 60430

We would like to thank the following people for the comments which helped us in the preparation of this textbook: Betty Habiger and her class at New Mexico State University at Grants, Johnnie Bellamy at Eastfield College, and all of the instructors who took the time to respond to our Peachtree survey.

We thank you for using our text. We believe that the use of this text will substantially increase your microcomputer skills in working with commercial accounting packages.

> Roger H. Hermanson
> Rosanne G. Walker

COMPUTERIZED ACCOUNTING WITH PEACHTREE COMPLETE ACCOUNTING:
VERSION 6.0

TABLE OF CONTENTS

Page

Chapter 1

INTRODUCTION TO PEACHTREE COMPLETE ACCOUNTING

Learning Objectives:

After studying this chapter, you should be able to:

1. Identify and describe the modules included in Peachtree Complete Accounting (PCA).

2. Describe how to operate PCA including—beginning and ending a session, using menus and starting programs, entering information, confirming entries, ending a screen, ending a program, and getting help.

3. Describe the function of control reports.

4. Discuss the importance of backing up data files.

5. Describe the meaning of different generations of files.

Chapter 1

Introduction To Peachtree Complete Accounting

Frame 1[1]

Peachtree Software has been a pioneer in the development of microcomputer accounting software. Since 1978, the company has constantly explored new ways to do a better job of computerizing the accounting function in businesses. Its commitment is to always provide powerful software that is easy to use.

Peachtree Complete Accounting (PCA) is the sixth generation of Peachtree Software's accounting programs for personal computers. Many enhancements have been included in this release.

Peachtree Complete Accounting represents much effort and creativity on the part of many people. Contributions made by those using the product are the most important. Product and enhancement ideas have come from many customers using the products in their businesses. Now this product is being introduced to students at colleges, universities, and other institutions of higher learning.

We welcome and encourage your comments and suggestions too. Tell us what you would like to see in future versions—what is important, what is helpful, and what is not. We appreciate your input. Send your suggestions regarding PCA to:

Peachtree Software, Inc.
1505 Pavilion Place
Norcross, Georgia 30093

Attn: Peachtree Complete Product Manager

Peachtree Complete Accounting Description & Features

This section gives a general description of Peachtree Complete Accounting and tells about some of the most useful features.

It takes a lot of effort to maintain accurate business records. Even if there is only one owner-employee, it is sometimes difficult to administer all of the paperwork in a timely manner. Peachtree Complete Accounting helps save time and gives a detailed picture of a company's financial position.

The ten modules work together to protect financial business information and organize it in an understandable form. The ten modules include:

- General Ledger
- Accounts Payable
- Accounts Receivable
- Invoicing
- Payroll

- Purchase Order
- Inventory
- Job Cost
- Fixed Assets
- Data Query

The purchase order, job cost, and data query modules are described in the Appendix at the end of the text.

Flexibility is the key to Peachtree Complete Accounting. All, or only a few, of the modules can be installed.

Each module performs as a personal accounting staff: it accepts the information and stores it in the proper areas. When the information is needed, Peachtree Complete Accounting provides the data in the form of reports or screen displays.

Because the modules work together, many operations that often require two or more steps may be accomplished with only one Peachtree Complete operation. For instance, when a customer invoice is posted, Peachtree Complete Accounting automatically:

- Updates the sale to the customer's account.

- Takes the items sold out of inventory.

- Creates General Ledger postings, including the sale and cost of sale as well as tax, freight, etc.

- Updates year-to-date sales of the item and year-to-date purchases by the customer.

General Features

Peachtree Complete Accounting is an excellent accounting system for any growing business. The modular format enables the installation of only the functions needed. And there is virtually no limit to the growth of a business when using PCA. It is easy to set up multiple departments or even multiple companies that can be consolidated through the General Ledger.

Peachtree Complete Accounting secures financial data with two levels of password security.

This most recent version of Peachtree Complete Accounting is simpler than ever to use. The new configuration allows loading the program much faster than before.

Peachtree Complete Accounting's error messages are written in plain English and accompanied by suggestions for correcting the problem. You will probably not encounter any of the serious error messages, called system errors but, if you do, see your instructor.

Use the pop-up menus to move through the program. The new Table Lookup feature gives you access to information stored in any module that interfaces with the program you are currently working in.

Peachtree Complete Accounting can generate over 450 financial reports, including invoices, statements, mailing labels and 1099 forms, as well as automatically calculate federal and state payroll taxes. The print utilities have been enhanced so that each computer can support up to four printers. You can print entire reports or select a range of fields. Reports can be sent to the screen, a specified printer, or saved on disk to print at your convenience.

Question Frame 1[1]

Indicate whether each of the following statements is true or false by writing "T" or "F" in the space provided.

_____ I.   There are ten modules in the Peachtree Complete Accounting package.

_____ 2.   The modules only work independently of one another, so data entered in one module cannot affect data in another module.

_____ 3.   Peachtree Complete Accounting should only be used for very small businesses that are going to remain small.

_____ 4.   Peachtree Complete Accounting can generate many reports and calculate several taxes.

Now turn to Answer Frame 1[1] on page 1-6 to check your answers.

Answer Frame 1[1]

1. True. The modules include General Ledger, Accounts Payable, Accounts Receivable, Invoicing, Payroll, Purchase Order, Inventory, Job Cost, Fixed Assets, and Data Query. Seven of the ten modules are covered in this text.

2. False. Many of the modules can be linked so that data entered into one of them affects data in another module. For instance, posting a company's invoice can increase the balance in the customer's accounts receivable account, take the items out of inventory, create General Ledger postings, and update year-to-date sales of the item and purchases by the customer.

3. False. Peachtree Complete Accounting can be used for growing businesses. There is virtually no limit to the growth of the businesses—multiple departments and even multiple companies can be accommodated.

4. True. Peachtree Complete Accounting can generate over 450 financial reports and can calculate various federal and state taxes.

If you missed any of the above, reread Frame 1[1] before continuing.

Frame 2[1]

Module Features

A brief description of each module included in PCA is given in this Section. General Ledger, Accounts Payable, Accounts Receivable, Inventory, Payroll, and Fixed Assets each has a separate chapter describing its functions thoroughly.

General Ledger should be activated first because this forces you to set up your complete chart of accounts (title, posting, subtotal and total accounts) since these account numbers are used by other modules. Normally when another module is activated, you are asked for General Ledger account numbers.

General Ledger

General Ledger (G/L) is the heart of the Peachtree Complete Accounting system. The General Ledger module records current financial transactions through journal entries and through the information it receives from other modules.

Through G/L, financial statements for the current period or previous periods can be printed. Peachtree Complete Accounting allows adjustments to previous periods and a printout of corrected financial statements reflecting the change. It is simple to compare current figures to budget or to year-to-date totals.

This version of Peachtree Complete makes it easy to add new department accounts based on an existing department. Combined financial statements for up to 32 companies can be produced at one time. G/L may be used alone or integrated with the rest of the Peachtree Complete Accounting system. When installed (linked) with the other modules, G/L is updated by Accounts Receivable, Invoicing (via Accounts Receivable), Inventory (via Invoicing and Accounts Receivable), Accounts Payable, Payroll, and Fixed Assets.

Accounts Payable

Accounts Payable (A/P) keeps track of the money owed to vendors. It helps decide which invoices to pay and then prints the checks. It tracks year-to-date purchases from each supplier, as well as year-to-date payments.

Accounts Payable produces invoices and payment transactions for transfer to General Ledger or for posting to a manual General Ledger. Vendors may be added on the fly without leaving the A/P program. This means that a new vendor can be added during processing. A vendor can be set up as a temporary vendor, which allows automatic deletion of vendors, if its account shows no activity and no balance at the end of a period.

Accounts Receivable and Invoicing

Accounts Receivable (A/R) provides information about the money customers owe. This is where all customer activity is recorded. Accounts Receivable will provide detailed information about customers' current balances and will prepare statements. Year-to-date sales by customer can be tracked, and sales tax reports can be generated with A/R. The program will also assess and post finance charges to customers' accounts.

A customer can be set up as a temporary customer. As with temporary vendors, the account will automatically be removed at the end of the period if it shows no activity and no balance.

Accounts Receivable creates G/L journal entries for its own activities and for the activities of the Invoicing module, sending postings summarizing these accounts to G/L. New customer accounts may be added during processing without leaving the A/R program.

A/R can be used with Invoicing and Inventory for simple, one-step billing. Inventory control and receivables management are no problem, since A/R works with Invoicing to process information about customer sales and returns. A/R and Invoicing also interact with Job Cost, sending the total billings and payments for each job tracked to the Job Cost module.

Invoicing must be used in conjunction with Accounts Receivable, and can be installed only after the A/R module is installed. Once in place, Invoicing permits sales and returns to be entered and invoices and credit memos to be printed. When using Invoicing with A/R and Inventory, billing, inventory control, and receivables management can be completed with only one step: entering the invoice.

Peachtree's batch entry of invoices lets invoices be edited prior to printing and posting them. And products and services can be included on the same invoice.

Invoicing updates A/R files with customer sales and returns, as well as provides tax information for sales tax reporting. G/L is updated through Accounts Receivable with sales and cost of sales information, and a record of items sold is sent to Inventory.

Purchase Order

The Purchase Order module is a new addition to Peachtree Complete. It must be installed after Accounts Payable has been installed. Purchase Order acts as a bridge between Inventory and Accounts Payable, allowing the entering of purchase orders, item receipts, and vendor invoices.

When receipts are entered, the quantity of items ordered and those received can be compared against new receipts. When entering vendor invoices, it is easy to reconcile the invoice with the quantities received and the price at which the items were ordered. Purchase Order automatically updates Accounts Payable files, which in turn update G/L.

This module is described in Appendix B at the end of the text.

Payroll

Payroll calculates each employee's pay and deductions and then prints payroll checks and tax reports. All types of employee wages can be calculated including hourly, salary, commission, and draw-against-commission.

Current tax laws have been incorporated into the program for federal and state taxes and deductions, including 401K plans and garnishments. The tax tables can be modified with updates published regularly by Peachtree Software. Printed and magnetic media W-2s are generated automatically.

Gross pay can be distributed to as many as ten G/L accounts. Payroll keeps updated records for each employee to provide current quarter-to-date and year-to-date figures. The Payroll module can be utilized independently or used to update G/L files automatically.

Inventory

The Inventory Module is invaluable for keeping track of the products and services sold by the business. Inventory will track item receipts, sales, returns, and adjustments.

Peachtree Complete Accounting's Inventory Module supports five costing types (LIFO, FIFO, Specific Unit, Standard Cost, and Average Cost). Should the product need tracking after the sale for warranty or legal reasons, that option is available with Peachtree Complete Accounting.

Products and services are stored in the same file in this inventory program. This enables the combination of products and services on the same invoice. It also allows the entering of extended descriptions for all inventory items.

Inventory also allows the set up of assembly items. An assembly is a group of products assembled together into an item. Assemblies are not covered in this text.

Job Cost

Job Cost monitors the cost and profitability of the projects a company performs. Job Cost allows estimates of costs to be prepared and comparisons of actual expenses to estimated expenses. Materials, equipment, labor, subcontractors, and other miscellaneous expenses can be tracked using this module. This module is described in Appendix A at the end of the text.

Fixed Assets

Fixed Assets calculates and records tax and accounting data for property, plant, and equipment, including depreciation expenses. It keeps track of the basis and depreciation of assets, investment tax credits (when applicable), and cost and depreciation information.

This module is updated with the latest tax law information and supports mid-quarter convention as well as a short taxable year. Up to three different sets of books can be maintained with individual information for an unlimited number of assets. Fixed Assets maintains tax books for filing federal tax returns, financial books with information to be transferred to General Ledger, as well as optional books for whatever purpose a business may have (such as state taxes).

Peachtree Data Query (PDQ)

Peachtree Data Query (PDQ) generates custom reports and graphs. Using PDQ, you can view, print, and analyze the data you enter in Peachtree Complete Accounting every day. PDQ is different in purpose and concept from the other modules of PCA; it is a tool you can use to supplement the reporting capabilities of each of the other modules.

The following chart shows the relationship between individual modules. (PDQ is not shown, because it can draw information from all the other modules.)

MODULE NAME	SENDS TO	RECEIVES DIRECTLY FROM
General Ledger	No other modules	Accounts Payable Accounts Receivable Payroll Fixed Assets
Accounts Payable	General Ledger Job Cost	Puchase Order
Accounts Receivable	General Ledger Job Cost	Invoicing
Invoicing	Accounts Receivable Inventory	No other modules
Payroll	General Ledger	Job Cost
Inventory	No other modules	Invoicing Purchase Order
Fixed Assets	General Ledger	No other modules
Job Cost	Payroll	Accounts Payable Accounts Receivable Invoicing
Purchase Order	Accounts Payable Inventory	No other modules

Question Frame 2[1]

Indicate whether each of the following statements is true or false by writing "T" or "F" in the space provided.

_____ 1. All of the other modules can be linked to General Ledger.

_____ 2. Accounts Receivable creates journal entries for its own activities and for one other module and sends these entries to General Ledger.

_____ 3. Both the Accounts Payable and Payroll modules print checks.

_____ 4. The Inventory module permits the use of several costing types.

_____ 5. Fixed Assets maintains information only for accounting purposes.

Now turn to Answer Frame 2[1] on Page 1-13 to check your answers.

Frame 3[1]

Operating PCA

This section gives you general information about using PCA; it can later be used as a reference. If you are unfamiliar with using DOS, you should study the appendix on DOS at the end of the text before reading this section. (Note to Student: This next section assumes that PCA has already been installed on the system you are using. Depending on the way your instructor has installed PCA, the initial start instructions may vary slightly. You should follow your instructor's steps.)

Beginning and Ending PCA

Follow these steps to start Peachtree Complete Accounting:

❖ Make the directory with your PCA programs the current directory.

Your programs are in a directory named PCA, so at the DOS prompt type:

CD\PCA and press [ENTER].

This directory was named when the PCA programs were installed on the hard disk of the computer you are using.

❖ Next, type PEACH and press [ENTER].

This is how you start PCA.

The first PCA screen appears, asking for the date. Notice that PCA provides a date. This is the date you entered when you started your computer, or it is the date stored in your computer's battery-powered calendar.

❖ You can change the date if you like. After you do this, press [ENTER]. Or, just press [ENTER] without changing it.

If you type a new date, leave out slashes and dashes—just type the numbers. For instance, type September 4, 1993 as **090493**.

To erase the date (before you start entering a new one) press [F9].

❖ Enter the two-character company ID -"WD"- for W. D. Peachtree. Or, press [F2] to view a pop up box listing company IDs and names, and then select the company from that box.

After you enter the company ID, PCA displays the PCA Main Menu. This is the menu from which you select a module to work with. You will also see the date on the left side of the screen on the second line:

```
================================================================
  MENU 6.00                 Peachtree Complete Accounting          COMPANY ID: WD
  09/04/92                   W. D. Peachtree & Company
================================================================
  ====================== PCA Main Menu ======================
    G  -  General Ledger
    A  -  Accounts Payable
    R  -  Accounts Receivable
    S  -  Invoicing
    I  -  Inventory
    P  -  Payroll
    F  -  Fixed Assets
    J  -  Job Cost
    O  -  Purchase Order
    U  -  Utilities
    Q  -  Peachtree Data Query


  =================================================

  F1-Help                                                    C N
```

You are ready to start.

<u>Ending PCA</u>

To end a PCA session, follow these instructions from the PCA Main Menu:

❖ Press 🖭.

PCA displays the *COMPANY ID* prompt.

❖ Press 🖭 to end Peachtree Complete Accounting.

The DOS prompt appears.

Answer Frame 2[1]

1. False. General Ledger can only be linked with Accounts Receivable, Invoicing (via Accounts Receivable), Inventory (via Invoicing and Accounts Receivable), Accounts Payable, Payroll, and Fixed Assets. It cannot be linked with Purchase Order or Job Cost.

2. True. Accounts Receivable creates journal entries for its own activities and those of Invoicing and sends them to General Ledger.

3. True. Accounts Payable prints checks to be sent to suppliers, and Payroll prints payroll checks.

4. True. The costing types permitted include LIFO, FIFO, Specific Unit, Standard Cost, and Average Cost.

5. False. Information is also maintained for tax purposes.

If you missed any of the above, reread Frame 2[1] before continuing.

Question Frame 3[1]

Indicate whether each of the following statements is true or false by writing "T" or "F" in the space provided.

_____ 1. To start Peachtree Complete Accounting, you type CD\PCA and press [ENTER]. Then you type PEACH and press [ENTER].

_____ 2. When you enter a new date, you must type the slash marks between the month, day, and year.

_____ 3. The company ID you will use for W. D. Peachtree is WP.

_____ 4. If you are at the PCA Main Menu and you want to end the session, you press [ESC] and then [F10].

Now turn to Answer Frame 3[1] on page 1-14 to check your answers.

Answer Frame 3[1]

1. True. These two simple commands will start PCA.

2. False. You should not type the slash marks. The computer will automatically enter the slash marks between the month, day, and year.

3. False. The ID you will use for W. D. Peachtree is WD. After you enter the company ID, PCA displays the PCA Main Menu.

4. True. Pressing **[ESC]** moves you back in the program to the COMPANY ID prompt. Pressing **[F10]** returns you to DOS.

If you missed any of the above, reread Frame 3[1] before continuing.

Frame 4[1]

Using Menus and Starting Programs

Peachtree Complete Accounting Menus

A menu is a list of choices you have. These choices are programs or other menus. The only way you can use PCA's programs is through menus.

The menu system in PCA has up to three levels. The first level, the PCA Main Menu, lets you select which module you want to use. You can also choose Utilities or Peachtree Data Query (if it has been installed) from the menu.

After you select a PCA module, the main menu for that module is displayed. This menu lets you select the type of program you want to run. The program types are usually Maintenance, Processing, and Reports. If you select Utilities, this menu contains a list of utility programs provided with PCA. (You will be instructed on how to use some of the options in the utilities module at a later time.)

After you select the type of program you want to run, a menu listing all available programs for that type are displayed.

The following screen shows the PCA menu system for General Ledger Processing programs (for example):

```
MENU 6.00                    Peachtree Complete Accounting      COMPANY ID: WD
09/04/92                      W. D. Peachtree & Company          Generation #: 11
═══════════════════════════════════════════════════════════════════════════════

_____ PCA Main Menu _____

  G -  General Ledger
  A -  Accounts Payable
  R -  Accounts Rec       _____General Ledger Main Menu_____
  S -  Invoicing          M - Maintenance Programs
  I -  Inventory          P - Processing Programs
  P -  Payroll            R - Report Programs _____General Ledger Processing Menu_____
  F -  Fixed Assets                           Q -  Query Account Status
  J -  Job Cost                               E -  Enter Transactions
  O -  Purchase Order                         X -  Delete Transactions
  U -  Utilities                              Z -  Edit Repeating Transactions
  Q -  Peachtree Data Query                   J -  Consolidate Companies
                                              S -  Transfer Summary Journals
                                              C -  Close Current Period


  F1-Help                        Shft F10 - Home            C N
```

As Peachtree Complete Accounting displays the menus, it overlaps them across your screen. That way you can see each of the selections you have already made.

<u>How to Make Menu Selections</u>

There are two ways you can make a choice from a menu:

1. Type the first letter of your choice, or

2. Use the ⬆ key or ⬇ key to move the highlight to the selection you want and press ⏎ to choose it.

You can always move back to a previous menu by pressing the ⎋ key. You can use other keys to move around menus:

- ⬅ ➡ ⬆ and ⬇ all move the highlight in the direction indicated.

- End moves the highlight to the last choice on your screen.

- Home moves the highlight to the first choice on your screen.

<u>Short-Cut Codes</u>

When you are at the PCA Main Menu, you can select a program by typing three letters:

1. A letter that represents the module.

2. A letter that represents the type of program.

3. A letter that stands for the program you want to select.

We call the three letters that select any program its **shortcut code**. Shortcut codes are a way of quickly selecting programs. For instance, the shortcut code for General Ledger's **Enter Transactions** is "GPE". This stands for:

General Ledger
Processing Programs
Enter Transactions

When you use shortcut codes you do not *do* anything unusual. Rather, you just remember the three letters for the program and type them.

If you are already at the main menu for a module, type only the last two letters of a shortcut code.

As you are working through the modules covered in this text, we recommend that you stay with the 3-level menu system. This system helps guide you a little more and makes finding programs easier. Later in your career if you are using PCA in a job situation you may choose to use the short-cut codes.

Question Frame 4[1]

Indicate whether each of the following statements is true or false by writing "T" or "F" in the space provided.

_____ 1.   For each of the modules (excluding Utilities and Peachtree Data Query) there are three levels of menus.

_____ 2.   PCA partially overlaps the three layers of menus.

_____ 3.   When you want to move back to a previous menu, you press the ▣ key.

_____ 4.   The short-cut codes should be used by an inexperienced user of PCA.

Now turn to Answer Frame 4[1] on page 1-18 to check your answers.

Answer Frame 4[1]

1. True. The first level is the PCA Main Menu, which lets you select the module you want to use. The second menu lets you select the type of program you want to run—maintenance, processing, or reports. The third menu lists all available programs for that type.

2. True. That way you can see each of the selections you have already made.

3. False. To move back to a previous menu, you press the [ESC] key.

4. False. The three-level menu system should be used by an inexperienced user of PCA.

If you missed any of the above, reread Frame 4[1] before continuing.

Frame 5[1]

Entering Information in Peachtree Complete Accounting

Once you choose a program from a menu, you are ready to enter new information or change existing information. (Or, for report programs, you are ready to enter or select some information about the report. For instance, in Payroll you might select which employees to include.)

To make an entry on one of Peachtree Complete Accounting's screens, simply fill in the blanks or type over any existing information. Then press one of these keys:

- [ENTER], [TAB], or [↓] to move to the next entry on the screen.

- [ESC], [SHIFT][TAB], or [↑] to move to the previous entry.

PCA Checks Your Entries

PCA tells you when you type an entry that does not "make sense" to it, and lets you correct the entry. It checks the type of entry you make. For instance it does not let you enter letters in a number or date field.

PCA checks that the size and content of each entry is valid. It performs these verifications as you go from one field to another. For example, for the W. D. Peachtree information used in this text, PCA expects that the G/L account numbers are either 5 or 6 digits. If you type an account number that has too many digits, or not enough, PCA displays a box similar to the following:

```
MENU 6.00                          Peachtree Complete Accounting
09/04/92                                                             Batch  S27-002


GENERAL INFORMATION

      Company Name .................................. :  Sample Company
      Address Line 1 .................................. :
      Address Line 2 .................................. :
      Address Line 3 .................................. :
      G/L Account # Size. (5 or 6)............. :  7
      ─────────────────────────────────────────────────────────
         Invalid entry.  The General Ledger account number size must be 5 or 6.



      PRESS ▣ TO CONTINUE
      ─────────────────────────────────────────────────────────

                                                                             N
```

The information you enter into PCA is always one of three types:

- characters

- dates

- numbers or amounts

The rules for entering each of these and special keys you can use for them are slightly different.

<u>Defaults PCA Provides</u>

As you use PCA, you will notice that it provides entries for some of the information each screen needs. These PCA-provided entries are called defaults. You can use these entries or change them. PCA provides them only for your convenience.

Defaults let you do less typing and enter your information faster. Some defaults are set through the module options for a module, others are set based on a previous entry in the field.

<u>Entering Characters</u>

When you enter characters, you can enter any combination of letters, numbers, and special characters such as punctuation marks. Hint: Use all upper case characters for any key fields (Item #, Customer ID, Vendor ID, Employee Code, Sales Tax Code, etc.).

When you are making an entry in a character field, you can use these keys to help you out:

- Press ▣ to erase the contents of the field.

- Press ◁ and ▷ to move one character to the left or right.

- Press <kbd>Home</kbd> or <kbd>F3</kbd> to go to beginning of the field.

- Press <kbd>End</kbd> or <kbd>F4</kbd> to go to the end of the field.

- Press <kbd>Ins</kbd> to be able to insert new characters before or between existing ones. If you do not press <kbd>Ins</kbd>, characters that you type will replace existing characters. When you press <kbd>Ins</kbd>, PCA displays an "I" at the bottom of your screen. This tells you that characters you type will be inserted without replacing existing characters.

- Press <kbd>Ins</kbd> a second time to resume typing over (replacing) existing characters. When you press <kbd>Ins</kbd> the second time, PCA removes the "I" at the bottom of your screen. This tells you that characters you type will replace existing characters.

Entering Dates

PCA requires that you enter dates using **MMDDYY** form. For example, type **090493** for September 4, 1993. Always omit the slashes when you type the date. PCA displays the slashes automatically. If you are entering a day or month less than 10, add a zero in front of the number, as in the example above.

You can use these keys as you enter dates:

- <kbd>F3</kbd> to erase the date.

- <kbd>←</kbd> and <kbd>→</kbd> to move one character to the left or right.

- <kbd>Home</kbd> or <kbd>F3</kbd> to move to the beginning of a date.

- <kbd>End</kbd> or <kbd>F4</kbd> to move to the end of a date.

Entering Numbers

When you are asked to enter numbers in PCA, follow these general rules:

- Enter only digits 0 through 9. You cannot enter letters.

- Do not enter commas.

- Do not enter dollar signs.

- Money amounts and other numbers are handled the same.

There are two kinds of numbers that you can enter in PCA—whole numbers (those without decimal points), and numbers with decimal points. PCA will display the decimal point if it is needed in the information you enter.

When you are asked to enter whole numbers, just type in the amount and press .

When you are asked to enter a number that has a decimal point, PCA places the cursor to the left of the decimal point. To enter a whole number, just type the amount and press <kbd>ENTER</kbd>. For example, type 1599 for 1,599.00.

To make a required decimal entry, type the whole number, press "." (period or decimal point) to move the cursor to the right of the decimal point, then type the decimal amount and press ⊞. For example, to enter 1,750.01, type 1750, press "." to move the cursor to the right of the decimal point, type 01 and press ⊞.

The "." key can be used to move the cursor from one side of the decimal point to the other. This is useful when correcting a previously entered amount. For example, suppose you entered 152.26 in a field that should have been 152.25. To correct this, move the cursor to the field, press "." to move the cursor to the right of the decimal point, type 25 and press ⊞.

Unless you are instructed otherwise, numbers are entered in PCA as positive numbers. If you are asked to enter a negative number, type a minus (-) sign **before** entering the number.

The only special key available when entering numbers is ⊞. Press this key to erase the current entry and replace it with 0.

Entering Debits and Credits

In PCA, debits are entered as positive amounts ("pluses") and credits are entered as negative numbers ("minuses"). You will get used to this procedure very quickly.

Question Frame 5[1]

Indicate whether each of the following statements is true or false by writing "T" or "F" in the space provided.

_____ 1.   When entering entries on a PCA screen, you can move the cursor by using several different methods.

_____ 2.   You should be very careful to avoid mistakes in entering data because PCA automatically accepts whatever you enter without verifying that data.

_____ 3.   Some defaults result from options selected during setup, while other defaults are based on a previous entry you have entered on a screen.

_____ 4.   When entering dates or numbers you can only use numbers, but when you enter characters you can use combinations of numbers, letters, and special characters (such as punctuation marks).

_____ 5.   To enter a negative number you place the number in parentheses.

Now turn to Answer Frame 5[1] on page 1-22 to check your answers.

Answer Frame 5[1]

1. True. To move to the next entry on the screen you can press ⌨ or use the arrow keys. To return to the previous entry you can press ⌨ or use the arrow keys.

2. False. While it is always advisable to be careful, PCA tells you when some entries do not make sense. For instance, it will not let you enter letters in a number or date field.

3. True. And the purpose of defaults is to save you some typing effort. A default is the computer guessing what your most likely response will be as you enter information.

4. True. These are the rules for entering characters, dates, and numbers.

5. False. To enter a negative number you type a minus sign in front of the number.

If you missed any of the above, reread Frame 5[1] before continuing.

Frame 6[1]

Confirming Your Entries: The "Accept Y/N" Prompt

PCA usually asks you to confirm your entries before they become permanent, or before it acts on them. It asks you whether you want to *ACCEPT* the information you have entered or changed.

The *ACCEPT* prompt gives you the chance to review the information you just entered. You can answer Y if you are satisfied with the information and want to accept it. Or, you can answer N if you want to make changes to what you entered. PCA then lets you make the changes as you want.

PCA also uses the *ACCEPT Y/N* prompt when you are looking at existing information, such as a customer record. When PCA displays the customer you ask for, it also says *ACCEPT Y/N*. Answer Y and press ⌨ to accept the customer information as it stands. Answer N and press ⌨ if you want to change it.

Multiple Screen Items

Some of PCA's programs use two or more screens for an item. In those cases, when you say Y at the ACCEPT Y/N prompt, you will see the next screen for the item.

Make entries on the second screen exactly as you did on the first. There are only two differences between the first screen and subsequent screens:

1. When you are at the *ACCEPT Y/N* prompt of subsequent screens, you can press ⌨ to return to the previous screen.

2. If you press ⌨ to undo changes on a subsequent screen, PCA undoes the changes you have made to *all* screens for the item.

<u>Undoing Entries or Changes</u>

PCA provides a means to undo the changes you've made on a screen. Whenever you see [F8]—Undo highlighted at the bottom of your screen, you can press the ⌨ key to do that.

This is convenient if you notice that you changed something you did not intend to change, or if you get part of the way through an entry and find you need more information.

Ending A Screen

Whenever you see [F10]—Done highlighted at the bottom of your screen, you can press ⌨ to end a screen. Often, you will get a chance to confirm the information on the screen, and decide whether to accept it.

Once you accept the information, PCA lets you add or change more information, or end the program.

In most cases, PCA displays an *ACCEPT (Y/N)* prompt to allow you to verify your entries.

Ending A Program

If you see [F10]—Menu highlighted at the bottom of your screen, you can press ⌨ to tell PCA that you are done with the program you are using. You'll return to the menu from which you selected the program.

The input screen is <u>not saved</u> to the hard disk until you press ⌨ to exit back to the menu (one of three levels of menus). To avoid damaged data files from power outages, etc., use ⌨ to exit to the menu periodically if entering a large volume of transactions.

If you see Shift [F10]—Home highlighted, you can press ⌨ and ⌨ together to return directly to the PCA Main Menu.

Getting Help with Your Entries

Peachtree Complete Accounting gives you two different types of help with your entries.

<u>[F1] - Help</u>

Press the 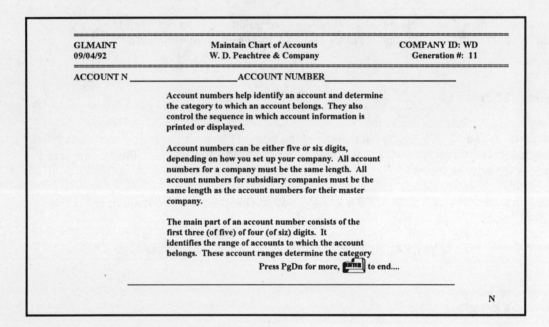 key whenever you want information about a choice you have or a piece of information you must enter. This feature lets you get information about PCA practically whenever you want it. It is particularly helpful when you want to know just what is allowed for a particular entry, or for what purposes PCA uses the entry.

This help is available whenever you see [F1]—Help highlighted at the bottom of your screen. When you press [F1] you will see a pop up box like this:

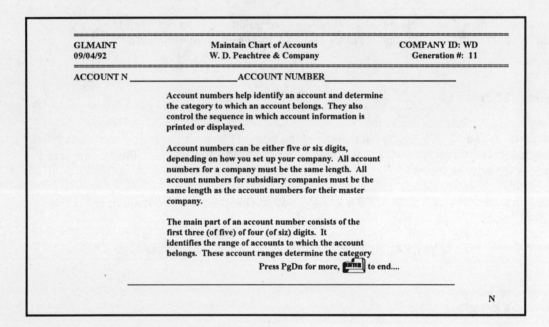

GLMAINT   Maintain Chart of Accounts   COMPANY ID: WD
09/04/92   W. D. Peachtree & Company   Generation #: 11

ACCOUNT N _____ACCOUNT NUMBER_____

Account numbers help identify an account and determine the category to which an account belongs. They also control the sequence in which account information is printed or displayed.

Account numbers can be either five or six digits, depending on how you set up your company. All account numbers for a company must be the same length. All account numbers for subsidiary companies must be the same length as the account numbers for their master company.

The main part of an account number consists of the first three (of five) of four (of siz) digits. It identifies the range of accounts to which the account belongs. These account ranges determine the category

Press PgDn for more, [ENTER] to end....

N

Some help messages have two (or more) screens. If there is more help than can be displayed in one box, you will see the words *PgDn for More*, [ENTER] *to end* at the bottom of the help box. Press [PG↓] to view additional information.

End help by pressing [ENTER].

<u>[F2] - Lookup</u>

Table lookups are a second kind of help. They show you a list of choices from which you can pick the entry you want. For instance, in Accounts Receivable's Enter Transactions, you can use [F2] to see a list of customers you might select:

```
============================================================
ARPROC1                    Enter Transactions          COMPANY ID: WD
09/04/92              W. D. Peachtree & Company         Generation #:  11
============================================================

Customer ID.:              _____SELECT CUSTOMER ID_____

                    ANDERA  -  Anita S. Anderson
                    ANDREC  -  Christine Andrews
                    CANNOP  -  Paul P. Cannon
                    COOPEG  -  Gloria S. Cooper
                    DUNCAF  -  Mrs. Fremont Duncan
                    DURAND  -  Dorothy Durand
                    FIELDJ  -  Jonathan S. Fields
                    GRAYC   -  Charles A. Gray
                    HENDEK  -  Kathy Henderson
                    HOLLOJ  -  James R. Holloway
                    JOHNSM  -  Michael H. Johnson
                    JONESE  -  Elizabeth A. Jones
         _____

                                                              N
```

Notice that the customers appear in order. They are arranged by Customer ID, beginning with the first customer.

Every module provides table lookups for you. You can look up things such as employees, customers, vendors, inventory items, and G/L account numbers. You can do a table lookup whenever you see [F2]—Lookup at the bottom of your screen.

Table lookup lets you find an item quickly. It shows you a name or description that goes along with the item so you can be sure you are selecting the right item. Table lookup also avoids your having to type long codes.

Once you press ⊞, these keys help you move around the pop up box containing your choices:

- ⬅⬇⬆ and ➡ move you to the next item in the direction you indicate.

- [Home] and [End] move you to first or last item displayed.

- ⊞ and ⊞ work when there are more choices than can be displayed in one box. They display the next or previous box of choices.

- ⊞ and ⊞ pressed together move you to the very first item in the list of choices.

Once you highlight the item you want to choose, press ⊞ to select it. If you want to erase the table lookup box without making a selection, press ⊞.

Focusing the Lookup

You can limit the items shown in a table lookup. If you press ⌨F2 at a blank field, the lookup begins with the first available choice. In the previous example, it began with the first customer. If there are many customers, you might have to look at many screens of customers to find the right one.

PCA allows you to enter as much of an entry as you know, and then ask it to do a lookup based on what you have typed. For example, suppose you know that the customer you want has an ID beginning with the letter "L". You can type **L** and then press ⌨F2. PCA starts the lookup with customers whose ID begins with L. Customers whose ID begins A through K are not included.

Using lookups this way is a lot faster. You can type as much of an entry as you know. In the above example, if you know that the customer you want has an ID beginning with "LI", you can type **LI** and then press ⌨F2. You will then see customers beginning LI at the top of your list.

Using Enter for a Lookup

You can press ⌨ENTER instead of ⌨F2 whenever the field on which you're doing a lookup is blank. PCA then begins a full table lookup for you. Some people find the ⌨ENTER key more convenient than ⌨F2.

Question Frame 6[1]

Indicate whether each of the following statements is true or false by writing "T" or "F" in the space provided.

_____ 1.   The purpose of the "Accept Y/N" prompt is to let you confirm your data entries before they become permanent.

_____ 2.   If you enter information on a screen and then want to eliminate that information and start the screen over, there is an easy way to accomplish this result.

_____ 3.   In working with screens in PCA you have to memorize what each function key will accomplish.

_____ 4.   PCA provides two ways of getting help.

Now turn to Answer Frame 6[1] on page 1-28 to check your answers.

Frame 7[1]

PCA's Audit Trails

This section discusses Peachtree Complete Accounting's control reports. These are reports that log changes and additions you make to your data. They are your audit trail—the reports that let you trace just what changes (or additions or deletions) you made and when you made each one.

It is important to keep track of what you enter into Peachtree Complete Accounting, and what you change. These reports help you do just that. They can be of vital importance in tracking errors, in tracing where various figures come from, and whenever you want to reconstruct what you did.

Control reports are different from PCA's other reports in several ways:

- You can not print them "on demand"—they print *as* you make changes. Typically, as you make each change, a line or lines prints on the report. You can print other reports whenever you like.

- You can not select them from a menu, as you can select other reports. Programs that produce control reports do so automatically as you enter or change information. You can set each module so that control reports are optional or required.

- You can not view control reports on your screen, as you can other reports. You must make permanent copies, either by printing them on paper or by printing them as disk files.

Each module has a module option called Force Control Reports. Y should always be chosen for this option, so PCA always prints your control reports. (NOTE: If you are working in a computer lab where several terminals are linked to a printer, you will have to save your reports on a disk file and print them later. Your instructor will give you the directions you need to do this.)

At the beginning of each program that can produce a control report, you will see the following prompt:

- Since Y has been selected as the default option to the Force Control Reports option, PCA displays the following message:

SET PAPER TO TOP OF FORM - PRESS 'ENTER' TO CONTINUE

Check that your printer is ready to print and press [ENTER]. (If you are working in a networked lab, you will follow a different procedure.)

Control reports are extremely important to accountants. They serve as audit trails and should be kept in a file according to the accountant's instructions. Your instructor is likely to ask you to turn in a copy of your control reports for each of the practice chapters in this text.

Answer Frame 6[1]

I.   True. And if the data are correct, you answer Y and press ▣. If they need to be corrected, you answer N and press ▣. Then you proceed to make the corrections.

2.   True. All you need to do to undo information already entered on a screen is to press ▣.

3.   False. The function keys that can be used at that point and what they will do are highlighted at the bottom of the screen.

4.   True. The ▣ key will provide information about a choice you have or a piece of information you must enter. The ▣ key will display a lookup table from which you can pick the entry you want. Whenever the field on which you are doing a lookup is blank, you can press ▣ and a full lookup table is provided.

If you missed any of the above, reread Frame 6[1] before continuing.

Frame 7[1] (Continued)

Backing Up Your Data Files

One of the most important responsibilities in record-keeping is safeguarding the information you enter. This section discusses how Peachtree Complete Accounting helps you safeguard your data: backups.

To backup means to make copies of your data files. Then, if something happens to your computer, to your hard disk, or even just to a single file, all the information it contains can be recovered from your backup copy. As you work through the practice chapters in this text, making backups of your data files is important. This procedure enables you to start where you left off if you take a break before finishing a module and someone else uses the computer you were using. You can restore the data files to the condition they were when you quit so you will not have to start at the beginning again.

Making backups is important for another reason. It is like buying insurance. If you expend a little time and energy on a regular basis, your backups are there when you need them. Consider what would happen if the power went out in the middle of updating your General Ledger. (Please don't think this cannot happen to you—it happens to *every* computer user at some time.)

When you are using most software packages, backups are something you must take care of yourself. You must learn the DOS BACKUP command, format a diskette or diskettes, figure out what files to backup, and find where they are. Because of this, many people fail to backup their information. All of their records—Payroll, General Ledger, Accounts Receivable, etc.,—could be destroyed through damage to their hard disk. All they would have left is reports, from which to re-enter all of their data. We know that computer technology is very reliable today, but we also know that computers do break down, and disk drives do get damaged.

Because of this, a backup utility has been included with PCA. It lets you quickly and easily backup your data from the Utilities Menu without leaving PCA.

When You Should Back Up

When you should backup your data files depends on how much information you have entered since your last backup. It does not depend on the time of day or day of the week.

Any time you are wondering whether to backup, consider whether it would take longer to make the backup or to re-enter everything you have entered since your last backup. If it would take longer to re-enter information, then backup.

You should always make sure you have a recent backup *before* you run programs that have the potential to change much information very quickly. If you do not have a very recent backup, make one before running these programs.

How Many Sets of Backup Diskettes Should You Keep?

We recommend that you keep enough backup sets so that you have backup information from at least the last three sessions. In order to have three sets of consecutive information, start by keeping three sets of backup diskettes the first time you backup your information. The second time, use one of these initial sets to backup that session's information. The third time, use another of these initial sets to backup that session's information. The remaining set becomes your oldest backup by default. The fourth session, use the set with the oldest information on it for that session's backup. Keep following this pattern and you will always have three consecutive sets of backup information.

In addition to these intermediate backups, you should prepare permanent backups. These permanent backups are the ones you do before you close a period. You should retain these backups for at least 12 months.

Interrelated Files

When you backup a module that is interrelated with other modules, all interrelated modules must also be backed up. For example, when you backup prior to "Post Invoices" in Invoicing, you need to also backup Accounts Receivable and Inventory, since all three modules have been updated. No longer when you select "Invoicing" to backup, are Accounts Receivable and Inventory automatically backed up. The same is true with "Purchase Order," which formerly also backed up Accounts Payable and Inventory.

Backup/Restore Data Files

Introduction

This program lets you backup the data files for any module you have installed.

It also lets you restore backup files from diskette to your hard drive.

Backup

If you need to interrupt your work before any session is completed, these backups can be used to restore your data files at the beginning of your next session. The backups are also important in the event of a system failure.

An example of when you may want to use this program is to make backups of the original W. D. Peachtree data files before you begin working this text. Then you will be able to restore the data files to their original condition at any time you need to. Normally, you will reset your data files by reloading the sample data. Both the reloading procedures and the restore function are described later in this section.

If your data files should become damaged, use this program to copy a good set of files from your last backup.

Before You Start

You can complete the backup process faster if you have enough formatted disks on hand before you start your backup. However, the program will allow you to format disks during the backup program.

All the files already on the backup diskette are erased if you go ahead with your backup. Because of this, you must use a separate backup diskette or set of diskettes, for each module.

Running the Program

After you select the program from the Utilities Menu, you must select whether you want to backup or restore data files, and then select a specific module or all modules or system files.

Formatting Disks During Backup

Your data files will be backed up to the drive specified when the program was installed. When the drive used for backup was chosen, you specify the size (density) of the disk that you use (360K, 1.2MB, etc.).

If you run out of formatted disks during the backup, you can format more disks without leaving the backup program. Simply put the unformatted disk in your drive then follow the instructions that appear on the screen.

If Peachtree Complete Accounting detects that the diskette you are using is not formatted, the following message displays:

General Failure Reading drive A
(F)ormat disk, (R)etry, (A)bort?

To format the disk, type **F** [ENTER].

When the format process is finished, the backup of your data files begins. If you want to interrupt the backup -- without saving any data onto your backup disk -- press [CTRL] and [C] at the same time. Then follow the instructions on your screen.

Peachtree Complete Accounting lists the files it backs up as it copies each one to your diskette.

If more diskettes are needed for the backup, Peachtree Complete Accounting asks for them.

Note: You cannot format a disk that is a different density than the type you set up in your company file. If you do, an error message will be displayed and you must insert another disk of the correct density.

Backing Up to a Different Disk

You can choose to backup to a disk drive other than the one originally specified when the program was installed. When the prompt asking you which drive you want to use for your backup is displayed, enter the letter of the drive you want to use. You must also specify the size (density) of the disk that you will use for the backup. A box will be displayed listing the valid sizes for the drive you entered.

After You Are Done

After you backup your files, label the diskette with the date, module name, and generation number. Always use a felt-tipped pen to write on floppy diskette labels.

In business, backup diskettes should be kept in a fireproof cabinet or safe. In the event of a disaster that ruins an office and the computer(s), the company will have its backups.

You will need to make a backup of all W. D. Peachtree data files <u>now</u> so that you can restore the data files to their original condition before working on a module in a practice chapter or problem. (Because of the integration among the modules, you must backup and restore <u>all</u> modules.) Here are the steps to do this:

BACKUP ALL MODULES

❖ From the PCA Main Menu, select "Utilities."

❖ From the Utilities Menu, select "Backup/Restore Data Files."

❖ Under Program Options, select "Backup Data Files."

❖ Under Backup Options, select "Backup All Module Files."

<u>Restore</u>

It is extremely important that you begin each module and each problem with the sample data for W. D. Peachtree in its original condition. Here are the steps to do this:

RESTORE ALL MODULES

❖ Obtain the original backup disk of W. D. Peachtree in its original condition.

❖ From the PCA Main Menu, select "Utilities."

❖ From the Utilities Menu, select "Backup/Restore Data Files."

❖ Under Program Options, select "Restore Data Files."

❖ Under Restore Options, select "Restore All Module Files."

Because of the integration among the modules you must restore <u>all</u> modules even if you only wish to work with one of them.

You <u>must</u> restore all data files to their original condition before working on a module in a practice chapter or a problem. You will be warned about restoring data files to their original condition through-out the text.

Peachtree Complete Accounting's Generations

Most of PCA's modules create a complete copy of their data files at specific times during the processing cycle. For most modules, the copy occurs when you run **Close Current Period**. Both the old files and the new copies remain on your hard disk. The old are useful if you need to print reports from a previous period or to use that period's information for other purposes. We call each of these sets of files a *generation* or a *data file generation.*

After a module creates a new set of files, it uses the new files until it creates yet another set of files. We call the set of files that you are using at any time the *current generation*. PCA stores the old set of files on your disk but never uses them unless you specifically tell it to do so.

Generation Numbers

Each of the files that makes up a generation has a number as part of each file name. This number is the **generation number**.

Whenever you use a module that has generations, it distinguishes between the sets of generations on your disk by the generation number.

Since both the current generation and one or more old generations remain on your disk, each module can distinguish between them only by the generation number in each file's name.

Manual Log

You should keep a manual log showing the generation number, module name, fiscal period (month)-ending date, and whether a transfer file was brought into General Ledger. This log is necessary if you are going to write any data query reports against older generations or for audits because the generation number increments to 99, and it needs to be identified to a period-ending date. Also, the generation number could be different for each module, especially Payroll -- which increments generation numbers for quarter-end and year-end closings. The transfer file column is handy so you will know if you have brought the summary journals in from Accounts Payable, Accounts Receivable, Payroll, and Fixed Assets. You cannot bring in these summaries more than once because PCA prevents this from occurring.

Question Frame 7[1]

Indicate whether each of the following statements is true or false by writing "T" or "F" in the space provided.

_____ 1. Control reports can only be printed "on demand," they can be selected from a menu, and they can be viewed on the screen.

_____ 2. The backup/restore program can be used to backup your data files at any time.

_____ 3. The restore option can be used to bring your data files for a module to any point at which you have prepared backup diskettes.

_____ 4. When you run the Close Current Period option, the old files are removed from your hard disk.

_____ 5. The generation numbers are similar for each module at any point in time.

Now turn to Answer Frame 7[1] on page 1-35 to check your answers.

Answer Frame 7[1]

1. False. Control reports cannot be printed "on demand." These reports print as you make changes. They cannot be selected from a menu (as you can select other reports), and they cannot be viewed on the screen.

2. True. For instance, this program can be used to backup the original data files.

3. True. And you will be asked to restore your data files to their original condition before working the end of chapter problems in this text. You use the Utilities module to accomplish this task.

4. False. Both the old files and the new copies remain on your hard disk. They will each have a different generation number.

5. False. The generation number could be different for each module, especially Payroll.

If you missed any of the above, reread Frame 7[1] before turning to the questions at the end of the chapter.

Name _____ ID # _____

INTRODUCTION TO PEACHTREE COMPLETE ACCOUNTING QUESTIONS

1. Describe the two steps that you must make at the DOS prompt to start PCA.

    _____

    _____

2. How would each of the following dates be typed in PCA?

    July 6, 1992 _____   May 25, 2000 _____

    November 8, 1993 _____   September 3, 1994 _____

3. What is the company ID that will be used in this text? _____

4. Describe three steps that will be taken to end a PCA session.

    _____

    _____

    _____

5. Define "menu" as the word relates to PCA. _____

    _____

    How many menu levels does PCA have? _____

6. Describe two ways that menu selection can be made in PCA.

    _____

    _____

7. Define the following words or terms as they relate to PCA.

    Default _____

    Backup _____

    Audit trail _____

Name _____ **ID #** _____

Lookup _____

Generation _____

8. If you are at the "Accept Y/N" prompt and you realize that you have made a mistake, how could you go about correcting it?

_____

_____

9. Name two ways that PCA provides help for you while you are working on the computer.

_____

_____

Name _____ ID # _____

INTRODUCTION TO PEACHTREE COMPLETE ACCOUNTING MATCHING

Instructions: Match the key symbol or screen indicator on the left with its function on the right.

Symbol/Indicator   **Function**   **Answer**

A. | Ins | 1. Moves down the list one screen.   _____

B. [DEL]   2. Discards entries or changes made to a screen.   _____

C. [ESC]   3. Clears the field.   _____

D. | Home | 4. Lets you return to the previous screen.   _____

E. [PG↓]   5. Returns you directly to the PCA Main Menu.   _____

F. | End | 6. Indicates you have finished making entries on a screen. _____

G. [F1]   7. Moves to the top of the list or to the first selection. _____

H. [F2]   8. Gives a Lookup Table.   _____

I. [F8]   9. Lets you enter information in a field with existing
                           information.   _____

J. [F9]   10. Moves to the last selection.   _____

K. [F10]   11. Gives you a help box.   _____

L. [SHIFT][F10]   12. Gets rid of the information in a selected field.   _____

Chapter 2

GENERAL LEDGER OVERVIEW

Learning Objectives:

After studying this chapter, you should be able to:

1. Identify the tasks involved in the accounting cycle that are performed by General Ledger.

2. Describe how General Ledger interacts with other Peachtree Complete Accounting modules, including Payroll, Accounts Payable, Accounts Receivable, and Fixed Assets.

3. Describe the four types of tasks performed by General Ledger, including entering transactions, printing financial statements and other reports, closing the fiscal period, and housekeeping and maintenance.

4. Identify some of the reports printed by General Ledger.

Chapter 2

General Ledger Overview

Frame 1[2]

How General Ledger Module Compares With A Manual Accounting System

You may have studied a manual accounting system in one of the Accounting Principles or Financial Accounting textbooks. If so, you may be wondering what the General Ledger module really does. In your textbook, the general ledger was defined as a collection of all of the ledger accounts for a company. You also learned that there was a general journal as well. The general journal recorded in chronological order all of the transactions that did not fit into one of the special journals, such as the Sales Journal, Cash Receipts Journal, Purchases Journal, or Cash Disbursements Journal.

The General Ledger module of PCA really is a combination general journal and general ledger. It records journal entries that are not entered into one of the other Peachtree Complete Accounting modules. Adjusting entries are an example of entries that would be entered into General Ledger. The module then posts all of the entries from all of the other modules to the general ledger. Then financial statements and certain other reports are prepared. Finally, the revenue and expense accounts are closed into the owner's equity account.

ther modules in the Peachtree Complete Accounting package that may act as special rnals include Payroll, Accounts Payable, Accounts Receivable, and Fixed Assets. When e modules are linked with General Ledger, any entries made in them are transferred to t eneral ledger accounts in General Ledger. If these modules are not linked with General Le r, you would have to manually summarize the information in those modules and pre e journal entries in General Ledger to enter the data into the general ledger accounts.

Question Frame 1^2

Indicate whether each of the following statements is true of false by writing "T" or "F" in the space provided.

_____ I.   The General Ledger module contains only a collection of all of the general ledger accounts for a company.

_____ 2.   Adjusting entries are an example of entries that would be entered into General Ledger.

_____ 3.   Other modules that may act as special journals include Payroll, Accounts Payable, Accounts Receivable, and Fixed Assets.

_____ 4.   Even if other modules are not linked with General Ledger, the information in them will be automatically transferred to General Ledger.

Now turn to Answer Frame 1^2 on page 2-4 to check your answers.

Answer Frame 1[2]

1. False. The General Ledger module contains both the general ledger accounts and the general journal.

2. True. Adjusting entries do not fit into any of the other modules and, therefore, are entered into General Ledger.

3. True. And when these modules are linked with General Ledger, any entries made in them are transferred to the general ledger accounts in General Ledger.

4. False. If these other modules are not linked with General Ledger, you would have to manually summarize the information in those modules and prepare journal entries in General Ledger to enter the data into the general ledger accounts.

If you missed any of the above, reread Frame 1[2] before continuing.

What General Ledger Does

General Ledger:

- Records and posts your current financial transactions to the proper accounts.

- Totals each account.

- Prints financial statements describing a company's current financial status and performance.

- Lets you use departments to organize and summarize financial data.

In short, General Ledger performs many of the tasks involved in the accounting cycle.

General Ledger produces comprehensive, up-to-date financial reports so you can compare current activity with budgeted figures or with financial figures from the previous year.

How General Ledger Interacts with Other PCA Modules

You can use General Ledger with some of the other Peachtree Complete Accounting modules. These modules can create summary journals for posting to General Ledger. Using all of PCA's modules and having them send information to one another saves you a lot of data entry and reduces errors.

For example, in Accounts Receivable (A/R) you enter sales, payments by customers, and service charges. You have accounts set up in General Ledger to handle these figures so, when you transfer this information into General Ledger, the Accounts Receivable figures go into the proper General Ledger accounts. If you did not use these two modules together, you would have to manually summarize your Accounts Receivable sales, payments by customers, and service charges and then post those amounts to the General Ledger accounts.

Four modules can create summary journals to transfer information into General Ledger:

1. Payroll
2. Accounts Payable
3. Accounts Receivable
4. Fixed Assets

Although PCA's Invoicing module does not transfer information directly to General Ledger, it does send information to Accounts Receivable and thus, indirectly to General Ledger.

You will create accounts in General Ledger that these other PCA modules need when they transfer information into General Ledger. The short sections below tell you about the General Ledger accounts these modules use. This is just an overview; details are provided in the next chapter.

Using Payroll with General Ledger - When you use Payroll with General Ledger, you need to know about the General Ledger accounts to which Payroll posts transactions. These accounts cover items such as the payroll checking account and the various FICA, insurance, withholding, and tax accounts. These topics are covered in Chapter 10.

Using Accounts Payable with General Ledger - When you use Accounts Payable with General Ledger, Accounts Payable posts transactions in some General Ledger accounts. These accounts are used to keep track of cash outflows, payable accounts, charged purchases, and discount purchases. Accounts Payable is further explained in Chapter 4.

Using Accounts Receivable with General Ledger - When you use Accounts Receivable with General Ledger, Accounts Receivable expects General Ledger to have certain accounts. Typically, these accounts handle sales for different types of products, returns, and different types of taxes. These types of transactions are discussed in Chapter 6.

Using Fixed Assets with General Ledger - When you use Fixed Assets with General Ledger, Fixed Assets can post transactions to General Ledger accounts. Chapter 12 describes Fixed Assets in more detail.

Because it is the most basic module, the detailed discussion of PCA modules begins with an Overview of General Ledger.

Question Frame 2^2

Indicate whether each of the following statements is true or false by writing "T" or "F" in the space provided.

____ 1.   General Ledger performs many of the tasks involved in the accounting cycle.

____ 2.   Linking modules creates a more efficient and effective accounting system.

____ 3.   The Invoicing module transfers information directly to General Ledger.

____ 4.   When the other modules are linked to General Ledger, you must make sure that you create the accounts in General Ledger that are needed by these other modules when they transfer the data to General Ledger.

Now turn to Answer Frame 2^2 on page 2-8 to check your answers.

Answer Frame 2²

1. True. General Ledger records and posts current transactions to the proper accounts, totals each account, prints financial statements, and organizes the data by department.

2. True. Linking the modules so they can pass information between them saves a lot of data entry effort and reduces errors.

3. False. The Invoicing module sends information to Accounts Receivable, and Accounts Receivable sends information to General Ledger. Thus, the transfer from Invoicing to General Ledger is indirect rather than direct.

4. True. Otherwise the data cannot be transferred.

If you missed any of the above, reread Frame 2² before continuing.

Frame 3²

General Ledger's Four Types of Tasks

Working with General Ledger is straightforward. During each fiscal period (usually a month long), most of the time that you work with General Ledger is spent entering transactions while keeping the General Ledger accounts in balance. At the end of the month, you will print financial statements and other reports. Then, after a bit of preparation, you will close the fiscal period.

This simple cycle is repeated each fiscal period: you enter transactions, produce financial reports, and close the period. Occasionally, you will perform some maintenance or housekeeping tasks, such as adding an account or updating budget data.

Thus, using General Ledger involves four types of tasks:

1. Entering transactions.
2. Printing financial statements and other reports.
3. Closing the fiscal period.
4. Housekeeping and maintenance.

The following sections explain what is involved in these types of tasks.

Entering Transactions

General Ledger provides these programs for entering and examining transactions:

*   **Enter Transactions**
*   **Delete Transactions**
*   **Transfer Summary Journals**
*   **Consolidate Companies**
*   **Query Account Status**

Use **Enter Transactions** to post journal entries to General Ledger for the current period. You also use this program to establish beginning balances for your accounts. You should always print a control report when you run this program. If the Year-to-Date option in the General Ledger Options File was set to "**Y**" before closing the period in which the transactions were entered, you can view transaction detail for a range of periods or year-to-date.

Use **Delete Transactions** to delete any incorrect transactions that you make. You can also enter adjusting transactions to offset amounts entered by mistake. You should also print a control report whenever you run this program.

Use **Transfer Summary Journals** to include in General Ledger transaction information from other PCA modules. This is usually done by a company near the end of the fiscal period.

Use **Consolidate Companies** if consolidated financial statements are needed. This is a very specialized program and will not be discussed in this text.

Use **Query Account Status** to examine an account's current activity and its beginning, current, and ending balances.

Question Frame 3[2]

____ 1.   Most of the activities you perform in General Ledger are quite routine.

____ 2.   There is only one way to correct any incorrect transaction that you make.

____ 3.   The Transfer Summary Journals option is generally used throughout the fiscal period.

____ 4.   The Query Account Status option is used to examine an account's current status.

Now turn to Answer Frame 3[2] on page 2-10 to check your answers.

Answer Frame 3²

I. True. Each fiscal period you enter transactions, produce financial statements, and close the period. Occasionally, you perform maintenance or housekeeping tasks.

2. False. You may either use the Delete Transactions option or enter adjusting transactions to offset amounts entered by mistake.

3. False. This option is usually done near the end of the fiscal period to transfer information in other modules to General Ledger.

4. True. This option is used to view an account's current activity, and its beginning, current, and ending balance.

If you missed any of the above, reread Frame 3² before continuing·

Frame 4²

Printing Financial Statements and Other Reports

These General Ledger programs let you print three financial statements:

- **Balance Sheet**
- **Income Statement**
- **Departmental Income Statements**

Use **Balance Sheet** to print a financial statement that summarizes the total assets, liabilities, and owner's equity for a company as of the close of an accounting period.

Use **Income Statement** to print a financial statement that shows the difference between Income (Revenue) account totals and Expense account totals—the Net Income—for a company for a given fiscal period.

Use **Departmental Income Statement** if a company uses departments. These income statements provide a detailed report on each department's income activity for a fiscal period.

Taken together, these three financial statements reflect the current financial state of a company. Each of these three programs can also print comparative financial statements; these statements compare current period figures either to figures budgeted for that period or to figures for the same period in the previous fiscal year.

You can interrupt the printing of a report at any time. Simply press [ESC] to do so. You will then be prompted "REPORT INTERRUPTED" "CONTINUE PRINTING - Y/N: N." If you want to continue printing the report, type Y and press [ENTER]. If you want to stop, press [ENTER] and you are returned to the menu.

The following General Ledger programs let you print three other reports:

- **Transaction Register**
- **Trial Balance**
- **Depreciation /Amortization Schedules**

Use **Transaction Register** to list transactions entered in the current period. You can tell General Ledger to order the transactions based on account numbers or on the type of transaction. You can have General Ledger print transactions based on the session in which they were entered. You should print a copy of the Transaction Register at the end of each of your sessions. You can use this to check the accuracy of your transactions.

Use **Trial Balance** to make sure that your General Ledger is in balance. You can run this report in detail or summary form. However, the detailed trial balance is preferred because it is important as an audit trail. The new Working Trial Balance is also the report that will be used most often to trace errors such as incorrect postings. This Trial Balance shows account numbers, account names, ending balances, adjustments (user fills in), and adjusted ending balances (user fills in). You should run a detailed Trial Balance before you attempt to print any financial statements (Balance Sheet, Income Statement, and Department Income Statement). You should also print a copy of the Trial Balance in Summary form at the end of each session. If General Ledger is out of balance, the Trial Balance and the Transaction Register help you track down the problem.

The Transaction Register or Trial Balance can be printed for a prior period, range of periods, or Year-to-date only if the Keep Year-to-Date option was set to Y in the General Ledger options file before closing the period in which the transactions were entered.

Use the **Depreciation/Amortization Schedules** to calculate and print:

- Asset depreciation using either Straight Line, Declining Balance, or Sum of the Year's Digits method.

- Amortization schedules using the declining balance method.

These schedules prepare information for posting to General Ledger but do not directly post transactions to General Ledger.

The **Depreciation/Amortization Schedules** program would only be used for depreciation schedules if the PCA Fixed Assets module is not being used. Fixed Assets provides more accurate and up-to-date depreciation information and is discussed in depth in Chapter 10.

Question Frame 4²

___ I. Three financial statements can be printed using the General Ledger module.

___ 2. Each financial statement can compare current period amounts only with amounts budgeted for that period.

___ 3. After transactions have been entered, you should print a transactions register.

___ 4. You should print a trial balance <u>after</u> you print any financial statements.

___ 5. The Depreciation/Amortization Schedules program should be used regardless of what other modules are being used.

Now turn to Answer Frame 4² on page 2-13 to check your answers.

Answer Frame 4[2]

I. True. The three financial statements are balance sheet, income statement, and departmental income statement.

2. False. The current period amounts can also be compared to amounts for the same period of the previous fiscal year.

3. True. This printout can be examined to check the accuracy of your transactions.

4. False. You should print a trial balance <u>before</u> you print any financial statements to make sure the accounts are in balance. If the accounts are not in balance, you need to find the error(s) and correct them before attempting to print financial statements.

5. False. If the Fixed Assets module is being used, the Depreciation/Amortization Schedules program should not be used.

If you missed any of the above, reread Frame 4[2] before continuing.

Frame 5[2]

Closing the Fiscal Period

At the end of the fiscal period (usually a month), you need to wrap up some loose ends and then close the fiscal period. In a manual system, this can be a lengthy or cumbersome process, but closing is relatively simple when PCA is used. Confirm that you have entered all of your regular transactions for the current period and that General Ledger is in balance. (Remember that the Transaction Register and Trial Balance will help you do this.) Once you print (and check) your financial statements for the period, your monthly tasks are done.

Then, use **Close Current Period** to close out the current fiscal period. This prepares General Ledger for processing the next month's activity. (NOTE: The year-end closing process is very similar. You will practice closing a fiscal year in the next chapter.)

Housekeeping and Maintenance

General Ledger provides these programs for housekeeping and maintenance:

- **Maintain Chart of Accounts**
- **Maintain General Ledger Options**
- **Edit Repeating Transactions**
- **List Chart of Accounts**
- **Prepare Next Year's Budget**

When General Ledger was first installed by your instructor, **Maintain Chart of Accounts** was used to enter the General Ledger accounts. You will use this program to add new accounts, change information for existing accounts, or delete obsolete accounts.

Use **Maintain General Ledger Options** to choose among options when General Ledger is initially set up. This was probably done by your instructor when PCA was installed.

Use **Edit Repeating Transactions** whenever you need to correct or remove an incorrect reversing transaction or remove a repeating transaction. Repeating transactions may include both adjusting and reversing entries.

Use **List Chart of Accounts** to print a listing of the information in your Chart of Accounts file. You can print all your accounts or a range of accounts.

When you close the last period in a fiscal year, you can use **Prepare Next Year's Budget** to create a budget for the new fiscal year based on the previous year's figures.

Question Frame 5[2]

____ l.   At the end of the fiscal period, just go ahead and print your financial statements without first checking anything else.

____ 2.   The Close Current Period option prepares General Ledger for processing the next period's activity.

____ 3.   The List Chart of Accounts and Maintain Chart of Accounts options can be used to view and update the chart of accounts.

____ 4.   "Repeating transactions" include entries to adjust the accounts that are similar from period to period (e.g., straight-line depreciation adjusting entries) and also may include reversing entries for some of the adjusting entries.

Now turn to Answer Frame 5[2] on page 2-15 to check your answers.

Answer Frame 5[2]

1. False. Before you print the financial statements, you need to confirm that you have entered all your regular transactions for the current period and that the General Ledger is in balance.

2. True. The closing process clears the revenue and expense accounts so that data for the next fiscal period can be entered into them.

3. True. The List Chart of Accounts option can be used to view the chart of accounts, and Maintain Chart of Accounts option can be used to update the chart of accounts.

4. True. Repeating entries are entries that are made at the end of each fiscal period. These entries may include both adjusting and reversing entries.

If you missed any of the above, reread Frame 5[2] before turning to the questions at the end of the chapter.

What's Next

Now that you have learned about General Ledger, you are ready to go on to the next chapter where you can practice and experiment with it. First, you may want to review the General Ledger Sample Reports at the end of the chapter to become familiar with the type of output you will produce in Chapter 3.

Name _____ ID # _____

GENERAL LEDGER OVERVIEW
QUESTIONS

1. **What four PCA modules can create summary journals to transfer information to General Ledger?**

    _____

    _____

    _____

    _____

2. **Name the four types of tasks involved in using General Ledger.**

    _____

    _____

    _____

    _____

3. **What are two functions performed by the program Enter Transactions?**

    _____

    _____

4. **Name three financial statements that you can print using General Ledger.**

    _____

    _____

    _____

5. What are three reports (other than financial statements) that can be printed using General Ledger?

_____

_____

_____

6. Name two reports that can help you track down the problem if General Ledger is out of balance.

_____

_____

7. What programs are used for housekeeping and maintenance in General Ledger?

_____

_____

_____

_____

_____

GENERAL LEDGER OVERVIEW
MATCHING

Instructions: Match each program name on the left with the proper program function on the right.

<u>Program Name</u>	<u>Program Function</u>	<u>Answer</u>
A. Query Account Status	1. Prints a financial statement summarizing Assets, Liabilities, and Owners' Equity at the end of a period.	_____
B. Transaction Register	2. Posts journal entries for the current period.	_____
C. Close Current Period	3. Lists transactions entered in the current period.	_____
D. Balance Sheet	4. Examines an account's balance.	_____
E. Delete Transactions	5. Prints a financial statement that shows profit or loss for a period.	_____
F. Maintain Chart of Accounts	6. Erases incorrect transactions.	_____
G. Edit Repeating Transactions	7. Makes sure that the general ledger is in balance.	_____
H. Trial Balance	8. Prepares General Ledger for processing the next month's activity.	_____
I. Enter Transactions	9. Adds or deletes accounts.	_____
J. Income Statement	10. Deletes an incorrect reversing transaction.	_____

GENERAL LEDGER

SAMPLE REPORTS

Standard Chart of Accounts

```
RUN DATE: 12/31/92        Standard Chart of Accts.           PAGE  1
RUN TIME: 12:58 PM              General Ledger
                               Chart Of Accounts
------------------------------------------------------------------------

ACCT    DESCRIPTION              TYP  M/D  GRP-END  COL
========================================================================

100     ASSETS                   1                  0
101     CURRENT ASSETS           1                  1
105     Cash                     2    M    11999    1
110     Cash - Operating         2                  1
115     Cash on Hand             2                  1
120     Accounts Receivable      2                  1
125     Due from Employees       2                  1
130     Allowance for Bad Debts  2                  1
135     Inventory                2                  1
140     Total Current Assets     4                  2
145     FIXED ASSETS             1                  1
147     Furniture & Fixtures     2                  1
150     Machinery & Equipment    2                  1
152     Buildings                2                  1
155     Land                     2                  1
157     Vehicles                 2                  1
160     Accumulated Depreciation 2                  1
165     Total Fixed Assets       4                  2
170     OTHER ASSETS             1                  1
172     Prepaid Expenses         2    M    18599    1
175     Prepaid Insurance        2                  1
180     Prepaid Advertising      2                  1
185     Prepaid Uniforms         2                  1
190     Deposits                 2                  1
195     Total Other Assets       4                  2
199     Total Assets             8                  3
200     LIABILITIES & EQUITY     1                  0
201     CURRENT LIABILITIES      1                  1
205     Accounts Payable         2                  1
210     Accrued Payroll          2                  1
215     Notes Payable - Bank     2                  1
220     Payroll Taxes Payable    2    M    23099    1
221     Federal Withholding Taxes 2                 1
222     State Withholding Taxes  2                  1
224     FICA                     2                  1
226     Federal Unemployment Tax 2                  1
228     State Unemployment Tax   2                  1
230     Earned Income Credit     2                  1
232     Fed. Income Tax Payable  2                  1
234     State Income Tax Payable 2                  1
236     Sales Tax Payable        2                  1
238     Industrial Ins. Payable  2                  1
240     Suspense                 2                  1
245     Total Current Liabilities 4                 2
250     LONG TERM LIABILITIES    1                  1
```

Standard Chart of Accounts

ACCT	DESCRIPTION	TYP	M/D	GRP-END	COL
255	Notes Payable - Bank	2			1
264	Total Long Term. Liab.	4			2
265	Total Liabilities	6			3
270	STOCKHOLDERS EQUITY	1			1
275	Common Stock	2			2
280	Retained Earnings	2			2
285	Current Earnings	2			2
298	Total Equity	6			3
299	Total Liab. & Equity	8			3
300	INCOME	1			
305	Sales	2			
315	Service	2			
320	Returns & Allowances	2			
325	Sales Discount	2			
330	Finance Charge Income	2			
340	Delivery Fee Income	2			
345	Miscellaneous Income	2			
399	Net Sales	4			
400	COST OF GOODS SOLD	1			
405	Cost of Sales	2			
420	Freight	2			
435	Purchase Discounts	2			
490	Total Cost of Goods Sold	4			
499	Gross Profit	9			
500	EXPENSES	1			
501	Salaries	2			
510	Payroll Taxes	2	M	51999	
514	FICA	2			
516	Fed. Unemployment Taxes	2			
518	State Unemployment Taxes	2			
520	Advertising	2			
525	Amortization	2			
530	Auto Expense	2			
535	Bad Debts	2			
540	Bank Service Charges	2			
545	Commissions	2			
550	Contributions	2			
555	Depreciation	2			
560	Dues & Subscriptions	2			
565	Employee Benefits	2			
570	Entertainment	2			
575	Freight	2			
580	Industrial Insurance	2			
583	Insurance	2	M	59999	
585	Fire & Theft Insurance	2			

Standard Chart of Accounts

```
RUN DATE: 12/31/92        Standard Chart of Accts.           PAGE  3
RUN TIME: 12:58 PM           General Ledger
                             Chart Of Accounts
-----------------------------------------------------------------------


ACCT    DESCRIPTION            TYP  M/D  GRP-END  COL
=======================================================================


590     Fleet Insurance         2
595     General Liability Ins.  2
598     Group Insurance         2
600     Interest Expense        2
605     Licenses                2
610     Miscellaneous Expense   2
615     Office Expense          2
620     Postage                 2
625     Professional Fees       2
630     Rent                    2
635     Repairs & Maintenance   2
640     Returned Checks         2
645     Taxes - Property        2
650     Taxes - Other           2
655     Telephone               2
660     Travel                  2
665     Uniforms                2
670     Utilities               2
698     Total Expenses          6
699     Net Operating Income    9
700     OTHER INCOME            1
710     Interest Income         2
720     Gain on Sale of Asset   2
799     Total Other Income      6
800     OTHER EXPENSES          1
810     Loss on Sale of Asset   2
849     Total Other Expenses    6
850     Income Before Taxes     9
855     Income Taxes            2
999     Net Income              9




*** CONTROL TOTALS ***        CONTROL           ACTUAL
MASTER FILE RECORDS               120              120
ACCOUNT HASH TOTAL          4,844,800        4,844,800



*** END OF - List Chart Of Accounts ***
```

W. D. Peachtree Chart of Accounts

RUN DATE: 12/31/92   W.D. Peachtree & Company   PAGE 1
RUN TIME: 1:56 PM   General Ledger
                           Chart Of Accounts

ACCT	DESCRIPTION	TYP	M/D	GRP-END	COL	CURRENT	NON-CURRENT	PRIOR PD ADJS	BEGIN BAL
100	ASSETS	1			0				
101	CURRENT ASSETS	1			1				
105	Cash	2	M	11999	1				
110	Cash - Operating	2			1	76,837.96	0.00	0.00	149,125.86
115	Cash on Hand	2			1	0.00	0.00	0.00	1,500.00
120	Accounts Receivable	2			1	0.00	0.00	0.00	120,869.86
125	Due from Employees	2			1	0.00	0.00	0.00	0.00
130	Allowance for Bad Debts	2			1	500.00-	0.00	0.00	5,500.00-
135	Inventory	2			1	38,240.78-	0.00	0.00	41,158.66
140	Total Current Assets	4			2				
145	FIXED ASSETS	1			1				
147	Furniture & Fixtures	2			1	0.00	0.00	0.00	5,667.00
150	Machinery & Equipment	2			1	0.00	0.00	0.00	34,014.50
152	Buildings	2			1	0.00	0.00	0.00	104,200.00
155	Land	2			1	0.00	0.00	0.00	25,000.00
157	Vehicles	2			1	0.00	0.00	0.00	52,093.00
160	Accumulated Depreciation	2			1	1,486.82-	0.00	0.00	47,841.23-
165	Total Fixed Assets	4			2				
170	OTHER ASSETS	1			1				
172	Prepaid Expenses	2	M	18599	1				
175	Prepaid Insurance	2			1	0.00	0.00	0.00	0.00
180	Prepaid Advertising	2			1	350.00-	0.00	0.00	700.00-
185	Prepaid Uniforms	2			1	74.00-	0.00	0.00	148.42
190	Deposits	2			1	0.00	0.00	0.00	1,000.00
195	Total Other Assets	4			2				
199	Total Assets	8			3				
200	LIABILITIES & EQUITY	1			0				
201	CURRENT LIABILITIES	1			1				
205	Accounts Payable	2			1	2,127.50-	0.00	0.00	28,307.40-
210	Accrued Payroll	2			1	0.00	0.00	0.00	0.00
215	Notes Payable - Bank	2			1	2,000.00	0.00	0.00	4,356.87-
220	Payroll Taxes Payable	2	M	23099	1				
221	Federal Withholding Taxes	2			1	0.00	0.00	0.00	7,151.40-
222	State Withholding Taxes	2			1	0.00	0.00	0.00	2,240.40-
224	FICA	2			1	0.00	0.00	0.00	8,377.51-

```
RUN DATE: 12/31/92        W.D. Peachtree & Company           PAGE   1
RUN TIME:  1:56 PM             General Ledger
                       Query Account Status Control Report

ACCOUNT   DESCRIPTION              TYPE        PTD BEGINNING BALANCE

11000   Cash - Operating       DETAIL ACCOUNT        149,125.86

SRC  REF    DATE    PE  PP  DESCRIPTION                   AMOUNT

2  11495  11/01/92  11  11  Peachtree Realty             2,500.00-
2  11560  11/04/92  11  11  Southern Bell                3,967.55-
2  11561  11/04/92  11  11  Atlanta Gas Light            1,123.55-
2  11562  11/04/92  11  11  Georgia Power Company        4,033.88-
2  11577  11/10/92  11  11  Bryan's Office Supply          176.88-
2  11578  11/10/92  11  11  Meyer's & Meyer's, CPA         500.00-
2  11622  11/20/92  11  11  Jones, Smith & Jones        11,000.00-
2  11623  11/20/92  11  11  U.S. Postmaster                600.00-
2  11624  11/20/92  11  11  Burns Auto Repair            1,189.54-
1  JE33   11/05/92  11  11  Cash Sales W/E 11/5/92     102,553.31
1  JE33   11/05/92  11  11  Serv. Sales W/E 11/5/92      3,455.00
1  JE33   11/05/92  11  11  Returns for W/E 11/5/92      4,078.95-

                                   DETAIL TOTAL:      76,837.96 *
                                   YTD TOTAL:        225,963.82 *


*** End Of Query Account Status Control Report ***
```

Transaction Register by Source Code

```
RUN DATE: 12/31/92        W.D. Peachtree & Company                    PAGE  1
RUN TIME:  2:03 PM              General Ledger
                             Transaction Register
===============================================================================

S BATCH  REF     DATE              DESCRIPTION        ACCT  PP PE      AMOUNT
===============================================================================

2  1 11495    11/01/92 Peachtree Realty              630   11 11    2,500.00
2  1 11495    11/01/92 Peachtree Realty              110   11 11    2,500.00-
                                                                        0.00 *

2  1 11560    11/04/92 Southern Bell                 655   11 11    3,967.55
2  1 11560    11/04/92 Southern Bell                 110   11 11    3,967.55-
                                                                        0.00 *

2  1 11561    11/04/92 Atlanta Gas Light             670   11 11    1,123.55
2  1 11561    11/04/92 Atlanta Gas Light             110   11 11    1,123.55-
                                                                        0.00 *

2  1 11562    11/04/92 Georgia Power Company         670   11 11    4,033.88
2  1 11562    11/04/92 Georgia Power Company         110   11 11    4,033.88-
                                                                        0.00 *

2  1 11577    11/10/92 Bryan's Office Supply         615   11 11      176.88
2  1 11577    11/10/92 Bryan's Office Supply         110   11 11      176.88-
                                                                        0.00 *

2  1 11578    11/10/92 Meyer's & Meyer's, CPA        625   11 11      500.00
2  1 11578    11/10/92 Meyer's & Meyer's, CPA        110   11 11      500.00-
                                                                        0.00 *


                    SOURCE TRANSACTIONS LISTED  =    18
                    SOURCE DEBITS      =        25,091.40
                    SOURCE CREDITS     =        25,091.40-
                                                ==========
                    DIFFERENCE         =             0.00

               *** End of - Transaction Register ***
```

```
RUN DATE: 12/31/92      W.D. Peachtree               any                    PAGE  1
RUN TIME:  2:06 PM            General Ledg
                          Transaction Regis

ACCT  BATCH    DESCRIPTION              REF     S   DATE      Pr       AMOUNT

110     1  Peachtree Realty          11495     2  11/01/92  11  11      2,500.00-
110     1  Southern Bell             11560     2  11/04/92  11  11      3,967.55-
110     1  Atlanta Gas Light         11561     2  11/04/92  11  11      1,123.55-
110     1  Georgia Power Company     11562     2  11/04/92  11  11      4,033.88-
110     1  Bryan's Office Supply     11577     2  11/10/92  11  11        176.88-
110     1  Meyer's & Meyer's, CPA    11578     2  11/10/92  11  11        500.00-
110     1  Jones, Smith & Jones      11622     2  11/20/92  11  11     11,000.00-
110     1  U.S. Postmaster           11623     2  11/20/92  11  11        600.00-
110     1  Burns Auto Repair         11624     2  11/20/92  11  11      1,189.54-
110     2  Cash Sales W/E 11/5/92    JE33      1  11/05/92  11  11    102,553.31
110     2  Serv. Sales W/E 11/5/92   JE33      1  11/05/92  11  11      3,455.00
110     2  Returns for W/E 11/5/92   JE33      1  11/05/92  11  11      4,078.95-
                                                                      76,837.96 *

130     4  Allowance for Bad Debts   JE50      3  11/30/92  11  11        500.00-

135     3  Cost of Sales             JE34      3  11/05/92  11  11     38,240.78-
```

```
TOTAL TRANSACTIONS LISTED  =      94
TOTAL DEBITS             =  177,957.76
TOTAL CREDITS           =  177,957.76-
                           ============
DIFFERENCE              =         0.00-
```

```
*** CONTROL TOTALS ***        CONTROL      ACTUAL
TRANSACTION COUNT               94           94
TRANSACTION TOTAL             0.00         0.00-
```

*** End of - Transaction Register ***

Summary Trial Balance

SUMMARY TRIAL BALANCE

ALL ACCOUNTS   PERIOD ENDING 11/30/92

| ------ACCOUNT------ | -BEGINNING- | ------------TRANSACTION------------ | | -----ENDING----- |
NUMBER DESCRIPTION	BALANCE	DESCRIPTION DATE PP PE S REFERENCE	AMOUNT	BALANCE
110 Cash - Operating	149,125.86		76,837.96 *	225,963.82 *
115 Cash on Hand	1,500.00		0.00 *	1,500.00 *
120 Accounts Receivable	120,869.86		0.00 *	120,869.86 *
125 Due from Employees	0.00		0.00 *	0.00 *
130 Allowance for Bad Debts	5,500.00-		500.00-*	6,000.00-*
135 Inventory	41,158.66		38,240.78-*	2,917.88 *
147 Furniture & Fixtures	5,667.00		0.00 *	5,667.00 *
150 Machinery & Equipment	34,014.50		0.00 *	34,014.50 *
152 Buildings	104,200.00		0.00 *	104,200.00 *
155 Land	25,000.00		0.00 *	25,000.00 *

TOTAL DEBITS	4,848,315.30	177,957.76	5,026,273.06
TOTAL CREDITS	4,848,315.30-	177,957.76-	5,026,273.06-

*** DIFFERENCE   0.00 *   0.00 *   0.00 *

	CONTROL	ACTUAL
*** CONTROL TOTALS ***		
TRANSACTION COUNT	94	94
TRANSACTION TOTAL	0.00	0.00-

*** End Of - SUMMARY TRIAL BALANCE ***

Working Trial Balance

RUN DATE: 12/31/92
RUN TIME: 3:05 PM

W.D. Peachtree & Company

WORKING TRIAL BALANCE

PERIOD ENDING 11/30/92

ALL ACCOUNTS

NUMBER	ACCOUNT DESCRIPTION	ENDING BALANCE	TRANSACTION REFERENCE	ADJUSTMENTS DEBIT	ADJUSTMENTS CREDIT	ADJUSTED BALANCE DEBIT	ADJUSTED BALANCE CREDIT
110	Cash - Operating	225,581.70					
115	Cash on Hand	1,500.00					
120	Accounts Receivable	120,869.86					
125	Due from Employees	0.00					
130	Allowance for Bad Debts	5,500.00-					
135	Inventory	99,672.02					
147	Furniture & Fixtures	5,667.00					
150	Machinery & Equipment	34,014.50					
152	Buildings	104,200.00					
155	Land	25,000.00					
157	Vehicles	52,093.00					

TOTAL DEBITS   5,122,909.32
TOTAL CREDITS   5,122,909.32-

*** DIFFERENCE   0.00 *

*** CONTROL TOTALS ***   CONTROL   ACTUAL
TRANSACTION COUNT   102   102
TRANSACTION TOTAL   0.00   0.00-

*** End Of - WORKING TRIAL BALANCE ***

Detail Trial Balance

DETAIL TRIAL BALANCE

ALL ACCOUNTS   PERIOD ENDING 11/30/92

NUMBER	DESCRIPTION	-BEGINNING- BALANCE	DESCRIPTION	DATE PP PE S REFERENCE	AMOUNT	---ENDING--- BALANCE
110	Cash - Operating	149,125.86				
			Peachtree Realty	11/01 11 11 2 11495	2,500.00-	
			Southern Bell	11/04 11 11 2 11560	3,967.55-	
			Atlanta Gas Light	11/04 11 11 2 11561	1,123.55-	
			Georgia Power Company	11/04 11 11 2 11562	4,033.88-	
			Bryan's Office Supply	11/10 11 11 2 11577	176.88-	
			Meyer's & Meyer's, CPA	11/10 11 11 2 11578	500.00-	
			Jones, Smith & Jones	11/20 11 11 2 11622	11,000.00-	
			U.S. Postmaster	11/20 11 11 2 11623	600.00-	
			Burns Auto Repair	11/20 11 11 2 11624	1,189.54-	
			Cash Sales W/E 11/5/92	11/05 11 11 1 JE33	102,553.31	
			Serv. Sales W/E 11/5/92	11/05 11 11 1 JE33	3,455.00	
			Returns for W/E 11/5/92	11/05 11 11 1 JE33	4,078.95-	
					76,837.96 *	225,963.82 *
115	Cash on Hand	1,500.00			0.00 *	1,500.00 *
120	Accounts Receivable	120,869.86			0.00 *	120,869.86 *
125	Due from Employees	0.00			0.00 *	0.00 *

TOTAL DEBITS	4,848,315.30	177,957.76	5,026,273.06
TOTAL CREDITS	4,848,315.30-	177,957.76-	5,026,273.06-
*** DIFFERENCE	0.00 *	0.00 *	0.00 *

*** CONTROL TOTALS ***	CONTROL	ACTUAL
TRANSACTION COUNT	94	94
TRANSACTION TOTAL	0.00	0.00-

*** End Of - DETAIL TRIAL BALANCE ***

Standard Balance Sheet

```
RUN DATE: 12/31/92          W.D. Peachtree & Company                    PAGE  1
RUN TIME:  2:17 PM
                                  Balance Sheet
                                 AS OF 11/30/92

                                     ASSETS
                                    ---------

CURRENT ASSETS
  Cash                             227,463.82
  Accounts Receivable              120,869.86
  Due from Employees                     0.00
  Allowance for Bad Debts           6,000.00-
  Inventory                         2,917.88
                                   ----------
       Total Current Assets                       345,251.56

FIXED ASSETS
  Furniture & Fixtures               5,667.00
  Machinery & Equipment             34,014.50
  Buildings                        104,200.00
  Land                              25,000.00
  Vehicles                          52,093.00
  Accumulated Depreciation          49,328.05-
                                   ----------
       Total Fixed Assets                         171,646.45

OTHER ASSETS
  Prepaid Expenses                     975.58-
  Deposits                          1,000.00
                                   ----------
       Total Other Assets                              24.42
                                                  ----------
            Total Assets                          516,922.43
                                                  ==========

                              LIABILITIES & EQUITY
                             ----------------------

CURRENT LIABILITIES
  Accounts Payable                  30,434.90
```

Comparative Balance Sheet

Balance Sheet
AS OF 11/30/92

	** THIS MONTH THIS YEAR **	** THIS MONTH LAST YEAR **
ASSETS		
CURRENT ASSETS		
Cash	227,463.82	0.00
Accounts Receivable	120,869.86	0.00
Due from Employees	0.00	0.00
Allowance for Bad Debts	6,000.00-	0.00
Inventory	2,917.88	0.00
Total Current Assets	345,251.56	0.00
FIXED ASSETS		
Furniture & Fixtures	5,667.00	0.00
Machinery & Equipment	34,014.50	0.00
Buildings	104,200.00	0.00
Land	25,000.00	0.00
Vehicles	52,093.00	0.00
Accumulated Depreciation	49,328.05-	0.00
Total Fixed Assets	171,646.45	0.00
OTHER ASSETS		
Prepaid Expenses	975.58-	0.00
Deposits	1,000.00	0.00
Total Other Assets	24.42	0.00
Total Assets	516,922.43	0.00

LIABILITIES & EQUITY

Comparative Balance Sheet Subsidiary Schedule

W.D. Peachtree & Company

Balance Sheet
AS OF 11/30/92

PAGE   3

	** THIS MONTH THIS YEAR **	** THIS MONTH LAST YEAR **
Cash		
Cash - Operating	225,963.82	0.00
Cash on Hand	1,500.00	0.00
	----------	----------
	227,463.82	0.00
Prepaid Expenses		
Prepaid Insurance	0.00	0.00
Prepaid Advertising	1,050.00-	0.00
Prepaid Uniforms	74.42	0.00
	----------	----------
	975.58-	0.00
Payroll Taxes Payable		
Federal Withholding Taxes	7,151.40	0.00
State Withholding Taxes	2,240.40	0.00
FICA	8,377.51	0.00
Federal Unemployment Tax	5,634.44	0.00
State Unemployment Tax	1,667.80	0.00
Earned Income Credit	0.00	0.00
	----------	----------
	25,071.55	0.00

*** SUBSIDIARY SCHEDULE ***

Standard Income Statement

Income Statement
AS OF 11/30/92

RATIO: INCOME	THIS MONTH	RATIO	11 MONTHS	RATIO
INCOME				
Sales	102,553.31	100.6	4,102,459.17	99.9
Service	3,455.00	3.4	138,783.00	3.4
Returns & Allowances	4,078.95-	4.0-	170,898.99-	4.2-
Sales Discount	0.00	0.0	19,758.92-	0.5-
Finance Charge Income	0.00	0.0	19,927.99	0.5
Delivery Fee Income	0.00	0.0	35,056.56	0.9
Net Sales	101,929.36	100.0	4,105,568.81	100.0
Travel	0.00	0.0	1,545.77	0.0
Uniforms	74.00	0.1	518.00	0.0
Utilities	5,157.43	5.1	51,376.88	1.3
Total Expenses	27,629.72	27.1	2,034,618.43	49.6
Net Operating Income	36,058.86	35.4	118,473.14	2.9
OTHER INCOME				
Total Other Income	0.00	0.0	0.00	0.0
OTHER EXPENSES				
Total Other Expenses	0.00	0.0	0.00	0.0
Income Before Taxes	36,058.86	35.4	118,473.14	2.9
Net Income	36,058.86	35.4	118,473.14	2.9

Comparative Income Statement

W.D. Peachtree & Company

Income Statement
AS OF 11/30/92

PAGE 1

RATIO: INCOME	THIS MONTH	RATIO	11 MONTHS	RATIO	BUDGET 11 MONTHS	LAST YEAR THIS MONTH	11 MONTHS
	** THIS MONTH THIS YEAR **				** THIS MONTH LAST YEAR **		
INCOME							
Sales	102,553.31	100.6	4,102,459.17	99.9	4,426,546.74	0.00	0.00
Service	3,455.00	3.4	138,783.00	3.4	149,050.00	0.00	0.00
Returns & Allowances	4,078.95-	4.0-	170,898.99-	4.2-	178,291.52-	0.00	0.00
Sales Discount	0.00	0.0	19,758.92-	0.5-	22,000.00-	0.00	0.00
Finance Charge Income	0.00	0.0	19,927.99	0.5	13,750.00	0.00	0.00
Delivery Fee Income	0.00	0.0	35,056.56	0.9	33,000.00	0.00	0.00
Net Sales	101,929.36	100.0	4,105,568.81	100.0	4,422,055.22	0.00	0.00
COST OF GOODS SOLD							
Cost of Sales	38,240.78	37.5	2,117,483.17	51.6	2,241,250.00	0.00	0.00
Freight	0.00	0.0	40,727.94	1.0	44,000.00	0.00	0.00
Purchase Discounts	0.00	0.0	205,733.87-	5.0-	233,750.00-	0.00	0.00
Total Cost of Goods Sold	38,240.78	37.5	1,952,477.24	47.6	2,051,500.00	0.00	0.00
Gross Profit	63,688.58	62.5	2,153,091.57	52.4	2,370,555.22	0.00	0.00
EXPENSES							
Salaries	0.00	0.0	1,436,288.58	35.0	1,566,583.26	0.00	0.00
Payroll Taxes	0.00	0.0	229,534.87	5.6	241,999.89	0.00	0.00
Income Before Taxes	36,058.86	35.4	118,473.14	2.9	201,984.20	0.00	0.00
Net Income	36,058.86	35.4	118,473.14	2.9	201,984.20	0.00	0.00

Comparative Income Statement Subsidiary Schedule

RUN DATE: 12/31/92
RUN TIME: 2:23 PM

W.D. Peachtree & Company

Income Statement
AS OF 11/30/92

PAGE 3

RATIO: INCOME

	----------THIS YEAR----------			-----BUDGET-----	-----LAST YEAR-----	
	THIS MONTH	RATIO	11 MONTHS	RATIO	11 MONTHS	THIS MONTH	11 MONTHS
	** THIS MONTH THIS YEAR **					** THIS MONTH LAST YEAR **	
	*** SUBSIDIARY SCHEDULE ***						
Sales							
Sales Men's Clothing	9,876.44	9.7	397,853.27	9.7	426,250.00	0.00	0.00
Sales Women's Clothing	10,016.57	9.8	415,358.48	10.1	444,583.37	0.00	0.00
Sales Children's Clothing	7,546.98	7.4	305,414.23	7.4	330,000.00	0.00	0.00
Sales Uniforms	2,448.73	2.4	101,269.60	2.5	105,380.00	0.00	0.00
Sales Athletic Shoes	5,866.45	5.8	217,478.63	5.3	233,750.00	0.00	0.00
Sales Other Shoes	4,640.38	4.6	190,273.13	4.6	203,500.00	0.00	0.00
Sales Appliances	17,090.40	16.8	692,735.60	16.9	748,000.00	0.00	0.00
Sales Electronics	14,110.90	13.8	562,866.93	13.7	609,583.37	0.00	0.00
Sales Hardware	12,234.56	12.0	481,553.37	11.7	522,500.00	0.00	0.00
Sales Sporting Goods	5,121.60	5.0	204,843.26	5.0	221,833.37	0.00	0.00
Sales Fencing & Gutters	11,980.50	11.8	470,820.72	11.5	514,250.00	0.00	0.00
Sales Hair Salon	1,619.80	1.6	61,991.95	1.5	66,916.63	0.00	0.00
	102,553.31	100.6	4,102,459.17	99.9	4,426,546.74	0.00	0.00
Service							
Service Appliances	550.00	0.5	21,335.00	0.5	22,000.00	0.00	0.00
Service Electronics	375.00	0.4	15,675.00	0.4	16,500.00	0.00	0.00
Service Hardware	155.00	0.2	5,870.00	0.1	_		0.00
Service Fencing & Gutters	1,225.00	1.2	51,710.00	1._	_000.00		0.00
Service Hair Salon	1,150.00	1.1			49,500.00		0.00
		_.4	138,783.00	3.4	149,050.00		0.00
Ret_							
Ret/Allow Men's Clothing	449.26-	0.4-	19,059.44-	0.5-	20,166.63-		0.00
Ret/Allow Women's Clothng	714.88-	0.7-	30,095.77-	0.7-	32,083.37-		0.00
Ret/Allow Children's Clth	256.06-	0.3-	11,664.68-	0.3-	11,000.00-		0.00
Ret/Allow Uniforms	107.40-	0.1-	4,626.96-	0.1-	4,583.37-		0.00
Ret/Allow Athletic Shoes	377.30-	0.4-	15,550.38-	0.4-	16,500.00-		0.00

Departmental Income Statement

```
RUN DATE: 12/31/92      W.D. Peachtree & Company              PAGE   1
RUN TIME:  2:32 PM
                       Department Income Statement
                          AS OF 11/30/92

50  Fencing & Gutters
RATIO: INCOME             THIS MONTH  RATIO     11 MONTHS  RATIO
=====================================================================
INCOME

  Sales Fencing & Gutters   11,980.50  91.5    470,820.72   90.9
  Service Fencing & Gutters  1,225.00   9.4     51,710.00   10.0
  Ret/Allow Fencing/Gutters    115.80-  0.9-     4,588.64-   0.9-
                           ----------  -----    ----------  -----
  Net Sales                 13,089.70 100.0    517,942.08  100.0

COST OF GOODS SOLD
  COS Fencing & Gutters      6,301.70  48.1    352,461.13   68.1
                           ----------  -----    ----------  -----
  Total Cost of Goods Sold   6,301.70  48.1    352,461.13   68.1
                           ----------  -----    ----------  -----
  Gross Profit               6,788.00  51.9    165,480.95   31.9

EXPENSES
  Salaries Fencing/Gutters       0.00   0.0    131,464.76   25.4
  Uniforms Fencing & Gutter     74.00   0.6        518.00    0.1
                           ----------  -----    ----------  -----
  Total Expenses                74.00   0.6    131,982.76   25.5
                           ----------  -----    ----------  -----
  Net Operating Income       6,714.00  51.3     33,498.19    6.5


  Income Before Taxes        6,714.00  51.3     33,498.19    6.5
                           ----------  -----    ----------  -----
  Net Income                 6,714.00  51.3     33,498.19    6.5
                           ==========  =====    ==========  =====
```

Depreciation Schedule

Depreciation Schedule

ASSET: COMPAQ COMPUTER S/N PV54-34592   METHOD: STRAIGHT LINE

YEAR	DEBIT DEPRECIATION EXPENSE	CREDIT ACCUMULATED DEPRECIATION	TOTAL ACCUMULATED DEPRECIATION	NET BOOK VALUE
1	750.00	750.00	750.00	7,500.00
2	750.00	750.00	1,500.00	6,750.00
3	750.00	750.00	2,250.00	6,000.00
4	750.00	750.00	3,000.00	5,250.00
5	750.00	750.00	3,750.00	4,500.00
6	750.00	750.00	4,500.00	3,750.00
7	750.00	750.00	5,250.00	3,000.00
8	750.00	750.00	6,000.00	2,250.00
9	750.00	750.00	6,750.00	1,500.00
10	750.00	750.00	7,500.00	750.00
TOTAL	7,500.00	7,500.00	7,500.00	0.00

Amortization Schedule

RUN DATE: 12/31/92   W.D. Peachtree & Company   PAGE 1
RUN TIME: 2:37 PM

Amortization Schedule

ITEM: COMPAQ COMPUTER LOAN   ANNUAL INTEREST RATE: 10.000
PRINCIPAL: 12,000.00   PAYMENTS PER YEAR: 12
TERM: 12 PAYMENTS

PMT. NO.	PAYMENT AMOUNT	EARNED INTEREST	PRINCIPAL REDUCTION	REMAINING BALANCE
				12,000.00
1	1,054.99	100.00	954.99	11,045.01
2	1,054.99	92.04	962.95	10,082.06
3	1,054.99	84.02	970.97	9,111.09
4	1,054.99	75.93	979.06	8,132.03
5	1,054.99	67.77	987.22	7,144.81
6	1,054.99	59.54	995.45	6,149.36
7	1,054.99	51.24	1,003.75	5,145.61
8	1,054.99	42.88	1,012.11	4,133.50
9	1,054.99	34.45	1,020.54	3,112.96
10	1,054.99	25.94	1,029.05	2,083.91
11	1,054.99	17.37	1,037.62	1,046.29
12	1,055.01	8.72	1,046.29	0.00
TOTAL	12,659.90	659.90	12,000.00	0.00

Maintain Chart of Accounts Control Report

```
RUN DATE: 12/31/92        W.D. Peachtree & Company              PAGE  1
RUN TIME:  2:39 PM              General Ledger
                    Maintain Chart of Accounts Control Report

                            CHANGE ACCOUNT

        FIELD                  CURRENT VALUE           ORIGINAL VALUE

ACCOUNT NUMBER.....:  11500
DESCRIPTION......:  Petty Cash                      : Cash on Hand
ACCOUNT TYPE (1-9):  2                              : 2
MASTER / DEPT....:                                  : .
BALANCE COL (0-3).:  1                              : 1

FISCAL PERIOD  1 . . :          1,500.00
FISCAL PERIOD  2 . . :          1,500.00
FISCAL PERIOD  3 . . :          1,500.00
FISCAL PERIOD  4 . . :          1,500.00
FISCAL PERIOD  5 . . :          1,500.00
FISCAL PERIOD  6 . . :          1,500.00
FISCAL PERIOD  7 . . :          1,500.00
FISCAL PERIOD  8 . . :          1,500.00
FISCAL PERIOD  9 . . :          1,500.00
FISCAL PERIOD 10 . . :          1,500.00
FISCAL PERIOD 11 . . :              0.00
FISCAL PERIOD 12 . . :              0.00
FISCAL PERIOD 13 . . :              0.00

BUDGET PERIOD  1 . . :              0.00                     0.00
BUDGET PERIOD  2 . . :              0.00                     0.00
BUDGET PERIOD  3 . . :              0.00                     0.00


ACCOUNT TOTALS:      ACCT. QTY.  ACCT. # HASH TOTAL
              BATCH      =  0         0
              ACTUAL     =  0         0
                          ----      ----
              DIFFERENCE =  0         0

*** End Of Maintain Chart of Accounts Control Report ***
```

Prepare Next Year's Budget Control Report

W.D. Peachtree & Company

Prepare Next Year's Budget Control Report

Using Prior Fiscal Information - Percentage Increase: 15.00

PD	CURR. BUDGET	NEXT BUDGET	PD	CURR. BUDGET	NEXT BUDGET	PD	CURR. BUDGET	NEXT BUDGET	PD	CURR. BUDGET	NEXT BUDGET
13500	Inventory										
1	55757.00	31991.42	4	78059.81	64256.71	7	92891.17	50201.17	10	137608.29	47332.46
2	44605.00	56269.58	5	92891.17	65534.49	8	89211.21	67043.27	11	126345.37	0.00
3	66908.40	65534.49	6	100362.61	54034.50	9	96682.64	75443.44	12	133816.81	0.00

*** End Of - Prepare Next Year's Budget Control Report ***

Enter Transactions Control Report

```
RUN DATE: 12/31/92        W.D. Peachtree & Company              PAGE  1
RUN TIME:  2:54 PM              General Ledger
                          Enter Transactions Control Report
----------------------------------------------------------------------------
SOURCE CODE: 3 MISCELLANEOUS JE                      ENTRY SESSION:  7
LN  REF     DATE      DESCRIPTION            ACCOUNT            AMOUNT
============================================================================
1   1408    11/30/92  11/92 SERVICE CHARGES   54000             43.50
2   1409    11/30/92  11/92 SERVICE CHARGES   11000             43.50-
    1410    11/30/92  RETURNED CHECK #38456   64000            147.56
4           11/30/92  RETURNED CHECK #38456   11000            147.56-
============================================================================
            TRANSACTIONS    DEBITS    CREDITS    BALANCE   ACCT. TOT.
TOTALS:          4          191.06    191.06-      0.00      140000
BATCH:           4                                           140000
            --------------------------------------------
DIFFERENCE:      0                                             0

*** End of Enter Transactions Control Report ***
```

Delete Transactions Control Report

RUN DATE: 12/31/92   W.D. Peachtree & Company   PAGE 1
RUN TIME: 2:59 PM   General Ledger
     Delete Transactions Control Report

SC	REFERENCE	DATE	DESCRIPTION	ENTRY SESSION	ACCOUNT	AMOUNT
3	JE50	11/30/92	Allowance for Bad Debts	4	13000	500.00-
3	JE50	11/30/92	Allowance for Bad Debts	4	53500	500.00

		TRANS. QTY.	ACCOUNT HASH NO.
TOTAL DEBITS	500.00	2	66500
TOTAL CREDITS	500.00-	2	66500
DIFFERENCE	0.00	0	0

*** End Of Delete Transactions Control Report ***

Chapter 3

GENERAL LEDGER: PRACTICING WITH A SAMPLE BUSINESS

Learning Objectives:

After studying this chapter you should be able to:

1. Perform General Ledger maintenance activities including—adding an account to your chart of accounts, setting up related department accounts, printing a list of all of the accounts, using some of PCA's standard features, and showing how to examine all the information in an account.

2. Perform daily and weekly activities including—entering regular transactions, entering reversing transactions, entering regular and repeating transactions, printing a transaction register and correcting errors, and keeping General Ledger in balance.

3. Perform monthly or fiscal period activities including—transferring summary journals, deleting obsolete repeating transactions, printing a detailed trial balance and financial statements, closing the current period, and examining reversed transactions.

4. Perform yearly activities including—making year-end adjustments, closing the fiscal year, adding an additional adjusting period and changing period ending dates, and preparing a budget for the new fiscal year.

Chapter 3

General Ledger: Practicing with a Sample Business

This chapter guides you through lessons that give you practical experience in working with General Ledger. Here, you will practice working with the General Ledger of W. D. Peachtree & Company, a fictitious business. The information contained in this company was created to help you practice with Peachtree Complete Accounting's modules.

Using a "hands-on" approach, you will work with the same General Ledger programs and perform the same kinds of tasks here that you may use later in an actual business.

The lessons in this chapter are grouped under these topics:

1. Maintenance activities.
2. Daily and weekly activities.
3. Monthly or fiscal period activities.
4. Yearly activities.

Topic 1, **Maintenance Activities**, shows you how to add an account with multiple departments. After you create an initial Chart of Accounts, you can add accounts as they are needed. You will also learn how to examine all the information in an existing account.

Topic 2, **Daily and Weekly Activities**, takes you through the General Ledger tasks that a business would do on a regular (daily or weekly) basis. These activities include entering different types of transactions, printing a transaction register to check your transactions, and correcting entry errors.

Topic 3, **Monthly or Fiscal Period Activities**, demonstrates activities that a business would typically do at the end of the month (or other accounting period). Among the topics included here are: deleting a repeating transaction, printing financial statements, printing transaction registers, and closing the current period.

Topic 4, **Yearly Activities**, guides you through closing the fiscal year and preparing a new budget based on the old fiscal year.

Introduction to W. D. Peachtree & Company

W. D. Peachtree & Company is a retail sales business, similar to many of the nation's large retailers. W. D. Peachtree & Company has a single location in Atlanta, Georgia.

In the following lessons, you will use examples from several of W. D. Peachtree & Company's departments. (The company has other departments, but they are not used in this chapter.) Each department's description is followed by the department number that General Ledger uses to identify the department.

- Men's Clothing (12)
- Women's Clothing (14)
- Children's Clothing (16)
- Uniforms (18)

The company's other departments that will be used in some of the other modules are:

- Athletic Shoes (23)
- Other Shoes (25)
- Appliances (31)
- Electronics (33)
- Hardware (35)
- Sporting Goods (42)
- Fencing and Gutters (50)
- Hair Salon (62)

Note that General Ledger has certain module options that govern the way General Ledger operates. W. D. Peachtree & Company has its Force Control Reports option set to Y. This setting ensures that General Ledger prints control reports as you go through the lessons here. Make sure your printer is "on-line" and ready to print before you start the lessons. Use the control reports (and other reports you will be instructed to print) to verify the changes you enter.

Beginning the Practice Session

```
                            WARNING

BEFORE CONTINUING, BE SURE THAT ALL DATA FILES HAVE BEEN RESTORED TO
THEIR ORIGINAL CONDITION.  IF YOU ARE UNSURE OF HOW TO RESTORE THESE
FILES, TURN TO THE INSTRUCTIONS FOUND ON PAGE 1-32 IN  CHAPTER 1.
```

This practice session guides you through typical General Ledger operations. You can complete the exercise in one session, or practice with one topic or lesson at a time. The choice is yours. *Please* do each step in the sequence shown here; some of the later lessons depend on earlier ones.

❖ Start Peachtree Complete Accounting by moving to the directory in which Peachtree Complete has been installed. Normally the directory is named PCA. Then, type **PEACH**, and press ⊞.

In a few moments the first screen will appear. PCA displays the system date, which it gets from your computer. (Either you entered this date when you last started your computer, or it is from your computer's internal calendar.)

❖ Press ⊞ to erase the date shown.

For this practice session you should use November 30, 1992, as the date. This date is convenient because it is the last day of November, the 11th fiscal period of the year. The General Ledger for W. D. Peachtree & Company has twelve fiscal periods that correspond to the calendar year.

❖ For the date 11/30/92, type **113092** and press ⊞.

You do not have to enter the slashes; PCA does that for you.

PCA asks you for a company ID. To use the information for W. D. Peachtree & Company, you must enter its company ID. For this example, WD is the company ID.

❖ Type **WD** and press ⊞.

PCA displays its **Main Menu.**

❖ Select **General Ledger** by highlighting it and pressing ⊞.

This starts PCA's General Ledger. PCA now displays the **General Ledger Main Menu**.

You are now ready to begin the practice session. Continue with Topic 1.

Topic 1 - Maintenance Activities

In General Ledger, there are two maintenance activities you should be familiar with: how to add an account to the Chart of Accounts and how to review an account's information. This section has two lessons:

1. The first lesson shows you how to create an account as well as a series of associated department accounts.

2. The second lesson shows you how to examine all the information in an account.

Lesson 1 - Adding an Account and Related Department Accounts

In this lesson you will learn how to:

- Add an account to your Chart of Accounts.
- Have General Ledger set up related department accounts for you.
- Print a list of all your accounts.
- Use some of PCA's standard features.

Here is the situation. Recently, W. D. Peachtree & Company decided to offer tailoring services for clothing. Each clothing department will charge separately for the tailoring service. You are going to create a tailoring fees account for each of the four clothing departments.

The four posting accounts for tailoring fees require a fifth account—a Department Control account. The Department Control account summarizes the figures for a group of department posting accounts.

❖ Because the Maintenance Programs are used to make changes select **Maintenance Programs** from the General Ledger Main Menu by pressing ▐ENTER▌, then select **Maintain Chart of Accounts**.

Because the Force Control Reports option has been set to Y, General Ledger asks you to set the paper on your printer to the *Top of Form*, that is, at the top of a new page. General Ledger is going to print a control report that lists the changes you make.

❖ Make sure your printer is ready to print and at the top of a new page. Then press ▐ENTER▌.

General Ledger now asks how many accounts you intend to change. You are going to add four department posting accounts and one Department Control account—a total of five accounts.

❖ Type **5** and press ▐ENTER▌ .

If you left out an account by mistake and added only four of the five accounts, General Ledger would tell you that the intended and actual numbers did not match.

General Ledger asks you for the **hash total** (a type of check figure) for the accounts you intend to change. The hash total is the sum of all the account numbers you are going to enter. In this practice case, the hash total will be 167560.

❖ Type **167560** for the hash total and press 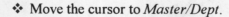.

To tell General Ledger to ignore either the number of accounts to change or the hash total, you would accept the default of zero.

After you enter the hash total, the cursor moves to the *ACCEPT (Y/N)* prompt. You can accept this information (leave it the way it is) or not accept it (in which case General Ledger lets you go back and change it).

❖ Check your entries and then respond to the accept prompt with **Y**. (Press [ENTER].)

General Ledger asks you for an account number. You are going to enter the Department Control account first. In this practice case, the Department Control account number is 33500.

❖ Type **33500** for the account number and press [ENTER].

General Ledger tells you that it could not find the account and asks if you want to add it.

❖ Since you do want to add the account, accept **Y**. (Press [ENTER].)

General Ledger asks you for a description for this account.

❖ Type **Tailoring** and press [ENTER].

General Ledger asks for the account type and supplies **2** as the default. You will learn about account types later.

❖ Press [F10] to accept 2 as the account type and to indicate that the current entries are correct.

General Ledger displays more account information and asks you to accept it.

❖ Since you still have other information to add for this account, type **N** and press [ENTER].

❖ Move the cursor to *Master/Dept*.

❖ Type **D** for *Master/Dept.*, and press [ENTER].

This signifies that the account is a Department Control account.

When you tell General Ledger that this is a Department Control account, it automatically fills in **33599** for the Group End number. The Group End specifies the last possible account that this account can sum. The account numbers for the other four accounts—the department posting accounts—must fall between 33500 (the number of the Department Control account) and 33599 (the last possible account to sum).

❖ Press [F10] to tell General Ledger that you are done.

General Ledger asks you to accept the displayed information.

When you add or change important information in General Ledger, it asks you to accept the information. This lets you check what is on the screen and choose whether or not that information becomes part of General Ledger. When responding to *ACCEPT (Y/N)*, you generally have four choices:

1. **Answer Y to accept the information**. The information you're accepting typically consists of transactions you have entered or accounts you have added or changed.

2. **Answer N to make changes to what you see.** Answer **N** if you notice a mistake or want to change any of the displayed information.

3. **Press [F8] to discard what you have typed**. For example, if you were in the process of renaming an account and changed your mind before accepting it, then it might be easier to discard what you have typed and start over. You can do this only if *[F8] - Undo* is highlighted at the bottom of your screen.

4. **Press [ESC] to move backwards in the program without either accepting or rejecting what you have typed.**

❖ Check the information you entered and, when you are satisfied with it, accept it by selecting **Y.** General Ledger will now give you an option to enter budget information for this account.

❖ When General Ledger asks if you want to enter budget information, answer **N**. (Press [ENTER].)

❖ General Ledger prints out a Maintain Chart of Accounts Control Report for Account Number 33500 that appears as follows. (Of course, your run time will likely be different.)

```
RUN DATE:  11/30/92              W.D. Peachtree & Company                PAGE 1
RUN TIME:    3:09 PM                  General Ledger
                                Maintain Chart Of Accounts Control Report
--------------------------------------------------------------------------------

                                          ADD ACCOUNT
            FIELD                         CURRENT VALUE
    ---------------------------      ---------------------------


    ACCOUNT NUMBER ...... :          33500
    DESCRIPTION ............... :    Tailoring
    ACCOUNT TYPE (1-9).... :         2
    MASTER / DEPT ........... :      D
    GROUP END ................. :    33599


    -----------------------------------------------------------------------------
    FISCAL PERIOD   1.......:                      0.00
    FISCAL PERIOD   2......:                       0.00
    FISCAL PERIOD   3......:                       0.00
    FISCAL PERIOD   4......:                       0.00
    FISCAL PERIOD   5......:                       0.00
    FISCAL PERIOD   6......:                       0.00
    FISCAL PERIOD   7......:                       0.00
    FISCAL PERIOD   8......:                       0.00
    FISCAL PERIOD   9......:                       0.00
    FISCAL PERIOD 10......:                        0.00
    FISCAL PERIOD 11......:                        0.00
    FISCAL PERIOD 12......:                        0.00
    FISCAL PERIOD 13......:                        0.00


    -----------------------------------------------------------------------------
    BUDGET PERIOD   1....:                         0.00
    BUDGET PERIOD   2....:                         0.00
    BUDGET PERIOD   3....:                         0.00
    BUDGET PERIOD   4....:                         0.00
    BUDGET PERIOD   5....:                         0.00
    BUDGET PERIOD   6....:                         0.00
    BUDGET PERIOD   7....:                         0.00
    BUDGET PERIOD   8....:                         0.00
    BUDGET PERIOD   9....:                         0.00
    BUDGET PERIOD 10....:                          0.00
    BUDGET PERIOD 11....:                          0.00
    BUDGET PERIOD 12....:                          0.00
    BUDGET PERIOD 13....:                          0.00
```

❖ When General Ledger asks you if you want to automatically create department accounts, answer **Y**. (Press 〔ENTER〕.)

This feature lets you create department posting accounts based on the Department Control account you just created. If you had not wanted to create department posting accounts, you would have answered **N**.

❖ Choose Selected Departments. (Type **S**.)

The screen asks you if you want to create department posting accounts for All Departments or Selected Departments. General Ledger asks you for a department number. Here is an easy way to look up what departments are available.

❖ Press **F2**.

General Ledger displays a "pop up" box that lists all available departments for W. D. Peachtree & Company. Pop up boxes, which allow you to look up possible responses, are available whenever you see *[F2] - LOOKUP* at the bottom of your screen.

❖ Select **12 - Men's Clothing** from the pop up box.

General Ledger creates a type **2** account with account number **33512** and the description **Tailoring Men's Clothing**.

General Ledger prints out a copy of this account. The printout appears as follows:

```
RUN DATE:  11/30/92          W.D. Peachtree & Company          PAGE 2
RUN TIME:    3:09 PM              General Ledger
                          Maintain Chart Of Accounts Control Report
-----------------------------------------------------------------------------
                                          ADD ACCOUNT
          FIELD                          CURRENT VALUE
------------------------------------     -------------------------------


ACCOUNT NUMBER ...... :          33512
DESCRIPTION .............. :      Tailoring Men's Clothing
ACCOUNT TYPE (1-9).... :          2
MASTER / DEPT ............ :


-----------------------------------------------------------------------------
FISCAL PERIOD   1.......:                      0.00
FISCAL PERIOD   2......:                       0.00
FISCAL PERIOD   3......:                       0.00
FISCAL PERIOD   4......:                       0.00
FISCAL PERIOD   5......:                       0.00
FISCAL PERIOD   6......:                       0.00
FISCAL PERIOD   7......:                       0.00
FISCAL PERIOD   8......:                       0.00
FISCAL PERIOD   9......:                       0.00
FISCAL PERIOD 10......:                        0.00
FISCAL PERIOD 11......:                        0.00
FISCAL PERIOD 12......:                        0.00
FISCAL PERIOD 13......:                        0.00


-----------------------------------------------------------------------------
BUDGET PERIOD   1....:                         0.00
BUDGET PERIOD   2....:                         0.00
BUDGET PERIOD   3....:                         0.00
BUDGET PERIOD   4....:                         0.00
BUDGET PERIOD   5....:                         0.00
BUDGET PERIOD   6....:                         0.00
BUDGET PERIOD   7....:                         0.00
BUDGET PERIOD   8....:                         0.00
BUDGET PERIOD   9....:                         0.00
BUDGET PERIOD 10....:                          0.00
BUDGET PERIOD 11....:                          0.00
BUDGET PERIOD 12....:                          0.00
BUDGET PERIOD 13....:                          0.00
```

Notice two things about this account:

- The account number consists of the main part of the Department Control account number (**335**) and the department number (**12**).

- Similarly, the description consists of the Department Control account description (**Tailoring**) and the department description (**Men's Clothing**).

Because the *entire* description can only be 25 characters, you should limit the size of both the Department Control account description and the department description. If the combined description is longer than 25 characters, General Ledger only uses the first 25 characters.

General Ledger asks you for another department number. Now you will see another way to look up what departments are available.

❖ Without typing anything, press ⌨.

General Ledger again displays the pop up box listing the available departments.

Pressing ⌨ looks up information only when General Ledger does not supply a default. If General Ledger had supplied a default department number and you had pressed ⌨, General Ledger would have created an account for the default department number.

If General Ledger does supply a default, you can usually press ⌨ to get rid of it and then use ⌨ to look up possible responses.

❖ Select **14 - Women's Clothing** from the pop up box.

General Ledger creates account number **33514** with the description **Tailoring Women's Clothing** and asks for yet another department number.

Again, General Ledger prints out a copy of the account just created.

❖ Press ⌨ and repeat the selection process for departments **16** and **18**.

General Ledger prints out copies of these accounts also.

❖ After General Ledger creates the posting account for department 18, press ⌨.

❖ When G/L asks for another account number, press ⌨ to indicate you are done.

General Ledger finishes printing the control report. The report appears as follows:

```
RUN DATE: 11/30/92          W.D. Peachtree & Company           PAGE 6
RUN TIME:   3:09 PM              General Ledger
                        Maintain Chart Of Accounts Control Report
------------------------------------------------------------------------------------
====================================================================================
    ACCOUNT TOTALS:              ACCT. QTY.     ACCT. # HASH TOTAL
                        BATCH   =      5              167,560
                        ACTUAL  =      5              167,560
                                    --------         -----------
                        DIFFERENCE =   0                  0

*** End Of Maintain Chart Of Accounts Control Report ***
```

Look at the end of the report. It shows the number of accounts and the hash total under "batch" and compares them to "actual." General Ledger shows you the difference between these sets of numbers. The difference should be zero. If there is a difference, you have made an error. You can correct your error by repeating the maintenance procedure from the beginning of this lesson, but you should only change the accounts that are in error.

Now that **Maintain Chart of Accounts** has been finished, General Ledger returns you to the General Ledger Maintenance Menu.

Now you are going to print a copy of your Chart of Accounts. Printing a copy is a good practice to follow whenever you add or change accounts. The following steps should be followed whenever you want to print a copy of your Chart of Accounts.

❖ Press [ESC] to reach the General Ledger Main Menu.

❖ Then select **Report Programs** and press [ENTER].

❖ Then select **List Chart of Accounts** and press [ENTER]. (Make sure that your printer is ready and your paper is set to the top of the form.)

❖ Select **NO DOLLAR AMOUNTS**, then select **ALL ACCOUNTS**.

General Ledger prints the new Chart of Accounts for W. D. Peachtree & Company. The accounts are listed in order by their account number. Find account number 33500 and its associated department accounts. Notice the traits these accounts have.

❖ Press [ESC] to return to the General Ledger Main Menu.

Note: If you are at a menu, you can always press [ESC] to return to a previous menu. In the remaining lessons, it is assumed that you can find your way around the menus.

Lesson 1 Summary

In this lesson you learned how to add accounts to your Chart of Accounts. You also learned a quick method for creating department posting accounts. You learned that department posting accounts get their account numbers from a combination of their Department Control account number and their department number. Along the way, you gained some familiarity with:

- Control reports and the type of information they give you.
- Using [F2] and [ENTER] to look up information.
- The *ACCEPT Y/N* prompt.

Finally, you learned how to print a copy of your Chart of Accounts.

Lesson 2 - Reviewing an Existing Account's Information

This lesson shows you how to examine all the information in an account. To look at an account's balance, activity, and transactions, you should use **Query Account Status**.

❖ To do this, first select **Processing Programs** from the General Ledger **Main Menu.** Then, from the General Ledger Processing Menu, select **Query Account Status**.

General Ledger asks for an account number.

If you know what account number you want to examine, just enter that number. However, if you don't remember the account number, then use 🖪 to look up information. Unfortunately, there are many account numbers so looking through all of them to find the one you want is neither efficient nor fun. You're in luck. There is a shortcut.

❖ For example, if you want to examine sales in the men's clothing department but you only remember that the account is in the 300 series, then: without pressing 🖱, type the number **300** and then press 🖪.

General Ledger displays a pop up box with W. D. Peachtree's accounts starting with account number *30000*. (If you had pressed 🖪 without typing anything, the box would start with the first account for W. D. Peachtree.)

The pop up box will show that the proper account number for Men's Clothing Sales is 30512.

❖ Select **30512** and press 🖱.

General Ledger shows you—for the Men's Clothing Sales account—the beginning balance, current activity, ending balance, adjustments, and transactions.

If you can't quite remember the account number but know that it starts with 300 (or 170 or whatever), then use this shortcut; it saves you having to use 🖪 and 🖪 to skim the entire list of accounts.

This shortcut is available anytime the pop up boxes are—when you see *[F2] - LOOKUP* at the bottom of your screen.

❖ The screen will ask you if you want to continue. Answer N. Press 🖱. Then press 🖪 to return to the General Ledger Processing Menu.

Lesson 2 Summary

In this lesson you learned how to examine an existing account's information. You also learned about a shortcut available with the 🖪 lookup feature. Use **Query Account Status** to look at an account's balances, activity, and transactions.

Topic 2 - Daily and Weekly Activities

Daily and weekly activities are those General Ledger activities performed on a regular basis to keep your company's General Ledger up-to-date. The lessons under this topic help you become familiar with these activities.

The most common General Ledger activity is entering transactions. Whether a company performs the activities shown here on a daily basis or a weekly basis depends on the volume of its General Ledger transactions. Some businesses have so few transactions that they only enter them once each month.

Topic 2 has five lessons:

1. Entering regular transactions.
2. Entering reversing transactions.
3. Entering regular and repeating transactions.
4. Printing a transaction register and correcting errors.
5. Keeping General Ledger in balance.

Just a reminder: before starting a lesson, prepare your printer for printing the control report. When you finish a lesson, review the control report and check the entries you made.

Lesson 1 - Entering Regular (Non-Repeating) Transactions *

In this lesson you will learn how to:

- Enter some regular transactions.
- Have General Ledger help check your work.

Consider the following situation. As an employee of W. D. Peachtree & Company, you receive the company's monthly bank statement. After reconciling the statement to the company's records, you have two adjusting entries to make:

1. The monthly service charge on your company's bank account ($43.50).
2. A check returned by the bank for insufficient funds from a walk-in customer ($147.56).

You are going to enter four line items (two transaction entries) to take care of these issues.

❖ From the General Ledger Processing Menu, select **Enter Transactions**.

After asking you to prepare your printer for the control report, G/L asks you how many transactions (See note at bottom of page) you plan to enter.

---

* Recall that journal entries are entered into General Ledger for transactions that are not entered into other modules that are linked with General Ledger. Adjusting entries are an example of such entries. When adjusting entries differ from period to period, consider them to be regular transactions in the sense that they must be individually (non-repeating) entered into General Ledger. Other entries that are entered into General Ledger individually would be entered in the manner illustrated here.

Comment: Because of the way W. D. Peachtree is set up, General Ledger usually asks you to prepare your printer for control reports when you start a program. The earlier lessons in this chapter should have given you a sense of how these things work. In the remaining lessons these important, but somewhat repetitive, topics are not discussed.

❖ The two entries require four lines of data to enter, so type **4** and press 🖮. (You can see what these four lines look like by turning to page 3-17.)

This lets General Ledger help check your work. If you enter more or less than four transactions in this session, General Ledger lets you know there is a problem.

Similar to an earlier lesson, General Ledger asks you the hash total for the transactions you intend to enter. The hash total is the sum of all the account numbers for which you plan to enter transactions.

❖ Enter **140000** for the hash total.

Because you are entering two transactions to account 11000, Cash-Operating, you count its account number twice in the hash total.

Having your transaction information clearly laid out makes computing the hash total easy.

❖ Check your entries, then accept them.

General Ledger then displays the date, the period ending date, and the entry session number.

The entry session number identifies all the transactions you enter during this **Enter Transactions** session. It is a good idea to jot down the entry session number on your paperwork (Transactions Setup Forms or whatever). The control report also contains the date and entry session number. General Ledger's **Transaction Register** lets you examine all the transactions for a given entry session.

General Ledger asks you to select a source code from a box of available source codes. The source code indicates the type of transactions you are going to enter.

❖ Select source code **3**, Miscellaneous journal entry.

W. D. Peachtree uses this source code for catch-all journal entries. General Ledger displays the following status information near the top of your screen:

- Today's date and the entry session number.
- The current source code and its description.
- The overall system balance and the total from the transactions entered so far in this session. At this point, both these amounts should be zero.

Note: The term "transactions" has a different meaning here than in accounting. Here a transaction means one part of a journal entry.

Besides this status information, General Ledger displays a line for you to enter your first transaction. The following table provides the information you will need in the next Section to enter the data.

Notice that the transactions are organized to be entered in balanced sets. For any financial event, you will always have at least two transactions—a credit and a debit—that cancel each other out. Often, you will have three or four transactions, for example, a single credit and two or three separate debits that total the amount of the credit.

Line	Ref. #	Date	Description	Acct #	Amount	Accept
1	1408	11/30/92	Service charges	54000	43.50	Y
2	1409	11/30/92	Service charges	11000	-43.50	Y
3	1410	11/30/92	Returned ck, #38456	64000	147.56	Y
4	1411	11/30/92	Returned ck, #38456	11000	-147.56	Y

Entering these four transactions will take care of both bank statement issues:

Note that, for W. D. Peachtree & Company:

- Account 54000, Bank Service Charges, is an Expense account.
- Account 11000, Cash-Operating, is an Asset account.
- Account 64000, Returned Checks, is an Expense account.

Remember that debits are entered as pluses and credits are entered as minuses.

❖ Using the table above, enter the first transaction.

General Ledger fills in the date for you.

If you cannot remember an account number, use ⬛ to search for the number you want. When using ⬛, G/L displays the account numbers in order. Use ⬛ and ⬛ to move through the numbers.

Once you enter an account number, G/L displays its title.

General Ledger supplies the dollar amount that will bring it into balance. Since G/L is already in balance, this amount is **0.00**. Replace it with **43.50**, the amount of the first transaction.

General Ledger asks you to accept the transaction entry.

❖ Check your work and answer **Y**.

After each transaction has been entered, General Ledger prints out the transaction.

General Ledger repeats the same account number on the next transaction line. If this is not the account number you want, type over the answer.

❖ Enter the remaining three transactions.

Both the overall system balance and the transaction total should again be zero.

❖ After you have entered the fourth transaction and G/L is prompting for a fifth one, press ▣.

General Ledger displays the number of transactions and the hash total at the bottom of your screen.

❖ Press ▣ to return to the source code selection screen.

G/L lets you select another source code (so you can enter more transactions) or leave the program.

❖ Press ▣ to leave Enter Transactions.

General Ledger completes the printing of the **Enter Transactions Control Report**, which appears as follows:

```
RUN DATE:  11/30/92          W.D. Peachtree & Company              PAGE 1
RUN TIME:   4:17 PM               General Ledger
                           Enter Transactions Control Report
-----------------------------------------------------------------------
SOURCE CODE: 3 MISCELLANEOUS JE                    ENTRY SESSION:  6
LN    REF        DATE        DESCRIPTION          ACCOUNT    AMOUNT
=======================================================================

1    1408      11/30/92     Service charges        54000       43.50
2    1409      11/30/92     Service charges        11000       43.50-
3    1410      11/30/92     Returned ck, #38456    64000      147.56
4    1411      11/30/92     Returned ck, #38456    11000      147.56-

=======================================================================
TOTALS:       TRANSACTIONS  DEBITS    CREDITS    BALANCE    ACCT. TOT.
                   4         191.06    191.06-     0.00       140000
BATCH:             4                                          140000
                  -----------------------------------------------------
DIFFERENCE:        0                                              0

      *** End Of Enter Transactions Control Report ***
```

❖ Examine the control report.

You will see a list of the transactions you entered. At the end of the report, G/L lists the number of transactions and the hash total. The actual and intended versions of these numbers should match.

Lesson 1 Summary

In this lesson you learned how to organize your transaction information and enter those transactions into General Ledger. You saw how to have General Ledger help check your work by entering the intended number of transactions and account hash totals.

You learned that General Ledger displays the system's balance status. You found out that the entry session number can be used to list a set of transactions. Finally, you saw how entering balanced sets of transactions helps keep General Ledger in balance.

Lesson 2 - Entering Reversing Transactions

Now that you have had some experience entering regular transactions, you are going to enter some transactions for payroll accrual purposes.

Consider this scenario. W. D. Peachtree's pay period for all clothing department employees ends on the 27th of November (the current fiscal period). Of course, clothing department employees still earn money on November 28th, 29th, and 30th, but they are not paid for it until the next fiscal period (December).

Reversing transactions are designed to handle accrual situations like this: where money is earned in one period but paid in another. General Ledger automatically transforms a *reversing* transaction entered in this fiscal period into a *reversed* transaction having an opposite dollar amount in the next fiscal period.

Here is a breakdown of the daily salaries and three-day totals for W. D. Peachtree & Company's four clothing departments:

Account	Description		Daily Amount	Three-Day Amount
50112	Salaries:	Men's Clothing	$275.00	$825.00
50114		Women's Clothing	300.00	900.00
50116		Children's Clothing	125.00	375.00
50118		Uniforms	100.00	300.00
	Salaries	Total	$800.00	$2400.00

Notice that the account numbers for all these Salary department accounts share the same first three digits. The last two digits of these account numbers are the department numbers.

Here are the reversing transactions you need to enter to take care of the clothing department salaries for the 28th, 29th, and 30th of November:

Ref. #	Description	Acct #	Amount	Accept
1412	Clothing Depts: 11/92	21000	-2400.00	Y
1413	Men's Clothing: 11/92	50112	825.00	Y
1414	Women's Clothing: 11/92	50114	900.00	Y
1415	Children's Clothing: 11/92	50116	375.00	Y
1416	Uniforms: 11/92	50118	300.00	Y

Note that, for W. D. Peachtree & Company:

- Account 21000, Accrued Payroll, is a Liability account.

- All the 501xx accounts—the Salary accounts for the clothing departments—are expense accounts.

Now it is time to enter these transactions.

❖ From the General Ledger Processing Menu, select **Enter Transactions**.

Check the current system balance; it should be zero.

❖ Type **5** when General Ledger asks how many transactions you plan to enter.

❖ Type **221460** for the hash total.

This is the sum of the account numbers for all five transactions.

❖ Check your entries, then accept them.

G/L displays the new entry session number along with other status information. If you need to check all transactions for an entry session at a later date, you will need this number.

❖ Jot down the entry session number (or save the control report that contains it) for future reference.

General Ledger asks you to select a source code.

❖ Select source code **7**, Reversing Journal Entry.

General Ledger is now ready for you to enter transactions.

❖ Enter all the transactions from the table below. Check the figures for each transaction before accepting it. General Ledger will print each line as you accept it.

Ref. #	Date	Description	Acct #	Amount	Accept
1412	11/30/92	Clothing Depts	21000	-2400.00	Y
1413	11/30/92	Men's Clothing	50112	825.00	Y
1414	11/30/92	Women's Clothing	50114	900.00	Y
1415	11/30/92	Children's Clothing	50116	375.00	Y
1416	11/30/92	Uniforms	50118	300.00	Y

When you are done, the system and transaction balances should be zero.

❖ Press ▨ to quit entering transactions and ▨ to return to the source code selection screen.

If you needed to enter other transactions that used a different source code, this is where you would have selected that source code.

By the way, you might want to get into the habit of organizing and entering your transactions by the source code they use. There are two excellent reasons to do so:

1. You can enter a series of transactions using the same source code into General Ledger without having to repeatedly enter that source code.

2. Most of the time, all the transactions that use a given source code should balance each other out. Entering all the same source code transactions together helps isolate your transactions into separate sets that are easier to keep in balance.

❖ Press ▣ to leave **Enter Transactions**. General Ledger will complete the Enter Transactions Control Report. The report will appear as follows:

```
RUN DATE: 11/30/92          W.D. Peachtree & Company              PAGE 1
RUN TIME:  4:42PM                  General Ledger
                             Enter Transactions Control Report
-----------------------------------------------------------------------------
SOURCE CODE: 7 REVERSING JE                          ENTRY SESSION:  7
LN    REF        DATE        DESCRIPTION           ACCOUNT      AMOUNT
=============================================================================

1    1412      11/30/92      Clothing Depts          21000     2,400.00-
2    1413      11/30/92      Men's Clothing          50112       825.00
3    1414      11/30/92      Women's Clothing        50114       900.00
4    1415      11/30/92      Children's Clothing     50116       375.00
5    1416      11/30/92      Uniforms                50118       300.00

=============================================================================
TOTALS:           TRANSACTIONS   DEBITS     CREDITS    BALANCE   ACCT. TOT.
                       5         2,400.00   2,400.00-   0.00      221460
BATCH:                 5                                          221460
                  -----------------------------------------------------------
DIFFERENCE:            0                                               0

       *** End Of Enter Transactions Control Report ***
```

Examine the control report.

You will see the transactions you entered as well as the number of transactions and hash total.

General Ledger will automatically transform a reversing transaction entered in this fiscal period (November) into a reversed transaction having an opposite dollar amount in the next fiscal period (December).

Lesson 2 Summary

In this lesson you learned how to use reversing transactions for accrual purposes. You saw how to handle a typical situation in which salaries earned in one fiscal period are paid in another.

Another example demonstrated how department accounts share the first three digits with their Department Control accounts.

Finally, you learned that organizing and entering your transactions by source code is not only efficient but also helps you keep General Ledger in balance.

Lesson 3 - Entering Regular and Repeating Transactions *

In this lesson you will learn how to:

- Enter repeating transactions.
- Plan for adjustments you have to make under certain conditions.

W. D. Peachtree & Company just paid for twelve months of insurance to provide coverage from November, 1992 through October, 1993. The amount, $3611.44, was paid through Peachtree Complete Accounting's Accounts Payable module.

This insurance payment was entered (in Accounts Payable) as a credit transaction. The same dollar amount was debited to a General Ledger Asset account called "Prepaid Insurance."

Now you are going to set up a series of *repeating* transactions; that is, transactions that repeatedly post amounts to the same accounts each fiscal period. The amount of these specific transactions should equal one-twelfth of the total annual cost of the insurance. Basically, this asset will be expensed each month by crediting the Prepaid Insurance account and debiting the account for the insurance expense.

W. D. Peachtree has three different types of insurance so the situation is a bit more complicated (but not much). This asset will be expensed by setting up four transactions—one for each of four accounts—that repeat each month:

1. Credit Prepaid Insurance (#17500), an Asset account.

2. Debit General Liability Insurance (#59500), an Expense account.

3. Debit Fire and Theft Insurance (#58500), an Expense account.

4. Debit Fleet Insurance (#59000), an Expense account that covers W. D. Peachtree's delivery trucks and company cars.

Here are the repeating transactions you will enter:

Ref. #	Date	Description	Acct #	Amount	Accept
1417	11/30/92	Monthly: 11/92 thru 10/93	17500	-300.00	Y
1418	11/30/92	Monthly: 11/92 thru 10/93	59500	55.00	Y
1419	11/30/92	Monthly: 11/92 thru 10/93	58500	82.00	Y
1420	11/30/92	Monthly: 11/92 thru 10/93	59000	163.00	Y

* Repeating transactions are adjusting entries that are identical month after month.

At the end of the 12-month period, these transactions account for $3600.00 of the $3611.44 so $11.44 remains to be handled during the final month of the insurance coverage (that is, during October, 1993). At the end of this 12-month coverage in October, two things need to happen:

1. You would need to enter a set of regular (non-repeating) transactions that deals with the remaining $11.44.

   For the Prepaid Insurance account (#17500), for example, you would enter a credit transaction for -$11.44 to have the total of $3611.44 come out right. You would also enter debits totaling $11.44 to the three insurance expense accounts.

2. You would have to delete the repeating transactions *before* you close this last period to which they apply (October, 1993). When you close a fiscal period, General Ledger takes any active repeating transactions and sets them up for the next fiscal period. Once these repeating transactions have outlived their usefulness, you must delete them before G/L sets them up for the next period.

Now enter the transactions.

❖ From the General Ledger Processing Menu, select **Enter Transactions**.

The current system balance should still be zero.

General Ledger asks how many transactions you plan to enter. Besides the four transactions above, you are going to add two other transactions you will learn about later.

❖ Type **6**.

❖ Type **239014** for the hash total.

This is the sum of the account numbers for all six transactions (including the two you will see later).

❖ Check and accept your entries.

❖ Write down the entry session number (or save the control report that contains it). You will need this number during the next lesson.

❖ Select source code **6**, Repeating journal entry.

❖ Enter the repeating transactions shown in the previous table. Remember to check each transaction's figures before accepting it. General Ledger will print each transaction as you accept it.

When you are done, the system balance and transaction total should both be zero.

❖ Press ▣ to quit entering transactions and ▣ to return to the source code selection screen.

The illustration regarding repeating transactions is now complete. Next, begins an illustration on how to correct an error.

❖ Select source code **1**, Cash Receipts, and enter these transactions:

Ref. #	Date	Description	Acct #	Amount	Accept
1421	11/30/92	Forgot to enter before	33512	-18.37	Y
1422	11/30/92	Forgot to enter before	11000	18.37	Y

These transactions cover a tailoring fee paid in cash to one of W. D. Peachtree's clothing departments. The transactions were not recorded previously. Account number 11000 is Cash-Operating, an Asset account. Account number 33512 is Tailoring Men's Clothing, a revenue account. The credit should have been to a different account as will be discussed in the next lesson.

Your General Ledger should still be in balance.

❖ General Ledger prints each line of the Enter Transactions Control Report as you accept it.

❖ Leave **Enter Transactions** by pressing 🔲 and then 🔲. Then press 🔲 again. The report will appear as follows:

```
RUN DATE: 11/30/92          W.D. Peachtree & Company               PAGE 2
RUN TIME:  7:08 PM                 General Ledger
                           Enter Transactions Control Report
-------------------------------------------------------------------------
SOURCE CODE: 1 CASH RECEIPTS                      ENTRY SESSION:  8
LN    REF        DATE       DESCRIPTION        ACCOUNT     AMOUNT
=========================================================================

5    1421      11/30/92     Forgot to enter before    33512       18.37-
6    1422      11/30/92     Forgot to enter before    11000       18.37

=========================================================================
TOTALS:      TRANSACTIONS   DEBITS   CREDITS   BALANCE   ACCT. TOT.
                  6         318.37   318.37-    0.00       239012
BATCH:            6                                        239014

             ------------------------------------------------------------
DIFFERENCE:       0                                            2

      *** End Of Enter Transactions Control Report ***
```

Examine the report. You will see on the control report that the intended and actual hash totals do not match. In the next lesson, you will see how to track down and correct the mistake.

Lesson 3 Summary

In this lesson you learned how to enter repeating transactions to deal with situations that repeat for a number of fiscal periods. You saw how to allocate an amount over a span of several fiscal periods and plan for the adjustments you have to make at the end of that time. You also learned that you must delete a set of repeating transactions *before* you close the last period to which they apply.

Lesson 4 - Printing a Transaction Register and Correcting Errors

In this lesson you will learn how to:

- Print a transaction register.
- Find and correct a transaction mistake.

The control report from the previous lesson showed a difference between your intended and actual hash totals. This is the idea behind entering the number and hash total of intended transactions: when the intended and actual numbers do not match, it alerts you to a mistake.

Often, you can find the mistake in your entries by printing a transaction register and comparing it with the paperwork (Transaction Setup Forms or whatever) from which you made the entries.

You will start with that approach. Follow this procedure to print a transaction register for the previous entry session:

❖ Press **ESC** to return to the General Ledger Main Menu, then select Report Programs. From the General Ledger Reports Menu, select **Transaction Register**.

❖ Then select **PRINT BY ACCOUNT NUMBER**.

Since you entered more than one source code, it does not make sense to print by source code.

G/L asks if you want to print a departmental transaction register.

❖ Answer **N**.

You do not want to print only department transactions since you do not know where the error occurred.

General Ledger asks you for the entry session number. You wrote it down during the last lesson or should have it on your control report.

❖ Enter the entry session number (8).

This number tells General Ledger to print all transactions for the current period entered during the entry session you specified. This list includes all transactions, regardless of their source code.

General Ledger prints your transaction register.

Nothing out of the ordinary should appear on the transaction register.

It turns out that the correct amount was entered to the wrong account number. There were two clues that this was the case:

1. General Ledger is still in balance even with the mistake. This means that the numbers that were entered were correct or just happened to balance each other out.

2. General Ledger discovered the error through an incorrect hash total. That means that either the account numbers were added incorrectly (and the wrong hash total was entered) or that an entry mistake was made (and one or more transactions were made to the wrong account).

You entered one of the regular transactions that covered the tailoring fee to the wrong account number. Sorry about that. You entered a credit of -$18.37 to account #33512 (Tailoring Men's Clothing). Fortunately, the hash total was computed using account #33514 (Tailoring Women's Clothing), which is where the transaction should in fact have been posted.

❖ When report is finished, press [F10].

Only one of the tailoring transactions was entered incorrectly; the other one was correct. Thus, two transactions are needed: one correcting transaction to fix (balance out) the mistake and a second transaction for the originally-intended entry.

Here they are:

Ref. #	Date	Description	Acct #	Amount	Accept
1423	11/30/92	Offset incorrect entry	33512	18.37	Y
1424	11/30/92	Forgot to enter before	33514	-18.37	Y

Notice that the correcting transaction (to #33512) is the same as the original entry except it has an opposite dollar amount. This step corrects the error while keeping an audit trail of both the original and the correcting transaction.

❖ Now these transactions will be entered into W. D. Peachtree & Company's General Ledger.

Press [ESC] to leave the General Ledger Reports Menu and return to the General Ledger Main Menu. Then select Processing Programs. Then select Enter Transactions from the General Ledger Processing Menu. The number of transactions is 2. The Hash Total is 67026. From the Select Source Code Menu, select Miscellaneous JE. Then enter the transactions using the data in the table above. After you have finished, press [F10] and then [ENTER]. Then press [F10] again.

Some companies like to keep an audit trail of *everything* that happens in their General Ledger, including mistakes. This is the approach used in this lesson.

Other companies prefer to avoid what they feel is unnecessary clutter. **Delete Transactions** can be used to get rid of mistakes and then to enter the originally-intended transaction. When you delete transactions, General Ledger asks you for the number and hash total of the transactions you intend to delete. After you enter an account number, G/L lets you remove any of that account's current transactions.

Lesson 4 Summary

In this lesson, you saw some good strategies for finding errors. These strategies include:

- Entering the number and hash total of your intended transactions.
- Always printing a control report so you are likely to know when an error occurs.
- Printing a transaction register for all transactions from a given entry session and comparing it with your paperwork.

You saw how to interpret a hash total error. After isolating the mistake, you learned how to correct the mistaken entry.

Lesson 5 - Keeping General Ledger in Balance

In this lesson, you will learn how to deal with General Ledger when it gets out of balance. G/L's behavior here depends on the setting of the Force Balance Transactions option. W. D. Peachtree & Company has this option set to Y.

Keeping G/L in balance is important. General Ledger will not let you print financial statements or close the current period unless G/L is in balance. This is true regardless of any module option settings.

❖ Select **Enter Transactions** from the General Ledger Processing Menu.

Start by entering a transaction that throws G/L out of balance. The number of transactions is 2. The Hash Total is 67036.

❖ Using source code **1**, enter only the first transaction below. That is, just type in the first line (Ref. # 1425) right now.

Ref. #	Date	Description	Acct #	Amount	Accept
1425	11/30/92	Testing balance	33518	2.00	Y
1426	11/30/92	Testing balance	33518	-2.00	Y

❖ After entering the first transaction (Ref. # 1425), notice the status of the Transaction Total near the top of the screen. Then try to leave **Enter Transactions** by pressing 📼.

General Ledger will not let you exit the program while G/L is out of balance. This is because W. D. Peachtree's Force Balance Transactions option—which forces you to keep G/L in balance—is set to Y. (If this option were set to N, G/L would have let you exit.)

❖ Press ▣ to continue. Then enter the second transaction using source code **1**. (The screen does not show the first transaction. You will see Line 2 with Ref. # 1425. Type 1426 in the Ref. # field and complete the transaction as shown above.)

General Ledger should be back in balance.

❖ Leave **Enter Transactions** by following the instructions on the screen (▣▣). General Ledger will print the following Enter Transactions Control Report:

```
RUN DATE:  11/30/92          W.D. Peachtree & Company              PAGE 1
RUN TIME:   8:11 PM                 General Ledger
                           Enter Transactions Control Report
------------------------------------------------------------------------------
SOURCE CODE:  1 CASH RECEIPTS                     ENTRY SESSION:  10
LN    REF        DATE       DESCRIPTION          ACCOUNT      AMOUNT
===============================================================================

1    1425      11/30/92    Testing balance        33518        2.00
2    1426      11/30/92    Testing balance        33518        2.00-

===============================================================================
TOTALS:       TRANSACTIONS  DEBITS    CREDITS    BALANCE    ACCT. TOT.
                  2          2.00      2.00-       0.00        67036
BATCH:            2                                            67036
                 ------------------------------------------------------
DIFFERENCE:       0                                               0

     *** End Of Enter Transactions Control Report ***
```

With Force Balance Transactions set to Y, **Delete Transactions** does the same thing: it will not let you leave if you delete one or more transactions that leave G/L out of balance.

The cardinal rule here is to *always* enter transactions in balanced sets.

Lesson 5 Summary

In this lesson, you saw what General Ledger does when it gets out of balance with the Force Balance Transactions option set to Y.

If you are tired, this may be a good point at which to end this session. If you decide to stop here make sure you have backed up your General Ledger data disk. When you continue this practice session at a later time you will have to follow the procedure now described.

I. Get to the PCA Main Menu by moving to the directory in which Peachtree Complete has been installed (probably PCA). Then type **PEACH.**
2. Select the Utilities option.
3. From the Utilities Menu, select Backup/Restore Data Files.
4. When asked to select a Program Option, choose Restore Data Files.
5. When asked to select a Restore Option, choose Restore Individual Module Files.
6. When asked to select a module, choose General Ledger.
7. Then follow the instructions on the screen.

These actions will restore the General Ledger data files to the point where you decide to end your session. This same routine can be used to restore data to any of the module data files in PCA.

Topic 3 - Monthly or Fiscal Period Activities

> If you ended your last session before this point, you should follow the procedures listed at the end of the Lesson 5 Summary. If you did not "take a break" at this point, you may just continue working.

Monthly or fiscal period tasks are activities you perform once during the month or fiscal period. Usually, you do these at the end of the fiscal period. The two key events that happen at this time are printing financial statements and closing the accounts for the current period.

By the time you finish the lessons in this topic, you will understand most of the things that General Ledger can do on a monthly (or other fiscal period) basis.

Topic 3 has four lessons:

1. Transferring summary journals.
2. Deleting obsolete repeating transactions.
3. Printing a detailed trial balance and financial statements.
4. Closing the current period.

Lesson 1 - Transferring Summary Journals

In this lesson you will learn how to transfer a summary journal from Accounts Payable, another Peachtree Complete Accounting module. Four of PCA's modules let you transfer information to General Ledger. When it gets information from other modules, General Ledger processes the information as a set of transactions to General Ledger accounts.

This lesson also shows you how to list the transferred transactions using **Transaction Register**.

W. D. Peachtree & Company uses Accounts Payable along with General Ledger and takes advantage of PCA's ability to receive postings (in summary journals) from other PCA modules.

Before starting this lesson, make sure W. D. Peachtree's General Ledger is in balance. If you have just finished another lesson, you should know your balance status. If you need to check on G/L's balance, run **Enter Transactions** and look at the displayed balance status. After confirming that G/L is in balance, continue with this lesson.

There are two other tasks you will usually perform before you run General Ledger and transfer any summary journals:

1. Finish any monthly work you have to do in the module(s) from which you are transferring the journal(s).

2. Run whatever program the module uses to create a summary journal for General Ledger. Often, this is the program that closes the accounts for the period for that module.

Comment: These steps will be explained in greater detail in future chapters. You do not have to worry about those tasks here. For W. D. Peachtree & Company, the summary journal for Accounts Payable has already been prepared.

❖ From the PCA Main Menu, select **General Ledger**.

❖ From the General Ledger Main Menu, select **Processing Programs**.

❖ From the General Ledger Processing Menu, select **Transfer Summary Journals**.

❖ Answer **N** when General Ledger asks if you want to process Payroll's summary journal.

G/L gives you the choice of whether or not to process certain PCA modules. Of the four modules that you can transfer summary journals from, General Ledger only asks you about the ones you have told it you want to use. (This is done by setting General Ledger's options.) W. D. Peachtree & Company has set their General Ledger options so that all four modules can transfer information to G/L.

❖ Answer **Y** when General Ledger asks if you want to process the Accounts Payable summary journal.

General Ledger shows you the "transfer path" for the Accounts Payable summary journal. This is the disk drive and directory where General Ledger looks to find the current period's A/P summary journal. (If you do not know what a directory is, see the Appendix, "DOS Fundamentals," at the end of the text.)

❖ Press [ENTER] to accept the suggested drive and directory.

If the suggested transfer path was wrong, you could have typed over the suggested answer.

General Ledger displays the date that the transfer file was created and asks you if you want to process it.

❖ Answer **Y** to confirm and start the transfer.

General Ledger processes transactions from the transfer summary journal and updates the current G/L activity balance. As it works, G/L displays the account number of the transactions it transfers. General Ledger uses the next available entry session number and the **A** source code for the transactions it transfers from A/P. General Ledger prints part of the **Transfer Summary Journals Control** at this point.

When it finishes processing the A/P summary journal file, G/L asks if you want to process any other A/P summary journal files. This lets you transfer another A/P summary journal from a different directory or from a diskette.

❖ Answer **N**.

Now that General Ledger has finished with A/P's summary journal, it asks if you want to process A/R's summary journal.

❖ Answer **N**. Answer **N** a second time when asked if you want to transfer the summary journal from Fixed Assets.

Since the program has nothing left to do, it stops and returns you to the General Ledger Processing Menu.

❖ Now that you are done, General Ledger finishes printing the control report. You should examine the control report. The report should appear as follows:

```
RUN DATE:  11/30/92        W.D. Peachtree & Company         PAGE 1
RUN TIME:   10:07 AM             General Ledger
                      Transfer Summary Journals Control Report
---------------------------------------------------------------------------
ACCT.    DESCRIPTION    REF.   SC    DATE      AMOUNT     ACTION
---------------------------------------------------------------------------
13500                          A   11/29/92   96,754.14   *** TRANSFERRED ***
20500                          A   11/29/92   96,754.14-  *** TRANSFERRED ***
---------------------------------------------------------------------------


TOTAL TRANSACTIONS ENTERED:        2
TOTAL DEBITS............................:       96,754.14
TOTAL CREDITS..........................:       96,754.14-
                                               ========
DIFFERENCE ...............................:        0.00

End Of - Transfer Summary Journals Control Report
```

If the account specified in A/P had not existed in General Ledger when you attempted to transfer that account's journal information, the control report would notify you of the problem.

Something else to watch for is confirmation that the journal is for General Ledger's current period. This is specified in the options for the module from which journals are transferred. Journals for periods other than General Ledger's current period cannot be transferred.

Next, you are going to print a transaction register by source code to isolate the transferred transactions.

❖ Press **ESC** to return to the General Ledger Main Menu.

❖ Then select **Report Programs**.

❖ Then select **Transaction Register** from the General Ledger Reports Menu.

Prepare your printer as usual.

❖ Select **PRINT BY SOURCE CODE**.

G/L asks if you want to print a departmental transaction register.

❖ Answer **N** and, when asked for the entry session number, enter it from that entry session's control report. (If you have continued working from Topic 2 lessons, then "11" should be the entry session number to be entered.)

❖ Enter **A** for the source code.

This tells General Ledger to print all transactions transferred from Accounts Payable earlier in this lesson. General Ledger begins printing the Transaction Register.

❖ When G/L again displays its print options, press ▩ to quit **Transaction Register**. General Ledger completes printing the Transaction Register.

This is an easy way to create a journal of transferred entries. You can do the same thing for any source code. For example, you can get a listing of all your catch-all journal entries by selecting source code 3 (Miscellaneous journal entry).

Lesson 1 Summary

In this lesson, you learned how to transfer a summary journal from another PCA module. You found out that, before you can transfer any summary journals, you have to:

1. Have G/L in balance.
2. Finish any monthly work in the module from which you are transferring.
3. Run the program that module uses (if any) to create a G/L summary journal.

You were warned about some common problems such as a missing G/L account and making sure that the journal is created for General Ledger's current period. Finally, you saw how to print a transaction register by source code to list the transferred transactions.

Lesson 2 - Deleting Obsolete Repeating Transactions

In this lesson you will learn how to delete obsolete repeating transactions. This is an easy task and an important one to remember: once you set up a repeating transaction, it repeats each fiscal period *until you delete it*.

W. D. Peachtree & Company made arrangements with an advertising firm to retain their services for a six-month period starting in June, 1992. The six-month contract expires this month (November), so you need to delete the repeating transactions that pertain to it.

But first you must enter these transactions as of June 1, 1992. These are the two repeating transactions:

Ref. #	Date	Description	Acct #	Amount	Accept
ADVERT	6/1/92	Magazine Ads w/ Wallace	52000	235.00	Y
ADVERT	6/1/92	Magazine Ads w/ Wallace	18000	-235.00	Y

Here debit Advertising (#52000), an Expense account and credit Prepaid Advertising (#18000), an Asset account.

❖ Select **Enter Transactions** from the General Ledger Processing Menu.

❖ The number of transactions is **2**.

❖ Type **7000** for the Hash Total and accept.

❖ As source code, select **Repeating JE**.

❖ Using the June 1, 1992 date, enter the transactions using the data in the above table. General Ledger will print the following **Enter Transactions Control Report** when you finish:

```
RUN DATE:  11/30/92          W.D. Peachtree & Company              PAGE 1
RUN TIME:  10:45 AM                General Ledger
                          Enter Transactions Control Report
-------------------------------------------------------------------------
SOURCE CODE: 6 REPEATING JE                    ENTRY SESSION:  12
LN    REF        DATE      DESCRIPTION          ACCOUNT    AMOUNT
=========================================================================

1    ADVERT    06/01/92    Magazine Ads w/Wallace   52000    235.00
2    ADVERT    06/01/92    Magazine Ads w/Wallace   18000    235.00-

=========================================================================
TOTALS:        TRANSACTIONS   DEBITS    CREDITS    BALANCE   ACCT. TOT.
                    2         235.00    235.00-    0.00       70000
BATCH:              2                                          7000
                 ----------------------------------------------------
DIFFERENCE:         0                                         63000-

*** End Of Enter Transactions Control Report ***
```

Now you are going to delete the repeating transactions you just created.

❖ From the General Ledger Processing Menu, select **Edit Repeating Transactions** .

Prepare your printer for the control report.

❖ When asked for an account number, enter **52000**.

General Ledger shows the first available repeating transaction in this account in the amount of $350.

❖ Select **S** to skip this transaction.

The next transaction for "Magazine Ads w/Wallace" is displayed. Notice that the transaction is dated with the date it was first entered, not the date of its posting (since that changes every period).

You could also select **E** to Edit a repeating transaction if the description or amount of the transaction changed.

❖ Select **D** to Delete the 2nd transaction ($235 for Magazine Ads w/Wallace).

General Ledger asks you to confirm your decision.

❖ Confirm the deletion, then enter account number **18000** and repeat the process.

❖ When done, press 🖭 to leave the program. General Ledger will print the Edit Repeating Transactions Control Report that appears as follows:

```
RUN DATE:  11/30/92          W.D. Peachtree & Company                 PAGE 1
RUN TIME:   10:56 AM               General Ledger
                      Edit Repeating Transactions Control Report
-----------------------------------------------------------------------------

                                            ENTRY
SC   REFERENCE   DATE      DESCRIPTION      SESSION   ACCOUNT  AMOUNT   ACT
=============================================================================
6    ADVERT      06/01/92  Magazine Ads w/Wallace  12   52000   235.00   DEL
6    ADVERT      06/01/92  Magazine Ads w/Wallace  12   18000   235.00-  DEL

-----------------------------------------------------------------------------

*** End Of Edit Repeating Transactions Control Report ***
```

You can use this program to delete reversing transactions as well as for deleting, editing, and reviewing repeating transactions.

If General Ledger was in balance before you started, it should remain in balance now. General Ledger usually creates the repeating transaction for the next period when the current period is closed, so it has not generated a new repeating transaction. And, once you delete the repeating transaction, General Ledger can no longer create one for the next period.

Lesson 2 Summary

In this lesson you learned how to delete repeating transactions. You need to know this because these transactions continue repeating each period until you delete them. You found out how to skip other repeating transactions in the same account. In an actual business you should keep a master list of repeating transactions and their expiration dates, and you should review it every month before you close the current period.

Lesson 3 - Printing a Detailed Trial Balance and Financial Statements

In this lesson you will learn how to:

• Print a detailed Trial Balance.
• Confirm that General Ledger is in balance.
• Print your financial statements.

Assume that it is near the end of the month for W. D. Peachtree & Company. All of your daily or weekly tasks are done. You have entered all your regular transactions into General Ledger for the current period. You have deleted any obsolete repeating transactions.

Now it is time to confirm that General Ledger is in balance, print a detailed Trial Balance to use as an audit trail, and print your financial statements.

❖ Select **Enter Transactions** from the General Ledger Processing Menu.

Watch for the system balance, which is only on your screen in the upper right-hand corner for a moment.   If you did not see the balance, press [F10], and again select **Enter Transactions** until you do see the system balance. Check the system balance; it should be zero.

❖ If, for some reason, General Ledger is not in balance, make any needed adjustments to bring it back into balance.

If you have done the previous lessons in this tutorial, you should not have to do anything here.

❖ Press [F10] to indicate you are done.

❖ Press [ESC] to go back to the General Ledger Main Menu. Then select Report Programs.

❖ Select **Trial Balance** from the General Ledger Reports Menu.

❖ Select **DETAIL TRIAL BALANCE**.

This provides transaction details along with the trial balance.

❖ Select **ALL ACCOUNTS**.

You can print a range of account numbers or all accounts.

❖ Answer **N** when asked if you want to print a departmental trial balance.

If you wanted a trial balance that listed only certain department accounts grouped by department number, you would answer this question **Y**.

❖ Answer **Y** when asked to print zero balance accounts with no activity.

General Ledger prints a detailed, 11 page, trial balance that shows the following for each account:

- The account number and description.
- The beginning balance.
- The account's transactions (including description, date, period, source code, reference, and amount).
- The ending balance.

This trial balance provides you with a report of all transactions during the period for audit trail purposes. The total amounts of debits and credits, and any difference between those amounts, is shown at the end of the trial balance. When the difference is zero, General Ledger is in balance.

❖ Make sure your General Ledger is in balance before continuing with this lesson.

General Ledger will not let you print financial statements if General Ledger is out of balance.

Now that you know your General Ledger is in balance and have a detailed Trial Balance for an audit trail of this period's activity, you are ready to print financial statements.

❖ Select **Balance Sheet** from the General Ledger Reports Menu.

Prepare your printer.

❖ Select **CURRENT PERIOD BALANCE SHEET**.

You want to print a Balance Sheet for the current period.

❖ Select **STANDARD BALANCE SHEET**.

You would select a comparative Balance Sheet if you wanted to compare the current period activity either to budget figures or to the same period last fiscal year. This option is discussed in Chapter 14.

❖ Answer **Y** when asked to print zero balance accounts.

This tells G/L to print an account's title and balance even if the account's balance is zero.

If you print financial statements from different companies that use identical Charts of Accounts, this lets you compare them easily.

❖ Answer **Y** when asked to print date and time on the Balance Sheet.

❖ Press ⌨ when you are prompted for a report heading. Type your name as the report footing. This will identify the balance sheet as yours.

❖ When you are asked to save the heading and footing, answer **Y**.

General Ledger prints a standard Balance Sheet for the current period for W. D. Peachtree & Company.

❖ Examine the Balance Sheet.

Do not be concerned that some of the balances appear to be unrealistic. The reason for this result is that data from the other modules has not been transferred to General Ledger. The only goal here is to show that Financial Statements can be produced. Analyzing Financial Statements is covered in Chapter 14.

Notice the accounts to which you made transactions (entries) in earlier lessons: the Prepaid Insurance and Prepaid Advertising accounts under "Other Assets" and the Accrued Payroll account under "Current Liabilities."

❖ Select **Income Statement** from the General Ledger Reports Menu.

Prepare your printer.

❖ Tell General Ledger to print an income statement for the **CURRENT** period, and to print a **STANDARD INCOME STATEMENT**.

❖ Answer **Y** when asked to print zero balance accounts.

❖ Answer **Y** when asked to print date and time on the income statement.

❖ Accept the default of **0.00** for the income ratio.

General Ledger compares the balance of each Income Statement account to a given amount to determine the *income ratio* of that account. Using 0.00 tells G/L to show the ratio of each account to your net sales. By comparing the income ratios for different periods you can see important trends in the relationship between net sales and expenses. (Further discussion of financial statement analysis can be found in Chapter 14.)

❖ Accept G/L's suggested report heading and report footing.

General Ledger prints a standard Income Statement for W. D. Peachtree & Company.

❖ Examine the Income Statement.

You should see the effect of your transactions on these accounts:
- Salaries
- Advertising
- Bank Service Charges
- Returned Checks
- Insurance

Lesson 3 Summary

In this lesson, you learned how to print a detailed Trial Balance to use as an audit trail. You found out that General Ledger will not print financial statements if it is out of balance. You saw how to print a Balance Sheet and Income Statement and were introduced to how the Income Statement's income ratio works.

Lesson 4 - Closing the Current Period

In this lesson you will learn how to prepare for closing, and then close, the current period.

When the end of the month (fiscal period) arrives, you should make sure you have entered all regular transactions into General Ledger for the current period. Among the things to take care of are summary journals, repeating transactions, reversing transactions for accruals, printing a detailed trial balance, making any final adjustments, and printing financial statements. You have seen how to do most of these tasks in previous lessons.

❖ Press **ESC** to return to the **General Ledger Main Menu**, and select **Processing Programs**.

❖ Select **Close Current Period** from the General Ledger Processing Menu.

General Ledger tells you it is ready to close period 11 on 11/30/92 and that the new period ending date is 12/31/92.

❖ Press **ENTER**.

General Ledger processes a series of files containing data for W. D. Peachtree & Company and displays status messages as it works.

Close Current Period adds all current amounts to year-to-date amounts and clears the current amounts to prepare General Ledger for the next period.

Now you are ready to start your daily or weekly cycle for the new fiscal period.

Lesson 4 Summary

In this lesson you learned how to close the current period. Some of the tasks you need to perform before closing the period were listed.

Topic 4 - Yearly Activities

Yearly activities are those tasks performed at the end of one fiscal year and at the start of another. These activities include tidying odds and ends at the year's end and making preparations for the new year.

Topic 4 has four lessons:

1. Making year-end adjustments.
2. Closing the fiscal year.
3. Adding an additional adjusting period and changing period ending dates.
4. Preparing a budget for the new fiscal year.

Lesson 1 - Making Year-end Adjustments

This lesson explains how to make year-end adjustments.

Assume that W. D. Peachtree & Company is still in fiscal period 12 (December), the last fiscal period of the year. Because W. D. Peachtree & Company does not use an additional adjusting period, any year-end adjustments must be made during this last fiscal period.

The only thing special about year-end adjustments is their timing: they should be entered before the last fiscal period of the year is closed. In all other respects, they are regular transactions.

The employees in one of W. D. Peachtree's departments—Fencing and Gutters (department 50)—wear company uniforms. (Right now, this is the only department that uses uniforms, but W. D. Peachtree has their accounts set up to accommodate uniforms used by other departments if needed.) The company handles the cost of the uniforms much like they do insurance costs. Here are the relevant facts:

- The total amount spent for uniforms was $592.42, paid as a credit through PCA's Accounts Payable module.

- The Asset account, Prepaid Uniforms (#18500), was debited for the same amount. This account covers all uniform costs, regardless of the department.

- There are two other relevant accounts, both Expense accounts: Uniforms (#66500), a Department Control account; and Uniforms Fencing & Gutters (#66550), the uniforms account for department 50.

- The uniforms were purchased in late April and, since they last about eight months, they are expensed for eight months—from May through December. Thus, there are two active repeating transactions:

  1. A credit for $74.00 to Prepaid Uniforms (the Asset account).

  2. A debit for $74.00 to Uniforms Fencing & Gutters (the Expense account).

Note that these two repeating transactions have already been applied to General Ledger for December. When you closed the period for November in an earlier lesson, these active repeating transactions were set up for December and immediately took effect. Since this is the final month for this set of repeating transactions and G/L has already applied them to their respective accounts, they are now obsolete.

In this section you will do three things to wrap up this situation for the year:

1. Delete the now-obsolete repeating transactions that handled the cost of the uniforms.

2. Use **Query Account Status** to examine the relevant accounts and see if any balance remains.

3. Do any necessary adjusting transactions to reconcile these accounts before closing the year.

❖ Press [ESC] to return to the General Ledger Main Menu. Then select Processing Programs.

❖ Select **Edit Repeating Transactions** from the General Ledger Processing Menu.

❖ Using the instructions for deleting that were covered earlier, delete these two repeating transactions: (Hint: Type in Acct # when prompted, and type in D to delete.)

Reference	Date	Description	Acct #	Amount	Accept
UNIFORMS	5/01/92	Uniform Purchase	18500	-74.00	Y
UNIFORMS	5/01/92	Uniform Purchase	66550	74.00	Y

❖ When done, press [F10] to leave the program. General Ledger will print the following Edit Repeating Transactions Control Report:

```
RUN DATE: 11/30/92            W.D. Peachtree & Company              PAGE 1
RUN TIME:  12:32 PM                  General Ledger
                       Edit Repeating Transactions Control Report
-----------------------------------------------------------------------------

                                            ENTRY
SC  REFERENCE  DATE   DESCRIPTION  SESSION   ACCOUNT AMOUNT  ACT
=============================================================================

6   UNIFORMS  05/01/92  Uniform Purchase    1     18500   74.00-   DEL
6   UNIFORMS  05/01/92  Uniform Purchase    1     66550   74.00    DEL
-----------------------------------------------------------------------------

*** End Of Edit Repeating Transactions Control Report ***
```

General Ledger should still be in balance.

❖ Select **Query Account Status** from the General Ledger Processing Menu.

❖ Type account number **18500** and examine the account's balance.

You will see $0.42—the difference between the total debited to this account ($592.42) and the amount credited by the repeating transaction (-$74.00) for eight months (-$592.00). This account needs an adjustment credit of -$0.42 to clean it up.

From this, you know that account number **66550** needs an adjustment debit of $0.42 to balance things out.

Here is a summary of the transactions:

Ref. #	Date	Description	Acct #	Amount	Accept
1427	12/31/92	Year-end adjustment	18500	-0.42	Y
1428	12/31/92	Year-end adjustment	66550	0.42	Y

❖ Leave **Query Account Status** (by entering **N** at the *CONTINUE* prompt). Press 🖰 and then select **Enter Transactions** and enter both of these year-end adjustments. (There are 2 transactions, and the Hash Total is 85050.) This is a MISCELLANEOUS JE. The date is 12/31/92.

General Ledger should remain in balance. (Press 🖰 to leave the program, and then press 🖰🖰 to print the Control Report).

General ledger will print the following control report during the procedure you have just followed.

```
RUN DATE:  11/30/92          W.D. Peachtree & Company              PAGE 1
RUN TIME:  12:39 PM                 General Ledger
                            Enter Transactions Control Report
------------------------------------------------------------------------
SOURCE CODE: 3 MISCELLANEOUS JE                     ENTRY SESSION:  1
LN   REF      DATE       DESCRIPTION            ACCOUNT      AMOUNT
========================================================================
1    1427    12/31/92    Year-end adjustment      18500        0.42-
2    1428    12/31/92    Year-end adjustment      66550        0.42
========================================================================
TOTALS:     TRANSACTIONS   DEBITS   CREDITS   BALANCE   ACCT. TOT.
                2          0.42     0.42-     0.00        85050
BATCH:          2                                        85050
            ------------------------------------------------------------
DIFFERENCE:     0                                           0

*** End Of Enter Transactions Control Report ***
```

Lesson 1 Summary

In this lesson you learned how to make year-end adjustments. Remember that when repeating transactions become obsolete, you must delete them. As suggested earlier, the best way to keep track of repeating transactions is to keep a list of each along with their intended expiration date. Refer to this list each month and delete any obsolete repeating transactions before you close the period.

Always examine the accounts to which the repeating transactions applied in case there are any final adjustments to be made. Dealing with the "pocket change" often left over in these accounts keeps the books clean.

Lesson 2 - Closing the Fiscal Year

This lesson provides tips on closing the fiscal year. There are three simple steps to this:

1. Do all the things that are usually done at the end of a regular fiscal period such as transferring summary journals and printing financial statements. The first three lessons under "Topic 3 - Monthly or Fiscal Period Activities" cover these tasks.

2. Make any needed year-end adjustments (like those in the preceding lesson) and confirm that G/L is in balance.

3. Close the last fiscal period of the year just as you would any other. (See the earlier lesson.) General Ledger does a few end-of-year tasks in addition to the regular period-closing tasks. For example, G/L computes and posts Current Earnings (the total earnings for the year) to the Retained Earnings account.

❖ Select **Close Current Period** from the General Ledger Processing Menu.

❖ Just follow the instructions on the screen to close the period. Answer **Y** at the prompts. (The closing process takes a while.)

Lesson 2 Summary

That concludes the closing process. The most important thing to remember is to make any final adjustments needed for end-of-year cleanup before you close the last period.

Optionally, you may want to print a detailed Trial Balance for the entire year. Some companies prefer to have this year-long audit trail and also find it useful for tax purposes. To do this, select **Trial Balance** from the General Ledger Reports Menu and specify Year-to-date Trial Balance.

Lesson 3 - Adding an Adjusting Period; Changing Period Ending Dates

In this lesson you will learn how to:

- Add an additional adjusting period to the fiscal year.
- Change period ending dates as needed.

If you have been doing the lessons, W. D. Peachtree & Company is now in period 1 (January, 1992). The first period of a new fiscal year is a good time to change some of General Ledger's options.

W. D. Peachtree & Company has decided to start using the Additional Adjusting Period. This lets them make any yearly adjustments to General Ledger in a special period designed for that purpose. Any adjustments made in this period clearly pertain to the entire year, not to any single period. The main advantage of this is that no single period has skewed (and misleading) financial data from year-end adjustments. When these adjustments are for trivial amounts, like those in the earlier lesson, this is an insignificant point. But if there are a lot of adjustments involving large numbers, the problem is significant.

❖ Return to the General Ledger Main Menu. (By now you should know how.) Then select **Maintenance Programs**.

❖ Select **Maintain General Ledger Options** from the General Ledger Maintenance Menu.

❖ Select **Set Module Options** and answer **N** when asked to accept General Ledger's displayed options.

General Ledger moves the cursor to the first item, *Controller Password.*

❖ Press ⌨ until you get to the second column of items.

You want to change the fiscal period information. The Number of Fiscal Periods option shows 12 periods. This number defines the number of *regular* fiscal periods, not the *total* number of fiscal periods, so you do not need to change it even though you are adding the additional adjusting period.

❖ Change the Additional Adjusting Period entry from **N** to **Y**.

Now you need to change some of the fiscal period ending dates so the additional adjusting period does not conflict with another fiscal period.

❖ Press ⌨ End (hold down ⌨ and simultaneously press End) which moves the cursor to current year.

❖ Press ⌨ to move to period 13's ending date.

❖ Type **12/31**.

This makes the last day of the fiscal year the ending date for the additional adjusting period.

❖ Press 🔲 to move to period 12's ending date and type **12/30**.

This ends the last regular fiscal period one day early to make room for the additional adjusting period.

❖ Press 🔲 to tell General Ledger you are done.

❖ Check and accept your entries. Then accept the remaining screens and press 🔲 again at the "Program Options" screen.

By the way, only three situations require that period ending dates be changed:

1. Changing the number of regular fiscal periods in your year. For example, if a company decides to go from a monthly system with twelve periods to a quarterly system with four periods, quarterly dates would be set for periods one through four. 🔲 would also be used to remove the dates in periods five through thirteen.

2. Changing the use of the additional adjusting period as was shown in this lesson. If you start using the adjusting period, repeat what we did in this lesson. If a company wants to quit using the adjusting period, it would set period 12 back to 12/31 and use 🔲 to remove the date in period 13.

3. Dealing with a leap year. In this case, February's ending date can just be changed to **02/28** or **02/29**.

Lesson 3 Summary

In this lesson you found out how to set up an additional adjusting period and change the necessary period ending dates. You also learned about the other circumstances in which you need to change these dates.

Lesson 4 - Preparing a Budget for the New Fiscal Year

This lesson shows you how to prepare a budget for an account for the new fiscal year. The budget for this account will be based on the account's figures from the fiscal year you just closed.

This procedure is illustrated by preparing a budget for account #54000, Bank Service Charges. This is one of W. D. Peachtree's Expense accounts. You entered a transaction to this account in an earlier lesson.

❖ From the General Ledger Maintenance Menu, select **Prepare Next Year's Budget**.

General Ledger asks if you want to use last year's fiscal information or last year's budget information.

❖ Select **USE LAST YEAR'S FISCAL INFORMATION**.

If you had wanted to base the new budget on last year's budget, you would have selected the other option.

General Ledger then asks if you want to change the budget based on last year's fiscal figures by amount or percentage.

❖ Select **CHANGE BY PERCENTAGE** to change these figures by a percentage.

General Ledger prompts you for a percentage.

❖ Enter **10.00** to increase the budget 10% over the actual figures spent in the previous fiscal year.

General Ledger asks if you want to prepare a budget for all the accounts or for a range of accounts.

❖ Select a **RANGE OF ACCOUNTS**.

G/L then asks for the beginning and ending account numbers for the range.

❖ Type **54000** for the beginning account number and accept 54000 for the ending account number.

General Ledger starts computing the new budget for account #54000. G/L prints the new budget for account #54000 on the control report, and then asks you to enter another range of accounts for which to compute budgets. The Prepare Next Year's Budget Control Report appears as follows:

```
RUN DATE: 11/30/92              W.D. Peachtree & Company                        PAGE 1
RUN TIME:  1:11 PM
                          Prepare Next Year's Budget Control Report
-------------------------------------------------------------------------------------------
              Using Prior Fiscal Information - Percentage Increase: 10.00

         CURR    NEXT           CURR    NEXT           CURR    NEXT           CURR    NEXT
   PD   BUDGET  BUDGET   PD    BUDGET  BUDGET   PD    BUDGET  BUDGET   PD    BUDGET BUDGET
-------------------------------------------------------------------------------------------
    54000  Bank Service Charges
   1   12.00   13.20    4    12.00   13.20    7    12.00   13.20   10    12.00   13.20
   2   12.00   13.20    5    12.00   13.20    8    12.00   13.20   11    12.00   47.85
   3   12.00   13.20    6    12.00   13.20    9    12.00   13.20   12    12.00    0.00
                                                                   13     0.00    0.00

*** End Of - Prepare Next Year's Budget Control Report ***
```

❖ Press [ESC] until you get back to G/L's Data Options Selection box. Then press [F10] to leave **Prepare Next Year's Budget**.

❖ Look at the control report.

The control report shows, for each of twelve fiscal periods, the last fiscal year's figures and the newly-computed budget. You should see a 10% increase over last year's figures for the Bank Service Charges account.

Notice that, if General Ledger has to adjust any figures to make the year's total come out right, it does so in the last regular fiscal period of the year.

Lesson 4 Summary

In this lesson you learned how to prepare budgets for the new fiscal year. You can do this for one account, a range of accounts, or for all accounts. You saw how to base the budget on last year's fiscal information and change that by a percentage. You can just as easily base it on last year's budget or alter the basis by a fixed amount.

Chapter 3

End of Chapter Problem

WARNING
BEFORE CONTINUING, BE SURE THAT ALL DATA FILES HAVE BEEN RESTORED TO THEIR ORIGINAL CONDITION. IF YOU ARE UNSURE OF HOW TO RESTORE THESE FILES, TURN TO THE INSTRUCTIONS FOUND ON PAGE 1-32 IN CHAPTER 1.

You should begin this practice set by entering the date as 11/30/92, then enter WD as the Company ID. The following transactions are similar to the transactions you entered during Chapter 3, so if you get stuck, look at the way a particular transaction was handled in that chapter. Unless told differently, all transactions should be dated 11/30/92.

Note: Since this is the first practice problem you will work, the input forms have been filled out for you. In the other end of chapter problems, you may want to prepare your own input forms before working the problem.

Problem Data

a. The management of W. D. Peachtree & Co. has decided to separate the company inventory by departments. This means that you will need to perform two tasks. First, you should set up a new Inventory account and 12 individual department accounts. (Hint: The easy way to set up the 12 individual department accounts is to answer "All Departments" to the Department Options prompt.) Second, you will need to transfer the balance from the old Inventory Account to some of the individual Inventory department accounts. Use the attached Chart of Accounts Setup Form to do the first task. Then use the Transactions Setup Form to perform the second task. The transfer of the balance to the departmental accounts will be handled in the same way you Entered Regular Transactions in Topic 1, Lesson 2.

<u>*Chart of Accounts Setup Form*</u>

Number of Accounts Changed: 13
Hash Total: 178461

Account Number: <u>13700</u>

Description: <u>New Inventory</u>
<u> </u>

Account Type (1-9): 2
Master/Dept: M Ⓓ BLANK   (Circle one)
Group End: <u>13799</u>
Balance Col (0-3): <u>1</u>

Department Numbers: _____
(for Dept. Control Accts) _____
_____
_____

Annual Budget Amount: _____.___

Per	Amount		Per	Amount
1	_____.__		8	_____.__
2	_____.__		9	_____.__
3	_____.__		10	_____.__
4	_____.__		11	_____.__
5	_____.__		12	_____.__
6	_____.__		13	_____.__
7	_____.__			

Transactions Setup Form

Number of Transactions: 3

Hash Total: 40964

Source Code: 3
Reference: 2113
Date: 11 30 92
Description: Transfer to Depar tments
Account: 13500
Amount: -2917.88

Source Code: 3
Reference: 2114
Date: 11 30 92
Description: Transfer to Depar tments
Account: 13731
Amount: 1213.12

Source Code: 3
Reference: 2115
Date: 11 30 92
Description: Transfer to Depar tments
Account: 13733
Amount: 1704.76

b. W. D. Peachtree & Co. purchased a new life insurance policy to cover the Senior Manager who is responsible for the clothing departments. The annual premium on this policy will have to be allocated to the four different departments for which the Senior Manager is responsible. Use the attached Chart of Accounts Setup Form and Transactions Setup Form to enter this transaction. Note: This transaction would normally be performed in the A/P Module. You are asked to enter it in the General Ledger Module so that you can become more familiar with how this Module operates. (Hint: You will need to first set up a new Prepaid Insurance Account and then make the entry to record the purchase of the policy (regular transaction). Then you will make a repeating transaction entry so that the system will allocate the cost of the policy to the four different departments each month.)

Chart of Accounts Setup Form

Number of Accounts: 1

Hash Total : 17550

Account Number: _ _17550

Description: Prepaid Ins. -Manager_____

Account Type (1-9): 2

Master/Dept: M   D   (BLANK)   (Circle one)

Group End: _ _ _ _ _ _ _

Balance Col (0-3): 1

Department Numbers: _ _ _ _ _ _ _ _ _ _ _ _
(for Dept. Control Accts) _ _ _ _ _ _ _ _ _ _ _ _
_ _ _ _ _ _ _ _ _ _ _ _

Annual Budget Amount: _ _ _ _ _ _ _ _ _ . _ _

Per	Amount		Per	Amount
1	_ _ _ _ _ _ _ . _ _		8	_ _ _ _ _ _ _ . _ _
2	_ _ _ _ _ _ _ . _ _		9	_ _ _ _ _ _ _ . _ _
3	_ _ _ _ _ _ _ . _ _		10	_ _ _ _ _ _ _ . _ _
4	_ _ _ _ _ _ _ . _ _		11	_ _ _ _ _ _ _ . _ _
5	_ _ _ _ _ _ _ . _ _		12	_ _ _ _ _ _ _ . _ _
6	_ _ _ _ _ _ _ . _ _		13	_ _ _ _ _ _ _ . _ _
7	_ _ _ _ _ _ _ . _ _			

Transactions Setup Form

Number of Transactions: 2

Hash Total: 28550

Source Code: 2

Reference: _____ 2 1 1 6

Date: 1 1 30 9 2

Description: Purchase New Life
Policy

Account: _ 1 7 5 5 0

Amount: _____ 3 6 0 0 . 0 0

Source Code: 2

Reference: _____ 2 1 1 7

Date: 1 1 30 9 2

Description: Purchase New Life
Policy

Account: _ 1 1 0 0 0

Amount: _____ - 3 6 0 0 . 0 0

(F10)

Source Code: __

Reference: __ __ __ __ __ __ __ __ __ __

Date: __ __ / __ __ / __ __

Description: __

__ __ __ __ __ __ __ __ __

Account: __ __ __ __ __ __

Amount: __ __ __ __ __ __ __ . __ __

Transactions Setup Form

Number of Transactions: 5

Hash Total: 218010

Source Code: **6**
Reference: _____ 2118
Date: 11/30/92
Description: Allocate Life Pol
icy_____
Account: _17550
Amount: _____ -300.00

Source Code: **6**
Reference: _____ 2119
Date: 11/30/92
Description: Allocate Life Pol
icy_____
Account: _50112
Amount: _____ 75.00

Source Code: **6**
Reference: _____ 2120
Date: 11/30/92
Description: Allocate Life Pol
icy_____
Account: _50114
Amount: _____ 75.00

Transactions Setup Form

Source Code: **6**

Reference: _____ 2121

Date: 11/30/92

Description: Allocate Life Pol icy

Account: _ 50116

Amount: _____ 75.00

Source Code: **6**

Reference: _____ 2122

Date: 11/30/92

Description: Allocate Life Pol icy

Account: _ 50118

Amount: _____ 75.00

Source Code: ___

Reference: _ _ _ _ _ _ _ _ _

Date: __ __/__ __/__ __

Description: _ _ _ _ _ _ _ _ _ _ _ _ _ _ _ _ _

_ _ _ _ _ _ _ _ _ _

Account: _ _ _ _ _ _ _

Amount: _ _ _ _ _ _ _ . _ _

---

c. In reviewing a detailed trial balance for the month of November an error has been discovered. The service sales credited to the Appliance department should have been credited to the Electronics department. Likewise, the service sales credited to the Electronics department should have been credited to the Appliance department. First, review the detailed information for each of these accounts (Appliance Sales Acct. No. 30531 and Electronics Sales Acct. No. 30533). Do this in the same manner as you did in Topic 2, Lesson 1, found in Chapter 3. Notice that $550.00 was credited to Appliance Sales for service and $375.00 was credited to Electronics Sales for service. These need to be reversed (but NOT through a reversing entry). Use the attached Transactions Setup Form to enter the corrections. (Hint: This is a regular transaction.)

Transactions Setup Form

Number of Transactions: 4

Hash Total: 122128

Source Code: 3
Reference: _ _ _ _ _ _ 2123
Date: 11 30 92
Description: Correction _ _ _ _ _ _ _ _
_ _ _ _ _ _ _ _
Account: _ 30531
Amount: _ _ _ _ _ 550.00

Source Code: 3
Reference: _ _ _ _ _ _ 2124
Date: 11 30 92
Description: Correction _ _ _ _ _ _ _
_ _ _ _ _ _ _
Account: _ 30531
Amount: _ _ _ _ _ - 375.00

Source Code: 3
Reference: _ _ _ _ _ _ 2125
Date: 11 30 92
Description: Correction _ _ _ _ _ _
_ _ _ _ _ _
Account: _ 30533
Amount: _ _ _ _ _ 375.00

Transactions Setup Form

Source Code: **3**

Reference: _____ **2126**

Date: **1 / 30 / 92**

Description: **Correction** _____

_____

Account: __ **30533**

Amount: _____ **-550.00**

Source Code: ___

Reference: _____

Date: __ __/ __ __/ __ __

Description: _____

_____

Account: _____ __

Amount: _____ · __ __

Source Code: ___

Reference: _____

Date: __ __/ __ __/ __ __

Description: _____

_____

Account: _____ __

Amount: _____ · __ __

---

d.   After reconciling the monthly bank statement, the service charge and returned check charges should be entered. Use the attached Transactions Setup Form to do this.

Transactions Setup Form

Number of Transactions: 7

Hash Total: 332000

Source Code: 3
Reference: _____ 2127
Date: 11 30 92
Description: Service charge_____
_____
Account: __54000
Amount: _____57.16

Source Code: 3
Reference: _____ 2128
Date: 11 30 92
Description: Service charge_____
_____
Account: __11000
Amount: _____-57.16

Source Code: 3
Reference: _____ 2129
Date: 11 30 92
Description: Returned check_____
#4578____
Account: __64000
Amount: _____714.14

Transactions Setup Form

Source Code: 3

Reference: _____ 2130

Date: 11 30 92

Description: Returned check #3490

Account: 64000

Amount: _____ 38.99

Source Code: 3

Reference: _____ 2131

Date: 11 30 92

Description: Returned check #567908

Account: 64000

Amount: _____ 123.15

Source Code: 3

Reference: _____ 2132

Date: 11 30 92

Description: Returned check #7658

Account: 64000

Amount: _____ 78.45

Transactions Setup Form

Source Code: **3**

Reference: _____ 2133

Date: 11 30 92

Description: Returned check- 4 checks

Account: 11000

Amount: -954.73

Source Code: ___

Reference: ___ ___ ___ ___ ___ ___ ___ ___

Date: ___ ___ / ___ ___ / ___ ___

Description: ___ ___ ___ ___ ___ ___ ___ ___ ___ ___ ___ ___ ___ ___ ___ ___ ___

___ ___ ___ ___ ___ ___ ___ ___ ___

Account: ___ ___ ___ ___ ___ ___

Amount: ___ ___ ___ ___ ___ ___ ___ . ___ ___

Source Code: ___

Reference: ___ ___ ___ ___ ___ ___ ___ ___

Date: ___ ___ / ___ ___ / ___ ___

Description: ___ ___ ___ ___ ___ ___ ___ ___ ___ ___ ___ ___ ___ ___ ___ ___ ___

___ ___ ___ ___ ___ ___ ___ ___ ___

Account: ___ ___ ___ ___ ___ ___

Amount: ___ ___ ___ ___ ___ ___ ___ . ___ ___

e.   The last pay period for the employees was 11/24/89. There are still four days left in November that the employees will earn their salary. However, the actual check will not be written until Friday, December 1. So, you need to recognize the four days of salaries for each department in this period. You will do this by making a reversing entry (Topic 2, Lesson 2). The Transactions Setup Forms are attached. Use them to make this entry.

Transactions Setup Form

Number of Transactions: 14

Hash Total: 643561

Source Code: 7
Reference: _____ 2134
Date: 11 30 92
Description: Clothing Departme
nt _____
Account: _21000
Amount: _____ -3200.00

Source Code: 7
Reference: _____ 2135
Date: 11 30 92
Description: Men's Clothing ___
_____
Account: _50112
Amount: _____ 1100.00

Source Code: 7
Reference: _____ 2136
Date: 11 30 92
Description: Women's Clothing_
_____
Account: _50114
Amount: _____ 1200.00

Transactions Setup Form

Source Code: _7_

Reference: _____ 2137

Date: 11 30 92

Description: Children's Clothing

Account: _ 50116

Amount: _____ 500.00

Source Code: _7_

Reference: _____ 2138

Date: 11 30 92

Description: Uniforms _____

Account: _ 50118

Amount: _____ 400.00

Source Code: _7_

Reference: _____ 2139

Date: 11 30 92

Description: Other Departments

Account: _ 21000

Amount: _____ -7850.00

Transactions Setup Form

Source Code: 7
Reference: _____ 2140
Date: 11 30 92
Description: Athletic Shoes_____
_____
Account: _50123
Amount: _____1500.00

Source Code: 7
Reference: _____ 2141
Date: 11 30 92
Description: Other Shoes_____
_____
Account: _50125
Amount: _____200.00

Source Code: 7
Reference: _____ 2142
Date: 11 30 92
Description: Appliances_____
_____
Account: _50131
Amount: _____2000.00

Transactions Setup Form

Source Code: _7_

Reference: _____ 2143

Date: _11_,_30_,_92_

Description: Electronics_____
_____

Account: __50133

Amount: _____ 1550.00

Source Code: _7_

Reference: _____ 2144

Date: _11_,_30_,_92_

Description: Hardware_____
_____

Account: __50135

Amount: _____ 700.00

Source Code: _7_

Reference: _____ 2145

Date: _11_,_30_,_92_

Description: Sporting Goods____
_____

Account: __50142

Amount: _____ 1475.00

Transactions Setup Form

Source Code: 7

Reference: 2146

Date: 11/30/92

Description: Fencing and Gutters

Account: 50150

Amount: 200.00

Source Code: 7

Reference: 2147

Date: 11/30/92

Description: Hair Salon

Account: 50162

Amount: 225.00

Source Code: ___

Reference: _____

Date: __ __/__ __/__ __

Description: _____

Account: _____

Amount: _____.__ __

---

f.   After all of the above transactions have been entered, you need to close the current period. Do this by first printing a summary trial balance and financial statements (Balance Sheet and Income Statement) for the current period (Topic 3, Lesson 3). Make sure the trial balance is in balance, then close the current period (Topic 4, Lesson 3).   Note: Normally you would also transfer summary journals and delete obsolete repeating transactions (Topics 1 & 2, Lesson 3), but for this practice set that is not necessary. (You may ignore the warning about the detailed trial balance in this problem.)

You will notice that the trial balance shows a small amount of inventory in only two departments. Normally, there would be inventory in each department, but for the purpose of this practice set the small amount of inventory is OK.

Chapter 4

ACCOUNTS PAYABLE OVERVIEW

Learning Objectives:

After studying this chapter, you should be able to:

1. Describe the purposes of Accounts Payable.

2. Describe setup and maintenance activities including—accounts payable module options, maintain vendors, and maintain automatic invoices.

3. Describe processing entries including—query vendors, enter invoices, enter credits, delete invoices, select invoices for payment, print pre-check register, print Accounts Payable checks, update Accounts Payable checks, void checks, create General Ledger journal entries, and close current period.

4. Describe accounts payable reports including—open invoices, cash requirements report, transaction register, ageing report, monthly check register, list vendors, list auto invoices, print 1099's, and 1099 magnetic media reporting.

5. Identify some of the reports printed by Accounts Payable.

Chapter 4

Accounts Payable Overview

Accounts Payable is the way a company keeps track of the amounts it owes to vendors. It also helps a company to save money by tracking discounts it will receive by paying vendors early. Missing these discounts can be very costly. Even with terms of 2/10, n/30 the annual rate of interest is 36%.

Accounts Payable lets a company store information about vendors and the invoices, credits, and discounts received from them. By using an effective management system for invoices, a company can save money.

How Accounts Payable Compares To A Manual Accounting System

In a manual accounting system, purchases on credit are recorded either in a special Purchases Journal or in a Voucher Register, and payments on accounts payable are recorded in the special Cash Disbursements Journal or in the Check Register (if the voucher system is used.) An Accounts Payable control account is maintained in the general ledger, and a subsidiary ledger is maintained showing an account for each supplier.

The Peachtree Complete Accounting module is used to record invoices (bills) received, record purchase discounts and purchase returns and allowances, print checks, and show summary journal entries that may be entered into General Ledger. The Module also prepares various reports such as a summary of all accounts payable transactions, a summary of unpaid invoices, an ageing report showing the age of all amounts owed, a monthly check register, and others.

What Accounts Payable Does

Accounts Payable records information about vendors, invoices (automatic and regular), and credits. Using this information, Accounts Payable helps you determine how much a company owes to its vendors and how to take advantage of early payment discounts. Accounts Payable calculates discount percentages and deducts them from the payment.

Accounts Payable information can be kept in summary or detail form. Journal entries can also be recorded in summary or detail for later transfer to PCA's General Ledger or for manual posting.

Additionally, 1099 information for vendors that may be needed for federal tax reporting can be stored and printed at the end of the year. Alternatively, Accounts Payable vendor information can be reported using magnetic media. (This is discussed in more detail later in this chapter.)

Programs and features in the Accounts Payable module include:

- Create General Ledger Journal Entries

- Update Accounts Payable Checks

- Updating to Job Cost with Accounts Payable Invoices

- Temporary Vendor Information

Question Frame 1[4]

Indicate whether each of the following statements is true of false by writing "T" or "F" in the space provided.

_____ I. The PCA Accounts Payable module is more than simply a Purchases Journal.

_____ 2. Accounts Payable records information about customers.

_____ 3. Accounts Payable can help make sure you do not miss discounts that may be taken.

_____ 4. Information regarding Accounts Payable cannot be transferred directly to General Ledger.

Now turn to Answer Frame 1[4] on page 4-5 to check your answers.

Answer Frame 1[4]

1. True. The Accounts Payable module records invoices, records purchase discounts and purchase returns and allowances, prints checks, shows summary entries, and prepares various reports. A Purchases Journal in a manual system merely records purchases of merchandise on account.

2. False. Accounts Payable records information about vendors (suppliers). Accounts Receivable records information about customers.

3. True. Accounts Payable shows how to take advantage of early payment discounts. This module calculates discount percentages and deducts them from the payment.

4. False. If Accounts Payable is linked with General Ledger, summary or detail data can be transferred directly to General Ledger at the end of the fiscal period.

If you missed any of the above, reread Frame 1[4] before continuing.

Frame 2[4]

Accounts Payable Functions Overview

Setup and Maintenance

Maintenance programs allow the set up of module options, vendors, and automatic invoices.

Accounts Payable Module Options is where all company information is set up. Any option can be changed after initial setup.

In **Maintain Vendors**, vendor information is entered on a permanent or temporary basis. Other information entered includes vendor remit-to address and specific 1099 type. Use this program to examine, add, or delete existing vendors.

In **Maintain Automatic Invoices,** repeating invoices are set up for fixed amounts payable to vendors. Repeating invoices would be set up for items such as rent, insurance, or mortgage payments, that are paid on a regular schedule. Specific billings can be set up to be issued for a specific number of months, or can be issued monthly, bi-monthly, quarterly, semi-annually, or annually. This program can also be used to examine, change, or delete existing automatic invoices.

Processing and Transaction Entry

After setting up Accounts Payable, processing programs are used to make regular entries and process the information. This is where both invoices and credits are entered. Processing is also where the invoices to be paid are selected, checks can be voided, and the period is closed.

Query Vendors permits a review of the current activity of specific vendors—whether or not there are outstanding invoices or credits, year-to-date figures, and payments made to them. Vendor activity can be viewed on the screen or printed in a report. If you keep historical detail (Y in Options file), you can query by all transactions or transactions from a range of periods. If you do not keep historical detail, you can only query current transactions.

In **Enter Invoices,** invoices from vendors are posted. When vendors send invoices, they are entered in this program. It is also where automatic invoices are processed, disallowed discounts are corrected, and prepaid invoices are posted. All the information here is stored in a transaction file until the month is closed.

Enter Credits is used to record open and specific credits from vendors. A credit can be an overpayment to a vendor or even a discount that was overlooked.

Delete Invoices purges an invoice, credit, or discount not allowed as long as no checks, credits, or other transactions exist for that particular invoice. This program is processed before the **Close Current Period** program is run.

Select Invoices for Payment is used to choose the invoices to pay. It can be run at any time during processing. Specific invoices can be paid individually or all invoices that are due by a certain date can be paid together. Invoices can be selected manually or automatically, by discount date or cash account. Specific credits can be chosen or any previously selected invoices can be changed any time before the checks are printed. This is where you can also enter a payment transaction for previously entered invoices that have been paid with a manual check.

The **Print Pre-Check Register** allows a preview of the checks to be written. This program should be run after **Select Invoices for Payment.**

Print A/P Checks prints a check for any vendor with at least one invoice marked for payment. Checks can be reprinted as many times as necessary before using the **Update A/P Checks** program.

Print Check Register gives a print-out that lists all the detail from the checks. The check register can be printed whenever required (as long as it is before **Update A/P Checks** is selected).

Update A/P Checks is the final step in the check-printing cycle. This program updates the invoice and vendor master files and marks invoices as paid.

Void Checks marks specific checks that have been written in error in the current month as being void. It also makes the corresponding invoices available for payment again. Reverse entries are created in the G/L transfer file.

Create G/L Journal Entries creates the journal entries for later transfer to General Ledger. Three options for selection are available within this program: List G/L Transfers, a listing of information for General Ledger; Consolidate G/L Transfers, where all transactions in the transaction file are consolidated; and Create G/L Transfers, a mandatory option that actually creates the journal entries for transfer. Create G/L Journal Entries provides a list of the transaction detail transferred to General Ledger. This program must be run prior to **Close Current Period.**

Close Current Period "ends" the current fiscal period. For all vendors, this process clears all paid or fully credited invoices from the current month and carries forward open invoices to the next month. It also creates a new generation of Accounts Payable files and increments the current fiscal period and generation numbers.

Question Frame 2[4]

Indicate whether each of the following statements is true or false by writing "T" or "F" in the space provided.

_____ 1.   There is no provision in Accounts Payable for preparing invoices that are similar each period.

_____ 2.   Processing programs are used more frequently than other types of programs.

_____ 3.   Accounts Payable prints checks for payment of invoices.

_____ 4.   The Create G/L Journal Entries option must be run <u>after</u> the option to Close Current Period.

Now turn to Answer Frame 2[4] on page 4-8 to check your answers.

Answer Frame 2⁴

1. False. The Maintain Automatic Invoices option can be used to prepare repeating invoices. Repeating invoices would be set up for items, such as rent, that are paid on a regular (e.g., monthly) schedule and have a fixed amount.

2. True. Processing programs are used to make regular entries and process the information. Both invoices and credits are entered. Invoices to be paid are selected, checks are voided, and the period is closed. Maintenance and report programs are used less frequently.

3. True. Accounts Payable prints a check for any vendor with at least one invoice marked for payment.

4. False. The Create G/L Journal Entries option must be run _prior to_ the Close Current Period option.

If you missed any of the above, reread Frame 2⁴ before continuing.

Frame 3⁴

Accounts Payable Reports

Accounts Payable reports print information on a variety of monthly activities, like open invoices, ageing, transaction and check registers, and automatic invoices.

Open Invoices is a list of all the unpaid invoices from vendors in vendor ID order. It shows the date each invoice was entered into the system, the total amount and due date of the invoice, the discount amount, the payments made on a particular invoice, whether or not it has been marked for payment, and the net amounts of all the invoices on the report.

The **Cash Requirements Report** lists all open invoices in order by due date showing the cash needed (on each due date) to pay the invoices. It also shows a running total of the cash necessary to pay all open invoices in Accounts Payable. In addition, the program groups all specific credits and associated transactions.

Transaction Register lists all the transactions in vendor ID order. It lists detailed activity for the current period; it also lists prior period activity if that option is selected.

The **Ageing Report** prints a one line ageing summary (or detailed listing) for each vendor, showing the total amounts of invoices due, the total of any open credits, and the total net amounts due. The total invoice amounts are aged as current, 1 - 30 days past due, 31 - 60 days past due, 61 - 90 days past due, or over 90 days past due.

The **Monthly Check Register** lists all checks written in the current period (in order by check number). This serves two purposes: to give a list of all checks written in the current period for reconciling the check register to bank statements and to provide an accurate audit trail. It also lists any void checks, prepaid invoices, and discounts. This report can be printed for all cash accounts or specific cash accounts identified.

List Vendors prints information on all or a range of vendors. This list includes year-to-date totals, last check printed, current balance, and vendor address and phone number.

List Auto Invoices prints a list of all the information for every automatic invoice in the automatic invoice file. Like **List Vendors,** there is the option of printing automatic invoices for all or a range of vendors.

Print 1099's makes a record of any earnings by non-employees (income not reported or otherwise withheld, like interest or dividend income). The 1099 form must be submitted to the federal government on a calendar-year basis.

1099 Magnetic Media Reporting produces a report for the Internal Revenue Service that shows the earnings for non-employees where no taxes have been withheld. This report is made on a diskette. Some states now require that 1099 information be submitted in this format.

Question Frame 3[4]

Indicate whether each of the following statements is true or false by writing "T" or "F" in the space provided.

_____ 1.   Accounts Payable can show you how much cash is needed to pay all of the open invoices.

_____ 2.   The Ageing Report uses age categories related to due dates of invoices.

_____ 3.   The Monthly Check Register lists all checks written in the current period in alphabetical order by vendor.

_____ 4.   The 1099 form is submitted only to the party who earned the income that was not reported or otherwise withheld.

Now turn to Answer Frame 3[4] on page 4-10 to check your answers.

Answer Frame 3[4]

1. True. The Cash Requirements Report shows a running total of the cash needed to pay all open invoices.

2. True. The categories are: current, 1-30 days past due, 31-60 days past due, 61-90 days past due, and over 90 days past due.

3. False. The Monthly Check Register lists all checks in the current period in order by check number. Having the checks in order by check number helps in reconciling the checking account.

4. False. A copy of each 1099 form must also be sent to the Internal Revenue Service so it can match the amount paid by the company against the amount reported as received by the vendor.

If you missed any of the above, reread Frame 3[4] before turning to the questions at the end of the chapter.

What's Next

Now that you are familiar with Accounts Payable, you are ready to begin Chapter 5. First, you may want to review the Accounts Payable sample reports at the end of this chapter. They will familiarize you with the reports you will produce in the next chapter.

Name _____ ID # _____

ACCOUNTS PAYABLE OVERVIEW
QUESTIONS

1. Briefly describe what Accounts Payable is used for in a business.

   _____

   _____

   _____

2. What are three programs that can be used to set up and maintain Accounts Payable?

   _____

   _____

   _____

3. What are four types of activities that can be performed as maintenance activities?

   _____

   _____

   _____

4. Name twelve processing programs that can be used in Accounts Payable.

   _____   _____

   _____   _____

   _____   _____

   _____   _____

   _____   _____

   _____   _____

Name _____ ID # _____

5. **What are nine reports that can be run in the Accounts Payable module?**

<u>Program Name</u>   <u>Program Function</u>

_____   _____

_____   _____

_____   _____

_____   _____

_____   _____

_____   _____

_____   _____

_____   _____

_____   _____

Name _____ ID # _____

ACCOUNTS PAYABLE OVERVIEW
MATCHING

Instructions: Match each program name on the left with the proper program function on the right.

Program Name	Program Function	Answer
A. Print Pre-Check Register	1. Posts invoices from vendors, corrects disallowed discounts, processes automatic invoices.	_____
B. Select Invoices for Payment	2. Allows current or historical vendor activity to be viewed on the screen or printed in a report.	_____
C. Maintain Vendors	3. Prints out all the detail from the checks.	_____
D. Create G/L Journal Entries	4. Enters vendor information, including vendor remit-to address.	_____
E. Void Checks	5. Chooses which invoices will be paid.	_____
F. Enter Invoices	6. Records open and specific credits from vendors (such as an overpayment).	_____
G. Query Vendors	7. Must be run prior to closing to create journal entries that will be transferred to the General Ledger.	_____
H. Print Check Register	8. Is run after Select Invoices for Payment to preview which checks are to be written.	_____
I. Update A/P Checks	9. Updates invoice and vendor master files and marks invoices as paid and is the final step in check printing cycle.	_____
J. Enter Credits	10. Makes an invoice available for payment again if a check was written incorrectly.	_____

ACCOUNTS PAYABLE

SAMPLE REPORTS

Pre-Check Register

RUN DATE: 12/31/92
RUN TIME: 3:22 PM

W.D. Peachtree & Company
Accounts Payable
Pre-Check Register

** CASH ACCOUNT: 1 11000

ID	INVOICE NUMBER	DATE	GROSS AMOUNT	DISCOUNT	NET AMOUNT	AMOUNT TO PAY	COMMENTS
BLASS PHIL BLASS MEN'S CLOTHING							
	9453BB08	11/05/92	1,432.66	0.00	1,432.66	1,432.66	
	9687BB08	11/25/92	1,113.44	0.00	1,113.44	1,113.44	
		TOTAL:	2,546.10	0.00	2,546.10	2,546.10	
WILSON WILSON, INC.							
	H02099765	10/31/92	19.50	0.00	19.50	19.50	
	H02099925	10/31/92	47.00	0.00	47.00	47.00	
	S006B08	10/31/92	124.40	0.00	124.40	124.40	
	S0100M20	10/31/92	71.11	0.00	71.11	71.11	
	S0500P11	10/31/92	220.00	0.00	220.00	220.00	
	TNT98400615	10/31/92	360.00	0.00	360.00	360.00	
		TOTAL:	842.01	0.00	842.01	842.01	
		RUN TOTAL:	3,388.11	0.00	3,388.11	3,388.11	

*** End of Pre-Check Register ***

Sample Check

0000344

YOUR COMPANY NAME

PHIL BLASS MEN'S CLOTHING
5867 HAMPTON HILL
WAREHOUSE #587
PHILADELPHIA, PA
48574-5867

INVOICE NUMBER	DATE	AMOUNT	AMOUNT	NET AMOUNT
9453BB08	11/05	1432.66	0.00	1432.66
9687BB08	11/25	1113.44	0.00	1113.44
			TOTAL =	$2,546.10

DATE
12/31/92

CHECK NUMBER
00000344

0000344

YOUR COMPANY NAME
ADDRESS
CITY, STATE ZIP CODE
PHONE AND FAX #

YOUR BANK NAME
ADDRESS
CITY, STATE ZIP CODE
00-00/000

00000344

DATE
12/31/92

AMOUNT
******$2,546.10

**** TWO THOUSAND FIVE HUNDRED FORTY SIX & 10/100 DOLLARS

SIGNATURE LINE IMPRINT

PAY

TO THE
ORDER
OF:

PHIL BLASS MEN'S CLOTHING
5867 HAMPTON HILL
WAREHOUSE #587
PHILADELPHIA, PA 48574-5867

⑈000344⑈ ⑈000000000⑈: ⑈00⑈000 00⑈

Check Register

RUN DATE: 12/31/92
RUN TIME: 6:40 PM

W.D. Peachtree & Company
Accounts Payable
Check Register

** CASH ACCOUNT: 1 11000

| CHECK | | VENDOR | | INVOICE | | DISCOUNT | |
NUMBER DATE	ID	NAME	INVOICE NUMBER	DATE	AMOUNT	AMOUNT	AMOUNT PAID
00000344 12/31/92	BLASS	PHIL BLASS MEN'S CLOTHING	9453B08	11/05/92	1,432.66	0.00	1,432.66
			9687B08	11/25/92	1,113.44	0.00	1,113.44
					Total Check Amount:		2,546.10
00000345 12/31/92	WILSON	WILSON, INC.	H02099765	10/31/92	19.50	0.00	19.50
			H02099925	10/31/92	47.00	0.00	47.00
			S006B08	10/31/92	124.40	0.00	124.40
			S0100W20	10/31/92	71.11	0.00	71.11
			S0500P11	10/31/92	220.00	0.00	220.00
			TNT98400615	10/31/92	360.00	0.00	360.00
					Total Check Amount:		842.01

Number Of Checks Written: 2   Total Checks Written: 3,388.11
================

*** End of Check Register ***

Monthly Check Register

```
RUN DATE: 12/31/92
RUN TIME:  3:23 PM
```

W.D. Peachtree & Company
Accounts Payable
Monthly Check Register

** Data Sorted By Check Number
** Cash Account: 1 11000

CHECK NUMBER	DATE	VENDOR ID	NAME	AMOUNT	DISCOUNT AMOUNT	CHECK AMOUNT
10000085	12/07/92	BLASS	PHIL BLASS MEN'S CLOTHING	472.00	0.00	472.00
10000086	12/07/92	BRATCH	BRATCHWORTH CLOTHES	106.56	0.00	106.56
10000087	12/07/92	CANNON	CANNON LINEN SUPPLIES	3,542.66	0.00	3,542.66
10000088	12/07/92	DIOR	CHRISTOPHER DIOR APPARELS	2,987.66	0.00	2,987.66
10000089	12/07/92	ELE001	BILL'S STEREO WAREHOUSE	600.00	0.00	600.00
10000090	12/07/92	ELE003	STEREO WAREHOUSE SUPPLIES	1,765.99	0.00	1,765.99
10000091	12/07/92	ELE012	STEREO CITY	2,258.70	0.00	2,258.70
10000092	12/07/92	ELE084	STEREO CITY DISTRIBUTORS	1,976.55	0.00	1,976.55
10000093	12/07/92	GVANNI	GVANNI FASHIONS, LTD.	534.44	0.00	534.44
10000094	12/07/92	HOLLYS	HOLLY'S FOODS	1,799.42	0.00	1,799.42
10000095	12/07/92	MAYTAB	MAYTAB APPLIANCES	843.00	0.00	843.00
10000096	12/07/92	NUMCO	NUMCO CLOTHING, LTD.	88.00	0.00	88.00
10000097	12/07/92	SACKS	SACKS 6TH AVENUE DISTRIB.	54.00	0.00	54.00
10000098	12/07/92	TARPAN	TARPAN KITCHEN APPLIANCES	4,481.88	0.00	4,481.88
			ACCOUNT TOTALS	21,510.86	0.00	21,510.86
			GRAND TOTALS	21,510.86	0.00	21,510.86

*** End of Monthly Check Register ***

```
RUN DATE: 12/31/92                    W.D. Peachtree & Company                              PAGE   1
RUN TIME:  3:24 PM                       Accounts Payable
                                           Query Vendor

VENDOR
  ID    NAME / ADDRESS           PHONE        AMOUNTS       CALENDAR     FISCAL        LAST CHECK

BRATCH  BRATCHWORTH CLOTHES                 YTD Purch:  9,746.75   9,746.75    9,746.75    No. : 10000086
        4867 MITCHELL BOULEVARD            YTD Paymt:  2,138.83   2,138.83    2,138.83    Amt.:    106.56
        LOS ANGELES, CALIFORNIA            Curr. Bal:  7,607.92                           Date: 12/07/92
                                           Net Pending:    0.00
   95860

                                            DISCOUNT                                                   DISC.
  INVOICE         AMOUNT DUE                  AMOUNT                                                    TAKEN PAY
 NUMBER / DATE    / DATE DUE                 / DATE      ACCOUNT - AMOUNT   ACCOUNT - AMOUNT   ACCOUNT - AMOUNT   ACCOUNT - AMOUNT

BB42520812         106.56                     0.00       13500   106.56    0   0.00          0   0.00          0   0.00          No  PD
   10/31/92                    11/30/92   01/01/00       0       0.00      0   0.00          0   0.00          0   0.00
                                                           A/P ACCOUNT 1 20500

BB42530807          62.16                     0.00       13500    62.16    0   0.00          0   0.00          0   0.00          No  NN
   10/31/92                    11/30/92   01/01/00       0       0.00      0   0.00          0   0.00          0   0.00
                                                           A/P ACCOUNT 1 20500

BB46378999       5,432.65                     0.00       13500 5,432.65    0   0.00          0   0.00          0   0.00          No  NN
   11/10/92                    12/10/92   01/01/00       0       0.00      0   0.00          0   0.00          0   0.00
                                                           A/P ACCOUNT 1 20500

BB46399765       2,113.11                     0.00       13500 2,113.11    0   0.00          0   0.00          0   0.00          No  NN
   11/24/92                    12/24/92   01/01/00       0       0.00      0   0.00          0   0.00          0   0.00
                                                           A/P ACCOUNT 1 20500

Chk # 10000086     106.56-                    0.00       0       0.00      0   0.00          0   0.00          0   0.00          No  CK
   12/07/92                    12/07/92   12/07/92       0       0.00      0   0.00          0   0.00          0   0.00
                                                           CASH ACCOUNT 1 11000

*** End of Query Vendor ***
```

Vendor File List

W.D. Peachtree & Company
Accounts Payable
Vendor File List

VENDOR ID	VENDOR NAME/ ADDRESS	PHONE/ CONTACT	FISCAL/CALENDAR YR AMTS		LAST CHECK		VENDOR TYPE	G/L ACCOUNT
AUTFNC	THIRD NATIONAL BANK OF GA	WILLIAM H. HAR	FIS PURCH:	0.00	NO.:	0		15700
	8764 PEACHTREE STREET		FIS PMTS:	0.00	AMT:	0.00	1099 TYPE:	
	SUITE 583		CAL PURCH:	0.00	DATE:	01/01/00	BOX:	
	ATLANTA, GA		CAL PMTS:	0.00			FED ID:	
	39384		CURRENT BALANCE:	0.00				
BLASS	PHIL BLASS MEN'S CLOTHING	215-555-1286	FIS PURCH:	7,131.78	NO.:	10000085		13500
	5867 HAMPTON HILL	RARREN P. OAKE	FIS PMTS:	4,584.76	AMT:	472.00	1099 TYPE:	
	WAREHOUSE #587		CAL PURCH:	7,131.78	DATE:	12/07/92	BOX:	
	PHILADELPHIA, PA		CAL PMTS:	4,584.76			FED ID:	
	48574-5867		CURRENT BALANCE:	2,546.10				
BRATCH	BRATCHWORTH CLOTHES		FIS PURCH:	9,746.75	NO.:	10000086	1099	13500
	4867 MITCHELL BOULEVARD	RYAN J. GUESS	FIS PMTS:	2,138.83	AMT:	106.56	1099 TYPE: M	
	LOS ANGELES, CALIFORNIA		CAL PURCH:	9,746.75	DATE:	12/07/92	BOX: 1	
	95860		CAL PMTS:	2,138.83			FED ID: 473-98-8376	
			CURRENT BALANCE:	7,607.92				
CANNON	CANNON LINEN SUPPLIES		FIS PURCH:	6,753.08	NO.:	10000087		13500
	12725 BOXWOOD COURT	BARRY MICHAELS	FIS PMTS:	3,642.66	AMT:	3,542.66	1099 TYPE:	
	SPRINGFIELD, MASS		CAL PURCH:	6,753.08	DATE:	12/07/92	BOX:	
	38387		CAL PMTS:	3,642.66			FED ID:	
			CURRENT BALANCE:	3,110.42				
CURTIS	CURTIS APPLIANCES		FIS PURCH:	2,655.78	NO.:	0		13500
	DISTRIBUTION CENTER "E"	ROBERT MCCAULL	FIS PMTS:	0.00	AMT:	0.00	1099 TYPE:	
	3748 EIGHTH STREET, NE		CAL PURCH:	2,655.78	DATE:	01/01/00	BOX:	
	CHICAGO, ILLINOIS		CAL PMTS:	0.00			FED ID:	
	93847		CURRENT BALANCE:	2,655.78				

RUN TOTALS:		
FIS PURCH:	26,287.39	
FIS PMTS:	10,366.25	AMT: 4,121.22
CAL PURCH:	26,287.39	
CAL PMTS:	10,366.25	
CURRENT BALANCE:	15,920.22	
VENDORS LISTED:	5	

*** End of Vendor File List ***

Open Invoice Report

RUN DATE: 12/31/92
RUN TIME: 3:28 PM

W.D. Peachtree & Company
Accounts Payable
Open Invoice Report

** A/P ACCOUNT: ALL

VENDOR ID	VENDOR NAME/ INVOICE NUMBER	ENTRY DATE	INVOICE AMOUNT	INVOICE DATE	DUE DATE	DISC. DATE	DISCOUNT AMOUNT	DATE	PAYMENTS	NET INVOICE	PAY
BLASS	PHIL BLASS MEN'S CLOTHING										
	9453BB08	11/05/92	1,432.66	11/05/92	12/05/92	0.00	0.00	01/01/00	0.00	1,432.66	YES
	9687BB08	11/05/92	1,113.44	11/25/92	12/25/92	0.00	0.00	01/01/00	0.00	1,113.44	YES
			2,546.10				0.00		0.00	2,546.10	
BRATCH	BRATCHWORTH CLOTHES										
	BB42530807	10/31/92	62.16	10/31/92	11/30/92	0.00	0.00	01/01/00	0.00	62.16	NO
	BB46378999	11/05/92	5,432.65	11/10/92	12/10/92	0.00	0.00	01/01/00	0.00	5,432.65	NO
	BB46399765	11/05/92	2,113.11	11/24/92	12/24/92	0.00	0.00	01/01/00	0.00	2,113.11	NO
			7,607.92				0.00		0.00	7,607.92	
CANNON	CANNON LINEN SUPPLIES										
	810987B50	11/05/92	2,334.54	11/19/92	12/19/92	0.00	0.00	01/01/00	0.00	2,334.54	NO
	811899B50	12/15/92	775.88	12/05/92	01/04/93	0.00	0.00	01/01/00	0.00	775.88	NO
			3,110.42				0.00		0.00	3,110.42	
CURTIS	CURTIS APPLIANCES										
	10060P10	10/31/92	1,100.00	10/31/92	11/30/92	0.00	0.00	01/01/00	0.00	1,100.00	NO
	10287P11	12/15/92	1,555.78	12/05/92	01/04/93	0.00	0.00	01/01/00	0.00	1,555.78	NO
			2,655.78				0.00		0.00	2,655.78	
	GRAND TOTALS		15,920.22				0.00		0.00	15,920.22	

TOTAL OPEN INVOICES 9

*** End of Open Invoice Report ***

Cash Requirements Report

RUN DATE: 12/31/92
RUN TIME: 3:29 PM

W.D. Peachtree & Company
Accounts Payable
Cash Requirements Report

PAGE 1

**DATA SORTED BY DUE DATE

DUE DATE/ VENDOR	VENDOR NAME	INVOICE NUMBER	INV.DATE	AMOUNT	DISCOUNT	NET	DAILY TOTAL	REQ. TO DATE
11/30/92								
BRATCH	BRATCHWORTH CLOTHES	BB42530807	10/31/92	62.16	0.00	62.16		
CURTIS	CURTIS APPLIANCES	10060P10	10/31/92	1,100.00	0.00	1,100.00		
ELE001	BILL'S STEREO WAREH	810534B100	10/31/92	55.56	0.00	55.56		
NUMCO	NUMCO CLOTHING, LTD	463487G20	10/31/92	105.00	0.00	105.00		
		81960813	10/31/92	71.50	0.00	71.50		
SACKS	SACKS 6TH AVENUE DI	46344475	10/31/92	51.75	0.00	51.75		
SCULLY	SCULLY HAIR PRODUCT	SC3SP7024	10/31/92	45.12	0.00	45.12		
SPEAR	SPEAR'S BEAUTY SUPP	SP7010	10/31/92	22.50	0.00	22.50		
STEWRT	STEWART'S APPARELS	FP398308	10/31/92	71.11	0.00	71.11		
WILSON	WILSON, INC.	H02099765	10/31/92	19.50	0.00	19.50		
		H02099925	10/31/92	47.00	0.00	47.00		
		S006B08	10/31/92	124.40	0.00	124.40		
		S0100M20	10/31/92	71.11	0.00	71.11		
		S0500P11	10/31/92	220.00	0.00	220.00		
		TN198400615	10/31/92	360.00	0.00	360.00	2,426.71	2,426.71
12/05/92								
BLASS	PHIL BLASS MEN'S CL	9453BB08	11/05/92	1,432.66	0.00	1,432.66	1,432.66	3,859.37
12/10/92								
BRATCH	BRATCHWORTH CLOTHES	BB46378999	11/10/92	5,432.65	0.00	5,432.65		
ELE006	JVP COMPUTERS & STE	811654E07	11/10/92	1,221.33	0.00	1,221.33	6,653.98	10,513.35
12/11/92								
ELE001	BILL'S STEREO WAREH	810765B100	11/11/92	2,322.54	0.00	2,322.54		
ELE010	TONY'S STEREO/ELECT	JVP9385433	11/11/92	2,114.65	0.00	2,114.65	4,437.19	14,950.54
12/12/92								
ELE001	BILL'S STEREO WAREH	811564B100	11/12/92	1,917.77	0.00	1,917.77	1,917.77	16,868.31
12/14/92								
ELE032	HARRIS ELECTRONICS	810999A20	11/14/92	1,234.55	0.00	1,234.55	1,234.55	18,102.86

*** End of Cash Requirements Report ***

Transaction Register

```
RUN DATE: 12/31/92              W.D. Peachtree & Company                                    PAGE  1
RUN TIME: 3:31 PM                   Accounts Payable
                          Transaction Register For Generation 12
```

VENDOR ID	VENDOR NAME/ INVOICE NUMBER	INVOICE DATE	DEBIT DISTRIBUTION ACCOUNT	AMOUNT ENTERED	INVOICES AP	PAYMENTS	DISC. TAKEN	CASH	ACT
BLASS	PHIL BLASS MEN'S CLOTHING								
	Check No. 10000085	12/07/92				472.00	0.00	472.00	1
				0.00	0.00	472.00	0.00	472.00	
BRATCH	BRATCHWORTH CLOTHES								
	Check No. 10000086	12/07/92				106.56	0.00	106.56	1
				0.00	0.00	106.56	0.00	106.56	
CANNON	CANNON LINEN SUPPLIES								
	811899B50	12/05/92	13500	775.88	775.88				1
	Check No. 10000087	12/07/92				3,542.66	0.00	3,542.66	1
				775.88	775.88	3,542.66	0.00	3,542.66	
CURTIS	CURTIS APPLIANCES								
	10287P11	12/05/92	13500	1,555.78	1,555.78				1
				1,555.78	1,555.78	0.00	0.00	0.00	
DIOR	CHRISTOPHER DIOR APPARELS								
	Check No. 10000088	12/07/92				2,987.66	0.00	2,987.66	1
				0.00	0.00	2,987.66	0.00	2,987.66	
ELE001	BILL'S STEREO WAREHOUSE								
	Check No. 10000089	12/07/92				600.00	0.00	600.00	1

	AMOUNT ENTERED	INVOICES AP	PAYMENTS	DISC. TAKEN	CASH
GENERATION 12 TOTALS	7,233.01	7,233.01	21,510.86	0.00	21,510.86
RUN TOTALS	7,233.01	7,233.01	21,510.86	0.00	21,510.86

*** End of Transaction Register ***

Ageing Report

```
RUN DATE: 12/31/92                        W.D. Peachtree & Company                                    PAGE  1
RUN TIME: 3:33 PM                            Accounts Payable
                                               Ageing Report
-----------------------------------------------------------------------------------------------------------------
** A/P ACCOUNT:  ALL

VENDOR   VENDOR NAME/
ID       INVOICE NUMBER     CURRENT    1 TO 30   31 TO 60   61 TO 90   OVER 90    CREDITS   TOTAL DUE
------   --------------

BLASS  PHIL BLASS MEN'S CLOTHING
       9453BB08                0.00   1,432.66       0.00       0.00      0.00      0.00    1,432.66
       9687BB08                       1,113.44                                              1,113.44
                              -------  --------   --------   --------   --------  --------  --------
       Vendor Totals:           0.00   2,546.10       0.00       0.00      0.00      0.00    2,546.10

BRATCH  BRATCHWORTH CLOTHES
        BB42530807                               62.16                                         62.16
        BB46378999             5,432.65                                                     5,432.65
        BB46399765             2,113.11                                                     2,113.11
                              -------  --------   --------   --------   --------  --------  --------
        Vendor Totals:          0.00   7,545.76      62.16       0.00      0.00      0.00    7,607.92

CANNON  CANNON LINEN SUPPLIES
        810987B50                      2,334.54                                             2,334.54
        811899B50              775.88                                                         775.88
                              -------  --------   --------   --------   --------  --------  --------
        Vendor Totals:         775.88  2,334.54       0.00       0.00      0.00      0.00    3,110.42

CURTIS  CURTIS APPLIANCES
        10060P10                                1,100.00                                    1,100.00
        10287P11             1,555.78                                                       1,555.78
                              -------  --------   --------   --------   --------  --------  --------
        VENDOR TOTALS:       1,555.78      0.00   1,100.00       0.00      0.00      0.00    2,655.78

                             ========  ========   ========   ========   ========  ========  ========
        RUN TOTALS:          2,331.66 12,426.40   1,162.16       0.00      0.00      0.00   15,920.22

                            *** End of Ageing Report ***
```

List Auto Invoices

W.D. Peachtree & Company
Accounts Payable
List Auto Invoices

VENDOR ID	VENDOR NAME	STATUS	INV. NO	AMOUNT DUE	DUE DAY	DISCOUNT DAY	DISCOUNT PERCENT	FREQ	NO	MONTHS BEG	LAST #	BILL ACCT	A/P ACCT	COMMENT
AUTFNC	THIRD NATIONAL BANK OF GA	A	01	357.45	15	0	0.00%	M	48	12	0	0	1	

ACCOUNT	AMOUNT	ACCOUNT	AMOUNT	ACCOUNT	AMOUNT
15700	357.45				

RUN TOTALS   INVOICES: 1   INVOICE DOLLARS: 357.45

*** End of List Auto Invoices ***

Vendor File Maintenance Control Report

```
RUN DATE: 12/31/92         W.D. Peachtree & Company              PAGE  1
RUN TIME: 5:58 PM               Accounts Payable
                        Vendor File Maintenance Control Report

                                  Add Vendor

Vendor   Field               Current Value
------   -----               -------------
ADVENT   Vendor Name       : ADVENT DISTRIBUTORS
         Address           : 303 NORTH MAIN STREET
         Address           : CANTON, LA
         Address           ..
         Postal Code       : 44222
         Telephone         : 318-564-5222
         Contact           : GEORGE FISH
         G/L Account       :  13500
         Temporary Vendor  : N
         1099 Employee     : N
         1099 Type         ..
         1099 Box          ..
         Federal ID Number: 444-22-8315
         Calendar YTD Pur. :               0.00
         Calendar YTD Pmt. :               0.00
         Fiscal YTD Pur.   :               0.00
         Fiscal YTD Pmt.   :               0.00

         *** End of Vendor File Maintenance Control Report ***
```

Auto Invoice File Maintenance Control Report

RUN DATE: 12/31/92   W.D. Peachtree & Company   PAGE 1
RUN TIME: 5:56 PM   Accounts Payable
           Auto Invoice File Maintenance Control Report

Add Auto Invoice

Vendor	Field	Current Value	
AUTFNC	Auto Invoice Num. :	01	
	Status A/I :	A	
	Amount Due :	357.45	
	Due Day :	15	
	Discount Day :	0	
	Discount Percent :	0.00	
	Number Of Months :	48	
	Month To Begin :	12	
	Frequency :	1	
	Last Month Billed:	0	
	# Of Month Billed:	0	
	A/P Account Code :	1	
	Comment :		
	Account/Amount 1 :	15700	357.45
	Account/Amount 2 :	0	0.00
	Account/Amount 3 :	0	0.00
	Account/Amount 4 :	0	0.00
	Account/Amount 5 :	0	0.00
	Account/Amount 6 :	0	0.00
	Account/Amount 7 :	0	0.00
	Account/Amount 8 :	0	0.00

*** End of Auto Invoice File Maintenance Control Report ***

Enter Invoices Control Report

```
RUN DATE: 12/31/92                      W.D. Peachtree & Company                                    PAGE   1
RUN TIME: 6:00 PM                           Accounts Payable
                                        Enter Invoices Control Report
-------------------------------------------------------------------------------------------------------------

VENDOR  VENDOR NAME/      INVOICE     DUE        DISCOUNT        DISTRIBUTION        PRE-   ACCOUNT
  ID      INVOICE NO.      DATE    AMOUNT/DATE  AMOUNT/DATE  ACCOUNT   AMOUNT        PAID   C/AP      COMMENT
-------------------------------------------------------------------------------------------------------------

ELE001 BILL'S STEREO WAREHOUSE
         55487            12/31/92   2,211.00     55.28      13500   2,211.00        N      0/1
                                    01/30/93    01/10/93


       TOTAL INVOICES ADDED:    1    2,211.00     55.28


*** End of Enter Invoices Control Report ***
```

Enter Open Credits Control Report

```
RUN DATE: 12/31/92                    W.D. Peachtree & Company                          PAGE   1
RUN TIME:  6:04 PM                         Accounts Payable
                                     Enter Open Credits Control Report
---------------------------------------------------------------------------------------------------

VENDOR   VENDOR NAME/        CREDIT                    DISTRIBUTION
ID       OPEN CREDIT NO.     DATE     CREDIT AMOUNT    ACCOUNT      AMOUNT      COMMENT
--------------------------   ------   -------------    ------------ ----------  ----------

BLASS  PHIL BLASS MEN'S CLOTHING
         EC-62154           12/31/92      300.00       13500         300.00     OPEN CREDIT

         TOTAL CREDITS ADDED:    1          300.00

*** End of Enter Open Credits Control Report ***
```

Enter Specific Credits Control Report

RUN DATE: 12/31/92   W.D. Peachtree & Company   PAGE   1
RUN TIME: 6:05 PM   Accounts Payable
                                            Enter Specific Credits Control Report

VENDOR   VENDOR NAME/   CREDIT   CREDIT   DISTRIBUTION
ID   INVOICE NO.   DATE   AMOUNT   ACCOUNT   AMOUNT   REFERENCE
------   -----------   ------   ------   -------   ------   ---------

ELE001   BILL'S STEREO WAREHOUSE
         810534B100   12/31/92   12.62   13500   12.62   EC-101

TOTAL CREDITS ADDED: 1

*** End of Enter Specific Credits Control Report ***

Delete Invoices Control Report

RUN DATE: 12/31/92
RUN TIME: 6:07 PM

W.D. Peachtree & Company
Accounts Payable
Delete Invoices Control Report

PAGE 1

VENDOR ID	VENDOR NAME/ INVOICE NO.	INVOICE DATE	AMOUNT/DATE	DISCOUNT AMOUNT/DATE	ACCOUNT	DISTRIBUTION AMOUNT	COMMENT
CANNON	CANNON LINEN SUPPLIES						
	810987B50	11/19/92	2,334.54 12/19/92	0.00 01/01/00	13500	2,334.54	

TOTAL INVOICES DELETED   1   2,334.54   0.00

*** End of Delete Invoices Control Report ***

Void Checks Control Report

```
RUN DATE: 12/31/92                                                              PAGE 1
RUN TIME:  6:08 PM

                          W.D. Peachtree & Company
                              Accounts Payable
                          Void Checks Control Report

                                                                                CASH
                        ------CHECK------    -------- AMOUNT --------           ACCT
VENDOR  VENDOR NAME     NUMBER    DATE        GROSS      DISCOUNT      NET       ----
------  -----------     ------    ----        -----      --------      ---
BLASS   PHIL BLASS MEN'S CLOTHING   10000085  12/07/92    472.00        0.00     472.00     1

            TOTAL CHECKS VOIDED:      1        472.00        0.00     472.00

*** End of Void Checks Control Report ***
```

List G/L Transfers

```
RUN DATE: 12/31/92          W.D. Peachtree & Company                    PAGE  1
RUN TIME:  6:10 PM                Accounts Payable
                                  List G/L Transfers

ACCOUNT SC REFERENCE   DATE            DESCRIPTION            DEBIT      CREDIT
------- -- ---------   --------        -----------            -----      ------
11000 A  10000085   12/07/92 BLASS  Cash                                  472.00
11000 A  10000086   12/07/92 BRATCH Cash                                  106.56
11000 A  10000087   12/07/92 CANNON Cash                                 3542.66
11000 A  10000088   12/07/92 DIOR   Cash                                 2987.66
11000 A  10000089   12/07/92 ELE001 Cash                                  600.00
11000 A  10000090   12/07/92 ELE003 Cash                                 1765.99
11000 A  10000091   12/07/92 ELE012 Cash                                  681.82
11000 A  10000091   12/07/92 ELE012 Cash                                 1576.88
11000 A  10000092   12/07/92 ELE084 Cash                                 1976.55
11000 A  10000093   12/07/92 GVANNI Cash                                  180.00
11000 A  10000093   12/07/92 GVANNI Cash                                  354.44
11000 A  10000094   12/07/92 HOLLYS Cash                                  789.66
11000 A  10000094   12/07/92 HOLLYS Cash                                 1009.76
11000 A  10000095   12/07/92 MAYTAB Cash                                  843.00
11000 A  10000096   12/07/92 NUMCO  Cash                                   88.00
11000 A  10000097   12/07/92 SACKS  Cash                                   54.00
11000 A  10000098   12/07/92 TARPAN Cash                                 4481.88
11000 A  Ck 10000   12/07/92 Cash Void Check          472.00

Account   11000 Total:                                 472.00   21510.86

13500 A  811899B5   12/05/92 CANNON - Invoice Dist.    775.88
13500 A  10287P11   12/05/92 CURTIS - Invoice Dist.   1555.78


20500 A  EC-101     12/31/92 ELE001 - Entered Invoices  12.62
20500 A  810987B5   11/19/92 CANNON - Deleted Invoice  2334.54
20500 A  Ck 10000   12/07/92 Payments Void Check                          472.00

Account   20500 Total:                               24158.02    9916.01


                                      Total:          34074.03   34074.03
                                                     ========== ==========

*** End of List G/L Transfers ***
```

Sample 1099

VOID ☐ CORRECTED ☐

PAYER'S name, street address, city, state, and ZIP code		OMB No. 1545-0115	
W. D. Peachtree & Company 3900 Peachtree Street Atlanta, GA 30309		19**92**	**Miscellaneous Income**

1 Rents $ 0.00	2 Royalties $ 0.00	3 Prizes, awards, etc. $ 0.00	5 Fishing boat proceeds $ 0.00	

PAYER'S Federal identification number	RECIPIENT'S identification number	4 Federal income tax withheld $ 0.00	6 Medical and health care payments $	7 Nonemployee compensation $ 12500.00	Copy C For Payer or State Copy
58-2468431	430-83-9320				

RECIPIENT'S name, address, and ZIP code	8 Substitute payments in lieu of dividends or interest $ 0.00	9 Payer made direct sales of $5,000 or more of consumer products to a buyer (recipient) for resale ▶ ☐	For Paperwork Reduction Act Notice and instructions for completing this form, see Instructions for Forms 1099, 1098, 5498, and W-2G.
Cal Cline 2301 Valley Heart Drive Atlanta, GA 30345	10 Crop insurance proceeds $ 0.00	11 State income tax withheld $ 0.00	
	12 State, Payer's state number		

Account number (optional)	2nd TIN Not. ☐

Form **1099-MISC**

Department of the Treasury – Internal Revenue Service 13 26/8063

Chapter 5

ACCOUNTS PAYABLE: PRACTICING WITH A SAMPLE BUSINESS

Learning Objectives:

After working this chapter you should be able to:

1. Perform customary Accounts Payable activities including—adding vendors, entering invoices (automatic and regular) and credits (open and specific) and printing checks.

2. Perform Special Accounts Payable activities including the creation of journal entries to the General Ledger, printing a transaction register, and closing the period.

Chapter 5

Accounts Payable: Practicing With a Sample Business

Certain module options govern the way Accounts Payable operates. W. D. Peachtree & Company's options are set to always force control reports, so you need your printer on-line and ready for these lessons. Use the control report as a method to verify the changes you enter.

Beginning the Practice Session

WARNING

BEFORE CONTINUING, BE SURE THAT ALL DATA FILES HAVE BEEN RESTORED TO THEIR ORIGINAL CONDITION. IF YOU ARE UNSURE OF HOW TO RESTORE THESE FILES, TURN TO THE INSTRUCTIONS FOUND ON PAGE 1-32 IN CHAPTER 1.

The lessons in this chapter guide you through typical Accounts Payable operations. You can complete the lessons in one session, or you can do them in several sessions. Start Peachtree Complete Accounting by changing to the directory in which you installed PCA, and then type **PEACH** 🖳.

❖ Press 🖳 to erase the date on your screen. For this tutorial you should use December 9, 1992 as the date. (All of the Peachtree Complete tutorials begin in November or December 1992.)

❖ Type **120992** 🖳.

❖ PCA asks you for a company ID.

❖ Type **WD** 🖳.

❖ Select **Accounts Payable**.

This starts PCA Accounts Payable. PCA displays the **Accounts Payable Main Menu**. You are now ready to begin the session.

Topic 1 - Working with Daily or Regular Activities

Everyday activities are the things that are done on a regular basis to keep Accounts Payable up-to-date.

This section has four lessons. You will learn how to:

1. Add a Vendor.

2. Enter an Automatic Invoice.

3. Enter an Invoice.

4. Enter a Specific and Open Credit.

Lesson 1: Adding a Vendor

W. D. Peachtree & Company has carried the same trash compactor in its appliance department for several years. It has now decided to order these trash compactors from a different vendor, Advent Distributors.

❖ Select **Maintenance Programs** from the **Accounts Payable Main Menu**. Press [ENTER].

❖ From the **Maintenance Programs Menu**, select **Maintain Vendors** and then press [ENTER].

Accounts Payable tells you to make sure that your printer is set to TOP OF FORM—that is, at the top of a new page. Accounts Payable is going to print a control report that will list your entries.

Note: Accounts Payable will ask you to do this as you begin each function.

❖ Make sure that your printer is ready to print and at the top on a new page. Then press [ENTER].

❖ At the **VENDOR ID** prompt, type **ADVENT**, and press [ENTER]. A prompt appears: *NOT ON FILE - ADD (Y/N): Y.*

❖ Accept the default (Y) and enter the vendor name: **ADVENT DISTRIBUTORS**, and press [ENTER].

❖ Now type the Advent's address in the next two lines:

303 North Main Street [ENTER]
Canton, GA [ENTER]

Skip the third line by just pressing [ENTER].

❖ Enter a **postal (zip) code - 44222**. Press ⏎ after entering the zip code.

❖ Enter a **Telephone Number - 404-394-0776** and press ⏎.

❖ Enter a **Contact Name: In this case, type Peter Lynch** ⏎.

The cursor will now be positioned on the General Ledger Account Number field. The default for this field is 0. Press the **F2** key and Accounts Payable displays a "pop up box" that contains all of the General Ledger chart of account numbers for W. D. Peachtree & Company. Position the highlighted bar on account number **13500** (inventory account) and press ⏎. The account number will now be displayed in the field. Press ⏎ once more.

The cursor is now positioned at the *TEMPORARY VENDOR (Y/N):* prompt.

❖ Accept the default **N** and press ⏎. The next field concerns 1099's. For purposes of this example, assume this vendor does not need a 1099.

❖ Accept the default **N** for the **1099 Vendor** prompt, by pressing ⏎ and Accounts Payable skips the 1099 Type and the 1099 Misc. Box prompts.

❖ Enter a **Federal ID number:** Use a Federal ID number, 107-24-4161, and press ⏎.

A Federal ID number is the federal taxpayer's number assigned to a vendor by the government. The next four fields are for fiscal and calendar year-to-date purchases and payments. This is a new vendor so these fields will be 0. Do not enter anything here.

❖ Press ⏎ at the **Calendar** and **Fiscal YTD Purchases and Payments** prompts to accept the defaults of **0**.

❖ Press **F10**, then accept the default, **Y,** at the *ACCEPT (Y/N):* prompt by pressing ⏎.

Accounts Payable displays at the bottom of the screen: *CHANGE VENDOR REMIT TO ADDRESS (Y/N)? N*

This appears in case you want to send remittance checks to an address other than the address entered at the beginning of this lesson. For example, vendors may prefer all payments sent to a home office address in another city.

❖ Accept the default **N** , and press ⏎.

Accounts Payable will print out a control report.

❖ Now you are back to the **VENDOR ID** prompt. Press **F10**.

Read the control report. Notice that the control report contains all the information that you entered in this lesson.

Lesson 1 Summary

You have just established a new vendor. This vendor has become a permanent record in the Vendor master file. You can now process transactions for this vendor.

Lesson 2: Entering an Automatic Invoice.

The **Maintain Automatic Invoice** program is used to establish repeating invoices such as rent, mortgage payments, and automobile loans, and usually consists of fixed amounts that are issued for a specific number of months on a regular basis.

W. D. Peachtree & Company has just purchased a new mini-van for small deliveries. The van was financed by a bank and will require monthly payments of $357.45 for the next four years. The payments are due on the 15th of each month, beginning in December.

❖ From the **Accounts Payable Maintenance Menu**, select **Maintain Auto Invoices**.

❖ At the **VENDOR ID** prompt, press the [F2] key and position the cursor on the **AUTFNC** Vendor ID (for Auto Financing) and press [ENTER].

Note: From now on, every time you enter information in a field during this tutorial, press [ENTER]. You will also follow this procedure when you see "Accept the screen".

❖ At the **Auto Invoice Number** prompt, enter **11** (for this example). A prompt will appear stating *NOT ON FILE - ADD (Y/N):Y*. Accept the default **Y**.

Accounts Payable displays the rest of the screen to enter the invoice information.

❖ Select **A** (for Active) at the **Status (A/I)** prompt.

This field determines whether this invoice is "Active" or "Inactive". The majority of all automatic invoices are active.

❖ Enter an **Amount Due** of **357.45**.

❖ Type **15** for the **Due Day**.

❖ Press [ENTER] at the **Discount Day** field to skip this field for this example.

Since you did not enter a Discount Day, the cursor skips over the **Discount Percent** field and goes to the **Number of Months** field.

❖ Type **48** for the **Number of Months**.

❖ Enter **12** for the **Month to Begin**.

This field records the month that you want billing to begin: Your choices are 1 through 12, to correspond with the twelve months of the year.

❖ At the **Frequency** field , which sets up the number of times the payment will be made, press the [F2]. Position the highlighted bar on the **1-Monthly** and press [ENTER]. The 1 - Monthly is displayed in the field.

❖ Accept the default, **0**, in the **Last Month Billed** field and Accounts Payable skips the **# of Months Billed** fields.

❖ Type **1** at the **Accounts Payable Account** prompt.

❖ Type **1762-87-73654 MINI-VAN** in the **Comment** field.

This comment will appear on some reports. It is generally used as a reference. You can enter account numbers, a brief description of an item, or anything else you believe is helpful.

The cursor will now be positioned on the **Distribution Account** field with a default account number because this number was entered when the vendor was established in the **Maintain Vendors** program. This is the account that the amount will be distributed to in General Ledger. You should accept the 15700 account by pressing [ENTER]. Then press [ENTER] to accept $357.45 in the **Amount Due** field. You must enter at least one distribution account and amount when entering invoices (and credits).

❖ Press [F10] to indicate you are done with this screen. The cursor is positioned at the bottom of the screen by the *ACCEPT (Y/N)* prompt. Accept the default **Y**, and press the [ENTER].

❖ Accounts Payable will display a message: *MAINTAIN JOB COST DISTRIBUTION (Y/N)? N* . Accept the *N* default and press [ENTER].

Note: Peachtree Accounting has the capability of integrating Accounts Payable with a Job Cost System. This is beyond the scope of this text and will not be discussed.

Accounts Payable prints the following Auto Invoice File Maintenance Control Report:

```
RUN DATE:  12/09/92          W.D. Peachtree & Company              PAGE 1
RUN TIME:  11:54 AM               Accounts Payable
                        Auto Invoice File Maintenance Control Report
-------------------------------------------------------------------------------------------------
                                   Add Auto Invoice
Vendor     Field                     Current Value
----------    --------------------        ------------------------------
AUTFNC  Auto Invoice Num.  :      11
           Status A/I              :      A
           Amount Due          :             357.45
           Due Day              :      15
           Discount Day        :       0
           Discount Percent   :              0.00
           Number Of Months :      48
           Month To Begin     :      12
           Frequency            :      1
           Last Month Billed  :      0
           # Of Month Billed  :      0
           A/P Account Code  :      1
           Comment              :      1762-87-73654  MINI VAN

           Account/Amount 1  :      15700                 357.45
           Account/Amount 2  :      0                        0.00
           Account/Amount 3  :      0                        0.00
           Account/Amount 4  :      0                        0.00
           Account/Amount 5  :      0                        0.00
           Account/Amount 6  :      0                        0.00
           Account/Amount 7  :      0                        0.00
           Account/Amount 8  :      0                        0.00

      *** End of Auto Invoice File Maintenance Control Report ***
```

❖ Accounts Payable returns to the **Auto Invoice Number** prompt. Press ▐ESC▌, then ▐F10▌.

Lesson 2 Summary

You have just entered an automatic invoice. You will learn how to process this invoice for payment in Lesson 3.

Lesson 3 - Entering an Invoice

In this lesson you are going to create an invoice, and add a vendor while processing. This means that the vendor will be added in the **Enter Invoice** program from the Accounts Payable Processing Menu. You will also process the auto invoice established in Lesson 2.

W. D. Peachtree & Company has just received a shipment of twenty compact disc players (coded as ELE004 by the company) for a special sale this month. The invoice from the Vendor, Mays Stereo, is number 55487 for $663.32, with a 2.5% discount offered for prompt payment.

❖ Return to the **Accounts Payable Main Menu** by pressing ▓▓▓. Then select **Processing Programs.**

❖ From the **Accounts Payable Processing Menu**, select **Enter Invoices.**

❖ Make sure your printer is ready and press ▓▓▓.

Accounts Payable then displays the following screen with the cursor positioned at the *ACCEPT (Y/N):Y* prompt.

```
=================================================================================
APPROC1                              Enter Invoices                    Company ID: WD
12/09/92                      W. D. PEACHTREE  & COMPANY                Generation #: 12
=================================================================================


Beginning Balances (Y/N):  N

Auto Invoices (Y/N):  N

Beginning Month/Day/Year For Auto Invoices:  12/09/92


Default Invoice Date:  12/09/92



Accept (Y/N):  Y
                                F10  - Menu        Shft F10 - Home
```

❖ Type **N** and press ▓▓▓ and the cursor moves to the *BEGINNING BALANCES (Y/N)* prompt.

❖ Accept the default, **N**, and press ▓▓▓ and the cursor moves to the **Auto Invoice (Y/N):** field.

This field determines whether or not you want to include automatic invoices in this process. If you answer Y Accounts Payable moves to the next field, Beginning Month/Day/Year For Auto Invoices:. The date entered here also determines which invoices Accounts Payable will pull from the Automatic Invoice file. If you enter N, Accounts Payable skips the Beginning Month/Day/Year For Auto Invoices: prompt and positions the cursor at the Default Invoice Date field. Default dates for both fields will be the system date.

❖ Type **Y** at the **Auto Invoice (Y/N):** field.

❖ Enter **121592** at the **Beginning Month/Day/Year** For Auto Invoices: prompt.

This makes the Auto Invoice entered in Lesson 2 available for transaction processing.

❖ Enter **121592** at the **Default Invoice Date:** field and press ⌨. Press ⌨ and accept this screen. Accounts Payable now displays the next screen.

❖ Type **ELE004** at the **Vendor ID** prompt. (Note: Be careful to type this exactly as it appears, including capitalizations.)

Accounts Payable displays: *NOT ON FILE - ADD (Y/N):Y*

❖ Accept the **Y** default and press ⌨.

Accounts Payable displays prompts for entry of vendor information. The cursor will be positioned at the Vendor Name prompt.

❖ Enter **MAYS STEREO DISTRIBUTORS**

❖ Enter the following address:

8837 Ellis Parkway
Suite 453
Atlanta, GA
30333

❖ Enter **404-651-4462** as the telephone number.

❖ **K. G. Mays** is your **Contact**.

❖ **13500** is the **G/L Account Number**.

❖ Press ⌨ and then accept the screen. Now you are ready to enter the invoice.

❖ At the **Invoice Number** field, enter **55487**.

❖ Accept the default **Invoice Date** by pressing ⌨.

❖ Enter an **Amount Due** of **663.32**.

❖ Accept the default **Due Date.**

❖ Enter a **Discount %** of **2.5**.

Accounts Payable calculates and displays the **Discount Amount**.

❖ Accept the **Discount Amount**.

   Accounts Payable displays the **Discount Date**.

❖ Accept the default date of 12/25/92.

❖ Type **1** at the **Accounts Payable Account Code** field.

❖ When prompted for Comment, press [ENTER].

❖ Accept the default **N** at the *PRE-PAID (Y/N):* prompt.

   Sometimes a company will prepare a check manually. If there are invoices that have been paid by a manually written check, you would enter **Y** here. Accounts Payable would then prompt for a Cash Account and Check Number. This check number would appear on the Monthly Check Register marked as "PREPAID".

❖ Accept the default **Distribution Account** and **Distribution Amount** displays. Press [F10] and then accept your entries.

❖ Accept the default **N** , for the *DISTRIBUTE TO JOB COST (Y/N):*

❖ Press [ESC] then [F10] to exit.

   Accounts Payable then prints the following Enter Invoices Control Report:

```
RUN DATE:  12/09/92              W.D. Peachtree & Company                PAGE 1
RUN TIME:     3:29 PM                 Accounts Payable
                                   Enter Invoices Control Report

----------------------------------------------------------------------------------------
VENDOR  VENDOR NAME/   INVOICE     DUE        DISCOUNT       DISTRIBUTION    PRE-  ACCOUNT
ID      INVOICE NO.    DATE     AMOUNT/DATE  AMOUNT/DATE   ACCOUNT AMOUNT   PAID  C/AP   COMMENT
----------------------------------------------------------------------------------------
ELE004 MAYS STEREO DISTRIBUTORS
        55487          12/15/92    663.32       16.58        13500   663.32    N    0/1
                                  01/14/93     12/25/92

AUTFNC THIRD NATIONAL BANK OF GA
   11 Auto Inv. - 12/15/92  12/15/92  357.45     0.00        15700   357.45    N    0/1  1762-87-73654
                                  12/15/92     01/01/00                                     MINI-VAN

        TOTAL INVOICES ADDED:  2   1,020.77     16.58

**** End of Enter Invoices Control Report ***
```

The **Accounts Payable Processing Menu** returns. Check your control report and verify your entries.

Lesson 3 Summary:

You have just learned how to enter an invoice while also adding a vendor. In addition, you learned how to process Automatic Invoices for transaction entry. All Automatic Invoices are processed in this manner.

Lesson 4: Entering A Credit

In this lesson you will enter a Specific Credit. Accounts Payable gives you the option of entering both Open and Specific Credits. An Open Credit is a credit that is applied to the vendor's account, and not to any one particular invoice. A Specific Credit is a credit taken against a specific invoice already entered into the Accounts Payable system.

In Lesson 3, W. D. Peachtree & Company purchased six compact disc players. One of these CD players arrived damaged. Mays Stereo Distributors issued a Credit Memo on December 16 for the damaged piece of equipment in the amount of $110.55.

From the **Accounts Payable Processing Menu**, select **Enter Credits.**

❖ Accept the default at the *BEGINNING BALANCES (Y/N): N* field.

❖ Enter a **Credit Date** of **121692.**

❖ From the Select Credit option box, select **S - Enter Specific Credits.**

❖ Type **ELE004** (Vendor ID for Mays) at the **Vendor ID** prompt.

❖ Use the [F2] key and select invoice **55487** (the original invoice number) from within the **Select Invoice** option box. Accounts Payable then displays the invoice detail. Accept the **Y** default at the *CORRECT INVOICE (Y/N):* prompt.

❖ Enter a **Credit Amount** of **110.55**.

❖ Type **55487-CR** as the **Ref. Code**.

This code uniquely identifies the specific credit. It generally is the Credit Memo number issued by the vendor and it is a required field of entry. Accounts Payable automatically distributes the credit amount to the General Ledger Account number selected when the original invoice was entered in the Enter Invoices program.

❖ Accept the default **Credit Amount** by pressing [ENTER].

❖ Press [F10] and accept the screen.

Accounts Payable prints the following Enter Specific Credits Control Report:

```
RUN DATE: 12/09/92                W.D. Peachtree & Company                    PAGE 1
RUN TIME:    6:26 PM                  Accounts Payable
                                Enter Specific Credits Control Report
--------------------------------------------------------------------------------------------
VENDOR    VENDOR NAME/     CREDIT      CREDIT     DISTRIBUTION
  ID      INVOICE NO.       DATE       AMOUNT       ACCOUNT       AMOUNT        REFERENCE
--------   ---------------   --------   ----------   ------------   ------------   ---------------
ELE004    MAYS STEREO DISTRIBUTORS
            55487          12/16/92     110.55       13500        110.55       55487-CR

        TOTAL CREDITS ADDED:  1         110.55

**** End of Enter Specific Credits Control Report ***
```

❖ Press [ESC] three times and then [↵]. The **Accounts Payable Processing Menu** returns. Examine your Control Report.

Lesson 4 Summary:

In this lesson you learned how to enter a credit taken against a specific invoice. Generally, if the credit memo does not reference a specific invoice, it is safe to assume that it should instead be entered as an open credit.

Topic 2: The Check Printing Cycle

In this section you learn the procedures necessary to complete the check printing cycle. The amount of activity that a company has in Accounts Payable determines the number of times in an accounting period that Accounts Payable checks need to be printed.

The check printing cycle can be completed as often as necessary within an accounting period. Some businesses may print Accounts Payable checks only once per month. Others may print Accounts Payable checks several times during a month. No matter how many times Accounts Payable checks are printed, the following programs should be used. The programs are merely described below. The lessons later in this section will show you how to use these programs.

1. Open Invoice Report

This report gives a complete listing for all Open Invoices by all or a range of General Ledger accounts in Vendor ID order. It is a good idea to run this report at the beginning of the check print cycle. Another helpful report to run would be the Cash Requirements Report. It is very similar to the Open Invoice Report with the exception that it lists all open invoices in due date order with a running total of the cash required to pay these open invoices.

2. Select Invoices for Payment

This program is used to choose those invoices that a company wishes to pay. Specific invoices can be selected or all invoices due by a certain date can be paid. Also, any invoices previously selected can be "unselected" before actually printing checks.

3. Print Pre-Check Register

This check register gives a list of all of the invoices selected for payment and a total amount of those invoices before the Accounts Payable checks are actually printed.

4. Print Accounts Payable Checks

This is the actual program used to print Accounts Payable checks. Checks may be reprinted as often as necessary, before the Update Accounts Payable Checks program is run.

5. Print Check Register

This check register is a detailed listing of all the checks that were actually printed.

6. Update Accounts Payable Checks

This is the last step in the check print cycle. This program must be run in order to update the vendor master and the transaction files with the check print transactions.

Lesson 1: Preparation for Printing Checks

In this lesson you will run through all the programs used in preparation of printing your Accounts Payable checks.

Open Invoice Report

❖ From the **Accounts Payable Report Menu**, select **Open Invoice Report**.

The first screen appears. Make sure your printer is on-line and the paper is set to the top of form. Press ▨.

❖ Accounts Payable displays the **Run Date** prompt. Press ▨ to accept the default date.

❖ At the **Select By A/P Account (Y/N):N** prompt, accept the N default and press ▨. This prompt gives the option of printing this report by specific Accounts Payable accounts or all of them.

❖ From the **Select Vendors** option box choose **All Vendors**.

All the invoices that W. D. Peachtree owes will be printed. (Total net invoices should be $93,514.63).

When it is finished, Accounts Payable returns to the **Accounts Payable Reports Menu**. Examine the report. Notice the invoices entered in Topic 1 of this tutorial. This report would be useful in a business to determine which invoices need to be paid immediately, or, if certain invoices should be paid to take advantage of discounts.

Select Invoices For Payment

❖ Press ▨ to return to the Accounts Payable Main Menu. Then select **Processing Programs**.

❖ From the Accounts Payable Processing Menu , choose **Select Invoices for Payment**. Accounts Payable displays the following screen:

```
========================================================================
APPROC2                      Select Invoices for Payment          Company ID:  WD
12/09/92                     W. D. PEACHTREE  & COMPANY            Generation #: 12
========================================================================


Cash Account Code: 1   11000

Auto Select (Y/N):  N

Beginning Discount Date:  12/09/92

Ending Discount Date:  12/16/92

Due Date:  12/09/92



Accept (Y/N):  Y
                                  F10  - Menu       Shft F10 - Home
```

Notice the cursor is positioned at the *ACCEPT (Y/N):Y* prompt. Change the default to N and press ▨▨. Now the cursor is at the *CASH ACCOUNT CODE* prompt, with a default account code of **1**. Press ▨▨. At the *AUTO SELECT (Y/N):N* prompt, change the default to **Y** and press ▨▨.

This means that the program will automatically select the invoices due for payment based on their discount and due dates.

❖ **Beginning Discount Date**: Enter **120192**.

This date is usually the current date.

❖ **Ending Discount Date**: Enter **123192**.

This date can be a date in the future. Accounts Payable automatically adds seven days to the Beginning Discount Date and displays that date. So, all invoices with discounts available within this time period are available for payment.

❖ **Due Date**: Enter **123192**.

This date is for invoices that you wish to pay without discounts.

❖ Press ▨▨ and Accounts Payable returns to the *ACCEPT (Y/N):Y* prompt. Accept the default.

Accounts Payable briefly displays the vendor ID and invoice numbers while it processes them for payment. An option appears for you to choose all or specific vendors.

❖ Select **A** for all vendors.

Each vendor will appear (the first one is Advent Distributor), followed by each invoice for that vendor. Another option box is displayed to let you **skip the vendor, mark all invoices to be paid, no invoices to be paid, individually choose the invoices,** or **manual payment.** This gives the opportunity to change any invoices that Accounts Payable automatically selected.

❖ Skip a few vendors and notice which invoices are marked for payment. After you are finished, press ▨▨, then ▨▨.

Print Pre-Check Register

❖ Select **Print Pre-Check Register** from the **Accounts Payable Processing Menu**. Make sure that your printer is ready and press ▨▨.

❖ At the **Run Date** prompt, accept today's default date and press ▨▨.

The Pre-Check Register report prints. When the report is finished, Accounts Payable returns to the **Accounts Payable Processing Menu**. Examine the report. All of the invoices available for payment that were marked in the **Select Invoices for Payment** program should appear on this register.

Now you are ready to print checks.

Print A/P Checks

❖ Select **Print A/P Checks** from the **Accounts Payable Processing Menu**.

For this exercise you will print checks on computer paper instead of check forms.

❖ Make sure your printer is ready and paper is positioned properly. Press [ENTER].

❖ At the **Check Printed Date:** prompt enter **123192**.

❖ Enter a **Starting Check Number: 100.**

❖ Accept the **Y** default at the **Print Check Mask** field. A "mask" (i.e., # facsimile) of your check is printed. This helps you see if your checks are aligned properly on the printer to avoid wasting them. (Check number 100 will be a void check used for the mask.) After the mask is printed, and checks are aligned properly, type **N** [ENTER], and the actual checks begin to print. Accounts Payable displays the Vendor ID and the invoice number as it prints the check. (The last check number printed will be No. 127, another void check.) When the checks have finished printing, a prompt appears:

PRINT CONTROL REPORT ON BLANK PAPER? (Y/N):

❖ Accept the N default. A control report will print showing the number of checks written (28) and the total amount ($86,428.09). Accounts Payable returns to the **Account Payable Processing Menu**.

Print Check Register

❖ From the **Accounts Payable Processing Menu** select **Print Check Register**.

Make sure your printer is ready and press [ENTER]. A detailed listing of your checks is printed, and A/P returns to the **Accounts Payable Processing Menu**.

Examine the Check Register closely. Make sure to match the following items to the numbers printed on the **Print A/P Checks** control report: total number of checks, total dollar amount of checks, and actual check numbers.

Update Accounts Payable Checks

❖ Select **Update A/P Checks** from the **Accounts Payable Processing Menu**.

A prompt appears as follows: *UPDATE CHECKS NOW (Y/N)?* **N.** Change the default to Y and press [ENTER].

A message is displayed on the screen while Accounts Payable processes the check transactions:

UPDATING CHECKS..., PLEASE WAIT.

When it is done, all check transactions have been updated to the Vendor master and Transaction files.

You have just completed the Check Printing Cycle. It may seem like a lot of detail work now, but once you are comfortable with it, you will understand why all the programs must be run in this specific order.

Topic 3: Some Special Activities

This section will cover activities that are performed at the end of the month (or other accounting period), as well as some other activities that are not generally a part of a daily routine.

Lesson 1 - Creating G/L Journal Entries

This program must be run in order to prepare the Accounts Payable transactions for transfer to the General Ledger module. It provides a list of all transfer information; consolidates all transactions that currently exist in the transaction file; and finally, creates the journal entries that will later be transferred into General Ledger.

This program must be run before **Close Current Period.** If there is a lot of activity in **Accounts Payable,** this program should be run on a regular basis throughout the accounting period, instead of once a month.

❖ From the **Accounts Payable Processing Menu** , select **Create G/L Journal Entries**.

❖ Make sure printer is ready. Press 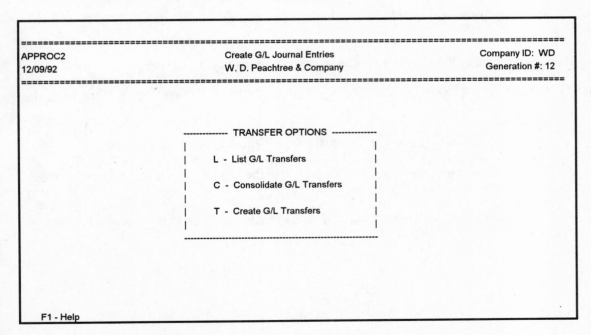.

❖ Accept the default **Run Date**.

A TRANSFER OPTION box will appear with three options:

```
=================================================================================
APPROC2                          Create G/L Journal Entries          Company ID:  WD
12/09/92                          W. D. Peachtree & Company           Generation #: 12
=================================================================================




                        -------------- TRANSFER OPTIONS --------------
                        |                                            |
                        |    L - List G/L Transfers                  |
                        |                                            |
                        |    C - Consolidate G/L Transfers           |
                        |                                            |
                        |    T - Create G/L Transfers                |
                        |                                            |
                        ----------------------------------------------




 F1 - Help
```

You will select all three options in the order that they are displayed.

❖ Select **L - List G/L Transfers**

A message will be displayed: *REPORT PRINTING...* while the list of Accounts Payable transactions are being printed. After printing, Accounts Payable returns to the TRANSFER OPTION box.

This report is an actual listing of the account debit and credit information that will be transferred to General Ledger.

❖ Select **C - Consolidate G/L Transfers**

(This consolidates all transfers to G/L. Sometimes a business will want a detail transfer and may skip this option. But you should use it here.)

Accounts Payable displays a "processing" message while processing transactions.

❖ Select **T - Create G/L Transfers**

This step creates the A/P summary journal for later transfer into G/L.

Lesson 2 - Printing the Transaction Register

The Transaction Register will provide a detailed listing of all the transactions that have occurred in the current period. This report should be used as an audit trail and reconciled with the **List G/L Transfers** Control Report.

❖ Return to the **Accounts Payable Main Menu** by pressing ▭. Then select **Report Programs**.

❖ From the **Accounts Payable Reports Menu**, select **Transaction Register**.

❖ At the *SET PAPER TO TOP OF FORM - PRESS 'ENTER' TO CONTINUE* prompt, press the ▭ *-Chg Device* key.

❖ When the **Select Device** option box appears, choose **Send Report to the Screen**.

Just for illustration here, this report will be printed to the screen. In a business, you would most likely send this report to a printer.

A message will appear at the bottom of the screen to let you know that the report will be sent to the screen.

❖ Press ⌨ to continue with the report.

❖ Accept the default **Run Date**.

❖ Accounts Payable displays the **Select Generations** option box. Choose **C - Current Generations**.

❖ From within the **Select Vendors** option box, choose **A - All Vendors**

❖ At the **List Job Cost Transactions** prompt, accept the N default.

Accounts Payable displays the report to your screen. Examine the report. Use your "Page Up", "Page Down", and ⌨⌨ to move around on the screen.

Press ⌨ three times and then ⌨ when you are finished viewing the report. Accounts Payable returns to the **Accounts Payable Reports Menu.**

Lesson 3 - Close Current Period

W. D. Peachtree & Company is now ready to close the fiscal as well as the calendar year.

❖ Press ⌨ to return to the **Accounts Payable Main Menu**. Then select **Processing Programs**.

❖ From the **Account Payable Processing Menu** , select **Close Current Period**.

Accounts Payable displays:

IS THIS THE END OF THE CALENDAR YEAR (Y/N)?

❖ Type **Y** ⌨ Accounts Payable then displays:

IS THIS THE END OF THE FISCAL YEAR (Y/N)?

❖ Change the default to **Y** ⌨.

Accounts Payable displays the Vendor Name and ID, as well as the invoice number while it's processing.

Chapter 5

End of Chapter Problem

```
WARNING

BEFORE CONTINUING, BE SURE THAT ALL DATA FILES HAVE BEEN RESTORED TO
THEIR ORIGINAL CONDITION.  IF YOU ARE UNSURE OF HOW TO RESTORE THESE
FILES, TURN TO THE INSTRUCTIONS FOUND ON PAGE 1-32 IN  CHAPTER 1.
```

NOTE: You may find it helpful to record the problem data on input forms before using
Accounts Payable. Master Input Forms are included in the last section of this
chapter. In some cases, you will need to make multiple copies of a form before you
begin. On the other hand, you may not need all of the input forms provided.

Problem Set Up

Before beginning this problem set, you will need to add the following vendors to the A/P File:

1:

Vendor ID	: GZE
Vendor Name	: GZE TELEPHONE CO.
Address	: Annex 68
Address	: Atlanta, GA
Address	:
Postal Code	: 30372
Telephone	: 404-652-9828
Contact	: Bill Stewart
G/L Account	: 655
Temporary Vendor	: N
1099 Employee (Vendor)	: N
Federal ID Number	: 58-0907158

2:

Vendor ID	: ATLHTG
Vendor Name	: ATLANTA HEATING CO.
Address	: Annex 72
Address	: Atlanta, GA
Address	:
Postal Code	: 30322
Telephone	: 404-872-9000

Contact	:	Chris Burroughs
G/L Account	:	670
Temporary Vendor	:	N
1099 Employee (Vendor)	:	N
Federal ID Number	:	52-0823168

3:

Vendor ID	:	POST
Vendor Name	:	US POSTAL SERVICE
Address	:	2968 Peach Street
Address	:	Atlanta, GA
Address	:	
Postal Code	:	69824
Telephone	:	404-870-8822
Contact	:	Bill Perry
G/L Account	:	620
Temporary Vendor	:	N
1099 Employee (Vendor)	:	N
Federal ID Number	:	99-9999999

4:

Vendor ID	:	TIMES
Vendor Name	:	ATLANTA TIMES
Address	:	P.O. Box 7200
Address	:	2313 Peach Street
Address	:	Atlanta, GA
Postal Code	:	32982-7200
Telephone	:	404-622-2100
Contact	:	Lynn Reagin
G/L Account	:	560
Temporary Vendor	:	N

1099 Employee (Vendor)   : N

Federal ID Number   : 52-8209246

5:

Vendor ID   : GANT

Vendor Name   : GANT ADVERTISING CO.

Address   : P.O. Box 720-A

Address   : 926 Clark Street

Address   : Roswell, GA

Postal Code   : 30262-720A

Telephone   : 404-892-6243

Contact   : Cathy Hendrix

G/L Account   : 520

Temporary Vendor   : N

1099 Employee (Vendor)   : N

Federal ID Number   : 68-5208245

6:

Vendor ID   : TILES

Vendor Name   : TILES OFFICE SUPPLY CO.

Address   : P.O.Box 6900

Address   : 324 Auburn Street

Address   : Atlanta, GA

Postal Code   : 30304-6900

Telephone   : 404-325-9243

Contact   : James Luger

G/L Account   : 615

Temporary Vendor   : N

1099 Employee (Vendor)   : N

Federal ID Number   : 82-8293690

Problem Data

a. 12/01/92   W. D. Peachtree received the following invoices. You should enter each invoice using the Enter Invoices program found in the Accounts Payable Processing Menu. Accept all defaults at the initial screen.

1:

Vendor ID	: GZE
Invoice Number	: 72-983-68
Invoice Date	: 11-30-92
Amount Due	: 236.89
Due Date	: 12-15-92
Discount %	: 0.00
Discount Amount	: 0.00
Discount Date	:
A/P Account Code	: 1
Comment	: Monthly Phone Bill
Prepaid	: N

Distribution:

Account	: 65500
Amount	: 236.89

2:

Vendor ID	: MAYTAB
Invoice Number	: 69-72A36
Invoice Date	: 11-28-92
Amount Due	: 4,564.92
Due Date	: 12-28-92
Discount %	: 2.50

Discount Amount	:	114.12
Discount Date	:	12-15-92
A/P Account Code	:	1
Comment	:	
Prepaid	:	N
Distribution:		
Account	:	13500
Amount	:	4,564.92

3:

Vendor ID	:	CANNON
Invoice Number	:	A1763-98
Invoice Date	:	11-25-92
Amount Due	:	7,420.82
Due Date	:	12-25-92
Discount %	:	1.00
Discount Amount	:	74.21
Discount Date	:	12-15-92
A/P Account Code	:	1
Comment	:	
Prepaid	:	N
Distribution:		
Account	:	13500
Amount	:	7,420.82

4:

Vendor ID	: ATLHTG
Invoice Number	: 727349982
Invoice Date	: 11-30-92
Amount Due	: 4,732.86
Due Date	: 12-30-92
Discount %	: 0.00
Discount Amount	: 0.00
Discount Date	:
A/P Account Code	: 1
Comment	: Monthly Utility Bill
Prepaid	: N
Distribution:	
Account	: 67000
Amount	: 4,732.86

b. 12/05/92 W. D. Peachtree & Co. received a credit from Christopher Dior Apparels (Vendor ID DIOR) in the amount of $45.34. This credit is for invoice number D91013222 (i.e. - this is a specific credit). The credit memo should be applied against Account number 13500 in the Distribution section. Do not process Beginning Balances. The Reference Code is CR-92.

c. 12/07/92 W. D. Peachtree & Co. has decided to pay its heating bill on an even-pay-per-month basis. This means that W. D. Peachtree & Co. will pay the same amount each month for its heating bill. You should set this up as an automatic invoice. Vendor ID is ATLHTG. Auto Invoice Number is 01. Status is A. W. D. Peachtree & Co.'s equal monthly payment is $215.00. The first due day is 1. No discounts are given by this vendor. The number of months is eleven. The month to begin is 1 and the frequency is monthly. The last month billed is 0 and the Accounts Payable account is 1. You should distribute this monthly payment to the utility expense account (67000).

d. 12/11/92 The following invoices were received today. For each invoice the A/P Account Code is 1, and you should distribute the total amount of each invoice to the General Ledger account as given. Note: Dates given for November and December are for the year 1992, and dates given for January are for 1993. Accept all defaults at the initial screen.

VENDOR ID	INVOICE NUMBER	INVOICE DATE	AMOUNT DUE	DUE DATE	DISCOUNT % OR AMT	DISCOUNT DATE
STEWRT	4567-2	11-25	$4,345.89	12-25	2%	12-15
WILSON	789-90	11-26	3,356.90	12-26	2.5%	12-15
GANT	4783	11-30	1,119.00	12-30	0	N/A
BLASS	23-899	11-30	987.20	12-15	0	N/A
DIOR	34-98AC	11-30	2,765.97	12-30	$2.75	12-20
ELE001	567834	12-05	8,001.56	1-05	1%	12-15
ELE006	78654	12-06	5,456.43	1-06	$5.23	12-21
HOLLYS	998	12-10	312.90	12-20	0	N/A
TIMES	PAPER	12-11	112.86	12-15	0	N/A

e. 12/15/92   W. D. Peachtree & Co. pays most invoices on the 15th of each month. Rather than allowing the computer to select the invoices for you, you should select invoices for payment by vendor. You should only select the following vendors for payment:

ATLHTG
BLASS
ELE001
STEWRT
TIMES, and
WILSON.

After you select each vendor then the computer asks for you to "Select Action." Select the option to "Mark All to Pay" for each vendor listed above. Accept the starting check number and allow a mask of the check. After you have selected the proper vendors, the Cash Requirement should equal $30,573.03. If yours does not, then compare your Pre-check Register with the one contained with this practice set. When the Cash Requirement agrees with the above figure, you should follow the steps as outlined in this chapter (Topic 2). <u>Caution</u>: Follow each step in the order given in the check printing cycle after "Select Invoices for Payment."

f. 12/20/92   W. D. Peachtree & Co. received notice of a vendor address change. Jackson Electronic's new address is P.O. Box 76, Pittsburgh, Pennsylvania 58393. Also, the new contact person is Glenn Cambridge. You should make these changes in Jackson Electronics' file (ELE873).

g. 12/27/92   W. D. Peachtree & Co. has purchased a new set of display racks from a new vendor. In order to even out cashflow, management decided to pay for these display racks over a nine month period beginning in January 1993. The <u>monthly</u> payment is $234.24. The new vendor is DISPLAY RACKS, INC., P. O. Box 1289, Atlanta, Ga. 30677. (Make the Vendor ID - RACK and the Federal ID-99-9999999). Their telephone number is 404-366-9900. The G/L Account for this vendor is Furniture and Fixtures (Hint: Press [F2] to locate G/L Account Number). Remember the A/P Accounts is always 1 for these exercises. Also, for the Automatic Invoice information the Due Day is 10 and No Discounts are given. Status will be "A." (Hint: remember this is auto invoice number 2.)

h. 12/29/92   The following invoices should be entered. Remember that the dates given for January are in 1993. Accept all defaults at the initial screen.

VENDOR ID	INVOICE NUMBER	INVOICE DATE	AMOUNT DUE	DUE DATE	DISCOUNT % OR AMT	DISCOUNT DATE
BRATCH	6753	12-15	$3,012.00	1-15	4%	1-05
CURTIS	43-PIA	12-20	2,546.54	1-10	2.54%	1-05
SPEAR	30-198	12-27	345.98	1-27	0	N/A
TILES	788	12-29	32.00	1-29	1%	1-10

i. 12/30/92   You should run the end of the period reports. These include:

1) Create G/L Journal Entries. Remember to select all three options.

2) Transaction Register - Current Generation Only, All Vendors.

3) Close the Current Period.

Note: If you receive warnings about deleting files at this point, you may ignore them by answering "Y" to continue.

Answer "Y" to both prompts regarding the end of the year.

ACCOUNTS PAYABLE

MASTER INPUT FORMS

Maintain Accounts Payable Options
Setup Form

Controller Password   __ __ __ __ __ __ __ __

Operator Password   __ __ __ __ __ __ __

Use Menus   Y   N   (Circle one)

Allow Changes/Deletions   Y   N

Force Control Reports   Y   N

Keep Historical Detail   Y   N

Current A/P Generation #   __ __

Current G/L Period   __ __

Report to G/L   Y   N

Post to Job Cost   Y   N

Transfer Vendor Name to G/L   Y   N

Use Expanded Vendor Lookup   Y   N

G/L Discount Account   __ __ __ __ __

Payer Federal ID Number   __ __ __ __ __ __ __ __ __ __

Use Pre-Printed Check Stub   Y   N

Print Company Name on Check   Y   N

Print Comment on Check Stub   Y   N

Code	Accounts Payable Account Number	Cash Account Number
1	__ __ __ __ __ __	__ __ __ __ __ __
2	__ __ __ __ __ __	__ __ __ __ __ __
3	__ __ __ __ __ __	__ __ __ __ __ __
4	__ __ __ __ __ __	__ __ __ __ __ __
5	__ __ __ __ __ __	__ __ __ __ __ __
6	__ __ __ __ __ __	__ __ __ __ __ __
7	__ __ __ __ __ __	__ __ __ __ __ __
8	__ __ __ __ __ __	__ __ __ __ __ __
9	__ __ __ __ __ __	__ __ __ __ __ __

Maintain Vendors Setup Form

Vendor ID ___ ___ ___ ___ ___ ___

Vendor Name ___ ___ ___ ___ ___ ___ ___ ___ ___ ___ ___ ___ ___ ___

___ ___ ___ ___ ___ ___ ___ ___ ___ ___ ___ ___ ___

Address ___ ___ ___ ___ ___ ___ ___ ___ ___ ___ ___ ___ ___ ___

___ ___ ___ ___ ___ ___ ___ ___ ___ ___ ___ ___ ___

Address ___ ___ ___ ___ ___ ___ ___ ___ ___ ___ ___ ___ ___ ___

___ ___ ___ ___ ___ ___ ___ ___ ___ ___ ___ ___ ___

Address ___ ___ ___ ___ ___ ___ ___ ___ ___ ___ ___ ___ ___ ___

___ ___ ___ ___ ___ ___ ___ ___ ___ ___ ___ ___ ___

Postal Code ___ ___ ___ ___ ___ ___ ___ ___ ___

Telephone ___ ___ ___ ___ ___ ___ ___ ___ ___ ___ ___ ___ ___ ___

Contact ___ ___ ___ ___ ___ ___ ___ ___ ___ ___ ___ ___ ___ ___

___ ___ ___ ___ ___ ___ ___ ___ ___ ___ ___

G/L Account Number ___ ___ ___ ___ ___ ___

Temporary Vendor Y N (Circle one)

1099 Vendor Y N

1099 Type A B D G I M O P R

1099 Misc Box 1 2 3 5 6 7 8

Federal ID Number ___ ___ ___ ___ ___ ___ ___ ___ ___ ___ ___

YTD Purchases

    Calendar ___ ___ ___,___ ___ ___,___ ___ ___.___ ___

    Fiscal ___ ___ ___,___ ___ ___,___ ___ ___.___ ___

YTD Payments

    Calendar ___ ___ ___,___ ___ ___,___ ___ ___.___ ___

    Fiscal ___ ___ ___,___ ___ ___,___ ___ ___.___ ___

Change Vendor Remit
To Address Line 1: __ __ __ __ __ __ __ __ __ __ __ __ __

__ __ __ __ __ __ __ __ __

Line 2: __ __ __ __ __ __ __ __ __ __ __ __ __

__ __ __ __ __ __ __ __ __

Line 3: __ __ __ __ __ __ __ __ __ __ __ __ __

__ __ __ __ __ __ __ __ __

Postal Code: __ __ __ __ __ __ __ __

Maintain Auto Invoices Setup Form

Vendor ID   __ __ __ __ __ __

Auto Invoice Number   __ __

Status   A   I   (Circle one)

Amount Due   __,__ __ __,__ __ __.__ __

Due Day   __ __

Discount Day   __ __

Discount Percent   __ __.__ __

Number of Months   __ __ __

Month to Begin   __ __

Frequency   __

Last Month Billed   __ __

# of Times Billed   __ __

A/P Account   __

Comment   __ __ __ __ __ __ __ __ __ __ __ __ __ __ __ __

                      __ __ __ __ __ __ __ __ __ __ __ __ __ __

Distribution

	Account	Amount
1.	__ __ __ __ __ __ __	__,__ __ __,__ __ __.__ __
2.	__ __ __ __ __ __ __	__,__ __ __,__ __ __.__ __
3.	__ __ __ __ __ __ __	__,__ __ __,__ __ __.__ __
4.	__ __ __ __ __ __ __	__,__ __ __,__ __ __.__ __
5.	__ __ __ __ __ __ __	__,__ __ __,__ __ __.__ __
6.	__ __ __ __ __ __ __	__,__ __ __,__ __ __.__ __
7.	__ __ __ __ __ __ __	__,__ __ __,__ __ __.__ __
8.	__ __ __ __ __ __ __	__,__ __ __,__ __ __.__ __

Enter Invoices Setup Form

Beginning Balances   Y N   (Circle one)

Auto Invoices   Y N

Beginning Month//Day/Year for Auto Invoices   __ __/ __ __/ __ __

Default Invoice Date   __ __/ __ __/ __ __

Vendor ID   __ __ __ __ __ __

Invoice Number   __ __ __ __ __ __ __ __ __ __ __ __

                                        __ __ __ __ __ __ __ __ __ __ __ __

Invoice Date   __ __/ __ __/ __ __

Amount Due   __,__ __ __,__ __ __.__ __

Due Date   __ __/ __ __/ __ __

Discount %   __ __.__ __

Discount Amount   __,__ __ __,__ __ __.__ __

Discount Date   __ __/ __ __/ __ __

A/P Account Code   __

Comment   __ __ __ __ __ __ __ __ __ __ __

                                        __ __ __ __ __ __ __ __ __ __

Pre-Paid   Y N   (Circle one)

Cash Account Code   __

Check Number   __ __ __ __ __ __ __

Distribution

	Account	Amount
1.	___ ___ ___ ___ ___	___,___ ___,___ ___ ___.___ ___
2.	___ ___ ___ ___ ___	___,___ ___,___ ___ ___.___ ___
3.	___ ___ ___ ___ ___	___,___ ___,___ ___ ___.___ ___
4.	___ ___ ___ ___ ___	___,___ ___,___ ___ ___.___ ___
5.	___ ___ ___ ___ ___	___,___ ___,___ ___ ___.___ ___
6.	___ ___ ___ ___ ___	___,___ ___,___ ___ ___.___ ___
7.	___ ___ ___ ___ ___	___,___ ___,___ ___ ___.___ ___
8.	___ ___ ___ ___ ___	___,___ ___,___ ___ ___.___ ___

Distribute to Job Cost

Amount to Distribute to Job Cost: ___,___ ___ ___,___ ___ ___.___ ___

Job Number	Phase Code	Cost Code	Amount
___ ___ ___ ___ ___ ___	___ ___	___ ___ ___ ___ ___	___,___ ___,___ ___ ___.___ ___
___ ___ ___ ___ ___ ___	___ ___	___ ___ ___ ___ ___	___,___ ___,___ ___ ___.___ ___
___ ___ ___ ___ ___ ___	___ ___	___ ___ ___ ___ ___	___,___ ___,___ ___ ___.___ ___
___ ___ ___ ___ ___ ___	___ ___	___ ___ ___ ___ ___	___,___ ___,___ ___ ___.___ ___
___ ___ ___ ___ ___ ___	___ ___	___ ___ ___ ___ ___	___,___ ___,___ ___ ___.___ ___

Enter Credits Setup Form

Beginning Balances (Y/N)? Y N (Circle one)

Credit Date ___ ___ / ___ ___ / ___ ___

Select one of the following:

Enter Open Credits

Enter Specific Credits

Open Credits

Vendor ID ___ ___ ___ ___ ___ ___

Invoice Number ___ ___ ___ ___ ___ ___ ___ ___

___ ___ ___ ___ ___ ___ ___ ___

___ ___ ___ ___ ___

Credit Date ___ ___ / ___ ___ / ___ ___

Credit Amount ___ ___ ___ ___ ___ ___ . ___ ___

A/P Account Code ___

Comment ___ ___ ___ ___ ___ ___ ___ ___

___ ___ ___ ___ ___ ___ ___ ___

___ ___ ___ ___ ___ ___

Distribution

	Account	Amount
1.	___ ___ ___ ___ ___ ___	___ , ___ ___ ___ , ___ ___ ___ . ___ ___
2.	___ ___ ___ ___ ___ ___	___ , ___ ___ ___ , ___ ___ ___ . ___ ___
3.	___ ___ ___ ___ ___ ___	___ , ___ ___ ___ , ___ ___ ___ . ___ ___
4.	___ ___ ___ ___ ___ ___	___ , ___ ___ ___ , ___ ___ ___ . ___ ___
5.	___ ___ ___ ___ ___ ___	___ , ___ ___ ___ , ___ ___ ___ . ___ ___
6.	___ ___ ___ ___ ___ ___	___ , ___ ___ ___ , ___ ___ ___ . ___ ___
7.	___ ___ ___ ___ ___ ___	___ , ___ ___ ___ , ___ ___ ___ . ___ ___
8.	___ ___ ___ ___ ___ ___	___ , ___ ___ ___ , ___ ___ ___ . ___ ___

Specific Credits

Vendor ID   __ __ __ __ __ __

Invoice Number   __ __ __ __ __ __ __ __ __ __ __ __

                               __ __ __ __ __ __ __ __ __

Credit Amount   __,__ __ __,__ __ __.__ __

Reference Code   __ __ __ __ __ __ __ __

Note: Other fields do appear on this screen, but they can't be changed.

----------------------------Distribution--Credit--------------

	Account	Amount	Amount
1.	__ __ __ __ __ __	__,__ __ __,__ __ __.__ __	__,__ __ __,__ __ __.__ __
2.	__ __ __ __ __ __	__,__ __ __,__ __ __.__ __	__,__ __ __,__ __ __.__ __
3.	__ __ __ __ __ __	__,__ __ __,__ __ __.__ __	__,__ __ __,__ __ __.__ __
4.	__ __ __ __ __ __	__,__ __ __,__ __ __.__ __	__,__ __ __,__ __ __.__ __
5.	__ __ __ __ __ __	__,__ __ __,__ __ __.__ __	__,__ __ __,__ __ __.__ __
6.	__ __ __ __ __ __	__,__ __ __,__ __ __.__ __	__,__ __ __,__ __ __.__ __
7.	__ __ __ __ __ __	__,__ __ __,__ __ __.__ __	__,__ __ __,__ __ __.__ __
8.	__ __ __ __ __ __	__,__ __ __,__ __ __.__ __	__,__ __ __,__ __ __.__ __

Chapter 6

ACCOUNTS RECEIVABLE AND INVOICING OVERVIEW

Learning Objectives:

After studying this chapter you should be able to:

1. Describe the functions performed by Accounts Receivable and Invoicing.

2. Perform everyday activities including—entering, printing, and posting invoices; entering transactions; and applying payments.

3. Perform statement and sales tasks including—reconciling open credits, ageing accounts receivable, applying service charges, printing customers' statements, and summarizing amounts owed to each tax authority.

4. Perform end of the period activities including—printing a transaction register report, closing the current period, and printing reports about customers and their accounts.

5. Identify some of the reports printed by Accounts Receivable and Invoicing.

Chapter 6

Accounts Receivable And Invoicing Overview

Accounts Receivable are the amounts that a company's customers owe it as a result of sales of services or goods to those customers. These accounts receivable are assets that appear as a current asset on the company's balance sheet. Invoices are bills a company sends its customers, listing what was purchased, when it was purchased, the amount due, and when it is due.

This chapter gives an overview of the Accounts Receivable and Invoicing modules. It describes how each module works, how they work together, and how they work with the other Peachtree Complete Accounting modules.

How Accounts Receivable Compares To A Manual Accounting System

In a manual accounting system, sales on credit are usually recorded in a special Sales Journal, and cash sales and collections on accounts receivable are recorded in a special Cash Receipts Journal along with other cash receipts transactions. Sales returns and allowances are normally recorded in the General Journal, and sales discounts are recorded in the Cash Receipts Journal. An Accounts Receivable control account is maintained in the general ledger, and a subsidiary ledger is maintained showing an account for each customer. Invoices are generally prepared manually by a clerk.

The Peachtree Complete Accounts Receivable module is used to record sales to customers; receipts from those customers; sales returns, allowances, and discounts; and sales taxes owed to each tax authority. A subsidiary Accounts Receivable Ledger is maintained, and the information needed to keep the Accounts Receivable control account current in the general ledger is automatically transferred to General Ledger if the two modules are linked. The module also produces customer statements and calculates service charges (if any).

An invoicing module can be used with Accounts Receivable to print invoices. Also, the Inventory module can be linked with Invoicing to automatically update inventory when sales and returns of inventory occur.

What Accounts Receivable and Invoicing Do

Accounts Receivable (A/R) and Invoicing track the amounts customers owe; they also track sales. Using A/R and Invoicing, you can record the daily activities of customers, prepare customer statements, send invoices, and calculate finance charges. You can also get detailed information including:

- A customer's year-to-date purchases and payments.
- A customer's current balance.
- The total amount owed to a company by all its customers.
- How much is owed to each tax authority.
- Audit trail reports.

You can use A/R and Invoicing together, or you can use A/R alone. However, you cannot use Invoicing without A/R. Invoicing operates using the information entered into A/R. This information includes customer account information, sales tax information, module options, and transaction/product code combinations. In the examples and problems in this text, Accounts Receivable will be used with Invoicing.

By itself, Accounts Receivable:

- Keeps track of the customers' daily account activities.
- Produces customer statements.
- Calculates service charges.
- Tracks the sales taxes owed by a company.
- Processes automatic customer transactions.
- Prepares receivables information for transfer to General Ledger.

When invoicing is used with A/R, then customer invoices can also be produced. There is a choice of invoice formats--product format, services format, or customized format (which is user controlled). If Inventory is used with A/R and Invoicing, inventory can be updated when sales and returns are processed. If you use A/R, Invoicing, and Job Cost, you can enter billing information into Invoicing for specific jobs and then track the information in Job Cost.

When to Use Invoicing

The Invoicing module should be used if a company sends invoices to customers. No matter how basic or how complex the invoicing needs are, using Invoicing with Accounts Receivable saves time and trouble. Together, the two modules produce invoices and record receivables transactions in just a few steps. In addition, Invoicing offers more sales tax flexibility and more discount flexibility than just Accounts Receivable alone.

When both the Inventory and Accounts Receivable modules are used, the Invoicing module should always be used also. Invoicing allows a company to invoice a customer, to record receivables transactions, and to update inventory. In addition, Invoicing tracks costs and provides a Back-Order Report listing items that could not be sold because they were out of stock.

If a company does not send invoices to customers and does not use the Inventory module, the Accounts Receivable module can be used alone. If a company is interested in tracking its receivables without tracking inventory and without sending invoices to customers, A/R can handle all its receivable needs.

Question Frame 1[6]

Indicate whether each of the following statements is true or false by writing "T" or "F" in the space provided.

_____ 1. The Accounts Receivable module performs exactly the same functions as does a Sales Journal in a manual system.

_____ 2. A Subsidiary Accounts Receivable Ledger is useful when using either the Accounts Receivable module or a manual system.

_____ 3. The Accounts Receivable module can be linked with several other modules.

_____ 4. Using Accounts Receivable and Invoicing together is a good idea if a company needs to send invoices to customers.

Now turn to Answer Frame 1[6] on Page 6-6 to check your answers.

Answer Frame 1[6]

1. False. One difference, for instance, is that collections on accounts receivable are recorded in the Accounts Receivable module but are not recorded in a Sales Journal in a manual system. Other differences exist as well.

2. True. It is always necessary to keep track of how much money each customer owes. The Subsidiary Accounts Receivable Ledger shows this information under either system.

3. True. Accounts receivable can be linked with Invoicing, Inventory, and General Ledger. It can also be linked with Job Cost, but Job Cost is beyond the scope of this text.

4. True. When used together, the two modules produce invoices and record receivables transactions in a single step. Also, Invoicing offers more sales tax flexibility and more discount flexibility than just Accounts Receivable alone.

If you missed any of the above, reread Frame 1[6] before continuing.

Frame 2[6]

Using Accounts Receivable and Invoicing

When using Accounts Receivable and Invoicing, three different kinds of activities are performed:

- maintenance
- processing
- reporting

This section gives you an overview of these types of activities.

Maintenance Activities

Maintenance activities are the tasks performed to keep Accounts Receivable and Invoicing information current and accurate. Maintenance includes entering or changing customer names, customer addresses, sales tax combinations, automatic transactions, and ship-to addresses. Invoicing uses Accounts Receivable Information, so most of the maintenance functions are done in Accounts Receivable. The programs used for maintenance are:

- Maintain Customers
- List Customer Accounts
- Maintain Ship-to Addresses
- Maintain Sales Tax Records
- List Sales Tax Records
- Maintain G/L Accounts Dist File
- Maintain Automatic Transactions

Use **Maintain Customers** to enter customer information including name, address, sales tax code, service charge code, and credit limit. You will also use this program to delete old customers, to change customer information, and to add new customers.

Use **List Customer Accounts** to print a list of the information entered into **Maintain Customers**. Print this list whenever you make a lot of changes to customer information or whenever you need a permanent reference list of customers.

Use **Maintain Ship-to Addresses** to enter or to change customers' shipping addresses. (You can also enter this information from **Maintain Customers**.)

Use **Maintain Sales Tax Records** to enter or to change the combinations of state, county, and city sales taxes used in a business. If the business operates in one location, it may have only one tax combination; if the business operates in several locations, it may have a number of different tax combinations.

Use **List Sales Tax Records** to print a list of the information entered into **Maintain Sales Tax Records**. Print this list whenever a lot of changes are made to sales tax combinations or whenever a permanent reference list of these combinations is needed.

Use **Maintain G/L Accounts Dist File** to control how A/R reports receivables information for a company's ledger. If PCA General Ledger (G/L) is used along with Accounts Receivable, then this information can be posted automatically to G/L. (**Dist** stands for distribution).

Use **Maintain Automatic Transactions** to set up transactions that Accounts Receivable can generate automatically. Once these transactions are set up, they will be generated as part of processing activities.

Processing Activities

Processing activities are the tasks performed to use Accounts Receivable and Invoicing in a business. They include:

- Daily tasks
- Statement tasks
- Sales tax tasks
- End of period tasks

Most of Accounts Receivable and Invoicing activities are processing activities.

Daily Tasks

Daily tasks are the tasks performed to enter customers' transactions and produce their invoices. The Accounts Receivable and Invoicing programs used for daily tasks are:

- **Enter Invoices**
- **Print Invoices**
- **Post Invoices**
- **Enter Transactions**
- **Apply Payments**

When you use Invoicing, use **Enter Invoices** to enter customer transactions that appear on printed invoices. (If Inventory is also used, the sales and returns entered in this program can also update inventory.) Using **Enter Invoices**, you can add new invoices, edit existing invoices, or delete existing invoices. Once you've entered your invoices, use **Print Invoices** to print them and then use **Post Invoices** to post the invoice transaction to your customers' accounts.

If you were only using Accounts Receivable, you would use **Enter Transactions** to enter most customer transactions. (You cannot print invoices for transactions entered into this program.)

Use **Apply Payments** to enter payments, credits, and other payment related transactions. Although you can enter payments into **Enter Transactions**, **Apply Payments** allows you to enter these transactions more quickly and easily.

Statement Tasks

Statement tasks are the tasks performed to produce customers' statements. The Accounts Receivable and Invoicing programs used for these tasks are:

- **Reconcile Open Credits**
- **Aged Receivables Report**
- **Apply Service Charges**
- **Customer Statements**

Use **Reconcile Open Credits** to apply a customer's credits to outstanding (unpaid) invoices.

Use **Aged Receivables Report** to age balance forward customers' accounts and to print an ageing summary.

Use **Apply Service Charges** to calculate customer's service charges. When you use Invoicing, you can also print service charge invoices using **Print Invoices**.

Use **Customer Statements** to print customers' statements.

Sales Tax Tasks

Sales tax tasks are the tasks performed to process sales taxes. You use only one program to complete this task, **Sales Tax Summary**.

Sales Tax Summary prints a list of the sales taxes collected during the period; it also summarizes the amounts owed each tax authority. It lists this information for all the cities, counties, and states for which taxes are collected.

Question Frame 2[6]

Indicate whether each of the following statements is true or false by writing "T" or "F" in the space provided.

_____ 1. Maintenance activities are the daily tasks that incorporate most of the Accounts Receivable and Invoicing activities.

_____ 2. Most maintenance functions are performed in Invoicing.

_____ 3. Daily tasks are the tasks performed to enter customers' transactions and produce their invoices.

_____ 4. More programs are used for statement tasks than for sales tax tasks.

Now turn to Answer Frame 2[6] on page 6-10 to check your answers.

Answer Frame 2[6]

1. False. The statement describes processing activities. Maintenance activities include entering or changing customer names, customer addresses, sales tax combinations, automatic transactions, and ship-to addresses. These generally are not daily tasks.

2. False. Most maintenance activities are performed in Accounts Receivable. Invoicing merely utilizes this information.

3. True. Daily tasks include enter invoices, print invoices, post invoices, enter transactions, and apply payments. These tasks include much of the effort in accounting for accounts receivable transactions.

4. True. Statement tasks include four programs, while sales tax tasks include only one program.

If you missed any of the above, reread Frame 2[6] before continuing.

Frame 3[6]

End of Period Tasks

End of period tasks are the tasks performed to close Accounts Receivable for the period. The Accounts Receivable and Invoicing programs used for these tasks are:

- **Transaction Register Report**
- **Create G/L Journal Entries**
- **Close Current Period**

Use **Transaction Register Report** to print a list of all the transactions entered during the period. The Transaction Register lists transactions entered through:

- **Enter Transactions**
- **Enter Invoices**
- **Apply Payments**
- **Apply Service Charges**

Use **Create G/L Journal Entries** to prepare receivables transactions for posting to the ledger. When PCA General Ledger is used, then this program prepares the Accounts Receivable summary journal entry for automatic posting to General Ledger.

Use **Close Current Period** to close the Accounts Receivable accounting period. This program calculates a balance forward on Balance Forward customers' accounts and then discards all current transactions.

Reporting Activities

Reporting activities are the tasks performed to get information about a company's receivables. Reporting activities include printing reports about customers and their accounts and about the invoices and transactions entered.

The Accounts Receivable and Invoicing programs used for reporting activities are:

- **Query Customer Accounts**
- **Query Inventory Items**
- **Inventory Activity Report**
- **Inventory Backorder Report**
- **Invoice Register**
- **Past Due Report**
- **Transaction Register Report**

Use **Query Customer Accounts** to review information about customers, their accounts, and their account activity. Just like "Query Vendors" in Accounts Payable, Accounts Receivable allows you to "query customers" by all transactions or transactions from a range of periods if "Keep historical detail" is set to Y in the options file. If not, you can only query current period transactions.

Use **Query Inventory Items** to review information about the items entered into PCA Inventory. You can use this program only if you use PCA Inventory.

If you use PCA Inventory, use **Inventory Activity Report** to list the changes made to inventory items by Invoicing. This report lists cost, sales, and profit information for each inventory stock item sold or returned through **Enter Invoices**. You can use this report only if you use PCA Inventory.

Use **Invoice Register** to print a list of all the invoices entered but not yet posted. The Invoice Register summarizes invoice information for unposted invoices. Once invoices are posted, they no longer appear on the Invoice Register.

Use **Inventory Backorder Report** to list the items that could not be sold in Invoicing because they were not in stock. This report can be used even if PCA Inventory is not used.

Use **Past Due Report** to list the past due status of customers' accounts. This report can be used to help the collection on past due accounts.

Use **Transaction Register Report** to list all the receivables transactions entered during the period.

Question Frame 3[6]

Indicate whether each of the following statements is true or false by writing "T" or "F" in the space provided.

_____ 1. End of period programs include one that prepares receivables transactions for posting to General Ledger.

_____ 2. Query programs are used to review information that already exists in the data files.

_____ 3. The programs with the word "Inventory" in their titles can only be used if the Inventory module is used.

_____ 4. The Transaction Register Report could be a very lengthy report.

Now turn to Answer Frame 3[6] on page 6-13 to check your answers.

Answer Frame 3[6]

1. **True.** The **Create G/L Journal Entries** program prepares receivable transactions for posting to General Ledger.

2. **True.** For instance, **Query Customer Accounts** is used to review information about customers, and **Query Inventory Items** is used to review information about inventory.

3. **False.** Although the **Query Inventory Items** and **Inventory Activity Report** programs can be used only if the Inventory module is used, the **Inventory Backorder Report** can be used even if the Inventory module is not used.

4. **True.** This report lists all of the receivables transactions entered during a period.

If you missed any of the above, reread Frame 3[6] before turning to the questions at the end of the chapter.

What's Next

Now that you have learned how Accounts Receivable works, you are ready to practice with a sample business. But first, you may want to review the sample reports generated by Accounts Receivable and Invoicing found at the end of this chapter. These reports are similar to the ones you will produce in the next chapter.

Name _____ ID# _____

ACCOUNTS RECEIVABLE AND
INVOICING OVERVIEW
QUESTIONS

1. **Briefly describe what A/R is used for in a business.**

    _____

    _____

    _____

2. **Name the seven maintenance programs and the function of each.**

Program Name	Program Function
_____	_____
_____	_____
_____	_____
_____	_____
_____	_____
_____	_____
_____	_____

3. **What are four tasks considered as processing activities?**

    _____

    _____

    _____

    _____

4. **Identify five processing programs. Put an asterisk (*) by the two that
    will be used when Accounts Receivable is used without Invoicing.**

    _____

    _____

Name _____ **ID#** _____

_____

_____

_____

5. Name the four programs used for statement tasks and the function of each.

<u>Program Name</u>   <u>Program Function</u>

_____   _____

_____   _____

_____   _____

_____   _____

6. What tasks are performed by Sales Tax Summary?

_____

_____

_____

7. Name three programs used for end of the period tasks and the function of each.

<u>Program Name</u>   <u>Program Function</u>

_____   _____

_____   _____

_____   _____

8. What are the four programs that generate transactions listed in the Transaction Register Report?

_____

_____

_____

_____

Name _____   ID# _____

9. **What are the seven report programs? Indicate the function of the three that will be used when Accounts Receivable is used without Invoicing or Inventory**

<u>Program Name</u>   <u>Program Function</u>

_____   _____

_____   _____

_____   _____

_____   _____

_____   _____

_____   _____

_____   _____

Name _____ ID# _____

ACCOUNTS RECEIVABLE AND INVOICING OVERVIEW MATCHING

Instructions: Match each program name on the left with the proper program function on the right.

Program Name	**Program Function**	**Answer**
A. Past Due Report	1. Lists the entire contents of the sales tax file.	_____
B. Maintain Customers	2. Calculates a balance forward on Balance Forward customers' accounts and then discards all current transactions.	_____
C. Apply Payments	3. Lists the status of customer accounts to help with the collection of past due accounts.	_____
D. Close Current Period	4. Used to add or delete customers.	_____
E. Aged Receivable Report	5. Prints customers' statements.	_____
F. List Sales Tax Records	6. Controls how Accounts Receivable reports receivables information to a company's ledger.	_____
G. Create General Ledger Journal Entries	7. Enters payments, credits, and other payment related transactions.	_____
H. Maintain General Ledger Accounts Dist File	8. Prints an ageing summary.	_____
I. Enter Transactions	9. Prepares receivable transactions for posting to the ledger.	_____
J. Customer Statements	10. Enters most customer transactions; also generates automatic transactions.	_____

ACCOUNTS RECEIVABLE
AND INVOICING
SAMPLE REPORTS

Customer Statement

YOUR COMPANY NAME
ADDRESS
CITY, STATE ZIP CODE
PHONE AND FAX #

STATEMENT

STATEMENT DATE:	12/31/92
ACCOUNT NUMBER:	**CANNOP**
PAGE:	**1**

AMOUNT REMITTED
$ _____

RETURN THIS PORTION OF STATEMENT
WITH YOUR PAYMENT.

Paul P. Cannon
956 Adams Drive
Apt. 45
Marietta, GA   30099

Happy Holidays from W.D. Peachtree & Company

INVOICE	DATE	TERMS OR REF.	CODE	DEBITS	CREDITS	BALANCE
023345	10/26/92		MC		15.90-	15.90-
023345	10/03/92		SA	254.26		254.26
023517	10/31/92		SA	1335.55		1335.55
023548	11/05/92		SA	15.00		15.00
				--------	--------	--------
				1604.81	15.90-	1588.91

CURRENT	1 - 30 PAST DUE	31 - 60 PAST DUE		TOTAL DUE	1588.91
---------	---------	---------			========
0.00	15.00	1573.91			========

OVER 60 PAST DUE	OPEN CR	TOTAL
---------	---------	---------
0.00	0.00	1588.91

Query Customer Accounts

```
RUN DATE: 12/31/92                    W.D. Peachtree & Company                         PAGE  1
RUN TIME:  6:48 PM                      Accounts Receivable
                                      Query Customer Accounts

Customer ID.....: ANDERA Anita S. Anderson
Current Transactions       321 Church Street
                           Decatur, GA              30078

Telephone #.....: 404/555-1212           -----LAST-----+------AMOUNT---
Customer Class..: A                      Debit           |    1122.54
Account Type....: Regular                Credit          |    -120.24
Service Chg Code: 3                      Payment         |    -200.00
Terms Code......: 1   2/10,NET 30        Service Charge  |       0.00
Sales Tax Code..: 001                    ------YTD------+------AMOUNT---
                                         Debit           |    2315.84
Credit Limit....:       1000.00          Credit          |    -120.24
Balance Forward.:       1392.49          Payment         |   -1003.11
Ship Addresses..: N                      Service Charge  |       0.00
Dunning Notices.: Y                      ---------------+----------------
Discount Percent:          0.00          Pending Invoices:        0.00
Print Statements: Y                      Adjusted Balance:     1192.49
Print Invoices..: Y

                  Trans.      Due    Discount  Disc.
Inv#  Transaction PC  Date      Date     Date    Rate   Amount   Comment
-----------------------------------------------------------------------------
023499 Payment      10/27/92    /  /     /  /    0.00   -200.00  CK
023499 Payment      11/03/92    /  /     /  /    0.00   -200.00  CK 3456
023499 Return     A 10/26/92    /  /     /  /    0.00   -120.24
023499 Sale       A 10/15/92 11/14/92 10/25/92  2.00   1122.54  Invoicing
023513 Sale       A 10/26/92 11/25/92 11/05/92  2.00    590.19
                                                       ==========
                   TOTAL TRANSACTIONS   5              1192.49
```

Transaction Register

W.D. Peachtree & Company
Accounts Receivable
Transaction Register

PAGE 1

CUST. ID	TRANSACTION TYPE	INVOICE NO.	GEN #	P C	TRANS. DATE	DUE DATE	DISCOUNT DATE	E.P. DISC%	COMMENT	CREDIT AMOUNT	DEBIT AMOUNT	NET AMOUNT
ANDERA	Payment	023499	11		11/03/92				CK 3456	200.00-		200.00-
ANDREC	Credit	0	11	A	11/03/92					50.00-		50.00-
	Payment	023489	11		11/03/92				CK 2112	350.00-		350.00-
	CUSTOMER TOTALS:									400.00-		400.00-
CANNOP	Sale	023548	11	A	11/05/92	12/05/92	11/15/92	2.00			15.00	15.00
COOPEG	Payment	023105	11		11/03/92				CK 7789	200.00-		200.00-
	GRAND TOTAL TRANSACTIONS:								5	800.00-	15.00	785.00-

*** END OF Transaction Register ***

Open Items Register

W.D. Peachtree & Company
Accounts Receivable
Open Items Register

PAGE 1

CUST. ID	TRANSACTION TYPE	INVOICE NO.	GEN #	P C	TRANS. DATE	DUE DATE	DISCOUNT DATE	E.P. DISC%	COMMENT	CREDIT AMOUNT	DEBIT AMOUNT	NET AMOUNT
CANNOP	Misc. Credit	023345	10	M	10/26/92			2.00		15.90-		15.90-
	Sale	023345	10	A	10/03/92	11/02/92	10/13/92	2.00			254.26	254.26
	Sale	023517	10	A	10/31/92	11/30/92	11/10/92	2.00			1,335.55	1,335.55
	Sale	023548	11	A	11/05/92	12/05/92	11/15/92	2.00			15.00	15.00
						CUSTOMER TOTALS:				15.90-	1,604.81	1,588.91
COOPEG	Credit	023105	10	A	10/26/92					106.00-		106.00-
	Payment	023105	10		10/27/92				CK	450.00-		450.00-
	Payment	023105	11		11/03/92				CK 7789	200.00-		200.00-
	Sale	023105	10	A	10/01/92	10/31/92	10/11/92	10.00			1,166.00	1,166.00
	Sale	023490	10		10/05/92	11/04/92	10/15/92	10.00	Invoicing		61.40	61.40
	Sale	023519	10	A	10/31/92	11/30/92	11/10/92	10.00			953.95	953.95
						CUSTOMER TOTALS:				756.00-	2,181.35	1,425.35
						GRAND TOTAL TRANSACTIONS:		10		771.90-	3,786.16	3,014.26

*** END OF Open Items Register ***

Summary Aged Receivables Report

W.D. Peachtree & Company
Accounts Receivable
Summary Aged Receivables Report

Ageing Date: 12/31/92

CUST. ID CUSTOMER NAME	INVOICE NUMBER DUE DATE	CURRENT	1 - 30 PAST DUE	31 - 60 PAST DUE	OVER 60 PAST DUE	OPEN CR	TOTAL
ANDERA Anita S. Anderson 404/555-1212	---- -----	0.00	0.00	1192.49	0.00	0.00	1192.49
ANDREC Christine Andrews 404/555-1212	---- -----	0.00	0.00	1114.21	0.00	50.00-	1064.21
CANNOP Paul P. Cannon 404/555-1212	---- -----	0.00	15.00	1573.91	0.00	0.00	1588.91
COOPEG Gloria S. Cooper 404/555-1212	---- -----	0.00	0.00	1015.35	410.00	0.00	1425.35
DURAND Dorothy Durand 404/555-1212	---- -----	18.09	2411.52				2429.61
TOTALS:		18.09	2426.52	4895.96	410.00	50.00-	7700.57

*** END OF Summary Aged Receivables Report ***

Detailed Aged Receivables Report

RUN DATE: 12/31/92
RUN TIME: 6:53 PM

W.D. Peachtree & Company
Accounts Receivable
Detailed Aged Receivables Report

PAGE 1

Ageing Date: 12/31/92

CUST. ID / CUSTOMER NAME	INVOICE NUMBER	DUE DATE	CURRENT	1 - 30 PAST DUE	31 - 60 PAST DUE	OVER 60 PAST DUE	OPEN CR	TOTAL
ANDERA Anita S. Anderson								
404/555-1212	023499	11/14/92			602.30			602.30
	023513	11/25/92			590.19			590.19
					1192.49			1192.49
ANDREC Christine Andrews								
404/555-1212	0	---					50.00-	50.00-
	023111	11/01/92			145.73			145.73
	023489	11/04/92			603.30			603.30
	023515	11/29/92			365.18			365.18
					1114.21		50.00-	1064.21
CANNOP Paul P. Cannon								
404/555-1212	023345	11/02/92			238.36			238.36
	023517	11/30/92			1335.55			1335.55
	023548	12/05/92		15.00				15.00
				15.00	1573.91			1588.91
COOPEG Gloria S. Cooper								
404/555-1212	023105	10/31/92				410.00		410.00
	023490	11/04/92			61.40			61.40
	023519	11/30/92			953.95			953.95
					1015.35	410.00		1425.35
TOTALS:			0.00	15.00	4895.96	410.00	50.00-	5270.96

*** END OF Detailed Aged Receivables Report ***

Summary Past Due Report

```
RUN DATE: 12/31/92        W.D. Peachtree & Company              PAGE  1
RUN TIME:  6:55 PM          Accounts Receivable
                              Past Due Report
Ageing Date: 12/31/92

CUST.ID   CUSTOMER NAME          PHONE         INVOICE  DUE DATE    AMOUNT
ANDREC   Christine Andrews     404/555-1212    -----    -----      1114.21

CANNOP   Paul P. Cannon        404/555-1212    -----    -----      1588.91

COOPEG   Gloria S. Cooper      404/555-1212    -----    -----      1425.35

DURAND   Dorothy Durand        404/555-1212    -----    -----      2411.52

FIELDJ   Jonathan S. Fields    404/555-1212    -----    -----      3226.71

GRAYC    Charles A. Gray       404/555-1212    -----    -----      3537.04

HENDEK   Kathy Henderson       404/555-1212    -----    -----      1249.69

HOLLOJ   James R. Holloway     404/555-1212    -----    -----      1033.75
                                                                 ==========
         TOTALS                                                   15587.18

*** END OF Past Due Report ***
```

Detailed Past Due Report

```
RUN DATE: 12/31/92       W.D. Peachtree & Company              PAGE  1
RUN TIME:  6:55 PM        Accounts Receivable
                          Past Due Report
--------------------------------------------------------------------------
Ageing Date: 12/31/92

CUST.ID   CUSTOMER NAME         PHONE        INVOICE  DUE DATE     AMOUNT
-------   -------------         -----        -------  --------     ------

ANDREC  Christine Andrews   404/555-1212  023111   11/01/92      145.73
                                          023489   11/04/92      603.30
                                          023515   11/29/92      365.18
                                                                -------
                                                                1114.21

CANNOP  Paul P. Cannon      404/555-1212  023345   11/02/92      238.36
                                          023517   11/30/92     1335.55
                                          023548   12/05/92       15.00
                                                                -------
                                                                1588.91

COOPEG  Gloria S. Cooper    404/555-1212  023105   10/31/92      410.00
                                          023490   11/04/92       61.40
                                          023519   11/30/92      953.95
                                                                -------
                                                                1425.35

                     TOTALS                                     ========
                                                                4128.47


*** END OF Past Due Report ***
```

List Customer Accounts

REPORT IS SORTED BY: Customer ID

CUST ID.	NAME-ADDRESS	TYPE	S.C. CODE	TERMS CODE	TAX CODE	DISC. %	CREDIT LIMIT	YTD DEBITS	YTD CREDITS	BALANCE
ANDERA	Anita S. Anderson	REGULAR	3	1	001	0.00	1000.00	2315.84	1123.35-	1192.49
	321 Church Street									
	Decatur, GA 30078									
	CONTACT.........: Anita Anderson									
	PHONE...........: 404/555-1212									
	SALESMAN........: BBS									
	DUNNING NOTICES..: Y									
	CUSTOMER CLASS...: A									
	SHIP-TO ADDRESSES.: N									
	PRINT STATEMENTS..: Y									
	PRINT INVOICES....: Y									
ANDREC	Christine Andrews	REGULAR	1	1	001	5.00	2000.00	1627.33	563.12-	1064.21
	444 Elm Street									
COOPEG	Gloria S. Cooper	REGULAR	2	4	001	0.00	3000.00	2181.35	756.00-	1425.35
	37 North Avenue									
	Atlanta, GA 30333									
	CONTACT.........: Gloria Cooper									
	PHONE...........: 404/555-1212									
	SALESMAN........: BBS									
	DUNNING NOTICES..: Y									
	CUSTOMER CLASS...: A									
	SHIP-TO ADDRESSES.: N									
	PRINT STATEMENTS..: Y									
	PRINT INVOICES....: Y									

GRAND TOTALS   4 CUSTOMERS LISTED

	YTD DEBITS	YTD CREDITS	BALANCE
	8070.65	2799.69-	5270.96

*** END OF List Customer Accounts ***

List Sales Tax Records

W.D. Peachtree & Company
Accounts Receivable
List Sales Tax Records

| | | | | | * * * * * * * TAX BRACKETS * * * * * * * | | | | | | | | | | | MAXIMUM |
CODE	NAME	SLS	FRE	TAX %	.00	.01	.02	.03	.04	.05	.06	.07	.08	.09	.10	TAXABLE
001	GEORGIA	T	T	4.000	0	0	0	0	0	0	0	0	0	0	0	
	FULTON			1.000	0	0	0	0	0	0	0	0	0	0	0	$0.00
	MARTA			1.000	0	0	0	0	0	0	0	0	0	0	0	$0.00

*** END OF List Sales Tax Records ***

Sales Tax Summary

W.D. Peachtree & Company
Accounts Receivable
Sales Tax Summary

PAGE 1

CODE	STATE NAME	COUNTY NAME	CITY NAME	SALES TAX	TAXABLE SALES	NON-TAXABLE SALES	TOTAL SALES
001	GEORGIA	FULTON	MARTA	52.33	1308.05	265.00	1573.05
				13.08	1308.05	265.00	1573.05
				13.08	1308.05	265.00	1573.05
			CITY TOTALS:	13.08	1308.05	265.00	1573.05
		COUNTY TOTALS:		13.08	1308.05	265.00	1573.05
	STATE TOTALS:			52.33	1308.05	265.00	1573.05

*** REPORT TOTALS ***

	SALES TAX	TAXABLE SALES	NON-TAXABLE SALES	TOTAL SALES
STATES:	52.33	1308.05	265.00	1573.05
COUNTIES:	13.08	1308.05	265.00	1573.05
CITIES:	13.08	1308.05	265.00	1573.05
TOTAL TAX:	78.49			

*** END OF Sales Tax Summary ***

Maintain Customer Control Report

```
RUN DATE: 12/31/92          W.D. Peachtree & Company                    PAGE  1
RUN TIME:  6:58 PM               Accounts Receivable
                          MAINTAIN CUSTOMER CONTROL REPORT - ADD
----------------------------------------------------------------------------------
Customer ID.....: MOOREK              Debit------
Customer Name...: KATHY MOORE            Last Date       01/01/00
Address.........: 1625 Revel Cove Dr.    Last Amt            0.00
Address.........:                        YTD  Amt            0.00
City, ST........: Conyers, GA         Credit-----
ZIP Code........: 30624                  Last Date       01/01/00
Telephone.......: 404-555-9223           Last Amt            0.00
Contact.........: Kathy Moore            YTD  Amt            0.00
Salesperson.....: Reba M.             Payments----
Customer Class..: A                      Last Date       01/01/00
Account Type....: R                      Last Amt            0.00
Service Chg Code: 1                      YTD  Amt            0.00
Terms Code......: 1                   Service Charges----
Sales Tax Code..: 001                    Last Date       01/01/00
Discount Percent:    5.00                Last Amt            0.00
Ship Addresses..: N                      YTD  Amt            0.00
Dunning Notices.: Y
Credit Limit....:         3,000.00
Print Statements: Y
Print Invoices..: Y

*** End Of - Maintain Customers Control Report ***
```

Maintain Sales Tax Control Report

```
                          NEW VALUE                   OLD VALUE
                         -----------                 -----------

Tax ID.......:001
Status.......:       A                           A
Sales Tax/Ex.:       T                           T
Frght Tax/Ex.:       T                           T
State Name...:       GEORGIA                     GEORGIA
State Tax %..:          4.00                         4.00
St. Brackets.:       N                           N
Bracket .00 :          0                            0
Bracket .01 :          0                            0


Bracket .09 :          0                            0
Bracket .10 :          0                            0
County Name..:       FULTON                      FULTON
County Tax %.:          2.00                         1.00
Max. Taxable.:          0.00                         0.00


City Name....:       MARTA                       MARTA
City Tax %...:          1.00                         1.00
Max. Taxable.:          0.00                         0.00
Co. Brackets.:       N                           N
Bracket .00 :          0                            0
Bracket .01 :          0                            0
Bracket .02 :          0                            0
Bracket .03 :          0                            0
Bracket .04 :          0                            0
Bracket .05 :          0                            0
Bracket .06 :          0                            0
Bracket .07 :          0                            0
Bracket .08 :          0                            0
Bracket .09 :          0                            0
Bracket .10 :          0                            0

*** End Of - Maintain Tax File Control Report ***
```

Maintain G/L Accounts Distribution File

```
RUN DATE: 12/31/92          W.D. Peachtree & Company              PAGE  1
RUN TIME:  7:02 PM              Accounts Receivable
                            Maintain G/L Account Dist File

TRANS.  PROD    ACCOUNT #
TYPE    CODE  CREDIT  DEBIT    DESCRIPTION
------  ----  ------  -----    -----------

AD       A    30531   12000    APPLIANCES
AD       C    30516   12000    CHILDREN'S CLOTHING
AD       D    30535   12000    HARDWARE
AD       E    30533   12000    ELECTRONICS
AD       F    30550   12000    FENCING & GUTTERS
AD       H    30562   12000    HAIR SALON
AD       L    30523   12000    ATHLETIC SHOES
AD       M    30512   12000    MEN'S CLOTHING
AD       O    30525   12000    OTHER SHOES
AD       S    30542   12000    SPORTING GOODS
AD       U    30518   12000    UNIFORMS
AD       W    30514   12000    WOMEN'S CLOTHING
BD            12000   13000    BAD DEBT
CI            23600   12000    CITY TAX
CO            23600   12000    COUNTY TAX
CP       A    13500   40531    APPLIANCES
CP       C    13500   40516    CHILDREN'S CLOTHING
CP       D    13500   40535    HARDWARE
CP       E    13500   40533    ELECTRONICS
CP       F    13500   40550    FENCING & GUTTERS
CP       H    13500   40562    HAIR SALON

SA       U    30518   12000    UNIFORMS
SA       W    30514   12000    WOMEN'S CLOTHING
SC            33000   12000    SERVICE CHARGE
SS       A    31531   12000    APPLIANCES
SS       D    31535   12000    HARDWARE
SS       E    31533   12000    ELECTRONICS
SS       F    31550   12000    FENCING & GUTTERS
SS       H    31562   12000    HAIR SALON
ST            23600   12000    STATE TAX

*** End Of - Maintain G/L Account Dist File ***
```

Maintain Distribution Control Report

```
RUN DATE: 12/31/92        W.D. Peachtree & Company                        PAGE  1
RUN TIME:  7:03 PM              Accounts Receivable
                     MAINTAIN DISTRIBUTION CONTROL REPORT - CHANGE

                            NEW VALUE                          OLD VALUE
                   ------------------------          ------------------------

Transaction ID.....: BD
Product Code.......:
Description........: BAD DEBT WRITEOFF             BAD DEBT
Sales Credit.......: 12000                        12000
Sales Debit........: 13000                        13000


*** End Of - Maintain G/L Distribution Accounts Control Report ***
```

Automatic Transactions Control Report

```
RUN DATE: 12/31/92                           W.D. Peachtree & Company                                           PAGE  1
RUN TIME: 7:04 PM                                Accounts Receivable
                                         Automatic Transactions Control Report

CUST.   TRN.  TRN.  PROD              TRANS.          STATE    COUNTY   CITY    TRMS                       BILL   START
ID      #     TYPE  CODE  STAT        AMOUNT   T/E    TAX      TAX      TAX     CODE   COMMENT   FRQ  PRDS  DATE
-----   ----  ----  ----  ----        ------   ---    -----    ------   -----   ----   -------   ---  ----  --------

MOOREK  01    SA    A     A           12.75    T      0.51     0.13     0.13    1      Service   M    12    12/31/92

*** END OF Automatic Transactions Control Report ***
```

Enter Transactions Control Report

W.D. Peachtree & Company
Accounts Receivable
Enter Transactions Control Report

PAGE 1

CUST ID	INV. NO	TRANSACTION TYPE	P C	TRANS DATE	DUE DATE	DISC DATE	E. P. DISC%	TRANS AMOUNT	COMMENT	CREDIT ACCT	CREDIT AMOUNT	DEBIT ACCT	DEBIT AMOUNT
MOOREK	023549	Sale	A	12/31/92	01/30/93	01/10/93	2.00	12.75	Service	30531	12.75-	12000	12.75
								0.77	State Tax	23600	0.51-	12000	0.51
									County Tax	23600	0.13-	12000	0.13
									City Tax	23600	0.13-	12000	0.13
						TOTAL TAX:		13.52			13.52-		13.52
MOOREK	019335	Begin. Bal.	A	10/31/92	11/30/92	11/10/92	2.00	752.99			752.99-		752.99
								45.18	State Tax		30.12-		30.12
									County Tax		7.53-		7.53
									City Tax		7.53-		7.53
						TOTAL TAX:		798.17			798.17-		798.17
								=========			=========		=========
								811.69			811.69-		811.69
								=========			=========		=========

*** End Of - Enter Transactions Control Report ***

Reconcile Open Credits Control Report

```
RUN DATE: 12/31/92                    W.D. Peachtree & Company                              PAGE  1
RUN TIME: 7:13 PM                        Accounts Receivable
                                        Reconcile Open Credits
---------------------------------------------------------------------------------------------------
              CUSTOMER    AVAILABLE      INVOICE    INVOICE    AMOUNT     CREDIT      NEW OPEN
CUST.ID       NAME        OPEN CREDIT    NUMBER     DATE       DUE        APPLIED     CREDIT BALANCE
-------       --------    -----------    -------    -------    ------     -------     --------------

ANDREC    Christine Andrews   50.00-     023111     11/01/92   145.73     50.00-          0.00
                                                               =======    =======      ========
                                                               145.73      50.00-         0.00

                                        REPORT TOTALS:         =======    =======      ========
                                                               145.73     50.00-          0.00


*** End Of Reconcile Open Credits Control Report ***
```

Apply Payments Control Report

W.D. Peachtree & Company
Accounts Receivable
Apply Payments Control Report

PAGE 1

CUST. ID.	INV. NO.	TRANSACTION TYPE	P C	TRANS. DATE	DUE DATE	DISC. DATE	E. P. DISC%	CASH AMOUNT	COMMENT	CREDIT ACCOUNT	CREDIT AMOUNT	DEBIT ACCOUNT	DEBIT AMOUNT
MOOREK	019335	PAYMENT		12/31/92	11/30/92	11/10/92	2.00	500.00	CK666	12000	500.00-	11000	500.00
							GRAND TOTALS:	500.00			500.00-		500.00

*** End Of - Apply Payments Control Report ***

Apply Service Charges Control Report

```
                              W.D. Peachtree & Company
                                 Accounts Receivable
                            Apply Service Charges Control Report
```

SERVICE CHARGES FOR 12/01/92 THROUGH 12/31/92

FINAL RUN
S.C. CREDIT ACCOUNT 33000
S.C. DEBIT ACCOUNT 12000
SERVICE CHARGE METHOD = AVERAGE DAILY BALANCE

CUST ID	CUSTOMER NAME	ACCOUNT TYPE	ANNUAL S.C. %	INVOICE NUMBER	DUE DATE	AMOUNT DUE	AMOUNT SUBJECT TO SVC CHGS	SERVICE CHG. AMOUNT	SVC CHG INVOICE	SVC CHG INV.DATE
ANDERA	Anita S. Anderson	REGULAR	18.00	023499	11/14/92	602.30	602.30	8.91	023550	12/31/92
				023513	11/25/92	590.19	590.19	8.73		
						1192.49	1192.49	17.64		
ANDREC	Christine Andrews	REGULAR	6.00	023111	11/01/92	145.73	145.73	2.00	023551	12/31/92
HOLLOJ	James R. Holloway	REGULAR	18.00	023502	11/25/92	121.43	121.43	2.00	023552	12/31/92
SMITHR	Robert M. Smith	TEMP	18.00	023536		1765.43	1765.43	26.12	023553	12/31/92
	REPORT TOTALS:					3225.08	3225.08	47.76		

*** End of Apply Service Charges Control Report ***

G/L Transfers List

```
RUN DATE: 12/31/92      W.D. Peachtree & Company              PAGE  1
RUN TIME: 7:14 PM          Accounts Receivable
                            G/L Transfers List
-----------------------------------------------------------------------------
Selection: List G/L Transfers

ACCOUNT  SC  REFERENCE   DATE      DESCRIPTION   TRANS. TYPE      AMOUNT
-------  --  ---------   --------  -----------   -----------   ----------
11000    R   Paymnt      11/03/92  CK 3456                        200.00
11000    R   Paymnt      11/03/92  CK 2112                        350.00
11000    R   Paymnt      11/03/92  CK 7789                        200.00
11000    R   Paymnt      11/03/92  CK 9098                        400.00
11000    R   Paymnt      11/03/92  CK 5598                         50.00
11000    R   Paymnt      11/03/92  CK 44321                      1250.00
11000    R   Paymnt      11/03/92  CK 1432                       1000.00
11000    R   Paymnt      11/03/92  CK 2341                        200.00
11000    R   Paymnt      11/03/92  CK 7654                        500.00
11000    R   Paymnt      12/31/92  CK666                          500.00
         --                                                    ----------
ACCOUNT TOTALS - Transactions :   10
                 Total Debits :       4650.00                    4650.00
                 Total Credits:          0.00

12000    R   Paymnt      11/03/92  CK 3456                        200.00-
12000    R   Paymnt      11/03/92  CK 2112                        350.00-

33000    R   023553      12/31/92  SERV. CHG.                      26.12-
         --                                                    ----------
ACCOUNT TOTALS - Transactions :    4
                 Total Debits :          0.00                     47.76-
                 Total Credits:         47.76-
=============================================================================
GRAND TOTALS - Transactions Processed:   82

Total Debits :      6,412.82
Total Credits:      6,412.82-
                 ----------
Difference   :          0.00                                       0.00

*** End Of - G/L Transfer List ***
```

Sample Invoice

YOUR COMPANY NAME
ADDRESS
CITY, STATE ZIP CODE
PHONE AND FAX #

INVOICE

INVOICE NUMBER: 023554

INVOICE DATE: 12/31/92

PAGE: 1

SOLD TO:
Charles A. Gray
3211 Summerville Road
Lawrenceville, GA   30055

SHIP TO:
Charles A. Gray
3211 Summerville Road
Lawrenceville, GA   30055

CUST. I.D.: GRAYC

P.O. NUMBER:

P.O. DATE: 12/31/92

OUR ORDER NO.:

SALESPERSON: BBS

SHIP VIA:
SHIP DATE: 12/31/92
DUE DATE: 01/30/93
TERMS: 2/10, NET 30

ITEM I.D. / DESC.	ORDERED	SHIPPED	UNIT	PRICE	NET	TX
APP0900210REF 21 CUBIC FT. RESIDENTIAL REFRIGERATOR	1.00	1.00	EACH	1100.0000	1100.00	T

SUBTOTAL: 1100.00
TAX: 66.00
PAYMENTS: 0.00
TOTAL: 1166.00

Invoice Register

Sales Invoicing

Invoice Register

INVOICE NUMBER	INVOICE DATE	CUST. ID	CUSTOMER NAME	TERMS	MERCHANDISE /SERVICES	OTHER CHARGES	FREIGHT	SALES TAX	INVOICE TOTAL
023545	11/08/92	COOPEG	Gloria S. Cooper	10/10,NET30	68.03	0.00	0.00	4.08	72.11
023546	11/08/92	HENDEK	Kathy Henderson	2/10,NET 30	413.10	0.00	0.00	24.78	437.88
023547	11/08/92	MILLEJ	Joel S. Miller	NET 30	149.95	0.00	0.00	9.00	158.95
023554	12/31/92	GRAYC	Charles A. Gray	2/10,NET 30	1100.00	0.00	0.00	66.00	1166.00
023555	12/31/92	MILLEJ	Joel S. Miller	NET 30	29.99	0.00	0.00	1.80	31.79
					1761.07	0.00	0.00	105.66	1866.73

NO. OF ITEMS LISTED: 5

REPORT SUMMARY TOTALS

	TAXABLE	NON-TAXABLE	GROSS
Sales..........:	1761.07	0.00	1761.07
Misc. Debits...:	0.00	0.00	0.00
Returns........:	0.00	0.00	0.00
Misc. Credits..:	0.00	0.00	0.00
Freight........:	0.00	0.00	0.00
Sub-Totals.....:	1761.07	0.00	1761.07
Credits........:	0.00	0.00	0.00
Payments.......:	0.00	0.00	0.00

	SALES TAXES	TAX REFUNDS	GROSS
State..........:	70.44	0.00	70.44
County.........:	17.61	0.00	17.61
City...........:	17.61	0.00	17.61
Tax Sub-Total..:	105.66	0.00	105.66

Report Total....:   1866.73

*** End Of - Invoice Register ***

Query Inventory Items Report

```
RUN DATE: 12/31/92          W.D. Peachtree & Company                    PAGE   1
RUN TIME: 7:21 PM                 Sales Invoicing
                              Query Inventory Items Report

ITEM TYPE: P               DEPARTMENT: APP         ITEM NUMBER: 090012OREF

ITEM DESCRIPTION..: COMMERCIAL REFRIGER.    ------- Extended Description -------
PRODUCT CODE.....: A                        20 CUBIC FT. COMMERCIAL REFRIGERATOR
LOCATION.........: WRHS-1
RECEIVING UNIT...: EACH
SELLING UNIT.....: EACH
CONVERSION FACTOR.: 1.00
VENDOR ID........: FRIGID
VENDOR ITEM #....: 900120
NEGATIVE QUANTITY.: N
COSTING METHOD...: CURRENT AVG.            SELLING PRICES
CURRENT COST.....: 356.8100000               PRICE A.........: 779.9900
LAST COST / UNIT.: 356.8100000               PRICE B.........: 669.9900
REORDER LEVEL....: 8.00                       PRICE C.........: 889.0000
REORDER QUANTITY.: 6.00
ON RO REPORT DATE.:  /  /

PTD ACTIVITY                               YTLP ACTIVITY

  SALES..........:      779.99               SALES..........:          0.00
  COST OF SALES..:      356.81               COST OF SALES..:          0.00

  BEGINNING QTY..:        5.00               # SOLD.........:          0.00
  # SOLD.........:        1.00               # RECEIVED.....:          0.00
  # RECEIVED.....:        4.00               # RETURNED.....:          0.00
  # RETURNED.....:        0.00               # ADJUSTED.....:          0.00
  # ADJUSTED.....:        0.00               # COMPONENTS...:          0.00
  # COMPONENTS...:        0.00

                                           ITEM VALUATION.........:   2854.48
CURRENT QTY-ON-HAND..:      8.00
(-) # UNITS PENDING..:      0.00           UNITS ON ORDER.........:      0.00
                        -------
# UNITS AVAILABLE....:      8.00
```

Invoicing Backorder Report

RUN TIME: 7:46 PM

W.D. Peachtree & Company
Sales Invoicing
Invoicing Backorder Report

PAGE 1

PRODUCT ID	S I	ITEM DESCRIPTION	P C	UNIT MEAS	INVOICE NUMBER	INVOICE DATE	QUANTITY BACKORDERED	UNIT COST	UNIT PRICE
PELE8100000SPC	E	MAIN ASSEMBLY: PORTA	E	EACH	023555	12/31/92	1.00	16.3710	29.9900

Total Items Listed: 1 → 1.00

*** End Of - Invoicing Backorder Report ***

Inventory Activity Report

RUN DATE: 12/31/92
RUN TIME: 7:25 PM

W.D. Peachtree & Company
Sales Invoicing
Inventory Activity Report

PRODUCT ID	P/C NUMBER	INVOICE NUMBER	ITEM DESCRIPTION	UNIT N MEAS S	QUANTITY ORDERED	QUANTITY SHIPPED	TOTAL COST	TOTAL SALES	PROFIT	PCT OF PROFIT
PAPP0900210REF	A	023554	21 CUBIC FT. RESIDEN	EACH	1.00	1.00	456.81	1100.00	643.19	58.47
PAPP10040TRA	A	023547	SUPERTRASH COMPACTOR	EACH	1.00	1.00	119.00	149.95	30.95	20.64
PCLC436781G	C	023545	GIRL'S BLUEJEANS	PAIR	2.00	2.00	10.90	25.00	14.10	56.40
PCLC463444	C	023545	ASSORTED COLORED TUB	PAIR	5.00	5.00	3.45	8.95	5.50	61.45

Sales:	UNITS	SALES	COST	PROFIT	% PROFIT
Stocked....:	14.00	1761.07	722.28	1038.79	58.99
Non-Stocked:	0.00	0.00	0.00	0.00	0.00
Services...:	0.00	0.00	0.00	0.00	0.00
Total......:	14.00	1761.07	722.28	1038.79	58.99

Returns:					
Stocked....:	0.00	0.00	0.00	0.00	0.00
Non-Stocked:	0.00	0.00	0.00	0.00	0.00
Services...:	0.00	0.00	0.00	0.00	0.00
Total......:	0.00	0.00	0.00	0.00	0.00

Totals:					
Stocked....:	14.00	1761.07	722.28	1038.79	58.99
Non-Stocked:	0.00	0.00	0.00	0.00	0.00
Services...:	0.00	0.00	0.00	0.00	0.00
Total......:	14.00	1761.07	722.28	1038.79	58.99

*** End Of - Inventory Activity Report ***

Post Invoices Control Report

W.D. Peachtree & Company
Sales Invoicing
Post Invoices Control Report

PAGE 1

Inv #	Inv Date	Cust ID	Customer Name	Invoice Amount	Item ID	Type	UOM	Number Posted	Status	Job
023545	11/08/92	COOPEG	Gloria S. Cooper	72.11						
					P CLC 463487G	SA	EACH	3.00	ok	
					P CLC 463444	SA	PAIR	5.00	ok	
					P CLC 436781G	SA	PAIR	2.00	ok	
023546	11/08/92	HENDEK	Kathy Henderson	437.88	P ELE 810544CDP	SA	EACH	1.00	ok	
023547	11/08/92	MILLEJ	Joel S. Miller	158.95	P APP 10040TRA	SA	EACH	1.00	ok	
023554	12/31/92	GRAYC	Charles A. Gray	1,166.00	P APP 0900210REF	SA	EACH	1.00	ok	
023555	12/31/92	MILLEJ	Joel S. Miller	31.79	P ELE 8100000SPC	SA	EACH	1.00	ok	

Totals..: Number of Invoices = 5   Amount = 1,866.73
Update to Job Cost = N at time of posting.

* * * End of Post Invoices Control Report * * *

Chapter 7

ACCOUNTS RECEIVABLE AND INVOICING: PRACTICING WITH A SAMPLE BUSINESS

Learning Objectives:

After studying this chapter you should be able to:

1. Perform maintenance activities including—adding or changing customer information and entering new automatic transactions.

2. Perform daily activities including—producing customer invoices, entering transactions, entering payments, and printing the transaction register.

3. Perform monthly activities including—preparing customer statements, preparing the sales tax summary, and closing the period.

Chapter 7

Accounts Receivable and Invoicing: Practicing with a Sample Business

This chapter guides you through lessons that give you practical experience with Accounts Receivable and Invoicing. You work with the customers of W.D. Peachtree & Company.

The lessons in this chapter are grouped into three topics:

1. Maintenance tasks.
2. Daily tasks.
3. Monthly tasks.

Topic 1, Maintenance Tasks, guides you through the tasks that must be completed before daily tasks can be performed. In general, these maintenance tasks will be performed whenever necessary.

Topic 2, Daily Tasks, guides you through the tasks that must be performed regularly to track receivables. Most of the tasks performed in Accounts Receivable and Invoicing are daily tasks. (Although they are called "daily tasks," they are actually tasks performed as often as is necessary to handle receivables transactions.)

Topic 3, Monthly Tasks, guides you through the tasks that must be performed to:

- Prepare customer statements.
- Pay sales taxes.
- Close your Accounts Receivable accounting period.

At W.D. Peachtree, these activities are all performed once a month.

About the Practice Session

You do not need to complete the lessons in this chapter in one session. However, you should complete all the lessons in a topic in one session. In addition, unless otherwise noted, you should complete the lessons in each topic in the order listed. In Accounts Receivable and Invoicing, the order in which you perform tasks is important.

To complete the lessons in this tutorial, you must have your printer turned on. W.D. Peachtree has set its options to force control reports, so you cannot complete many of the lessons unless you have your printer ready. The control reports (as well as the other reports you will print in the tutorial) help you verify the changes you make to Accounts Receivable and Invoicing.

About W.D. Peachtree's Data

In this session, you will work with sample data created for W.D. Peachtree & Company. Since most of Accounts Receivable revolves around customers and their transactions, you should get to know the customers for whom you will be entering transactions.

Mary Wortham is a new customer. She just purchased a duplex, so she came to W.D. Peachtree to buy trash compactors for both units. For Mary Wortham, you will:

- Enter her as a new W.D. Peachtree customer.
- Enter a shipping address for her trash compactor purchase.
- Bill her for the purchase.

Bill Parker has been a W.D. Peachtree customer for many years. He recently purchased a maintenance agreement for his W.D. Peachtree trash compactor. In addition, he made an early payment on a pocket TV he bought at W.D. Peachtree. For Bill Parker, you will:

- Set up an automatic billing transaction to handle his maintenance agreement.
- Bill him for his first maintenance agreement payment.
- Enter a payment and include an early payment discount.

Darryl Tracer has had a W.D. Peachtree charge card for several years. Recently, Mr. Tracer asked to have his credit limit increased. He travels frequently and for long periods of time, so his account often becomes overdue. However, he always makes his payments. For Darryl Tracer, you will:

- Increase his credit limit, give him a volume discount, and remove dunning notices from his statements.
- Enter a payment.
- Apply a service charge to his account.

In completing the steps of this practice session, you will also complete the following tasks for W.D. Peachtree:

- Print customer statements.
- Prepare the company's sales taxes for payment.
- Close the receivables accounting period.

Beginning the Practice Session

WARNING

BEFORE CONTINUING, BE SURE THAT ALL DATA FILES HAVE BEEN RESTORED TO THEIR ORIGINAL CONDITION. IF YOU ARE UNSURE OF HOW TO RESTORE THESE FILES, TURN TO THE INSTRUCTIONS FOUND ON PAGE 1-32 IN CHAPTER 1.

Please note that this chapter is not a simulation. You do not use a sample Accounts Receivable program. To complete the lessons, you actually use Accounts Receivable and Invoicing along with sample data from W.D. Peachtree. Since you actually use A/R and Invoicing for the tutorial, you must start the programs as you would if you were using them for a real business.

Note: Because you use sample data, it is important that you follow the instructions in this chapter. In particular, enter the dates indicated in the examples; never enter different dates.

❖ Start Peachtree Complete Accounting by changing to the directory in which Peachtree Complete is installed. Type PEACH and then press ⌨.

In a few moments, you will see the first PCA screen. The only information PCA provides here is the date (which should be today's date).

❖ Press ⌨ to erase the date shown.

For this example, use 11/30/92 as the date.

❖ Type **113092** and press ⌨.

The next screen appears. On this screen, you enter the company ID.

❖ Type **WD** for the company ID.

PCA displays the PCA Main Menu.

❖ Select **Accounts Receivable**.

Most of the receivables tasks are completed in Accounts Receivable. However, when you complete the Invoicing lessons in this session, you will return to the PCA Main Menu to select Invoicing.

PCA starts Accounts Receivable and displays the Accounts Receivable Main Menu.

You are now ready to begin the session. The lessons in the chapter are arranged in the order in which you would normally do them in a business. So, you should begin with Lesson 1 of Topic 1. Remember, you must have your printer turned on and ready to print in this session.

Topic 1: Maintenance Tasks

Maintenance tasks involve adding or changing information that can affect the rest of the daily tasks. Maintenance tasks will not necessarily occur every day, but, when they do, they must be completed before daily and monthly tasks are started. For example, it makes sense to enter a customer's new address (a maintenance task) before entering his or her invoice (a daily task).

Unlike daily and monthly tasks, the order in which maintenance tasks are performed is not crucial. The tasks needed should dictate the order to follow.

Topic 1 has two lessons; they concentrate on the management of W.D. Peachtree's Accounts Receivable and Invoicing data. In this topic, you will:

1. Enter a new customer and change information for an existing customer.

2. Enter a new automatic transaction.

Lesson 1: Adding or Changing Customer Information

In this lesson, you will learn how to add new customers to Accounts Receivable and how to change account information for existing customers. In this lesson, you will:

*   Enter a new customer, Mary Wortham.
*   Change account information for an existing customer, Darryl Tracer.
*   Check the additions and changes you made.

Step 1: Enter a New Customer

W.D. Peachtree & Company receives an order from Mary Wortham for two trash compactors. She wants them delivered and installed at a new duplex she recently purchased. Since she has never made a purchase at W.D. Peachtree, you will need to enter Ms. Wortham into Accounts Receivable. Step 1 helps you complete this task.

❖ From the Account Receivable Main Menu, select **Maintenance Programs**.

❖ From the Accounts Receivable Maintenance Menu, select **Maintain Customers**.

Accounts Receivable displays the message:

SET PAPER TO TOP OF FORM - PRESS 'ENTER' TO CONTINUE.

Before you can print a control report, your printer must be on-line and ready to print.

❖ Make sure you printer is on-line, then press .

The screen clears. Accounts Receivable asks for a customer ID.

Accounts Receivable identifies customers by the six-character ID assigned to each of them. Whenever you want to enter transactions for customers or review their accounts, you must enter their IDs.

W.D. Peachtree assigns customer IDs using the first five letters of a customer's last name and the initial of the first name. In this lesson, you will enter a new customer, Mary Wortham. Using W.D. Peachtree's system, you will assign WORTHM to Mary Wortham.

❖ Type **WORTHM** (use all capital letters) and press ⌤.

Accounts Receivable does not recognize WORTHM as the ID of an existing customer. So, Accounts Receivable asks:

CUSTOMER NOT FOUND
ADD (Y/N).

❖ Accept the **Y** default and press ⌤.

Accounts Receivable displays the following screen:

```
===========================================================================
ARMAINT1                        Maintain Customers              COMPANY ID: WD
11/30/92                    W.D. Peachtree & Company            GENERATION #: 11
===========================================================================
Customer    ID: WORTHM                          Debit——————————————————
Customer Name:                                    Last Date          01/01/00
Address.............:                             Last Amt               0.00
Address.............:                             YTD  Amt               0.00
City, ST...........:                            Credit—————————————————
ZIP Code...........:                              Last Date          01/01/00
Telephone..........:                              Last Amt               0.00
Contact.............:                             YTD  Amt               0.00
Salesperson......:                              Payments————————————————
                                                  Last Date          01/01/00
Customer Class....:   A    Service Chg Code:  1   Last Amt               0.00
Account Type........:  R   Print Statements..:  Y YTD  Amt               0.00
Terms Code..........: 1    Print Invoices.......:  Y Service Charges——————————
Sales Tax Code....:  001                          Last Date          01/01/00
Discount Percent...:    0.00                      Last Amt               0.00
Ship Addresses.....:  N                           YTD Amt                0.00
Dunning Notices....:  Y
Credit Limit...........:          0.00          Balance                  0.00

  F1-Help                              F8 - Undo    F10 - Done      C
```

When a new customer is entered into Accounts Receivable, the information requested by this screen will need to be entered. Some of this information—such as name and address—will be provided by the customer. Some of the information—such as account type and customer class—will be selected by the business.

❖ Enter the following information for Mary Wortham. After you enter an item (such as name), press ▣; the cursor moves to the next field. Continue entering information.

Customer ID	WORTHM		
Customer Name	Mary Wortham		
Address	5310 Roswell Road		
Address	Apartment 3-G		
City, ST	Atlanta, GA		
ZIP Code	30316		
Telephone	555-9436		
Contact	Mary Wortham		
Salesperson	Brenda S		
Customer Class	3		
Account Type	R		
Terms Code	2		
Sales Tax Code	001		
Discount Percent	0.00		
Ship Addresses	Y	**Service Chg Code**	2
Dunning Notices	N	**Print Statements**	Y
Credit Limit	2500.00	**Print Invoices**	Y

Notice that as you enter information, Accounts Receivable sometimes displays the following message at the bottom of your screen:

F2 —LOOKUP

Whenever this message appears, you can press ▣ to select from a list of possible entries. For example, if you press ▣ while the cursor is at Service Chg Code, Accounts Receivable would display a list of possible service charge codes.

Notice the right side of your screen lists Debit, Credit, Payments, and Service Charges information. Accounts Receivable collects this information as customer transactions and invoices are entered. When entering a new customer, do not make any entries here.

❖ Press ▣ when you have entered all the customer information and you are certain it is correct.

Accounts Receivable asks, *ACCEPT (Y/N)*.

❖ Accept the **Y** default and press ▣.

Accounts Receivable prints the control report. Then, it asks:

EDIT SHIP-TO ADDRESSES (Y/N)?

(This prompt appears because you set Ship Addresses to Y.)

❖ Since Mary has shipping addresses, type **Y** and press ▣.

The following screen appears:

```
================================================================================
ARMAINT1                         Maintain Customers                  COMPANY ID: WD
11/30/92                       W.D. Peachtree & Company               GENERATION #: 11
================================================================================
Customer    ID: WORTHM


SHIPPING ID.....:
_____

Name................:
Address.............:
Address.............:
City, ST.............:
ZIP Code...........:
Telephone.........:




F1-Help        F2 - Lookup                          F10 - Done                C
```

Accounts Receivable identifies a customer's different shipping addresses by the six-character ID assigned to each address. Whenever entering invoices for a customer, a shipping address can be selected by entering the ID assigned to that shipping address.

❖ Enter **1210MH** for Shipping ID for this example.

Since you have not entered any shipping addresses for Mary Wortham yet, Accounts Receivable does not recognize 1210MH. So, Accounts Receivable asks:

ADDRESS NOT FOUND
ADD (Y/N).

❖ Accept the **Y** default and press [ENTER].

On this new screen, enter the following information.

Name	Tenant/Mary Wortham
Address	1210 Marietta Highway
Address	Building 1
City, ST	Marietta, GA
ZIP Code	30062
Telephone	555-9436

Remember, press [ENTER] to move around the screen.

❖ Press [F10] when you have entered all the shipping information and you are certain it is correct.

Accounts Receivable asks, *ACCEPT (Y/N)*.

❖ Accept the **Y** default and press ▇▇▇.

The cursor returns to Shipping ID. If Mary Wortham had additional shipping addresses, you could continue to enter them now. (You must assign a unique shipping ID to each shipping address a customer has.)

Note: Shipping addresses can be entered using either **Maintain Customers** or **Maintain Ship-to Addresses** in Accounts Receivable. (Use **Maintain Customers** when both account information and shipping addresses for a customer must be entered. Use **Maintain Ship-to Addresses** when only shipping addresses are needed.) In Invoicing, shipping addresses can be entered using **Maintain Ship-to Addresses**.

❖ Press ▇▇▇ to tell Accounts Receivable you are finished entering shipping addresses.

The screen clears; A/R asks for another customer ID.

Step 2: Change Customer Information

W.D. Peachtree has decided to increase Darryl Tracer's credit limit to $3,000 and to offer him better terms on his account. In addition, Mr. Tracer travels often and for long periods of time. So, W.D. Peachtree has decided to remove dunning notices from his statements. Step 2 helps you make these changes to Darryl Tracer's account.

To make changes to a customer's account information, you will use **Maintain Customers**, the program you are already using.

❖ Enter **TRACED**, Darryl Tracer's customer ID. (Be sure to use all capital letters.)

Any time you want to display a customer's account information, just enter his or her ID. Accounts Receivable displays the customer's account information on your screen.

Notice that, for Darryl Tracer, Accounts Receivable displays information in the Debit, Credit, Payments, and Service Charges fields. As transactions were entered on his account, Accounts Receivable updated each of these fields.

❖ Make the following changes to Darryl Tracer's account. (Hint: Do not accept Y at the prompt.)

Terms Code	4
Dunning Notices	N
Credit Limit	3000.00

Use ▇▇ or ▇▇▇ to move the cursor to these fields.

In Accounts Receivable, a credit limit does not prohibit you from entering a customer's transactions. If a customer reaches his credit limit while you are adding a debit transaction, Accounts Receivable simply displays a message asking if you want to continue with the transaction.

❖ When you have entered all the correct information, press [F9].

Accounts Receivable asks, *ACCEPT (Y/N)*.

❖ Accept the **Y** default and press [ENTER].

Accounts Receivable prints the control report shown on the next page and then asks, *EDIT BALANCE FORWARD AGEING (Y/N)*.

A/R allows the definition of two types of customers: Balance Forward and Regular. (Account Type determines whether a customer's account is Balance Forward (B) or Regular (R).) After the period, Accounts Receivable keeps transaction detail for Regular customers. For Balance Forward customers, though, Accounts Receivable discards transaction detail; instead, Accounts Receivable calculates an account balance and keeps ageing information. So, whenever a Balance Forward customer's account information is changed, Accounts Receivable will ask if his ageing information should be edited.

You do not need to make any changes to Darryl Tracer's ageing, but you should review that information just for practice.

❖ Type **Y** and press [ENTER].

Accounts Receivable displays the Balance Forward Ageing screen for Darryl Tracer.

❖ When you are finished reviewing Darryl's ageing, press [F9].

Accounts Receivable asks, *ACCEPT (Y/N)*.

❖ Accept the **Y** default and press [ENTER].

A/R prints a control report and ageing information.

Accounts Receivable asks for another customer ID.

```
RUN DATE:  11/30/92              W. D. Peachtree & Company              Page 2
RUN TIME:  10:38  AM                Accounts Receivable
                    MAINTAIN CUSTOMER CONTROL REPORT - CHANGE
-------------------------------------------------------------------------------
                              NEW VALUE                    OLD VALUE
                              ----------------             ----------------

Customer ID............:      TRACED
Cust. Name       ......:      Darryl Tracer                Darryl Tracer
Address 1        ......:      990 Benson Drive             990 Benson Drive
Address 2        ......:      Apt. 5                       Apt. 5
City, State      .....:       Atlanta, GA                  Atlanta, GA
Zip Code         .....:       30303                        30303
Telephone        ......:      404/555-1212                 404/555-1212
Contact          .......:     Darryl Tracer                Darryl Tracer
Salesperson      .......:     GMC                          GMC
Customer Class   .......:     A                            A
Account Type     .......:     B                            B
Service Chg Code ....:        1                            1
Terms Code       ......:      4                            2
Sales Tax Code   .....:       001                          001
Discount Percent ......:         0.00                         0.00
Ship Addresses   ......:      N                            N
Dunning Notices  ......:      N                            Y
Credit Limit     ......:          3,000.00                     2,700.00
Print Statements.......:      Y                            Y
Print Invoices ..........:    Y                            Y
Last Debit Date  .......:     11/05/92                     11/05/92
Last Debit Amt   ........:        250.00                       250.00
YTD Debit Amt    .......:       1,475.00                     1,475.00
Last Credit Date .......:     01/01/00                     01/01/00
Last Credit Amt. .......:          0.00                         0.00
YTD Credit Amt.........:           0.00                         0.00
Last Paymt Date.......:       01/01/00                     01/01/00
Last Paymt Amt........:            0.00                         0.00
YTD Payment Amt ...:               0.00                         0.00
Last S.C. Date..........:     01/01/00                     01/01/00
Last S.C. Amt..........:           0.00                         0.00
YTD S.C. Amt ..........:           0.00                         0.00


Balance Forward Ageing Information:

Current.....................:     250.00                       250.00
 1 - 30 Days............:         125.00                       125.00
31 - 60 Days............:       1,100.00                     1,100.00
Over 60 Days...........:           0.00                         0.00

*** End Of - Maintain Customers Control Report ***
```

❖ You have entered all your new customers and made all your changes to your existing customers' accounts, so press 🔲 to tell Accounts Receivable you are finished with **Maintain Customers**.

Step 3: Review the Control Report

Any time changes are made to the receivables information, the printed copy of the changes should be checked. Even though you may think your entries were all correct, you may discover errors when reviewing a printed copy.

As information for a customer in **Maintain Customers** is entered or changed, Accounts Receivable prints a control report listing the customer's account information. Check the control report for Mary and Darryl. Compare the information listed on the report to the information listed in Steps 1 and 2. If you see an error, return to **Maintain Customers** to make the necessary changes. (In Step 2, you made changes to Darryl Tracer's account. If you have trouble making corrections, review this lesson.) Remember, even though you are following a practice example, it is important that you enter the correct information.

Lesson 1: Summary

In this lesson, you learned how to add a new customer and how to change account information for an existing customer. To accomplish both tasks, you used **Maintain Customers**. Before you can enter transactions for a new customer, you must enter him or her into Accounts Receivable. Before you enter transactions for an existing customer, you should make any necessary changes to his or her account.

In this lesson, you also learned how to add shipping addresses for a customer in **Maintain Customers**. You learned when to use **Maintain Ship-to Addresses** and when to use **Maintain Customers** to complete that task. Finally, you learned to review control reports when you are finished with any task.

Lesson 2: Enter a New Automatic Transaction

In this lesson, you will learn how to set up an automatic transaction. An automatic transaction is a specific transaction made to a customer's account on a regular interval and for a set number of times. Each time the transaction occurs, it is for the same amount and has the same invoice terms. Since these transactions are exactly the same, Accounts Receivable can generate them for you automatically. This lesson teaches you how to set up an automatic transaction for Bill Parker's maintenance agreement.

Bill Parker has purchased a two year maintenance agreement for his W.D. Peachtree trash compactor. W.D. Peachtree charges customers a fixed fee every month for maintenance agreements. Since maintenance agreements are for a fixed amount and for a set interval, they can be handled by Accounts Receivable as automatic transactions.

To have Accounts Receivable handle a transaction automatically, you must know:

- The amount of the transaction. (For Bill Parker, it is $7.50.)

- How frequently the transaction should be made: weekly; bi-weekly; once a month; once every two months; once a quarter; twice a year; or once a year. (Bill should be billed every month.)

- For how many periods the transaction should be made. (Bill Parker purchased a two year maintenance agreement, so his transaction should be made 24 times, the number of months he will be billed.)

To set up automatic transactions, you must use **Maintain Automatic Transactions**.

❖ Select **Maintain Automatic Transactions** from the Accounts Receivable Maintenance Menu.

Accounts Receivable reminds you to make sure you paper is at the top of a new page.

❖ Make sure your printer is ready, then press 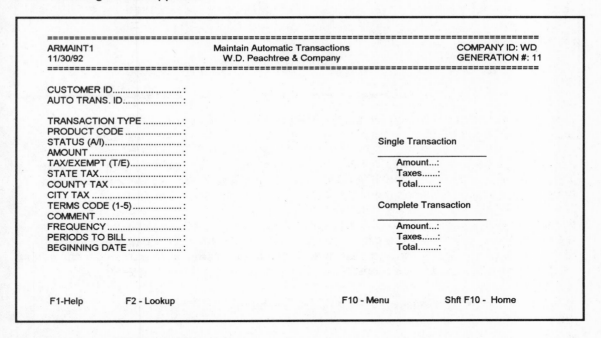.

The following screen appears:

```
===============================================================================
ARMAINT1                    Maintain Automatic Transactions          COMPANY ID: WD
11/30/92                       W.D. Peachtree & Company               GENERATION #: 11
===============================================================================

CUSTOMER ID..........................:
AUTO TRANS. ID.......................:

TRANSACTION TYPE ...............:
PRODUCT CODE .....................:
STATUS (A/I)...........................:              Single Transaction
AMOUNT ................................:            _____
TAX/EXEMPT (T/E)..................:                   Amount...:
STATE TAX............................:                Taxes......:
COUNTY TAX .........................:                 Total........:
CITY TAX ..............................:
TERMS CODE (1-5)..................:              Complete Transaction
COMMENT ..............................:            _____
FREQUENCY ..........................:                Amount...:
PERIODS TO BILL ....................:                Taxes......:
BEGINNING DATE ...................:                  Total........:



F1-Help        F2 - Lookup                F10 - Menu        Shft F10 - Home
```

The cursor is at Customer ID.

❖ Enter **PARKEB**, Bill Parker's customer ID. (Be sure to use all capital letters.)

The cursor moves to Auto Trans. ID. Accounts Receivable identifies a customer's automatic transactions using automatic transaction IDs. Bill Parker does not have any automatic transactions, so you will be entering his first automatic transaction.

❖ Enter **1** for Auto Trans. ID (for his first).

Since Bill Parker does not have any automatic transactions, Accounts Receivable asks,

> *AUTOMATIC TRANSACTION NOT FOUND.*
> *ADD (Y/N).:Y*

❖ Accept the **Y** default and press ⬛.

❖ Enter the following information for Bill Parker:

Transaction Type	MD
Product Code	M
Status (A/I)	A
Amount	7.50
Tax/Exempt	E
Terms Code (1-5)	1
Comment	Trash C.

In some states, such as Georgia, maintenance agreements which involve only labor are tax exempt; Bill Parker purchased a maintenance agreement that involves only labor.

Notice that, when you entered E for Tax/Exempt, Accounts Receivable skipped over State Tax, County Tax, and City Tax. If you had entered T instead, Accounts Receivable would have automatically calculated the state, county, and city tax for the transaction.

Notice that when you move the cursor to Terms Code, Accounts Receivable displays 4 as the terms code. Whenever you enter transactions for a customer, Accounts Receivable always displays the terms code you assigned to him in **Maintain Customers**. You can enter a different terms code or just accept the code displayed.

❖ When the cursor is at Frequency, press ⬛, the look-up key.

Accounts Receivable displays the possible entries you can make for Frequency. For Accounts Receivable to handle a transaction automatically, the transaction must occur with one of the listed frequencies.

❖ Since Bill Parker's maintenance agreement requires him to pay a monthly fee, select **M** for monthly. (You can select an entry by using ⬛ or ⬛ to move the cursor to the appropriate selection. Then, press ⬛.)

The cursor moves to Periods to Bill.

Bill Parker's maintenance agreement is for two years, so Accounts Receivable should generate his transaction once each month for the next 24 months.

❖ Enter **24** for Periods to Bill.

The cursor moves to Beginning Date.

❖ Bill Parker's maintenance agreement begins this period, so accept **11/30/92** for Beginning Date.

Notice that after you enter the beginning date for the transaction, Accounts Receivable calculates the total for a single transaction ($7.50) and the total for all transactions ($180.00).

❖ Press 🔲 when you are certain all the transaction information you have entered is correct. Then, accept the automatic transaction.

Accounts Receivable prints the following control report for your entry. Then, the screen clears and the cursor moves to Auto Trans. ID. Press 🔲 and the cursor moves to Customer ID.

RUN DATE: 11/30/92					W. D. Peachtree & Company								PAGE 1
RUN TIME: 2:33 PM					Accounts Receivable								
					Automatic Transactions Control Report								

CUST. ID	TRN. #	TRN. TYPE	PROD CODE	STAT	TRANS. AMOUNT	T/E	STATE TAX	COUNTY TAX	CITY TAX	TRMS CODE	COMMENT	FRQ	BILL PRDS	START DATE
PARKEB	1	MD	M	A	7.50	E	0.00	0.00	0.00	1	Trash C.	M	24	11/30/92

*** END OF Automatic Transactions Control Report ***

❖ Review the control report. Make sure the information you entered is correct. If necessary, re-enter Bill Parker's ID and his automatic transaction ID so you can edit the information you entered.

❖ While the cursor is at Customer ID, press 🔲 to tell Accounts Receivable you are finished with **Maintain Automatic Transactions**.

❖ Press 🔲🔲 to return to the PCA Main Menu.

Lesson 2: Summary

In this lesson, you learned how to set up a transaction so that it is handled automatically by Accounts Receivable. Before you can generate any automatic transactions, you must enter the automatic transaction into **Maintain Automatic Transactions**.

Remember, Accounts Receivable can process a transaction automatically only if it is for a set amount, for a specific length of time, and at a regular interval.

In this lesson, you were also reminded how to use 🔲 to view a list of possible entries. Remember, you can use 🔲 only when you see *F2 - LOOKUP* at the bottom of the screen.

Topic 2: Daily Tasks

Daily tasks are the tasks that must be performed to enter customers' transactions. The volume of receivables business determines how often a company will complete daily tasks. In a business, these tasks may be performed once a day, twice a day, or only once a week.

Topic 2 has four lessons; they concentrate on entering customer transactions. In this topic, you will:

1. Enter and print invoices in Invoicing.
2. Enter a down payment and correct a sale transaction in Accounts Receivable.
3. Make a payment.
4. Print a list of all the customer transactions you entered.

Lesson 1 explains how to record customer transactions and produce invoices.

Lesson 2 explains how to enter a down payment into Accounts Receivable. Since sooner or later you will need to correct transaction errors, this lesson also explains how to enter offsetting and correcting transactions. Finally, this lesson explains how to generate an automatic transaction.

Lesson 3 helps you enter a customer's payment. This lesson explains how to review a customer's account as well as how early payment discounts work.

Lesson 4 shows you how to print a list of all the customer transactions you entered in this topic.

Note: Unlike maintenance tasks, the order in which you perform daily tasks is very important. So, complete the lessons in the order described.

Lesson 1: Producing Customer Invoices

To produce an invoice for a customer, you must complete up to four different steps:

1. Enter and print the invoice.
2. If necessary, edit the invoice and reprint it.
3. Print the Invoice Register.
4. Post the invoice.

This lesson covers all these steps.

Step 1: Enter and Print an Invoice.

Mary Wortham purchased two trash compactors. She wants them delivered and installed, so you will need to enter her sale as well as her delivery and installation charges.

❖ From the PCA Main Menu, select **Invoicing**.

❖ Then, from the Invoicing Main Menu, select **Processing Programs**. Finally, select **Enter Invoices**.

Invoicing asks, *PROCESS REPEATING INVOICES (Y/N)*.

❖ Accept the **N** default and press [ENTER].

Next, Invoicing allows you to select the type of invoice you will enter: Current or Repeating. Like Accounts Receivable, Invoicing allows you to set up repeating invoices; once you set up these invoices, Invoicing can generate them for you automatically.

Mary's purchase was a one-time transaction; so, you will enter a current invoice.

❖ Select **Current Invoice**.

Invoicing asks, *PRINT INVOICE ALIGNMENT GUIDE (Y/N)*.

Using **Enter Invoices**, you can print each invoice you enter as you enter it. (Or, you can use **Print Invoices** to print all the invoices you entered but have not yet posted.)

❖ Since you are not using invoice forms for this lesson, you do not need to print an alignment guide so type **N** and press [ENTER].

Invoicing asks, *INVOICE OR CREDIT MEMO (I/C)*.

Invoicing allows you to enter both invoices and credit memos. The only difference between a credit memo and an invoice is the title: invoices have "Invoice" printed on them and credit memos have "Credit Memo" printed on them.

❖ Select **Invoice**.

Invoicing displays Invoice Date and lists the current system date—that date should be 11/30/92. The invoice date is the date Invoicing prints on the invoice and uses to calculate the discount date and due date for the invoice.

❖ Mary made her purchase on **11/29/92**, so enter that date. Then, accept your entries.

Finally, Invoicing displays the Process Options pop up box. As you know already, a pop up box is simply a box that appears on your screen and allows you to select from a list of options. From the Process Options pop up box, you can:

- Add an invoice.
- Edit an invoice.
- Cancel an invoice.

❖ Select **Add Invoice**.

The following screen appears:

```
================================================================================
SIPROC1                              Enter Invoices                    COMPANY ID: WD
11/30/92                        W.D. Peachtree & Company
================================================================================
INVOICE NUMBER ........:  023549      Current Invoices                    Add Inv.

CUSTOMER ID:

SOLD TO:                                      SHIP TO:



P. O. NUMBER.......:                          SALES
P. O. DATE ............:                       TAX:
SALESMAN ............:
TERMS CODE .......:
SHIP DATE ............:
SHIPPED VIA .........:
JOB/ORDER NO....:




F1-Help         F2 - Lookup
```

To enter an invoice for a customer, you must first enter a customer ID. Remember, you assigned WORTHM as Mary Wortham's ID in the Maintenance Task lessons.

❖ Enter Mary Wortham's customer ID.

Notice that Invoicing automatically assigns an invoice number to this invoice. W.D. Peachtree has set up Accounts Receivable to assign invoice numbers automatically.

Invoicing displays Mary's address for the sold-to address. The cursor is at Ship-To ID. Enter 1210MH.

Invoicing displays the ship-to address. The cursor is on the first line of that address.

❖ Press ⌨ at each line of the ship-to address.

Enter the following information for Mary's invoice:

P.O. Date	11/29/92
Salesman	Trudy
Terms Code	2
Ship Date	12/02/92
Shipped Via	Roadway
Sales Tax Code	001

Just leave all other fields blank (for this exercise).

❖ Press 【F10】 to tell Invoicing you are finished entering information on this screen. Then, accept the information you have entered.

The screen clears. On this new screen, Invoicing allows you to enter, line by line, the transactions for the customer's invoice.

For Mary Wortham, you will need to enter three different transactions:

- The sale of two trash compactors.
- Freight for delivery of the items.
- A charge for the installation.

Each of these transactions has a different transaction type assigned to it. (A transaction type is just a two-letter code that makes it faster and easier for you to enter transactions. The transaction types used in Invoicing are the same as the ones used in Accounts Receivable.) The transaction type for the sale is SA.

❖ While the cursor is at Typ, enter **SA**.

W.D Peachtree uses all the PCA modules, so Invoicing helps with the selling and returning of Inventory items. When the cursor is at any of the following fields, you can press 【F2】 to display a list of possible entries for inventory items:

- Product ID
- Prod CD
- Price CD

If W.D. Peachtree did not use Inventory, then you could not have used 【F2】 to look up this inventory information. Instead, you would have had to enter this information yourself.

❖ Press 【F2】 while the cursor is at Product ID.

Invoicing displays a list of possible inventory items and their product IDs.

❖ Move the cursor down to select the trash compactor (**APP1400040TRA**) and press 【ENTER】.

Invoicing displays the trash compactor description.

❖ Accept the displayed description.

Invoicing displays the trash compactor product code.

❖ Accept the displayed product code (A).

Now, Invoicing displays the unit of measure for the trash compactor.

❖ Accept the displayed unit of measure as well (EACH). Then, enter **2** for Quantity Ordered.

Invoicing assumes you will ship the number of items ordered, so it displays 2 for Quantity Shipped.

❖ Press ⌨ to accept 2 as the number of trash compactors shipped.

❖ Press [F2] to select the price code for the trash compactors.

Invoicing displays the possible prices for the item. (This information was entered into Inventory.)

❖ Select **A**, $499.99, as the price of the item.

Invoicing displays the price selected.

❖ Accept the displayed price. Then, enter **10** for the discount percent (Disc Pct).

For new customers, W.D. Peachtree offers a 10 percent discount on the first purchase.

❖ Enter **T** to let Invoicing know the sale transaction is taxable.

Invoicing calculates the net amount of the transaction ($899.98) and asks, *ACCEPT (Y/N)*.

❖ Accept the sale transaction.

The cursor moves to Typ for the next transaction. Invoicing allows an unlimited number of transactions per invoice to be entered.

Now that you have entered the trash compactor sale, you need to enter the delivery (freight of $20) and installation charges in the amount of $25. (Both are tax exempt transactions.)

❖ Enter the following transactions exactly as shown.

Typ	FR
Misc. Comment	DELIVERY CHARGES
Amount	20.00
T/E	E
Typ	MD
Prod CD	D
Misc. Comment	INSTALLATION CHARGES
Amount	25.00
T/E	E

Notice that you entered different information for the freight (FR) and miscellaneous debit (MD) transactions than you did for the sale transaction. Invoicing asks only for the information it needs to process the transaction.

❖ After you have entered and accepted all three transactions for Mary Wortham, press [F2].

Invoicing calculates the subtotal, tax, and total amounts of the invoice. Then, Invoicing asks, *INVOICE COMPLETE (Y/N)*.

Notice the bottom of your screen. While the *INVOICE COMPLETE* prompt is on your screen, you can press:

F1	For help.
F5	To list all the lines of the invoice.
F6	To add more transactions to the invoice.
F7	To edit any of the lines of the invoice.
F8	To delete any lines from the invoice.

❖ Accept the **Y** default and press **ENTER** to tell Invoicing the invoice is complete.

Invoicing asks, *PRINT INVOICE (Y/N)*.

In this lesson, this is the only invoice that will be entered. So, it is easier for you to print the invoice here through **Enter Invoices** than through **Print Invoices**.

❖ Type **Y** and press **ENTER** to tell Invoicing to print the invoice.

❖ Make sure your printer is ready, then press **ENTER**.

Invoicing prompts for the Invoice Format: Standard, Sales, Service, or Customized.

❖ Select **Standard Invoice** for the product sales layout.

Invoicing prints the following invoice you just entered. The screen clears and the cursor returns to Customer ID.

```
┌─────────────────────────────────────────────────────────────────────────┐
│                                                      **********          │
│  W. D. Peachtree & Company                           *        *          │
│  3900 Peachtree Street                             *  I N V O I C E  *    │
│  Atlanta, GA 30309                                   *        *          │
│                                                      **********          │
│                                                                          │
│                                        Invoice Number:  023549           │
│                                                                          │
│                                          Invoice Date:  11/29/92         │
│                                                                          │
│                                                 Page:   1                │
│                                                                          │
│  Sold  Mary Wortham                 Ship   Tenet/Mary Wortham            │
│  To:   5310 Roswell Road            To:    1210 Marietta Highway         │
│        Apartment 3-G                       Building 1                     │
│        Atlanta, GA                         Marietta, GA                   │
│               30316                                 30062                 │
│                                                                          │
│                                     Cust I.D..........:  WORTHM           │
│  Ship Via....: Roadway              P.O. Number..:                        │
│  Ship Date: 12/02/92                P.O. Date.......:  11/29/92           │
│  Due Date.: 12/29/92                Job/Order No.  :                      │
│  Terms......: NET 30                Salesperson ...:  Trudy               │
│                                                                          │
│  Item I.D./Desc.      Ordered    Shipped    Unit   Price     Net    TX    │
│  ----------------------------------------------------------------------   │
│  APP1400040TRA          2.00       2.00    EACH   499.9900  999.98   T    │
│     TRASH COMPACTOR                                                       │
│  Discount On Above                                           100.00-      │
│                                                                          │
│  DELIVERY CHARGES                                             20.00   E   │
│                                                                          │
│  INSTALLATION CHARGES                                         25.00   E   │
│                                                                          │
│                                     Subtotal ..:            944.98        │
│                                     Tax .........:          54.00         │
│                                     Total .......:         998.98         │
└─────────────────────────────────────────────────────────────────────────┘
```

Step 2: Edit an Invoice.

Review the invoice you just printed. Notice the freight transaction. W.D. Peachtree charges customers $20.00 per appliance delivered. Since Mary bought two trash compactors, you need to charge her $40.00 for freight. So, you will have to edit this invoice.

Remember, **Enter Invoices** allows you to:

- Add a new invoice.
- Edit an existing, unposted invoice.
- Cancel an existing, unposted invoice.

You are already in **Enter Invoices**, so you just need to return to the Process Options pop up box, the pop up box that lets you choose from these options.

❖ While the cursor is at Customer ID, press ⌨️[ESC].

The Process Options pop up box appears.

❖ Select **Edit Invoice**.

The cursor returns to Invoice Number.

❖ Press ⌨️[F2] to see a list of possible unposted invoices. Select the invoice for Mary Wortham.

❖ The program displays a warning box. Press ⌨️[ENTER] to continue.

You could make changes to the invoice header information by typing **N** at the ACCEPT (Y/N) prompt.

❖ Press ⌨️[ENTER] to accept the screen with the invoice header information.

Invoicing displays the transactions you entered for this invoice and displays the message:

END OF INVOICE - SELECT NEXT FUNCTION

❖ Press ⌨️[F7] to tell Invoicing you want to edit one of the lines of the invoice.

Invoicing displays the message:

ENTER THE NUMBER OF THE LINE TO EDIT.

❖ Enter line number **2** for the freight transaction.

(Invoicing lists the line number of a transaction in the column labeled "LN.")

The cursor is at Misc. Comment. Change the description to "DELIVERY CHARGES - FOR TWO UNITS." Then press ⌨️[ENTER] and the cursor moves to amount.

❖ Enter **$40.00** as the amount. (The transaction will still be tax exempt.)

Invoicing asks, *ACCEPT (Y/N)*.

❖ Accept the transaction.

Invoicing again displays the message:

ENTER THE NUMBER OF THE LINE TO EDIT.

❖ Press 【F10】 to tell Invoicing you are finished editing transactions.

❖ Tell Invoicing the transaction is complete, then reprint the invoice. The program displays a warning box informing you that the invoice has already been printed. Type **Y** and press 【ENTER】 to continue.

The screen clears; the cursor returns to Invoice Number.

Review the invoice you just printed; make sure the new information you entered is correct. If necessary, re-edit the invoice.

❖ When you have a correct, printed invoice, press 【ESC】 and 【F10】 to tell Invoicing you are finished adding, entering, and canceling invoices.

The Invoicing Processing Menu returns.

❖ Press 【ESC】 to return to the Invoicing Main Menu.

Step 3: Print Invoices.

Generally, when invoices are entered, more than just one invoice are entered at a time. So, invoices will probably be printed in a group rather than one at a time. In this step, you will print the invoice you entered for Mary Wortham as well as several other invoices already entered for you.

❖ From the Invoicing Main Menu, select **Report Programs**. Then, select **Print Invoices**.

❖ Press 【ENTER】 when the program prompts "Do you want to allow other programs to update your Invoicing files while invoices are being printed?"

Invoicing allows you to print current, posted, or backorder invoices.

❖ Select **Current Invoices**.

You can print all invoices or just a range of invoices.

❖ Select **All Invoices**.

There are three invoice formats -- Standard Sales, Service, and Customized.

❖ Select **Standard Invoice**.

Invoicing asks, *PRINT ALIGNMENT GUIDE (Y/N)*. If you were using preprinted invoices, you would probably want to print an alignment guide so you could make sure your invoice forms were properly aligned in your printer. But, here you are not using invoice forms.

❖ Type **N** and press 【ENTER】.

Invoicing prints all the unposted invoices; the Invoicing Reports Menu returns.

Step 4: Print the Invoice Register.

Before invoices are posted, the Invoice Register should always be printed. This report lists the transactions entered from all unposted invoices; it serves as an archive of Invoicing activities.

❖ From the Invoicing Report Programs, select **Invoice Register**.

❖ Make sure your printer is at the top of a new page. Then, press ▣.

Invoicing asks for the report date and displays the current tutorial date.

A report date is simply the date Invoicing prints on the report. Both Accounts Receivable and Invoicing ask for a report date any time a report is printed. For the most part, report dates are not used for calculations.

❖ Press ▣ to accept the displayed report date.

Invoicing prints the Invoice Register. The Invoicing Reports Menu returns.

❖ Press ▣ to return to the Invoicing Main Menu.

Review the Invoice Register. Notice that it does not list each individual transaction you entered. Instead, the Invoice Register organizes the transactions into four groups:

- Merchandise/Services
- Other Charges
- Freight
- Sales Tax

The sale of the trash compactors is listed under Merchandise/Services; the installation charges are listed under Other Charges; the freight is listed under Freight; and, the sales tax on the sale is listed under Sales Tax.

Notice, also, that the Invoice Register contains a Report Summary Totals section. This section totals the taxable and non-taxable transactions for all the unposted invoices.

Step 5: Post Invoices.

The final step in processing the customers' invoices is to post the invoice transactions to the customers' accounts. Invoices should be posted only after you have:

- Corrected any invoice errors.
- Printed all invoices.
- Printed the Invoice Register.

When invoices are posted, Invoicing posts the transactions from the invoices to the customers' accounts. It also clears the Invoice Register. As a result, this report must be printed before invoices are posted.

If the Accounts Receivable, Invoicing, and Inventory modules are all used by a company, then posting invoices also updates Inventory. Invoicing reduces the quantity on hand for each item sold in Invoicing and increases the quantity on hand for each item returned in Invoicing. (Sales or returns entered into Accounts Receivable do not affect Inventory.)

❖ From the Invoicing Main Menu, select **Processing Programs**. Then, select **Post Invoices**.

❖ Next, the program asks whether you want to Post Current Invoices or Delete Previously Posted Invoices. Select **Post Current Invoices**.

The program allows you to post all invoices, a range of invoice dates, or a range of invoice numbers.

❖ Select **All Invoices.**

Next, the program recommends a backup, tells the user that the posting of invoices will preclude editing those invoices, and asks user to select *POST INVOICES (Y/N): N.*

❖ Type **Y** and press [ENTER] to post all W.D. Peachtree invoices.

Invoicing posts all unposted invoices and prints the following control report.

```
RUN DATE:  11/30/92                              W. D. Peachtree & Company                         PAGE 1
RUN TIME:  11:52 AM                                   Sales Invoicing
                                                 Post Invoices Control Report
------------------------------------------------------------------------------------------------------------
Inv #   Inv Date   Cust ID    Customer Name      Invoice Amount   Item ID          Type   UOM    Number Posted   Status   Job
------  --------   -------    -------------      --------------   -------          ----   ---    -------------   ------   ---

023545 11/08/92   COOPEG     Gloria S. Cooper        72.11
                                                                  P CLC 463487G    SA     EACH        3.00         ok
                                                                  P CLC 463444     SA     PAIR        5.00         ok
                                                                  P CLC 436781G    SA     PAIR        2.00         ok
023546 11/08/92   HENDEK     Kathy Henderson        437.88
                                                                  P ELE 810544CDP  SA     EACH        1.00         ok
023547 11/08/92   MILLEJ     Joel S. Miller         158.95
                                                                  P APP 10040TRA   SA     EACH        1.00         ok
023549 11/29/92   WORTHM     Mary Wortham         1,018.98
                                                                  P APP 1400040TRA SA     EACH        2.00         ok


Totals.:  Number of Invoices =        4  Amount =      1,687.92
Update to Job Cost = N at time of posting.


                *** End of Post Invoices Control Report ***
```

Then, the Invoicing Processing Menu returns.

❖ Press [SHIFT] [F10] to return to the PCA Main Menu.

Lesson 1: Summary

In this lesson, you learned how to enter, edit, post, and print invoices. You learned how to print invoices from both **Enter Invoices** and **Print Invoices**.

This lesson taught you how and when to print an Invoice Register. Whenever you enter invoices, be sure to print this report and, in particular, to print it before you post invoices.

Lesson 2: Entering Transactions

Since W.D. Peachtree uses both Accounts Receivable and Invoicing, the lessons in this session have you enter into Accounts Receivable only those transactions that should not appear on an invoice since Invoicing handles all of the other information automatically. If W.D. Peachtree did not use Invoicing, then you would have to enter all customer transactions directly into A/R.

Accounts Receivable does not produce invoices. So, when you enter a transaction into Accounts Receivable, those transactions cannot appear on invoices. They do, however, appear on customer statements. (Transactions entered into Invoicing appear on both invoices and statements.)

When a transaction is entered into Accounts Receivable, it is automatically posted to the customer's account. You do not need to post transactions entered into Accounts Receivable.

In this lesson you will learn how to use Accounts Receivable to enter customers' transactions. You will:

1. Generate an automatic transaction—Bill Parker's maintenance agreement.

2. Enter a down payment—Mary Wortham's down payment on her trash compactors.

3. Make a correction to a sale transaction.

Step 1: Generate an Automatic Transaction

Assume that it is time to bill Bill Parker for the first installment of his maintenance agreement. You have already set up his maintenance agreement as an automatic transaction, so all you need to do is generate that transaction.

❖ From the PCA Main Menu, select **Accounts Receivable**. Then, select **Processing Programs** and, finally, **Enter Transactions**.

❖ Make sure your printer is ready, then press ⌨️.

Accounts Receivable displays Transaction Date and lists the current tutorial date. The date you enter here becomes the default date Accounts Receivable displays for all the transactions you enter.

❖ Accept the displayed date.

Accounts Receivable asks, *GENERATE AUTOMATIC TRANSACTIONS? (Y/N)*

❖ Enter **Y**.

Accounts Receivable prints the first part of a control report.

When automatic transactions are generated, Accounts Receivable reviews each automatic transaction set up in **Maintain Automatic Transactions**. For Accounts Receivable to generate a transaction:

- The automatic transaction must be active (Status = A).
- The beginning date of the automatic transaction must be on or before the transaction date just entered.

When Accounts Receivable generates a transaction, it posts a transaction to the customer's account based on the information entered for the automatic transaction. So, when you generate Bill Parker's maintenance agreement, Accounts Receivable will post a $7.50 miscellaneous debit to his account.

No matter how often you generate transactions, Accounts Receivable never generates a transaction more frequently than specified by the automatic transaction.

Accounts Receivable displays the message:

AUTO TRANSACTIONS COMPLETE. 1 TRANSACTIONS GENERATED
PRESS 'ENTER'

❖ Press ⌨.

The screen clears. The cursor is at Customer ID.

Step 2: Enter a Down Payment

After Mary Wortham ordered her trash compactors, she made a down payment on her purchase. You have already entered her sale into Invoicing. In this step, you will enter her down payment.

❖ Enter Mary Wortham's customer ID.

If you do not remember her ID, use ⌨ to look it up. Use ⌨ to find her ID.

Accounts Receivable displays Mary Wortham's name, account balance, and credit limit. The cursor is at Trans. Type.

Accounts Receivable doesn't have a down payment transaction, so W.D. Peachtree uses a payment transaction (Transaction Type = PA) for down payments.

❖ Enter **PA** for the transaction type.

The cursor moves to Product Code.

❖ Press ⌨ to leave the Product Code blank.

The following screen appears:

```
================================================================================
ARPROC                              Enter Transactions              COMPANY ID: WD
11/30/92                        W.D. Peachtree & Company             GENERATION #: 11
================================================================================
CUSTOMER ID:   WORTHM      Mary Wortham                    Balance:          1018.98
Trans. Type.:  PA    Payment                               Credit Limit:     2500.00
Product Code:        PAYMENT

Invoice     Terms      Terms          Trans.      Due      Discount    Trans.                      T
Number      Code       Description     Date       Date      Date       Amount      Comment         E
----------  ---------  -------------  ---------  --------  ---------  ----------   ----------      ---

                                              State Tax....:           0.00
                                              County Tax.:             0.00
                                              City Tax......:          0.00
                                                                   _____
                                              Invoice Total:           0.00




F1-Help        F2 - Lookup                                F10 - Done                   C
```

To post a transaction to an already existing invoice (the trash compactor invoice in Lesson 1), you just enter the number of that invoice.

❖ Use ⌨ to select Mary Wortham's trash compactor invoice.

The cursor moves to Trans. Date. A/R automatically displays the transaction date you entered when you first entered **Enter Transactions**.

At W.D. Peachtree, transactions are entered in batches rather than as they occur. Accounts Receivable uses the transaction date (along with the invoice terms) to calculate the invoice due date and the discount date.

❖ Mary made her down payment on **11/29/92**; enter that date.

The cursor moves to Trans. Amount.

❖ Enter **$250.00** for Mary's down payment.

❖ Type **Down Paymt** for Comment then press ⌨.

❖ Press ⌨ to tell Accounts Receivable you are finished with the transaction. Then, accept the transaction.

Accounts Receivable lists the transaction on the control report. The screen clears and the cursor returns to Customer ID. The control report appears as follows:

```
RUN DATE: 11/30/92                              W. D. Peachtree & Company                              PAGE 1
RUN TIME: 12:06 PM                                 Accounts Receivable
                                             Enter Transactions Control Report
-------------------------------------------------------------------------------------------------------------
CUST    INV.   TRANSACTION   P    TRANS    DUE     DISC.    E.P.    TRANS              CREDIT   CREDIT   DEBIT   DEBIT
ID      NO       TYPE        C    DATE     DATE    DATE     DISC%   AMOUNT   COMMENT   ACCT     AMOUNT   ACCT    AMOUNT
-------------------------------------------------------------------------------------------------------------
PARKEB  023550  Misc. Debit  M  11/30/92 12/30/92 12/10/92  2.00    7.50    Trash C.   30512    7.50-   12000    7.50

WORTHM  023549  Payment         11/29/92   / /      / /     0.00   250.00-  Down Paymt  12000  250.00-  11000   250.00
                                                                   ==========                ==========       ==========
                                                                     242.50-                   257.50-          257.50
                                                                   ==========                ==========       ==========

*** End Of - Enter Transactions Control Report ***
```

Review the control report; it lists two transactions: the down payment you just entered and the maintenance agreement transaction you generated in Step 1.

Press [F8] to return to the Accounts Receivable Processing Menu.

Step 3: Correct a Transaction Error

Suppose Mary Wortham tells you that you have charged her $30 too much for each of the two trash compactors sold to her on invoice 023549. Since invoices have been posted and mailed, you need to correct in Accounts Receivable (unless the customer needs a credit memo mailed to them).

Follow these instructions to correct the error:

❖ Select **Enter Transactions**. Then type in 11/30/92 as the transaction date.

❖ Answer "N" to Generate Automatic Transaction.

❖ Enter Mary Wortham's customer ID.

❖ Enter **MC** for the transaction type (miscellaneous credit).

To correct a sales error such as the one in this example, you use a miscellaneous credit.

❖ Type **A** and press [ENTER] at Product Code.

❖ Enter the number for Mary's trash compactor invoice. (If you do not remember it, use [F2].)

❖ Accept the displayed date as the transaction date.

❖ Enter **60.00** for the credit amount.

❖ Enter "Correction" as comment.

❖ Accept **T** to indicate that the original transaction was taxable and PCA will add sales tax to the credit.

❖ Press 💾 to tell Accounts Receivable you are finished entering this transaction. Then, accept the transaction.

Accounts Receivable prints the transaction on the control report; the cursor returns to Customer ID. Then press 💾 and A/R will complete the control report.

Check your control report. It lists the offsetting credit (for $63.60).

If you made any errors, make the necessary corrections.

❖ Return to the Accounts Receivable Main Menu.

Lesson 2: Summary

In this lesson, you learned how to generate automatic transactions, how to enter transactions, and how to correct transaction errors.

If W.D. Peachtree did not use Invoicing, then you would have entered all the W.D. Peachtree customers' transactions into **Enter Transactions**. You would have entered Mary Wortham's sale, freight, and installation charges as well as her down payment into Accounts Receivable.

Note: Sales and returns entered into Accounts Receivable do not affect Inventory. So, when you use **Enter Transactions** to record sales and returns, you will not enter product identification information. Instead, you just enter the transaction information.

Lesson 3: Enter Payments

An important part of using Accounts Receivable and Invoicing is entering customers' payments. Any of the following programs can be used to enter payments:

- **Apply Payments**
- **Enter Transactions**
- **Enter Invoices**

However, **Apply Payments** is specifically designed for payments and payment related transactions. So, using that program, these transactions can be entered more quickly.

In this lesson you will learn how to:

1. Review customers' accounts.

2. Enter a payment on a Regular account—Bill Parker's pays for a TV he bought ($179.54).

3. Enter a payment on a Balance Forward account—Darryl Tracer makes a payment to his account ($1,000).

Step 1: Review Customer Account

Before you enter Bill Parker's and Darryl Tracer's payments, you should review their accounts. Reviewing their accounts before you enter their payments helps you become familiar with all their invoices.

❖ From the Accounts Receivable Main Menu, select **Processing Programs**. Then, select **Query Customer Accounts**.

The screen clears; the cursor is at Customer ID.

To review a customer's account, you must enter the proper ID.

❖ Enter **TRACED**, Darryl Tracer's customer ID.

Accounts Receivable uses two screens to display a customer's account information.

1. The first screen displays the customer's current balance and address as well as his last and year-to-date payments, credits, debits, and service charges.

2. The second screen displays his account activity.

❖ You need to review Darryl's account activity, so press .

Accounts Receivable displays all Darryl's current open invoices from the lowest numbered invoice to the highest.

❖ When you are finished reviewing Darryl's account activity, press .

The screen clears; the cursor is at Customer ID.

Accounts Receivable asks for another customer ID.

❖ Enter **PARKEB**, Bill Parker's customer ID.

Accounts Receivable displays Bill Parker's account information.

❖ At the *PRESS 'ENTER' TO CONTINUE* prompt, enter **P**.

Accounts Receivable prints a copy of Bill Parker's account information and his account activity. (You could have printed Darryl Tracer's account information also.)

❖ Press 〔ESC〕.

Accounts Receivable asks for another customer ID.

❖ Review all the other customers' accounts. (Use 〔F2〕 if you cannot remember their IDs.) Use 〔PgDn〕 to scroll to later names.

You should notice:

- Since Mary Wortham is a new customer, her account activities include only the information you entered in this chapter.

- Bill Parker's account activities include the maintenance agreement transaction you generated.

- Darryl Tracer's account information includes the changes you made in Topic 1, Maintenance Tasks.

❖ While the cursor is at Customer ID, press 〔F10〕 to return to the Accounts Receivable Processing Menu.

Step 2: Enter a Payment to a Regular Account

Bill Parker bought a TV several days ago. W.D. Peachtree offers customers a discount if they pay on or before the invoice discount date. In Accounts Receivable, if a customer pays on or before the discount date, Accounts Receivable automatically includes an early payment discount transaction with the payment transaction.

You have the following information about Bill Parker's payment:

Check Number	1372
Check Amount	179.54
Payment Date	11/30/92

❖ From the Accounts Receivable Processing menu, select **Apply Payments**.

For Regular customers, you can enter any of the following transaction types in this program:

- Adjustment
- Bad Debt Write-off
- Credit
- Early Payment Discount
- Payment

❖ Make sure your printer is ready for the control report; press ⌨.

Accounts Receivable displays Transaction Date and lists the current tutorial date. The date you enter for Transaction Date becomes the date of all the transactions you enter. Unlike in **Enter Transactions**, you cannot change this date.

❖ Assume that both Darryl Tracer and Bill Parker made payments on 11/30/92; so accept the displayed transaction date.

The screen clears; the cursor is at Customer ID.

❖ Enter Bill Parker's customer ID.

Accounts Receivable lists Bill's name and account balance. The cursor is at Reference.

Reference is only for your information; Accounts Receivable does not process the information. W.D. Peachtree always uses the customer's check number as a payment reference, but, in your own business, you might use Reference for something else.

❖ Enter Bill Parker's check number. (See top of this page.) Then, enter the amount of Bill Parker's check.

The following screen appears:

```
========================================================================================
ARPROC                              Apply Payments                      COMPANY ID: WD
11/30/92                        W.D. Peachtree & Company                 GENERATION #: 11
========================================================================================
CUSTOMER ID:   PARKEB          Bill Parker

Reference........:   CK1372              Amount:          179.54        Balance:         206.99
                     Undistributed:                       179.54

Invoice      Due         Trans.       Prod.      Invoice       Amount
Number       Date        Type         Code       Amount        To Apply
-----------  ----------  -----------  ---------  ------------  ------------
023544




F1-Help          F2 - Lookup                                                            C
```

The cursor is at Invoice Number. For Regular customers, you must apply payments to specific invoices.

❖ Press ⌨ to select from a list of his invoices.

Accounts Receivable lists all Bill Parker's debit-balance invoices: a $7.50 invoice (for the maintenance agreement) and a $199.49 invoice (for the TV). Notice the asterisks beside the open invoices.

❖ Select the $199.49 invoice.

Accounts Receivable displays the invoice due date and the invoice amount; the cursor moves to Trans. Type. Since an early payment discount can be taken on the invoice, accept EP (early payment) for the transaction type.

Even though Bill Parker's sale was for $199.49, he was offered a 10% discount if he paid before 12/05/92. So, Bill Parker sent a check for $179.54, the sale total less 10%.

❖ Press ⌨ to accept the early payment transaction type.

The cursor moves to Product Code.

❖ Press ⌨ to leave the Product Code blank.

❖ The cursor moves to Amount to Apply. Press ⌨ to accept $19.95. Then, accept the transaction. Accounts Receivable begins printing a Control Report.

Accounts Receivable displays the invoice due date and invoice amount; then, Accounts Receivable displays PA (Payment) for the transaction type.

❖ Press ⌨ to accept the transaction type.

❖ Press ⌨ to leave the Product Code blank.

The cursor moves to Amount to Apply. Bill Parker's invoice was for $199.49, his discount was for $19.95, so his payment is for $179.54.

Accounts Receivable automatically displays a payment transaction for the check amount.

❖ Accept the amount of Bill Parker's payment.

❖ Accept the transaction.

Accounts Receivable reduces Undistributed to 0.00. (As soon as you enter transactions which reduce Undistributed to zero, Accounts Receivable considers the transaction complete.)

Accounts Receivable asks for another customer ID.

Step 3: Enter a Payment on a Balance Forward Account

Darryl Tracer has made a $1000.00 payment on his account. You have the following information about Darryl's payment:

Check Number	3407
Check Amount	1000.00
Payment Date	11/30/92

❖ Enter Darryl Tracer's customer ID.

❖ Enter his check number and check amount.

The following screen appears:

```
===========================================================================
ARPROC                            Apply Payments                 COMPANY ID: WD
11/30/92                      W.D. Peachtree & Company            GENERATION #: 11
===========================================================================
CUSTOMER ID:   TRACED          Darryl Tracer

Reference........:  CK3407          Amount:         1000.00    Balance:      1475.00
                    Undistributed:                  1000.00

Trans.      Prod.      Amount                      Aged
Type        Code       To Apply                    Balances
----------  --------   -----------                 -------------
  PA                                  Over  60           0.00
                                      31 - 60        1100.00
                                       1 - 30         125.00
                                      Current         250.00




F1-Help        F2 - Lookup                       F10 - Done                   C
```

Notice that this screen is different from the screen you saw when you entered Bill Parker's payment. When you enter payments to Balance Forward accounts such as this one, Accounts Receivable requires you to apply payments to ageing periods rather than to invoices.

Notice that Darryl has current, past due 1 - 30 days, and past due 31 - 60 days balances. None of these balances is exactly $1000.00. So, you can apply Mr. Tracer's payment to several ageing period balances.

The cursor is at Trans. Type. Accounts Receivable always displays the transaction type you last entered. So, Accounts Receivable automatically displays PA for the transaction type.

❖ Press **F2** to look up the transaction type and the product code.

Notice that Accounts Receivable lists only two transaction types:

- Payment
- Credit

For Balance Forward customers, you can enter only these transaction types into **Apply Payments**.

❖ Accept the payment transaction type. Press ⌨ at Prod. Code.

Accounts Receivable automatically distributes the amount of the check. It applies the check from the oldest ageing period to the newest until the Undistributed equals zero.

For example:

Amount Applied	Ageing Period	Aged Balance
$ 0.00	Over 60	$ 0.00
1000.00	31 - 60	1100.00
0.00	1 - 30	125.00
0.00	Current	250.00

❖ Press ⌨.

❖ Accept the transaction.

The screen clears; the cursor is at Customer ID. Press ⌨ to conclude the transaction.

❖ You have entered all your payments, so return to the Accounts Receivable Main Menu.

Carefully review the Apply Payments Control Report. If you made any errors, return to **Enter Transactions** to make corrections. (To reverse a payment, first set up an adjustment transaction, AD, with a new product code which will credit Cash and debit Accounts Receivable.)

Lesson 3: Summary

In this lesson, you learned how to enter payments for both Regular and Balance Forward customers. For a Regular customer, you always apply payments to specific invoices. For Balance Forward customers, you apply payments to ageing period balances.

You also learned how to enter a payment before the discount date: A/R automatically includes an early payment transaction.

Lesson 4: Print the Transaction Register

After you enter transactions, you should always print a Transaction Register. The Transaction Register is a complete record of customer transactions; it lists all the transactions entered in both Accounts Receivable and Invoicing. Saving a Transaction Register is more convenient than saving all the control reports. This lesson helps you print this report.

❖ Go to the Accounts Receivable Reports menu and select **Transaction Register Report**.

❖ Make sure your printer is ready, then press [ENTER].

A/R asks for the report date and displays the current date. (Remember, the report date is simply the date printed on the report.)

❖ Accept the current date.

A/R asks for the type of report, Transaction Register or Open Items Register.

❖ Select **Transaction Register**.

❖ Then select **All Transactions**.

❖ Next, select **Current Generation**.

After Accounts Receivable prints the register, the Reports menu returns.

Notice that the report lists all the transactions you entered in this topic: the transactions entered using **Enter Transactions**, **Enter Invoices**, and **Apply Payments**. Notice, also, that the automatic transaction you generated for Bill Parker appears on this report.

Lesson 4: Summary

The Transaction Register lists all the transactions made on customers' accounts during the current period. It lists the transactions entered as well as the transactions generated automatically by Accounts Receivable.

A Transaction Register should always be printed as part of your daily tasks. The report should be kept as an audit trail.

Topic 3: Monthly Tasks

Monthly tasks are the tasks that must be performed to prepare customers' statements, prepare sales taxes for payment, and close Accounts Receivable accounting period. At W.D. Peachtree, these tasks are performed once a month.

Topic 3 has three lessons:

1. Statement Activities
2. Sales Tax Activities
3. End of Period Activities

Lesson 1 explains the tasks needed to print customers' statements. They include ageing Balance Forward customers' accounts and reconciling any open credits on Regular customers' accounts. Service charges are also applied before statements are printed.

Lesson 2 explains how to print the Sales Tax Summary; this report lists the sales taxes charged during the period. This lesson also explains how to prepare Accounts Receivable to charge sales taxes for the next accounting period.

Lesson 3 explains how to close the current Accounts Receivable period. The lesson also explains the reports that should be printed before closing the period so there is an archive of the period's activities.

The order in which monthly tasks are performed is very important. So, be sure you complete the lessons in this topic in the order listed.

Lesson 1: Statement Activities

W.D. Peachtree sends out customer statements at the end of every month. To send statements, four different steps need to be completed:

1. Age the Balance Forward customers' accounts.
2. Reconcile open credits on the Regular customers' accounts.
3. Apply service charges to customers with past due amounts.
4. Print the statements.

This lesson covers all these steps.

Step 1: Age Balance Forward Customers' Accounts

Accounts Receivable ages Regular customers' accounts based on the age of each invoice. So, on any day, Regular customers' invoices can become past due. For Balance Forward customers, though, Accounts Receivable ages the account only when an **Aged Receivables Report** is run.

To help you understand how Accounts Receivable ages Balance Forward accounts, review Darryl Tracer's account before you age it.

❖ Return to the Accounts Receivable Main Menu and select **Maintenance Programs**. Then select **Maintain Customers**.

Query Customer Accounts does not list ageing information, so you must use **Maintain Customers** to view this information.

❖ Enter Darryl Tracer's ID and accept the first screen of account information.

❖ At the prompt, select to edit balance forward ageing.

Accounts Receivable displays the ageing information for Darryl Tracer.

❖ After you have reviewed his ageing period balances press ⬛ and then, accept the screen and return to the menu.

After Balance Forward customers' accounts are aged, you can compare Darryl Tracer's new ageing period balances to the balances Accounts Receivable just displayed.

❖ Return to the Accounts Receivable Main Menu and select Report Programs. From the Accounts Receivable Reports Menu, select **Aged Receivables Report**.

Accounts Receivable asks for the Report date and displays the current tutorial date.

❖ Accept the displayed date.

You can print the Aged Receivables Report for all customers, just Regular customers, or just Balance Forward customers.

❖ Select **All Customers**.

Accounts Receivable asks:

UPDATE BALANCE FORWARD AGEING (Y/N)?

Your response to this prompt determines whether Accounts Receivable ages the Balance Forward customers' accounts. If you enter N, Accounts Receivable does not age these accounts; if you enter Y, then Accounts Receivable does age Balance Forward accounts.

When Accounts Receivable ages Balance Forward accounts, it transfers ageing period balances:

• The Current balance becomes the Past Due 1 - 30 Days balance.

• The Past Due 1 - 30 Days balance becomes the Past Due 31 - 60 Days balance.

• The Past Due 31 - 60 Days is added to the existing Past Due 60 or More Days balance.

❖ Enter **Y**.

Accounts Receivable asks for the Ageing Date and displays 10/31/92.

Accounts Receivable ages Regular customers' accounts using the length of the ageing period (30 days for W.D. Peachtree), the due date of each invoice, and the date you enter for Ageing Date.

❖ Type 11/30/92 for the ageing date.

Accounts Receivable can print either a detailed or a summary report.

❖ Select **Detailed**.

Accounts Receivable allows you to print the report for all customers or just for a range of customers.

❖ Select **All Customers**.

Accounts Receivable prints the report.   The Accounts Receivable Reports Menu returns.

Review the Aged Receivables Report. Notice that Accounts Receivable prints ageing information for all customers even if they do not have past due invoices or past due amounts. Darryl Tracer has past due amounts. Since he is a Balance Forward customer, Accounts Receivable does not list invoices; it just lists ageing period balances.

❖ Return to **Maintain Customers** and review Darryl Tracer's ageing period balances.

Notice that Accounts Receivable simply moved each balance one ageing period.

Balance	Before Ageing	After Ageing
Current	$250.00	$0.00
Past Due 1 - 30	125.00	250.00
Past Due 31 - 60	100.00	125.00
Past Due 60 +	0.00	100.00

Step 2: Reconcile Open Credits

Before service charges are applied to customers' accounts, any open credits Regular customers might have should be reconciled. (Since Accounts Receivable does not keep invoice detail for Balance Forward customers, monthly tasks automatically reconcile Balance Forward customers' open credits.) When you reconcile open credits, you apply any outstanding credits a customer has to any open invoices of the customer.

To help you understand how Accounts Receivable reconciles open credits, review Christine Andrew's account before you reconcile credits.

❖ Return to the processing program, **Query Customer Accounts**, and review Christine Andrew's account.

❖ Print her account and activity information.

❖ Return to the Accounts Receivable Processing Menu.

Review Christine Andrew's invoice information. Notice that she has invoice #023111 for $145.73 and a $50.00 credit.

Next, you will reconcile the credit.

❖ From the Accounts Receivable Processing Menu, select **Reconcile Open Credits**.

❖ Make sure your printer is ready to print the control report, then press ▣.

Accounts Receivable allows you to reconcile open credits for all customers or just for a range of customers.

❖ Select **All Customers**.

You can reconcile credits manually or automatically. When you reconcile credits automatically, Accounts Receivable applies open credit to invoices based on the invoice number. (It applies credits to invoices with the lowest invoice number until all the credit has been applied.)

❖ Select **Review Each Customer**.

When you reconcile credits manually, you can either select the invoice to which a credit should be applied or have Accounts Receivable select for you.

❖ Select **Apply Credit to Specific Invoice**.

Reconciling open credits is an internal process; credits are simply applied, they are not created.

❖ Press ▣ and select Invoice #023111.

❖ Type **Y** and press ▣ to apply the $50 credit to Invoice #023111.

Review the control report. It lists the amount of credit each customer has available and the invoices to which that credit was applied. Christine Andrews was the only customer with an open credit.

The Accounts Receivable Processing Menu returns.

❖ Return to **Query Customer Accounts** to review Christine Andrew's account.

Notice that the $50.00 credit has been applied to the $145.73 invoice. As a result, the invoice balance is now $95.73.

Step 3: Apply Service Charges

W.D. Peachtree applies service charges to past due accounts. So, before you can print W.D. Peachtree statements, you must apply service charges.

❖ From the Accounts Receivable Processing Menu, select **Apply Service Charges**.

❖ Make sure your printer is ready to print a control report.

Accounts Receivable asks for an ending date and displays the current tutorial date as the ending date.

Accounts Receivable applies services charges to invoices which have a due date within a specific date range. You specify the date range by entering a starting date and an ending date.

❖ Accept 11/30/92 as the ending date.

Accounts Receivable displays a starting date that is 30 days prior to the ending date. (W.D. Peachtree uses a 30 day ageing period.)

❖ Accept the displayed starting date.

You can perform a service charges trial run. For a trial run, Accounts Receivable calculates each customer's service charge and prints a control report listing those charges. However, Accounts Receivable does not actually apply the charges to the customers' accounts yet.

❖ Enter **F** for a final run.

Accounts Receivable asks if you want to create invoices. If Invoicing is used, service charge invoices can be printed. (They list only the customer's service charge.) Service charges appear on customer statements, so W.D. Peachtree does not send separate service charge invoices.

❖ Do not create invoices. (Answer **N**.)

Accounts Receivable asks, *REVIEW EACH CUSTOMER (Y/N)*.

If you review accounts, Accounts Receivable displays account and service charge information for each customer who is subject to a service charge. Accounts Receivable does not apply service charges unless you accept the charge. Although you cannot change the charge, you can choose not to apply it.

❖ Do not review each customer. (Answer **N**.)

Accounts Receivable applies service charges automatically. The service charges are based on the service charge options selected in **A/R Module Options** and the service charge code assigned to each customer's account. W.D. Peachtree calculates service charges based on each customer's average daily balance. In addition, W.D. Peachtree charges a $2.00 minimum service charge.

The Accounts Receivable Reports Menu returns.

Review the Apply Service Charges Control Report. *Notice that Darryl Tracer was charged a service charge.*

Step 4: Print Customer Statements

Now that you have reconciled open credits and have applied service charges, you can print statements.

❖ Return to the Accounts Receivable Main Menu and select **Report Programs**. From the Accounts Receivable Reports Menu, select **Customer Statements**.

❖ Press ⌨ when the program prompts "Do you want to allow other programs to update your A/R files while statements are being printed? N"

Accounts Receivable displays the current tutorial date as the statement date—the date Accounts Receivable prints on each statement. Then, Accounts Receivable asks for the statement ageing date. That date controls the ageing information printed on statements for Regular customers. (Accounts Receivable prints statement ageing information only for Regular customers.) The last day of the current period should always be entered for that date.

❖ Accept **11/30/92** as the statement date and for the statement ageing date.

Accounts Receivable asks if you want to print a statement message. If statement messages are used, they appear at the bottom of each statement.

❖ Enter **Ask about our special Time Option Plan accounts.** as the message.

Accounts Receivable asks, *PRINT DUNNING MESSAGES (Y/N).*

(Dunning messages are comments to customers concerning any overdue amounts.)

❖ W.D. Peachtree does not use dunning messages, so enter **N**.

Accounts Receivable asks, *PRINT ZERO BALANCE STATEMENTS (Y/N)?*

❖ W.D. Peachtree does not send a statement to a customer if his account balance is zero; enter **N**.

Accounts Receivable can print customer statements in customer ID order or in customer class order.

❖ Select **Customer ID**.

Accounts Receivable can print statements for all your customers or just for a range of customers.

❖ Select **Range of Customers**. Then select **CANNOP** as the beginning customer ID and **DURAND** as the ending customer ID.

Accounts Receivable asks if it should print an alignment guide.

❖ Since you will print the statements on standard printer paper in this exercise, do not print an alignment guide.

Accounts Receivable prints a statement for three of W.D. Peachtree's customers. Then press ▥ until ▥ appears at the bottom of the screen. Then press ▥. The Accounts Receivable Reports Menu returns.

❖ Review each customer's statement.

For Regular customers, the statement lists all debit and credit transactions on all open invoices and all current invoices. The statement also summarizes the total debit and credit transactions made on the customers' account and lists the customer's account balance. If the customer has any past due invoices, the statement lists the account ageing as well.

For Balance Forward customers, the statement lists all current period transactions as well as the customer's balance forward.

Along with the customer statements, Accounts Receivable prints a summary statement. That statement lists the total:

• Number of statements printed.
• Due for the customers for whom statements were printed.
• Due for each ageing period for those customers.

Lesson 1: Summary

In this lesson, you learned the tasks you must complete to print customer statements. You learned that you should always age Balance Forward customers' accounts and reconcile Regular customers' open credits *before* you print statements. In addition, if service charges are applied, you learned to apply them before statements are printed.

Lesson 2: Sales Tax Activities

W.D. Peachtree pays sales tax at the end of every month.   The Sales Tax Summary lists the sales activity for the month. Using this report, W.D. Peachtree knows how much to pay each tax authority (each state, county, or city government).

To complete sales tax activities, you must:

1. Print the Sales Tax Summary
2. Clear sales tax accumulators

This lesson explains both these tasks.

Step 1: Print the Sales Tax Summary

❖ From the Accounts Receivable Reports menu, select **Sales Tax Summary**.

❖ Accept the current tutorial date as the report date. Check your printer and press .

Accounts Receivable prints the Sales Tax Summary.

❖ Review the Sales Tax Summary.

The Sales Tax Summary totals the taxes charged for all the states, counties, and cities for which W.D. Peachtree must charge taxes. Since, W.D. Peachtree operates in only one location (Atlanta, Georgia), the report lists only one tax code.

Step 2: Clear the Sales Tax Accumulators

The Sales Tax Summary lists accumulated tax information. Accounts Receivable accumulates this information until the sales tax accumulators are cleared. W.D. Peachtree pays sales taxes every month. So, W.D. Peachtree clears sales tax accumulators at the end of each month. After Accounts Receivable prints the Sales Tax Summary, Accounts Receivable asks which sales tax accumulators you want to clear:

- Clear State Totals
- Clear County Totals
- Clear City Totals
- Clear All Totals

❖ Select Clear All Totals.

Accounts Receivable asks, *DELETE DEACTIVATED RECORDS (Y/N)*.

Accounts Receivable allows you to use an unlimited number of sales tax codes. So, sales tax codes may be entered before they become active; for example, a sales tax code might be entered before a sales tax increase takes effect. Also, an active code can be made inactive; for example, a code that is no longer needed would be deactivated.

Accounts Receivable allows the deletion of inactive sales tax codes after the Sales Tax Summary is printed and after the sales tax accumulators are cleared. However, if you decide to delete deactivated sales tax codes, you must delete all deactivated sales tax codes. You cannot select the codes you will delete.

❖ W.D. Peachtree does not have any deactivated sales tax records, so do not delete deactivated codes.

❖ Accept your entries.

Then press 🖫.

The Accounts Receivable Reports Menu returns.

Lesson 2: Summary

In this lesson, you learned how to print a list of all the sales taxes you charged during the period. You learned how to prepare Accounts Receivable to accumulate sales taxes for the next period and how to delete deactivated sales tax codes.

Lesson 3: End of Period Activities

The final monthly task to be completed is closing the period. To close the period, you must:

1. Print the end of period reports.
2. Prepare A/R transactions for the company ledger.
3. Close the period.

This lesson shows you how to complete each of these tasks.

Step 1: Print End of Period Reports

At the end of every month, W.D. Peachtree archives all the receivables transactions from the current period. To archive these transactions, W.D. Peachtree prints three different reports:

1. Transaction Register
2. Aged Receivables Report
3. Past Due Report

In this step, you will print all three reports.

❖ To print the Transaction Register from the Accounts Receivable Reports Menu, select **Transaction Register Report**. Accept the report date of 11/30/92. Then select **Transaction Register**. Then Select **All Transactions** and **Current Generation**.

A/R prints the Transaction Register.

❖ To print the Aged Receivables Report, select **Aged Receivables Report**. Be sure to select **All Customers** and **Summary**. In addition, do not update the Balance Forward customers—you have already completed that task. Use **11/30/92** for the ageing date.

❖ To print the Past Due Report, select **Past Due Report**. Accept 11/30/92 as the report date and as the last aged date. Be sure to select **Detailed Ageing** and **All Customers**.

❖ Review each report.

On the Transaction Register, notice that the final report lists the transactions you entered in the Daily Tasks lessons as well as the service charges entered in the Statement Activities lessons. Although you did not enter the transactions, Accounts Receivable entered them for you. Since the Transaction Register lists all the transactions made on a customer's account, it lists the service charges as well.

On the Aged Receivables Report, notice that the report lists each customer's open invoices, the ageing status of those invoices, and the total amount due in each ageing period. The report also summarizes the ageing information for all customers. Finally, since the report lists each customer's phone number, this report could be used as a collection list.

On the Past Due Report, notice that the report lists only a customer's past due invoices; it does not, however, provide ageing information. Like the Aged Receivable Report, the Past Due Report lists each customer's phone number so the report could be used as a collection list.

Step 2: Prepare A/R Transactions for the Company Ledger

Before the period can be closed, the current period transactions must be prepared for the W.D. Peachtree company ledger. W.D. Peachtree uses PCA General Ledger, so you will prepare these transactions for automatic posting to General Ledger.

❖ Return to the Accounts Receivable Main Menu and select Processing Programs. From the Accounts Receivable Processing menu, select **Create G/L Journal Entries**.

❖ Check your printer and press [ENTER].

The Transfer Options pop up box appears. From this pop up box, you can select:
- List G/L Transfers
- Consolidate G/L Transfers
- Create G/L Transfers

The List G/L Transfers option prints a detailed listing of the current period transactions and the G/L account numbers to which those transactions should be posted. The Consolidate G/L Transfers option (automatically consolidated by PCA even if you don't select) summarizes the current period transactions by the assigned G/L account numbers and prints a list of those consolidated transactions. The Create G/L Transfers option creates the A/R summary journal for PCA General Ledger; once this journal is created, the A/R transactions can be transferred automatically from the G/L Processing Menu.

❖ W.D. Peachtree uses PCA General Ledger, so select **Create G/L Transfers**.

At the warning prompt, select **Y** to continue. Accept 11/30/92 as the posting date.

Accounts Receivable lists the current period transactions; it groups them by the G/L account number assigned to those transactions.

The Accounts Receivable Processing Menu returns.

Step 3: Close the Period

Now that you have created the A/R summary journal for automatic posting to General Ledger, you can close the period.

❖ From the Accounts Receivable Processing menu, select **Close Current Period**.

Accounts Receivable asks for the period ending date.

When the period is closed, Accounts Receivable replaces the product code of every transaction dated on or before the period ending date. Accounts Receivable replaces the product code with an asterisk (*) to signify the transaction is no longer current.

❖ Accept **11/30/92** as the period ending date.

Accounts Receivable asks, *END OF YEAR (Y/N)*.

❖ Accept the default **N**, and then accept your entries.

Accounts Receivable closes the current period for W.D. Peachtree. It clears the Transaction Register so that the next time this report is printed, it will list only the transactions entered during that new period.

For Regular customers, **Close Current Period** discards all closed invoices. (Accounts Receivable considers an invoice closed when its balance is zero.) Open invoices remain available for the next period.

For Balance Forward customers, **Close Current Period** calculates the customer's net balance; this balance becomes the customer's balance forward for the next period. Then, Accounts Receivable discards all invoice information. This process will take a while to perform.

Lesson 3: Summary

In this lesson you learned how to close the current A/R period. You learned the effects closing the period has on Regular customers' accounts and on Balance Forward customers' accounts. In addition, you learned how, when closing a period, Accounts Receivable summarizes all the current period transactions for General Ledger.

Now that you have completed the Accounts Receivable and Invoicing practice session, you have a very good idea of how the two modules work in a business. You also understand how the two modules work with each other to handle almost all receivables tasks.

Chapter 7

End of Chapter Problem

```
                            WARNING

BEFORE CONTINUING, BE SURE THAT ALL DATA FILES HAVE BEEN RESTORED TO
THEIR ORIGINAL CONDITION.  IF YOU ARE UNSURE OF HOW TO RESTORE THESE
FILES, TURN TO THE INSTRUCTIONS FOUND ON PAGE 1-32 IN  CHAPTER 1.
```

NOTE: You may find it helpful to record the problem data on input forms before using Accounts Receivable. Master Input Forms are included in the last section of this chapter. In some cases, you will need to make multiple copies of a form before you begin. On the other hand, you may not need all of the input forms provided.

Problem Data

a. 11/03/92 Use the following information to enter new customer data.

1: Susan Edwards
3050 Tailor Lane
Atlanta, Ga 30303
(404) 662-9800
Salesperson: Martin
Customer Class: 3
Regular Account; Terms Code 1; Sales Tax Code 001; Credit Limit, $5,000; Dunning notices, statements and invoices to be printed; Service Charge Code 3.

2: Arthur Roundtable
P.O. Box 1713
3122 Market Street
Decatur, GA 32798-1713
(404) 622-9120
Shipping Address: 1960 Parker Road
Lithonia, GA 30058
(404) 482-2612
Salesperson: Milam
Customer Class: 3
Regular Account; Terms Code 2; Sales Tax Code 001; Credit Limit, $7,000; Dunning notices, statements and invoices to be printed; Service Charge Code 3;

3:        John Sheffield
        P.O. Box 19A
        1312 Madison Ave.
        Atlanta, GA 36298-19A
        (404) 998-1613
        Salesperson: Buford
        Customer Class: A
        Regular Account; Terms Code 3; Sales Tax Code 001; No different Shipping
        Addresses; Credit Limit, $500; No Dunning Notices to be printed; Service Charge
        Code 3; Statements and invoices to be printed.

4:        Thomas Ethan
        1733 Knight Circle
        Roswell, GA 33229
        (404) 629-1312
        Shipping Address: 2122 South Main Street
                               Job Site 69B
                               Sandy Springs, GA 31318
                               (404) 531-6220
        Salesperson: Martin
        Customer Class: 3
        Regular account; Terms Code 1; Sales Tax Code 001; Credit limit, $4000; Dunning
        notices, statements and invoices to be printed; Service Charge Code 4.

b. 11/07/92   Use the following information to enter customer transactions. DO NOT generate
                  Automatic Transactions at this time. (Hint: Use the A/R Processing Programs and
                  Enter Transactions to do this.) NOTE: Normally these transactions would be done
                  in the Invoicing Module so that the Inventory Module would be updated for
                  quantities sold and returned.

1:        Gloria Cooper bought a new refrigerator on November 7, 1992. The discount date
        is the same. The due date is in one month. The terms of the purchase are 'Net 30'.
        The cost was $612.00 and is taxable. The final bill will be $648.72. (Hint:
        Remember to use [F2]-Lookup and accept the invoice number given.)

2:        Susan Edwards also bought an appliance on November 7, 1992, with similar
        payment dates. However, the terms of purchase are '2/10, Net 30'. The sales price
        of the dishwasher was $249.98. The total cost with tax amounted to $264.98.

c. 11/08/92   The following information should be used to process invoices. NOTE: DO NOT
                  process repeating invoices. Choose the Current Invoice option. Also, all of these
                  invoices are new invoices. (Hint: Use the Invoicing Module and print each invoice
                  as you enter it.) Since you will be printing on standard paper, the invoice alignment
                  guide is not needed. Invoice date is 11-08-92.

1:        Susan Edwards purchased a Compact Disc Player, Item No. ELE810544CDP on
        November 8, 1992, from salesperson, Barbara Brown Scarborough (BBS). The
        terms were 2/10, Net 30, and the product was shipped on the purchase date by
        Roadway (RDW). Susan paid $459.00 plus tax. She also had to pay for freight
        charges (tax-exempt) totalling $25.00. The total cost was $511.54.

2:    Arthur Roundtable ordered five 21 cubic foot Residential Refrigerators, Item APP0900210REF from Calvin on October 30, 1992. He also ordered three Deluxe Dishwashers, Item APP1200040DIS. The purchase order number was A1749-2 and was shipped to his Lithonia, GA address by Smith on November 8, 1992, with terms of Net 30. The freight on the shipment came to $75.23 (tax-exempt). The cost of the refrigerators was $779.99 each and the cost of the dishwashers was $549.99 each. Because of the large order, Arthur received a 2% discount. The total invoice came to $5,840.49.

3:    Thomas Mitchell bought one set of High Quality Floor Speakers, Item ELE810104SPK for $298.89 at a 5% discount from Barbara Brown Scarborough (BBS) on November 8, 1992. The terms were 2/10, Net 30, and the order was picked up (P/U) by the customer at the warehouse. The total cost came to $300.99.

4:    Charles Gray bought a 20 cubic foot Commercial Refrigerator from Mrs. Scarborough (BBS) under terms of Net 60. The item number was APP0900120REF and cost $779.99. Mr. Gray received a 1% discount for being a loyal customer. The freight cost was $23.12 (tax-exempt), and a miscellaneous debit charge (MD) for set-up on delivery (tax-exempt) came to $15.00. The refrigerator was delivered by a local company, Periwinkle (PWK). Even though Mr. Gray exceeded his credit limit, the store manager approved the sale. The total cost came to $856.64.

d. 11/13/92   The following customers paid on their account. You should apply each payment using Apply Payments in the A/R Module. The transaction date is 11-13-92. The product code should be blank for all transactions.

ID	Customer Name	Amount Paid	Check Number	Apply to Inv. No.
ANDREC	Christine Andrews	$525.00	1210	023489
COOPEG	Gloria S. Cooper	200.00	2530	023105
FIELDJ	Jonathan Fields	1000.00	98	N/A
HENDEK	Kathy Henderson	1249.69	1250	023500
MILLEJ	Joel S. Miller	131.23	6239	023505

e. 11/14/92   Susan Edwards has decided to purchase a two year service contract on her newly purchased Compact Disc Player. This will be a miscellaneous debit for $21.00 to be billed quarterly for the eight quarters beginning on January 1, 1993. This is a tax exempt item. Use term code 1 and "C. Disc Plr" as a comment. (Hint: Use the Maintain Programs option and DO NOT print a list of automatic transactions.)

f. 11/21/92   Mrs. Fremont Duncan (Customer ID - DUNCAF) has notified you of her address change. Her new address is 1374 Hightower Trl., Conyers, GA 30208. Her new telephone number is 483-0021. You should make the necessary changes in Mrs. Duncan's file.

g. 11/24/92 Use the following information to enter the new invoices and credits. Use the Invoicing Module but do NOT generate Automatic Invoices. (Hint: You have one invoice and three credits to enter. You will need to process the invoice, then process the credits; they can not be done at the same time. Choose the current invoice option and the add invoice option for both the invoice and the credits.)

1: John Sheffield bought a Dual Cassette Player with Auto Reverse from Calvin on November 24, 1992. The customer picked up (P/U) his purchase at the loading dock. The purchase price was $355.00 ($376.30 with tax).

2: Thomas Mitchell returned the ten heating ducts (HAC9900101FURN) he purchased on November 24, 1992, from Barbara Brown Scarborough. He originally purchased the items at $24.99 at a 5% discount. The total credit on his invoice came to $251.64. (Hint: Use transaction type of RE to update the Inventory Module).

3: James Holloway received a 10% credit on the Stereo Amplifiers he purchased on October 5, 1992, that were shipped on November 24, 1992, because they did not perform as advertised. His total credit came to $18.89. (Hint: Use transaction type of CR for Non-Taxable Credit. Transaction types of MC or AD could have been used).

4: Lisa Williams received an adjustment on the 10 feet of gutters she ordered on October 15, 1992. The gutters were shipped on November 24, 1992. Due to the late shipment, she received an adjustment of $11.67. (Hint: Use transaction type of AD for Non-Taxable Adjustment and precede the amount with a minus sign. Transaction types of MC or CR could have been used).

h. 11/27/92 Print the Invoice Register and then run Post Invoices and post all invoices.

i. 11/27/92 Use the following information to enter new transactions. DO NOT generate automatic transactions (Hint: Use A/R Enter Transactions to do this). NOTE: Normally these transactions would be done in the Invoicing Module so that the Inventory Module would be updated for quantities sold and returned.

1: Thomas Ethan bought a gate for $325.10 on November 27, 1992 (terms 2/10, Net/30). (Terms Code = 1).

2: Charles Gray returned a refrigerator on November 27, 1992. He received a $1,100.00 credit on invoice number 023488. (Hint: Use transaction type RE and compute sales tax. Use "Ret. Ref." as your comment.)

3: On November 27, 1992, Gloria Cooper returned a pair of blue jeans (product code C), receiving a $13.00 credit on invoice number 023490. (Hint: Use transaction type RE and compute sales tax. Use "Ret. Bljen" for a comment).

4: Anita Anderson purchased a washing machine on November 27, 1992, for $200.00 (terms 2/10, Net/30). The Sales Manager approved her purchase even though it exceeded her credit limit. (Terms Code = 1).

5: On November 27, 1992, Paul Cannon was charged $45 for repair work (transaction type SA, product code E). The invoice is tax-exempt and is due by December 27, 1992.

6:      On November 27, 1992, Dorothy Durand purchased a wide screen TV for $2411.52 (due on December 27, 1992; terms code 2). It is OK to exceed this customer's credit limit.

7:      On November 27, 1992, Michael Johnson was charged $35.00 for a service call (transaction type SA, product code E, terms code = 1). The amount is tax-exempt and is due on December 27, 1992. It is OK to exceed this customer's credit limit.

j.   11/30/92   It is time to run the end of the month reports and statements. You should follow the steps as outlined in this chapter in Topic 3 in the exact order as given. In other words, you should do the following activities in this order:

1) Statements,
2) Sales Tax, and then
3) End of the Period.

Do not forget that within each of three activities you need to perform several different tasks. See top of next page for specific tasks which should be performed.

The following are different dates and options you should choose for each task:

Task			Option to Select
Ageing	Report Date :	11/30/92	All Customers
	Ageing Date :	11/30/92	Update balance forward ageing
			Detailed Ageing
Reconcile Open Credits			All Customers
			Automatic
Service Charge	Ending Date :	11/30/92	DO NOT review each customer
	Starting Date :	10/31/92	DO NOT create invoices
Statements	Statement Date :	11/30/92	No statement or dunning messages
	Statement Ageing Date :	11/30/92	No zero balance statements
			Range of Customers
			Beg. Customer ID: FIELDJ
			End Customer ID: MARSHJ
Sales Tax	Report Date :	11/30/92	Clear all totals
			DO NOT delete deactivated records
Trans. Register	Report Date :	11/30/92	All Transactions
			Current Generation
Ageing	Report Date:	11/30/92	All Customers
	Ageing Date:	11/30/92	DO NOT update balance forward ageing
			Summary Ageing
Past Due	Report Date :	11/30/92	
	Last Aged Date :	11/30/92	Summary Ageing
			Range of Customers:
			Beg. Customer ID: ANDERA
			End. Customer ID: DURAND
Creating G/L Transfers	Posting Date :	11/30/92	Create G/L Transfers
Ending Period	Period Ending Date :	11/30/92	Not the End of Year **

You will get a series of warning messages. Answer **Y at each question to complete the problem.

ACCOUNTS RECEIVABLE

AND INVOICING

MASTER INPUT FORMS

A/R Module Options Setup Form

Controller Password: __ __ __ __ __ __ __ __

Operator Password: __ __ __ __ __ __ __ __

Use Menus: Y   N   (Circle one)

Allow Changes/Deletions: Y   N

Force Control Reports: Y   N

Keep Historical Detail: Y   N

Current G/L Period: __ __

Post to General Ledger: Y   N

Consolidate A/R Trans: Y   N

Check Credit Limit: Y   N

Generation Number: __ __

Print Company Name: Y   N

Print Titles: Y   N

Use Expanded Lookups: Y   N

Auto Numbering: Y   N

Start Number: __ __ __ __ __ __

End Number: __ __ __ __ __ __

Reset Number: __ __ __ __ __ __

Service Charge Options

     Customer Types: 0   1   2   3

     Amount or Percentage: A   P

     Min Amount: __ __ __ __ __.__ __

     Include Past Charges: Y   N

     Avg Daily/Ending Bal: A   E

     Service Chg Amts/Pcts

         Code 1:   __ __.__ __

         Code 2:   __ __.__ __

         Code 3:   __ __.__ __

         Code 4:   __ __.__ __

Age Period Length: __ __ __

Dunning Messages

    Extended Messages: Y   N

    Period 1: _____

    Period 2: _____

    Period 3: _____

Terms Code 1   **Description:** _____

                          Discount Pct: __ __.__ __

                          Discount Days: __ __

                          Due Days: __ __

Terms Code 2   **Description:** _____

                          Discount Pct: __ __.__ __

                          Discount Days: __ __

                          Due Days: __ __

Terms Code 3   **Description:** _____

                          Discount Pct: __ __.__ __

                          Discount Days: __ __

                          Due Days: __ __

Terms Code 4   **Description:** _____

                          Discount Pct: __ __.__ __

                          Discount Days: __ __

                          Due Days: __ __

Terms Code 5   **Description:** _____

                          Discount Pct: __ __.__ __

                          Discount Date: __ __ __ __ __

                          Force Nxt Month: Y   N

                          Due Date: __ __ __ __ __

                          Force Nxt Month: Y   N

Invoicing Module Options
Setup Form

Use Menus:	Y N (Circle one)
Use Inventory in Invoicing:	Y N
Automatic Invoice Numbering:	Y N
Starting Invoice Number:	__ __ __ __ __ __
Ending Invoice Number:	__ __ __ __ __ __
Reset Invoice Number:	__ __ __ __ __
Update to Job Cost:	Y N
Print Company Name on Invoice:	Y N
Print Field Titles on Invoice:	Y N
Print Inventory Dept. Code:	Y N

Invoice Message:

__ __ __ __ __ __ __ __ __ __ __ __ __ __ __ __

__ __ __ __ __ __ __ __ __ __ __ __ __ __ __ __

__ __ __ __ __ __ __ __ __ __ __ __ __ __ __ __

__ __ __ __ __ __ __ __ __ __ __ __ __ __ __ __

__ __ __ __ __ __ __ __ __ __ __ __ __ __ __ __

__ __ __ __ __ __ __ __ __ __ __ __ __ __ __ __

__ __ __ __ __ __ __ __ __ __ __ __ __ __ __ __

__ __ __ __ __ __ __ __ __ __ __ __ __ __ __ __

__ __ __ __ __ __ __ __ __ __ __ __ __ __ __ __

__ __ __ __ __ __ __ __ __ __ __ __ __ __ __ __

__ __ __ __ __ __ __ __ __ __ __ __ __ __ __ __

__ __ __ __ __ __ __ __ __ __ __ __ __ __ __ __

Transaction/Product Code Setup Form

Trans. Type: ___ __

Product Code: __

Description: __ __ __ __ __ __ __ __ __ __

            __ __ __ __ __ __ __ __ __ __

Account #, Credit: __ __ __ __ __ __

Account #, Debit: __ __ __ __ __ __

Trans. Type: ___ __

Product Code: __

Description: __ __ __ __ __ __ __ __ __ __

            __ __ __ __ __ __ __ __ __ __

Account #, Credit: __ __ __ __ __ __

Account #, Debit: __ __ __ __ __ __

Trans. Type: ___ __

Product Code: __

Description: __ __ __ __ __ __ __ __ __ __

            __ __ __ __ __ __ __ __ __ __

Account #, Credit: __ __ __ __ __ __

Account #, Debit: __ __ __ __ __ __

Sales Tax Setup Form

Sales Tax Code: __ __ __

Sales Taxable/Exempt: T E (Circle one)

Freight Taxable/Exempt: T E

State_____

Name: __ __ __ __ __ __ __ __ __

__ __ __ __ __ __ __ __ __

__ __

Tax Percentage: __ __.__ __ __

Use Tax Brackets: Y N

County_____

Name: __ __ __ __ __ __ __ __

__ __ __ __ __ __ __ __

__ __

Tax Percentage: __ __.__ __ __

Maximum Taxable __ __ __ __ __ __.__ __

Use Tax Brackets: Y N

Tax Brackets		
State	**County**	**City**
.00 __ __	__ __	__ __
.01 __ __	__ __	__ __
.02 __ __	__ __	__ __
.03 __ __	__ __	__ __
.04 __ __	__ __	__ __
.05 __ __	__ __	__ __
.06 __ __	__ __	__ __
.07 __ __	__ __	__ __
.08 __ __	__ __	__ __
.09 __ __	__ __	__ __
.10 __ __	__ __	__ __

City_____

Name: __ __ __ __ __ __ __ __ __

__ __ __ __ __ __ __ __

__ __

Tax Percentage: __ __.__ __ __

Maximum Taxable __ __ __ __ __ __.__ __

Use Tax Brackets: Y N

Automatic Transactions Setup Form

Customer ID: ___ ___ ___ ___ ___ ___

Auto Trans. ID: ___ ___

Transaction Type: ___ ___

Product Code: ___

Status (A/I):   A I   (Circle one)

Amount: ___ ___ ___ ___ ___ ___ ___.___ ___

Tax/Exempt (T/E):   T E

State Tax: ___ ___ ___ ___ ___ ___ ___.___ ___

County Tax: ___ ___ ___ ___ ___ ___ ___.___ ___

City Tax: ___ ___ ___ ___ ___ ___ ___.___ ___

Terms Code (1-5):   1 2 3 4 5

Comment: ___ ___ ___ ___ ___ ___ ___ ___ ___ ___

Frequency: W T M B Q S A

Periods to Bill: ___ ___ ___ ___

Beginning Date: ___ ___/___ ___/___ ___

Customer Information Setup Form

Customer ID: — — — — — —

Customer Name: — — — — — — — — — — — — — — —

— — — — — — — — — — — — — —

Address: — — — — — — — — — — — — — — —

— — — — — — — — — — — — — —

Address: — — — — — — — — — — — — — — —

— — — — — — — — — — — — — —

City, ST: — — — — — — — — — — — — — — —

— — — — — — — — — — — — — —

ZIP Code: — — — — — — — — —

Telephone: — — — — — — — — — —

Contact: — — — — — — — — — — — —

— — — — — — — — — — — — — —

Salesperson: — — — — — — — —

Customer Class: — —

Account Type: R B T (Circle one)

Terms Code: 1 2 3 4 5

Sales Tax Code: — — —

Discount Percent: — — . — —

Ship Addresses: Y N

Dunning Notices: Y N

Credit Limit: — — — — — — — — . — —

Service Chg Code: 1 2 3 4

Print Statements: Y N

Print Invoices: Y N

Balance Forward Ageing (Only for Balance Forward Customers)

Current: — — — — — — — — — . — —

1 - 30 Days: — — — — — — — — — . — —

31 - 60 Days: — — — — — — — — . — —

Over 60 Days: — — — — — — — . — —

Debit_____

Last Date: __ __ / __ __ / __ __

Last Amt: __ __ __ __ __ __ __ __ __ . __ __

YTD Amt: __ __ __ __ __ __ __ __ __ . __ __

Credit_____

Last Date: __ __ / __ __ / __ __

Last Amt: __ __ __ __ __ __ __ . __ __

YTD Amt: __ __ __ __ __ __ __ __ . __ __

Payments_____

Last Date: __ __ / __ __ / __ __

Last Amt: __ __ __ __ __ __ __ __ __ . __ __

YTD Amt: __ __ __ __ __ __ __ __ . __ __

Service Charges_____

Last Date: __ __ / __ __ / __ __

Last Amt: __ __ __ __ __ __ __ __ . __ __

YTD Amt: __ __ __ __ __ __ __ __ . __ __

Customer Shipping Addresses Setup Form

Customer ID: __ __ __ __ __ __

Shipping ID: __ __ __ __ __ __

Customer Name: __ __ __ __ __ __ __ __ __ __ __ __ __ __
__ __ __ __ __ __ __ __ __ __

Address: __ __ __ __ __ __ __ __ __ __ __ __ __ __
__ __ __ __ __ __ __ __ __ __

Address: __ __ __ __ __ __ __ __ __ __ __ __ __ __
__ __ __ __ __ __ __ __ __ __

City, ST: __ __ __ __ __ __ __ __ __ __ __ __ __ __
__ __ __ __ __ __ __ __ __ __

ZIP Code: __ __ __ __ __ __ __ __ __ __

Telephone: __ __ __ __ __ __ __ __ __ __ __

Shipping ID: __ __ __ __ __ __

Customer Name: __ __ __ __ __ __ __ __ __ __ __ __ __ __
__ __ __ __ __ __ __ __ __ __

Address: __ __ __ __ __ __ __ __ __ __ __ __ __ __
__ __ __ __ __ __ __ __ __ __

Address: __ __ __ __ __ __ __ __ __ __ __ __ __ __
__ __ __ __ __ __ __ __ __ __

City, ST: __ __ __ __ __ __ __ __ __ __ __ __ __ __
__ __ __ __ __ __ __ __ __ __

ZIP Code: __ __ __ __ __ __ __ __ __ __

Telephone: __ __ __ __ __ __ __ __ __ __ __

Customer Transactions Setup Form

Customer ID: __ __ __ __ __ __

Trans. Type: __ __

Product Code: __

Invoice Number: __ __ __ __ __

Terms Code: __

Trans. Date: __ __/__ __/__ __

Due Date: __ __/__ __/__ __

Discount Date: __ __/__ __/__ __

Trans. Amount: __ __ __ __ __ __ __ __.__ __

Comment: __ __ __ __ __ __ __ __

T/E: T E (Circle one)

State Tax: __ __ __ __ __ __ __.__ __

County Tax: __ __ __ __ __ __ __.__ __

City Tax: __ __ __ __ __ __ __.__ __

Chapter 8

INVENTORY OVERVIEW

<u>Learning Objectives:</u>

After studying this chapter, you should be able to:

1. Describe the functions performed by Inventory.

2. Perform everyday activities including—making changes to an inventory item, entering a receipt of goods, selling an item from inventory, and changing the selling price of a group of items.

3. Perform monthly tasks including—printing a Departmental Summary, printing a Period-to-Date Report, printing a Transaction Register, and closing the period.

4. Identify some of the reports printed by Inventory.

Chapter 8

Inventory Overview

Inventory keeps track of one of the most important assets of a business: the goods that it sells. A business cannot be well managed and profitable without proper control of its inventory.

How Inventory Compares To A Manual System

In a manual accounting system, the periodic method of inventory is used frequently. Under the periodic method, the inventory account is only brought up to date at the end of the accounting period based on taking a physical inventory. Keeping track of each unit of inventory as it comes into the business or leaves the business is considered to be too cumbersome.

In a computerized accounting system it is much easier to use the perpetual inventory method. Under this method each unit of inventory is tracked as it enters or leaves the business so that the inventory account is kept perpetually up to date. The Peachtree Complete Accounting package uses the perpetual inventory method. When Inventory is linked to Accounts Receivable and Accounts Receivable is linked to General Ledger, the inventory account in the general ledger is updated as often as you run "Post Invoices" and then "Create General Ledger Journal Entries" in Accounts Receivable and then run "Transfer Summary Journals" in G/L.

A company needs to carefully manage its inventory. Too little inventory on hand will lead to lost sales. Too much inventory on hand is an inefficient use of financial resources and can lead to excess spoilage and/or obsolescence. Peachtree Complete Accounting allows you to know at all times how much inventory of a particular item is on hand. It also reminds you when you need to reorder certain items.

Peachtree Complete allows you to use the FIFO, LIFO, average, or specific identification inventory methods. The module also allows the use of a standard, or preset cost.

What Inventory Does

For each item, inventory tracks the following information for the current month (or fiscal period) as well as for the year through the end of the previous period:

- sales and quantity sold
- cost of sales
- quantity returned
- quantity received
- quantity adjusted
- quantity used as components of assemblies*

In Inventory, each item has its own identification code consisting of an item type (product or service), a department code, and an item number.

Inventory gives you the choice of five costing methods for each item you stock:

- **Standard Cost**, which is a term for a predetermined or target cost: a costing method that lets a company set the cost for an item. Inventory does not change the cost unless it is directed to do so.

- **Average Cost**, which provides a weighted average cost that Inventory re-calculates every time new stock is received.

- **FIFO**, which is standard First In, First Out costing.

- **LIFO**, which is standard Last In, First Out costing. If you select either LIFO or FIFO, Inventory tracks the cost of items in each shipment received.

- **Specific Unit Costing,** which tracks the cost of each unit of stock on an individual basis. It also tracks the serial number (or other identification number) of each unit in stock. Optionally, you can track the serial number and sale information after it is sold.

(You should refer to a Principles of Accounting textbook if you need a review of these costing methods. For instance, see Hermanson, Edwards, and Salmonson, *Accounting Principles* (4th Edition), Richard D. Irwin, Inc., pp. 385-391.)

Inventory calculates the cost of each item according to the costing type you select.

---

* This is a very specialized topic and is beyond the scope of this text.

Question Frame 1[8]

Indicate whether each of the following statements is true or false by writing "T" or "F" in the space provided.

_____ I.   Under the perpetual method, the inventory account is only brought up to date at the end of the accounting period.

_____ 2.   Computerized accounting systems generally use the perpetual method of inventory.

_____ 3.   The inventory module gives you a choice of five costing methods.

_____ 4.   Under the average cost method, the Inventory module recalculates the average cost every time you sell an item.

Now turn to Answer Frame 1[8] on page 8-6 to check your answers.

Answer Frame 1[8]

1.   False. The perpetual method keeps the Inventory account perpetually up to date. The *Periodic* method only brings the Inventory account up to date at the end of the accounting period.

2.   True. Computerized accounting systems make the use of the perpetual method more feasible than does a manual system.

3.   True. You have a choice of five costing methods—standard, average, FIFO, LIFO, or specific unit costing.

4.   False. The Inventory module calculates a new average cost every time you *buy* a new item.

If you missed any of the above, reread Frame 1[8] before continuing.

Inventory Functions Overview

Setup and Maintenance

When Inventory is first set up, **Maintain Inventory Items** will be used to enter information about a company's inventory items. After the initial set up, this program will be used at any time to add new items, change price or other information for existing items, or to delete items that are no longer needed.

When you have a price change for a group of items, you will use **Change Inventory Item Prices** to change the prices. You will use it to increase or decrease prices. These price changes can be either a fixed amount or a percentage, and you may apply each change to all inventory items or a range of inventory items.

Processing and Transaction Entry

After inventory information has been entered, you will use **Enter Inventory Transactions** to record inventory activity as it occurs: sales (SAL), receipts (REC), returns (RET), and adjustments (ADJ).

If you are interfacing with Invoicing, sales and returns transactions are not entered in Inventory but are transferred from Invoicing when you "post invoices." Entering sales and returns in Invoicing rather than in Inventory will keep both Inventory and Accounts Receivable updated. Also, if you are interfacing with Purchase Order, all receipts transactions are entered in the Purchase Order module and not in Inventory.

At the end of the month (or other fiscal period), you will use **Close Current Period** to update year-to-date (of closing) information and reset the program in preparation for the next month's information. (You need to choose the end of year option of this program when preparing to close the entire year's activity.)

Question Frame 2^8

Indicate whether each of the following statements is true or false by writing "T" or "F" in the space provided.

____ 1. **Maintain Inventory Items** is used to enter information about a company's inventory items.

____ 2. When you have a price change for a group of items you use the **Change Inventory Item Prices** option and must change all items by a fixed percentage.

____ 3. The **Enter Inventory Transactions** option is used to record inventory activity during the period.

____ 4. There are two closing options for the Inventory module.

Now turn to Answer Frame 2^8 on page 8-8 to check your answers.

Answer Frame 2[8]

1. True. And after initial set up, this same program is used at any time to add new items, change price or other information for existing items, or to delete items that are no longer needed.

2. False. The prices may be changed either by a fixed percentage or fixed dollar amount.

3. True. Transactions involving sales, receipts, returns, and adjustments of inventory are entered using this option.

4. True. You use the **Close Current Period** option at the end of a month to update year-to-date information and reset the program in preparation for the next month's information. You use the end of year option to close the entire year's activity.

If you missed any of the above, reread Frame 2[8] before continuing.

Frame 3[8]

Inventory Reporting

Inventory provides several types of reports to help keep track of activity, including reports on both period-to-date and year-to-date activity. These reports give profit margins for the reporting period based on the costing method selected. Reports can be run as needed or on a preset schedule.

- The **Inventory Price List** shows the item name, vendor information, current on-hand balance, and three pricing levels. This report is especially useful to the employees responsible for purchasing inventory.

- The **Inventory Status Report** lists inventory items showing the beginning period balance, all period activity, and the ending period balance. This report could be used by many people within a business. For example, salespeople might need to know the inventory balance before making a large sale to a customer.

- The **Departmental Summary** lists a summary of departmental activity with the total investment, year-to-date sales, percentage of sales by department, and profit margins. This report provides information to departmental managers to help them make decisions.

- The **Reorder Items Report** lists the items that are at or below their reorder level. This report provides information to the employees who are responsible for making sure they do not run out of an inventory item.

- The **Inventory Valuation Report** gives the value (cost) of all the inventory items or a range of inventory items and shows how the value of each item contributes to the total inventory value (cost). This report is probably most often used by accountants for financial reporting.

- Inventory has the capability of tracking information when **Specific Units** or **Assembly/Component Items** are used. These topics are beyond the scope of this text.

- The **Query Inventory Items** option reports on the activity of a specific inventory item. This feature can be used throughout the month by anyone who has a question about an inventory item.

- The **Physical Inventory Report** lists inventory items in a way so that the report can be used to help take a physical inventory count. Printing quantity-on-hand is optional for this report. The employees responsible for counting the inventory could use this report to write down the item quantities as they are counted.

- The **To-Date Reports** program gives the choice of two reports: the **Year-to-Date Report** and the **Period-to-Date Report**. Each shows net sales, cost of goods sold, profit margin, and average selling price for the year-to-date or period-to-date. These reports may be run any time during the month to provide profit information to managers.

- The **List Inventory Items** feature provides a detailed list of the inventory items showing all information for each item. This report allows employees to examine the inventory items in detail.

- The **Transaction Register** can be printed to keep a permanent record of all transactions involving inventory items.

Question Frame 3[8]

Indicate whether each of the following statements is true or false by writing "T" or "F" in the space provided.

_____ 1. The inventory price list shows the item name, vendor information, current on-hand balance, and three pricing levels.

_____ 2. Salespersons might be wise to use the Inventory Status Report before making a large sale to a customer.

_____ 3. The report most often used by accountants for financial reporting is probably the Physical Inventory Report.

_____ 4. The To-Date Reports program shows net sales, cost of goods sold, profit margin, and average selling price only for period-to-date.

Now turn to Answer Frame 3[8] on page 8-10 to check your answers.

Answer Frame 3^8

1. True. This report is especially useful to the employees responsible for purchasing inventory.

2. True. The salesperson should make sure the goods are on hand before making the sale.

3. False. The Inventory Valuation Report gives the value (cost) of all the inventory items and is probably used most often by accountants for financial reporting. The Physical Inventory Report is useful when counting inventory items.

4. False. The report can also show this information for year-to-date.

If you missed any of the above, reread Frame 3^8 before turning to the questions at the end of the chapter.

What's Next

Before working Chapter 9, you may want to review the sample Inventory reports at the end of this chapter so that you will be familiar with the output generated when practicing with W. D. Peachtree.

Name _____ ID # _____

INVENTORY OVERVIEW
QUESTIONS

1. What types of information does Inventory track for each inventory item?

    _____

    _____

    _____

    _____

    _____

    _____

2. Name the five costing methods available in Inventory.

    _____

    _____

    _____

    _____

    _____

3. Name two programs that can be used in the setup and maintenance of Inventory and identify their functions.

    Program Name   **Program Function**

    _____   _____

    _____   _____

4. What two steps does the Close Current Period program perform in Inventory?

    _____

    _____

Name _____ ID # _____

5. Identify eight Inventory report programs and the purpose they serve.

<u>Report Program Name</u>   <u>Purpose of Report</u>

_____   _____

_____   _____

_____   _____

_____   _____

_____   _____

_____   _____

_____   _____

_____   _____

Name _____ ID # _____

INVENTORY OVERVIEW
MATCHING

Instructions: Match each program name on the left with the proper program function on the right.

Program Name	**Program Function**	**Answer**
A. Physical Inventory Report	1. Prints the only PCA report that shows sales information by department.	_____
B. Inventory Price List	2. Adds new inventory items, changes information about existing items, or deletes items from inventory.	_____
C. Maintain Inventory Items	3. Records receipts and sales of inventory.	_____
D. Period-to-Date Report	4. Lists all inventory items and their balances.	_____
E. Change Inventory Item Prices	5. Finds out the activity of a specific inventory item.	_____
F. Query Inventory Items	6. Increases (or decreases) inventory prices.	_____
G. Enter Inventory Transactions	7. Shows inventory profit information to managers at the end of a period.	_____
H. Departmental Summary	8. Lists inventory items to help count inventory.	_____
I. Reorder Items Report	9. Shows information about an inventory item's vendor or pricing levels.	_____
J. Inventory Status Report	10. Lists inventory items that may be below their reorder level.	_____

INVENTORY

SAMPLE REPORTS

Query Inventory Items Report

RUN DATE: 12/31/92   W.D. Peachtree & Company   PAGE 1
RUN TIME: 8:13 PM   Inventory Control
Query Inventory Items Report

```
ITEM TYPE: P        DEPARTMENT: APP        ITEM NUMBER: 1200040DIS

ITEM DESCRIPTION..: DISHWASHER        ------- Extended Description -------
PRODUCT CODE.....: A                  DELUXE DISHWASHER WITH OPTIONAL BUTCHER
LOCATION........: WRHS-1              BLOCK TOP ORDERED AT NO EXTRA COST FROM
RECEIVING UNIT..: EACH                HARRIS CABINETS (555-3989)
SELLING UNIT....: EACH
CONVERSION FACTOR.: 1.00
VENDOR ID........: MAYTAB
VENDOR ITEM #....: DIS092721
NEGATIVE QUANTITY.: N
COSTING METHOD...: CURRENT AVG.
CURRENT COST.....: 267.8600000        SELLING PRICES
LAST COST / UNIT.: 267.8600000          PRICE A.........: 599.9900
REORDER LEVEL....: 8.00                  PRICE B.........: 549.9900
REORDER QUANTITY.: 8.00                  PRICE C.........: 499.9000
ON RO REPORT DATE.: / /

PTD ACTIVITY                          YTLP ACTIVITY

  SALES...........: 0.00                SALES...........: 0.00
  COST OF SALES...: 0.00                COST OF SALES...: 0.00

  BEGINNING QTY...: 7.00
  # SOLD..........: 0.00              # SOLD...........: 0.00
  # RECEIVED......: 6.00              # RECEIVED.......: 0.00
  # RETURNED......: 0.00              # RETURNED.......: 0.00
  # ADJUSTED......: 0.00              # ADJUSTED.......: 0.00
  # COMPONENTS....: 0.00              # COMPONENTS.....: 0.00

CURRENT QTY-ON-HAND.: 13.00           ITEM VALUATION....: 3482.18
(-) # UNITS PENDING.: 0.00
                     -------
# UNITS AVAILABLE...: 13.00           UNITS ON ORDER....: 0.00
```

Inventory Status Report

W.D. Peachtree & Company
Inventory Control
Inventory Status Report

DEPARTMENT: APP

ITEM NUMBER	DESCRIPTION	BEGINNING BALANCE	SALES	RETURNS	RECEIPTS	ADJMTS.	COMPNTS	UNITS PENDING	UNITS AVAILABLE
0900120REF	COMMERCIAL REFRIGER.	5.00	1.00	0.00	4.00	0.00	0.00	0.00	8.00
0900121REF	COMMERCIAL REFRIGER.	5.00	0.00	0.00	0.00	0.00	0.00	0.00	5.00
0900122REF	COMMERCIAL REFRIGER.	2.00	0.00	0.00	4.00	0.00	0.00	0.00	6.00
0900210REF	RESIDENTIAL REFRIG.	2.00	1.00	0.00	5.00	0.00	0.00	0.00	6.00
1001010VE	OVEN, COMMERCIAL	13.00	0.00	0.00	0.00	0.00	0.00	0.00	13.00
10040TRA	SUPERTRASH COMPACTOR	10.00	1.00	0.00	0.00	0.00	0.00	0.00	9.00
1100101OVE	OVEN, COMMERCIAL	13.00	0.00	0.00	0.00	0.00	0.00	0.00	13.00
1100102MOV	MICROWAVE OVEN	8.00	4.00	1.00	2.00	0.00	0.00	0.00	7.00
1200040DIS	DISHWASHER	7.00	0.00	0.00	6.00	0.00	0.00	0.00	13.00
1400040TRA	TRASH COMPACTOR	4.00	1.00	0.00	0.00	0.00	0.00	0.00	3.00

DEPARTMENT TOTALS

NUMBER OF ITEMS:	10.00					0.00	83.00

GRAND TOTALS:

NUMBER OF ITEMS:	10.00					0.00	83.00

*** End of Inventory Status Report ***

Transaction Register

RUN DATE: 12/31/92   W.D. Peachtree & Company   PAGE 1
RUN TIME: 8:14 PM   Inventory Control
Transaction Register Report

ITEM TYPE: P

DEPT	GEN #	DATE	TRAN	ITEM #	QUANTITY	UNIT PRICE	UNIT COST	TOTAL PRICE	TOTAL COST
APP	12	12/02/92	REC	0900120REF	4.00	0.00	356.8100000	0.00	1427.24
		12/02/92	REC	0900122REF	4.00	0.00	456.8100000	0.00	1827.24
		12/02/92	REC	0900210REF	5.00	0.00	456.8100000	0.00	2284.05
		12/02/92	REC	1200040DIS	6.00	0.00	267.8600000	0.00	1607.16
		12/02/92	SAL	0900120REF	1.00	779.99	356.8100000	779.99	356.81-
		12/02/92	SAL	1100101OVE	1.00	700.00	344.7600000	700.00	344.76-
		12/02/92	SAL	1100101OVE	1.00-	700.00	344.7600000	700.00-	344.76
		12/02/92	SAL	1400040TRA	1.00	499.99	210.7500000	499.99	210.75-
		12/02/92	REC	1100102MOV	1.00	0.00	125.0000000	0.00	125.00
		12/02/92	SAL	1100102MOV	1.00	212.89	125.0000000	212.89	125.00-
		12/02/92	RET	1100102MOV	1.00	212.89	125.0000000	212.89-	125.00
		12/02/92	SAL	1100102MOV	1.00	212.89	125.0000000	212.89	125.00-
		12/02/92	REC	1100102MOV	1.00	0.00	125.0000000	0.00	125.00
		12/02/92	SAL	1100102MOV	1.00	212.89	125.0000000	212.89	125.00-
		12/02/92	SAL	1100102MOV	1.00	212.89	125.0000000	212.89	125.00-
		12/31/92	SAI	10040TRA	1.00	149.95	119.0000000	149.95	119.00-
		12/31/92	SAI	0900210REF	1.00	1100.00	456.8100000	1100.00	456.81-

GENERATION TOTALS: 3168.60   5877.32

DEPARTMENT TOTALS: 3168.60   5877.32

CLC	12	12/02/92	REC	436781G	24.00	0.00	5.4500000	0.00	130.80
		12/02/92	REC	463487G	4.00	0.00	5.2500000	0.00	21.00
		12/02/92	REC	463781	144.00	0.00	0.7500000	0.00	108.00
		12/02/92	SAL	463487G	2.00	10.99	5.2500000	21.98	10.50-

GRAND TOTALS......:   5673.38   20508.05
                                                ============ =============

*** End of the Transaction Register Report ***

Inventory Valuation Report

```
RUN DATE: 12/31/92                    W.D. Peachtree & Company                                    PAGE   1
RUN TIME:  8:18 PM                         Inventory Control
                                      Inventory Valuation Report
------------------------------------------------------------------------------------------------------------
                                          CURRENT          ITEM        % TOTAL     TOTAL INVENTORY
DEPT    ITEM ID      DESCRIPTION       QTY-ON-HAND      VALUATION      VALUATION       VALUATION
----    -------      -----------       -----------      ---------      ---------    ---------------
APP    0900120REF    COMMERCIAL REFRIGER.      8.00     2854.4800        4.90%          $58,261.13
       0900121REF    COMMERCIAL REFRIGER.      5.00     1949.5000        3.35%
       0900122REF    COMMERCIAL REFRIGER.      6.00     2740.8600        4.70%
       0900210REF    RESIDENTIAL REFRIG.       6.00     2740.8600        4.70%
       100101OVE     OVEN, COMMERCIAL         13.00     4481.8800        7.69%
       10040TRA      SUPERTRASH COMPACTOR      9.00     1071.0000        1.84%
       1100101OVE    OVEN, COMMERCIAL         13.00     4481.8800        7.69%
       1100102MOV    MICROWAVE OVEN            7.00      875.0000        1.50%
       1200040DIS    DISHWASHER               13.00     3482.1800        5.98%
       1400040TRA    TRASH COMPACTOR           3.00      632.2500        1.09%
                                           ----------   ----------     ----------
DEPARTMENT TOTALS:                            83.00    25309.8900       43.44%
     # ITEMS:      10.00                   ==========   ==========     ==========
GRAND TOTALS.....:                            83.00    25309.8900       43.44%
     # ITEMS:      10.00                   ==========   ==========     ==========


                                  *** End of Inventory Valuation Report ***
```

Inventory Price List

RUN DATE: 12/31/92   W.D. Peachtree & Company   PAGE 1
RUN TIME: 8:18 PM   Inventory Control
Inventory Price List

DEPARTMENT: APP

ITEM NUMBER	P C	DESCRIPTION	VENDOR ID	VENDOR ITEM #	SELL UNIT	QUANTITY AVAILABLE	PRICE A	PRICE B	PRICE C
0900120REF	A	COMMERCIAL REFRIGER.	FRIGID	900120	EACH	8.00	779.9900	669.9900	889.0000
0900121REF	A	COMMERCIAL REFRIGER.	FRIGID	900121	EACH	5.00	900.0000	999.9999	1099.9999
0900122REF	A	COMMERCIAL REFRIGER.	FRIGID	0900122	EACH	6.00	1100.0000	888.8800	1250.5500
0900210REF	A	RESIDENTIAL REFRIG.	FRIGID		EACH	6.00	1100.0000	888.8800	779.9900
1001010VE	A	OVEN, COMMERCIAL	TARPAN	TRPN11934	EACH	13.00	700.0000	675.0000	599.9900
10040TRA	A	SUPERTRASH COMPACTOR	ACME	COMP-XL	EACH	9.00	149.9500	145.9500	139.9500
1100101OVE	A	OVEN, COMMERCIAL	TARPAN	TRPN11934	EACH	13.00	700.0000	675.0000	599.9900
1100102MOV	A	MICROWAVE OVEN	MAYTAB		EACH	7.00	212.8900	199.9900	0.0000
120004DIS	A	DISHWASHER	MAYTAB	DIS092721	EACH	13.00	599.9900	549.9900	499.9900
1400040TRA	A	TRASH COMPACTOR	MAYTAB		EACH	3.00	499.9900	449.9900	399.3300

DEPARTMENT TOTALS: NUMBER OF ITEMS: 10.00   NUMBER OF UNITS: 83.00

GRAND TOTALS: NUMBER OF ITEMS: 10.00   NUMBER OF UNITS: 83.00

*** End of Inventory Price List Report ***

Departmental Summary Report

W.D. Peachtree & Company
Inventory Control
Departmental Summary Report

PAGE 1

ITEM TYPE: P

TOTAL INVENTORY VALUE: 58261.13

DEPT	ITEM VALUATION	% TOTAL VALUATION	YTD SALES AMOUNT	YTD SALES % TOTAL	COST OF SALES YTD AMOUNT	COST % TOTAL	YTD MARGIN AMOUNT	% TOTAL MARGIN
APP	25309.89	43.44%	3168.60	56.32%	1518.37	62.89%	1650.23	51.39%
CLC	566.45	0.97%	152.51	2.71%	67.85	2.81%	84.66	2.64%
CLM	1161.32	1.99%	149.46	2.66%	58.50	2.42%	90.96	2.83%
CLW	1385.56	2.38%	193.99	3.45%	80.00	3.31%	113.99	3.55%
ELE	23291.16	39.98%	1961.03	34.86%	689.47	28.56%	1271.56	39.60%
HAC	2618.64	4.49%	0.00	0.00%	0.00	0.00%	0.00	0.00%
HDW	203.75	0.35%	0.00	0.00%	0.00	0.00%	0.00	0.00%
SHA	2529.74	4.34%	0.00	0.00%	0.00	0.00%	0.00	0.00%
SLN	391.62	0.67%	0.00	0.00%	0.00	0.00%	0.00	0.00%
SPO	803.01	1.38%	0.00	0.00%	0.00	0.00%	0.00	0.00%
TOTALS:	58261.13		5625.59		2414.19		3211.40	

*** End of Departmental Summary Report ***

Reorder Items Report

```
RUN DATE: 12/31/92                        W.D. Peachtree & Company                                    PAGE  1
RUN TIME:  8:24 PM                            Inventory Control
                                            Reorder Items Report
----------------------------------------------------------------------------------------------------------------
   YOUR                          VENDOR  P          REORDER   WEEKS SINCE   REORDER    DATE    FIRST
  ITEM ID       DESCRIPTION      ITEM #  C QTY AVAIL  LEVEL   LAST ON RPT   QUANTITY  ORDERED  TIME?
----------------------------------------------------------------------------------------------------------------
ELE-8100000SPC  PORT. RADIO SPECIAL  WD       E    9.00    10.00        0         20.00    _____   *YES*
ELE-810060PTV   COLORTRONIC TV     CURTIS     E   11.00    20.00        0         10.00    _____   *YES*
ELE-810340TV    COLOR TELEVISION   ELE001 340TV E    3.00    20.00        0         10.00    _____   *YES*

TOTAL ITEMS BELOW REORDER LEVEL = 3

                          *** End of Reorder Items Report ***
```

Physical Inventory Report

W.D. Peachtree & Company
Inventory Control
Physical Inventory Report

DEPARTMENT: APP

ITEM NUMBER	P C	DESCRIPTION	LOCATION	VENDOR ID	VENDOR ITEM #	SELL UNIT	QTY-ON-HAND CALCULATED	QTY-ON-HAND ACTUAL	COMMENTS
0900120REF	A	COMMERCIAL REFRIGER.	WRHS-1	FRIGID	900120	EACH	8.00		
0900121REF	A	COMMERCIAL REFRIGER.	WRHS-1	FRIGID	900121	EACH	5.00		
0900122REF	A	COMMERCIAL REFRIGER.	WRHS-1	FRIGID	0900122	EACH	6.00		
0900210REF	A	RESIDENTIAL REFRIG.	WRHS-1	FRIGID		EACH	6.00		
100101OVE	A	OVEN, COMMERCIAL	WRHS-1	TARPAN	TRPN11934	EACH	13.00		
10040TRA	A	SUPERTRASH COMPACTOR	BIN 2-2	ACME	COMP-XL	EACH	9.00		
110010OVE	A	OVEN, COMMERCIAL	WRHS	TARPAN	TRPN11934	EACH	13.00		
1100102MOV	A	MICROWAVE OVEN		MAYTAB		EACH	7.00		
1200040DIS	A	DISHWASHER	WRHS-1	MAYTAB	DIS092721	EACH	13.00		
1400040TRA	A	TRASH COMPACTOR	WRHS-1	MAYTAB		EACH	3.00		

DEPARTMENT TOTALS: NUMBER OF ITEMS: 10.00   NUMBER OF UNITS: 83.00

GRAND TOTALS: NUMBER OF ITEMS: 10.00   NUMBER OF UNITS: 83.00

*** End of Physical Inventory Report ***

Period To Date Report

```
RUN DATE: 12/31/92                    W.D. Peachtree & Company                                    PAGE  1
RUN TIME:  8:26 PM                         Inventory Control
                                         Period To Date Report
```

DEPARTMENT: APP   ITEM TYPE: P

ITEM #	P C	DESCRIPTION	NET SALES UNITS	NET SALES AMOUNT	COST OF GOODS SOLD AMOUNT	COST OF GOODS SOLD % SALES	MARGIN AMOUNT	MARGIN % SALES	AVG SELLING PRICE
0900120REF	A	COMMERCIAL REFRIGER.	1.00	779.99	356.81	45.75	423.18	54.25	779.9900
0900121REF	A	COMMERCIAL REFRIGER.	0.00	0.00	0.00	0.00	0.00	0.00	0.0000
0900122REF	A	COMMERCIAL REFRIGER.	0.00	0.00	0.00	0.00	0.00	0.00	0.0000
0900210REF	A	RESIDENTIAL REFRIG.	1.00	1100.00	456.81	41.53	643.19	58.47	1100.0000
1001010VE	A	OVEN, COMMERCIAL	0.00	0.00	0.00	0.00	0.00	0.00	0.0000
10040TRA	A	SUPERTRASH COMPACTOR	1.00	149.95	119.00	79.36	30.95	20.64	149.9500
1100101OVE	A	OVEN, COMMERCIAL	0.00	0.00	0.00	0.00	0.00	0.00	0.0000
1100102MOV	A	MICROWAVE OVEN	3.00	638.67	375.00	58.72	263.67	41.28	212.8900
1200040DIS	A	DISHWASHER	0.00	0.00	0.00	0.00	0.00	0.00	0.0000
1400040TRA	A	TRASH COMPACTOR	1.00	499.99	210.75	42.15	289.24	57.85	499.9900
DEPARTMENT APP TOTALS:				3168.60	1518.37	47.92	1650.23	52.08	
GRAND TOTALS:				3168.60	1518.37	47.92	1650.23	52.08	

*** End of Inventory Period To Date Report ***

Year To Date Report

```
                          W.D. Peachtree & Company                              PAGE  1
                             Inventory Control
                             Year To Date Report
```

DEPARTMENT: APP   ITEM TYPE: P

ITEM #	P C	DESCRIPTION	NET SALES UNITS	NET SALES AMOUNT	COST OF GOODS SOLD AMOUNT	COST OF GOODS SOLD % SALES	MARGIN AMOUNT	MARGIN % SALES	AVG SELLING PRICE
0900120REF	A	COMMERCIAL REFRIGER.	1.00	779.99	356.81	45.75	423.18	54.25	779.9900
0900121REF	A	COMMERCIAL REFRIGER.	0.00	0.00	0.00	0.00	0.00	0.00	0.0000
0900122REF	A	COMMERCIAL REFRIGER.	0.00	0.00	0.00	0.00	0.00	0.00	0.0000
0900210REF	A	RESIDENTIAL REFRIG.	1.00	1100.00	456.81	41.53	643.19	58.47	1100.0000
100101OVE	A	OVEN, COMMERCIAL	0.00	0.00	0.00	0.00	0.00	0.00	0.0000
10040TRA	A	SUPERTRASH COMPACTOR	1.00	149.95	119.00	79.36	30.95	20.64	149.9500
1100101OVE	A	OVEN, COMMERCIAL	0.00	0.00	0.00	0.00	0.00	0.00	0.0000
1100102MOV	A	MICROWAVE OVEN	3.00	638.67	375.00	58.72	263.67	41.28	212.8900
1200040DIS	A	DISHWASHER	0.00	0.00	0.00	0.00	0.00	0.00	0.0000
1400040TRA	A	TRASH COMPACTOR	1.00	499.99	210.75	42.15	289.24	57.85	499.9900
DEPARTMENT APP TOTALS:				3168.60	1518.37	47.92	1650.23	52.08	
GRAND TOTALS:				3168.60	1518.37	47.92	1650.23	52.08	

*** End of Inventory Year To Date Report ***

List Inventory Items Report

```
RUN DATE: 12/31/92                    W.D. Peachtree & Company                    PAGE 1
RUN TIME:  8:26 PM                         Inventory Control
                                      List Inventory Items Report
-----------------------------------------------------------------------------------------
DEPARTMENT: APP

ITEM TYPE        :  P                                  :  P
ITEM NUMBER      :  0900120REF                         :  0900121REF
PRODUCT CODE     :  A                                  :  A
LOCATION         :  WRHS-1                             :  WRHS-1
DESCRIPTION      :  COMMERCIAL REFRIGER.               :  COMMERCIAL REFRIGER.
EXT. DESCRPTN    :  Y                                  :  Y
EXT DESCRPTN     :  20 CUBIC FT. COMMERCIAL REFRIGERATOR :  21 CUBIC FT. COMMERCIAL REFRIGERATOR
                                                          AVAILABLE WITH 2-YR WARRANTY AT NO EXTRA
                                                          COST

RECVG UNITS      :  EACH                               :  EACH
SELLING UNITS    :  EACH                               :  EACH
CONVRSN FACTOR:     1.00                                   1.00
VENDOR ID        :  FRIGID                             :  FRIGID
VENDOR ITEM #  :    900120                             :  900121
NEG. QUANTITY  :    N                                  :  N
COSTING TYPE   :    A                                  :  A
COMPONENT ITEM:     S                                  :  S
CURRENT COST   :             356.8100000               :           389.8999999
ITEM VALUATION:             2854.48                    :          1949.50
LST COST/UNIT  :             356.8100000               :             0.0000000
TAX STATUS     :    T                                  :  T
SELLING PRICES
     PRICE A    :             779.9900               :           900.0000
     PRICE B    :             669.9900               :           999.9999
     PRICE C    :             889.0000               :          1099.9999
REORDER LEVEL  :                8.00                 :             8.00
REORDER QTY    :                6.00                 :            10.00
ON RO RPT DATE:               /  /                   :            /  /


DEPARTMENT TOTALS
TOTAL VALUE:      25309.89   NUMBER OF ITEMS:   10.00   NUMBER OF UNITS:   83.00
GRAND TOTALS
TOTAL VALUE:      25309.89   NUMBER OF ITEMS:   10.00   NUMBER OF UNITS:   83.00

                        *** End of List Inventory Items Report ***
```

Specific Units on Hand Report

```
RUN DATE: 12/31/92                      W.D. Peachtree & Company                              PAGE  1
RUN TIME:  8:30 PM                           Inventory Control
                                        Specific Units On Hand Report
---------------------------------------------------------------------------------------------------
  ITEM ID          DESCRIPTION          SERIAL NUMBER        UNIT COST       STATUS
---------------------------------------------------------------------------------------------------

PELE810340TV       COLOR TELEVISION     938384729            345.0000000        A
                                        49875845             345.0000000        A
                                        94857845             345.0000000        A


*** End of Specific Units On Hand Report ***
```

Specific Units Sold Report

W.D. Peachtree & Company
Inventory Control
Specific Units Sold Report

SERIAL NUMBER	PURCHASE DATE	OPTIONAL DATE	CUSTOMER ID	CUSTOMER NAME	UNIT PRICE	UNIT COST	COMMENT
PELE810340TV	- COLOR TELEVISION						
883847302	12/02/92	12/02/92	MATHIS	MATHIS, WILLIAM A.	555.99	345.00	SEVICE WARRANTY RENEWAL

*** End of Specific Units Sold Report ***

Maintain Inventory Items Control Report

```
RUN DATE: 12/31/92                    W.D. Peachtree & Company                                    PAGE 1
RUN TIME: 8:34 PM                         Inventory Control
                                   Maintain Inventory Items Control Report

                                    --------------- CHANGES ---------------
     ITEM ID              FIELD            CURRENT VALUE                      INITIAL VALUE
   -----------         -----------       --------------                    ----------------
   PAPP10040TRA        DESCRIPTION.....:  SUPERTRASH COMPACTOR               SUPERTRASH COMPACTOR
                       EXT. DESCR. FLAG :  Y                                 N
                       EXT. DESCRIPTION :  Advent SuperTrash Compactor. Note this
                                           Model 60JL is now serviced by Yankee
                                           Repairs.  For 24-hour service, call
                                           555-1212.

                       PRODUCT CODE.....:  A                                 A
                       PRIMARY LOCATION.:  BIN 2-2                           BIN 2-2
                       RECEIVING UNIT...:  EACH                             EACH
                       SELLING UNIT.....:  EACH                             EACH
                       CONVERSION FACTOR:  1.00                             1.00
                       VENDER I.D.......:  ACME                             ACME
                       VENDER ITEM #....:  COMP-XL                          COMP-XL
                       NEGATIVE QUANTITY:  N                                N
                       COSTING TYPE.....:  S                                S
                       COMPONENT ITEM...:  S                                S
                       CURRENT COST.....:  119.0000000                      119.0000000
                       LAST COST/UNIT...:  0.0000000                        0.0000000
                       SELLING PRICES
                           PRICE A......:  149.9500                         149.9500
                           PRICE B......:  145.9500                         145.9500
                           PRICE C......:  139.9500                         139.9500
                       ITEM TAX STATUS..:  T                                T
                       REORDER LEVEL....:  10.00                            10.00
                       REORDER QUANTITY :  6.00                             6.00
                       ON REORDER REPORT:   /   /                            /   /
                       YTLP ACTIVITY:
                           SALES........:  0.00                             0.00
                           COST OF SALES:  0.00                             0.00
                           # SOLD.......:  0.00                             0.00
                           # RECEIVED...:  0.00                             0.00
                           # RETURNED...:  0.00                             0.00
                           # ADJUSTED...:  0.00                             0.00
                           # COMPONENTS.:  0.00                             0.00

*** End of MAINTAIN INVENTORY ITEMS Control Report ***
```

Change Item Prices Control Report

```
RUN DATE: 12/31/92                      W.D. Peachtree & Company                               PAGE  1
RUN TIME:  8:36 PM                          Inventory Control
                                     Change Item Prices Control Report
------------------------------------------------------------------------------------------------------------
TYPE OF CHANGE: PERCENT       7.50
------- PRICE A -------      ------- PRICE B -------       ------- PRICE C -------
OLD         CHANGE       NEW      OLD        CHANGE       NEW       OLD        CHANGE       NEW
------------------------      ------------------------       ------------------------

------ APP ------

10040TRA    - SUPERTRASH COMPACTOR

149.9500    11.2463   161.1963    145.9500   10.9462   156.8963    139.9500   10.4963   150.4463


TOTAL NUMBER OF ITEMS CHANGED.....:  1
TOTAL NUMBER OF ITEMS NOT CHANGED.:  0


*** End of CHANGE INVENTORY ITEMS PRICES Control Report ***
```

Change Costing Type Control Report

```
RUN DATE: 12/31/92          W.D. Peachtree & Company               PAGE   1
RUN TIME:  8:37 PM               Inventory Control
                          Change Costing Type Control Report
-------------------------------------------------------------------------------
                                                         COSTING TYPE CHANGED
                              ITEM                        FROM          TO
    ITEM ID                DESCRIPTION                    ====         ====
-------------------     --------------------             ------       ------
PAPP10040TRA            SUPERTRASH COMPACTOR              S            A


TOTAL NUMBER OF ITEMS CHANGED:  1


*** End of CHANGE INVENTORY COSTING TYPE Control Report ***
```

Maintain Specific Unit History Control Report

```
RUN DATE: 12/31/92        W.D. Peachtree & Company              PAGE   1
RUN TIME:  8:41 PM             Inventory Control
                        Maintain Specific Unit History

    FIELD                  NOW                        WAS
------------------   -------------------      -------------------
ITEM ID.........:    PELE810340TV
UNIT SERIAL #...:    883847302
ITEM DESCRIPTION:    COLOR TELEVISION            COLOR TELEVISION
OPTIONAL DATE...:    12/02/92                    12/02/92
CUSTOMER NAME...:    MATHIS, SHARON              MATHIS, WILLIAM A.
CUSTOMER ID....:     MATHIS                      MATHIS
UNIT PRICE......:           555.9900                   555.9900
UNIT COST.......:           345.0000000                345.0000000
COMMENT.........:    SEVICE WARRANTY RENEWAL     SEVICE WARRANTY RENEWAL


*** End of Maintain Specific Unit History Control Report ***
```

Enter Transactions Control Report

W.D. Peachtree & Company
Inventory Control
Enter Transactions Control Report

DATE	T/C	ITEM ID	P C	TRANSACTION QUANTITY	SALES AMOUNT	EFFECT ON INV. QTY.	EFFECT ON INV. VALUE	COMMENT	WARNING MESSAGE
12/31/92	REC	PELE810340TV	E	1.00 *	0.00	1.00	345.00		

SALE TOTALS :	0.00	0.00	0.00
RETURN TOTALS :	0.00	0.00	0.00
RECEIPT TOTALS:		1.00	345.00
ADJUST TOTALS :		0.00	0.00
	==========	==========	==========
	0.00	1.00	345.00

* - Quantity reflects RECEIVING units.

*** End of Enter Transactions Control Report ***

Chapter 9

INVENTORY: PRACTICING WITH A SAMPLE BUSINESS

Learning Objectives:

After working this chapter you should be able to:

1. Perform everyday inventory activities including—making changes to an inventory item, entering a receipt of goods, selling an item from inventory, and changing the selling price of a group of items.

2. Perform monthly inventory activities including—printing a departmental summary, printing a period-to-date report, printing a transaction register, and closing the period.

Chapter 9

Inventory: Practicing with a Sample Business

This section guides you through lessons that give you practical experience in working with Inventory. You work with the inventory of W.D. Peachtree & Company.

The lessons in this chapter are grouped under two topics:

1.   Everyday Activities.
2.   Monthly Tasks.

Topic 1 - Everyday Activities takes you through inventory activities you do frequently. These tasks include changing information about an item, entering receipts, recording sales, and changing inventory prices.

Topic 2 - Monthly Tasks demonstrates typical activities you do at the end of a month or other accounting period.

Practice With W. D. Peachtree & Company

In this practice session, you use examples from several of W.D. Peachtree & Company's departments. Here is a list of the departments used in this chapter. Each department description is followed by the department code Inventory uses to identify the department:

- Men's Clothing (CLM)
- Women's Clothing (CLW)
- Children's Clothing (CLC)
- Large Appliances (APP)
- Electronics (ELE)
- Sporting Goods (SPO)

W.D. Peachtree & Company's options are set to always print control reports, so you need your printer on-line and ready for these lessons. Use the control reports as a method to verify the changes you enter.

Beginning the Session

```
WARNING

BEFORE CONTINUING, BE SURE THAT ALL DATA FILES HAVE BEEN RESTORED TO
THEIR ORIGINAL CONDITION.  IF YOU ARE UNSURE OF HOW TO RESTORE THESE
FILES, TURN TO THE INSTRUCTIONS FOUND ON PAGE 1-32 IN  CHAPTER 1.
```

The lessons in this chapter guide you through typical Inventory operations. You can complete the lessons in one session or you can do them in several sessions. .

❖ Start Peachtree Complete Accounting by changing to the directory in which you installed Peachtree Complete and typing **PEACH** [ENTER].

❖ Press [F9] to erase the date shown on your screen.

For this session we want to use December 2, 1992 as the date.

❖ For the date 12/2/92 type **120292** and press [ENTER].

PCA asks you for a company ID.

❖ Type **WD** [ENTER].

PCA displays its **Main Menu.**

❖ Select **Inventory** by highlighting it and pressing [ENTER].

This starts PCA Inventory. PCA displays the **Inventory Main Menu**.

You are now ready to begin the practice session. Continue with Topic 1.

Topic 1 - Everyday Activities

Everyday activities are the things you do on a regular basis to keep your inventory up-to-date.

The lessons in this topic help you become familiar with some of the functions used on an everyday basis. Topic 1 has four lessons:

1. Make changes to an inventory item.
2. Enter a receipt of goods.
3. Sell an item from inventory.
4. Change the selling price of a group of items.

Lesson 1 - Make Changes To An Inventory Item

This lesson shows you how to make changes to an inventory item.

W.D. Peachtree & Company has carried the same trash compactor in its appliance department for several years. It has now decided to change vendors (suppliers). You are going to make the types of changes that might come about when a company decides to switch vendors for an item of inventory.

❖ Select **Maintenance Programs** from the Inventory Main Menu.

❖ From the Maintenance Programs Menu, select **Maintain Inventory Items**.

Inventory tells you to make sure that your printer is set to *TOP OF FORM.*

Note: Inventory will ask you to do this as you begin each Inventory function. However, it will not be mentioned from here on.

❖ Make sure that your printer is ready to print and at the top of a new page. Then press .

Inventory now asks for three pieces of information, one at a time:

- item type
- department code
- item number

These pieces of information form the **item identification** for each inventory item. They are different for each item. This is the item identification for the trash compactor:

Item Type	Dept. Code	Item Number
P	APP	10040TRA

❖ For *ITEM TYPE,* press to accept the default of P (Product).

Now you will see a way to look up departments.

❖ Press **[ENTER]** at the *DEPT* prompt. Do not type anything else.

Inventory displays a "pop up box" that has the department codes for all of W.D. Peachtree's departments.

❖ Select **APP** (Large Appliances) by pressing **[ENTER]**.

If you wanted to select another department, you could move the highlighted bar to it (using the arrow keys) and then press **[ENTER]**.

Now you will see how to look up an item number. Because you may have many hundreds of items in this department, looking through a list of all of them would take a long time. Here is a shortcut.

❖ Type the number **10** (as a starting point) and then press **[F2]**. Do **not** press **[ENTER]** yet.

Inventory shows you a pop up box that only has items that are products, are stocked by department APP, and begin with 10.

You can type as many numbers or letters as you like before you press **[F2]**.

The pop up boxes are always available when you see *[F2] - LOOKUP* at the bottom of your screen.

❖ Select item number **10040TRA** (for Supertrash Compactor) by moving the highlight to it and pressing **[ENTER]**.

Inventory displays the following information for this item:

```
==================================================================================
INMAINT1                        Maintain Inventory Items            COMPANY ID: WD
12/02/92                        W.D. Peachtree & Company            GENERATION #: 12
==================================================================================

ITEM TYPE (P/S): P           DEPARTMENT : APP           ITEM NUMBER : 10040TRA

        ITEM DESCRIPTION ............:  SUPERTRASH COMPACTOR
        EXT DESCRIPTION...............:  N
        PRODUCT CODE..................:  A
        LOCATION ..........................:  BIN 2-2
        RECEIVING UNIT ................:  EACH
        SELLING UNIT ....................:  EACH
        CONVERSION FACTOR .......:          1.00
        VENDOR ID.........................:  ACME          REORDER LEVEL ....................:          10.00
        VENDOR ITEM #.................:  COMP-XL       REORDER QUANTITY.............:           6.00
        NEG QUANTITY ...................:  N             ON REORDER RPT DATE.......:     /  /
        COSTING TYPE ...................:  S
        COMPONENT ITEM ..............:  S             SELLING PRICES
        CURRENT COST ..................:      119.0000000     PRICE A........................:         149.9500
        LAST COST/UNIT................:        0.0000000     PRICE B........................:         145.9500
        ITEM TAX STATUS ..............:  T                     PRICE C ........................:         139.9500

ACCEPT (Y/N) : Y           (D = DELETE RECORD FROM FILE)
                                 F8 - Undo                                              C
```

Check that the item description is *SUPERTRASH COMPACTOR*. If it is not, press **[ESC]** and re-enter the correct item number.

Notice that the cursor is on *ACCEPT (Y/N)*, at the bottom of the screen. You can accept this information—leave it the way it is **(Y)**—or not accept it **(N)**, and change it.

❖ Because a change is needed in the extended description, Type **N** at the accept prompt.

Inventory moves the cursor to the first field, *ITEM DESCRIPTION*.

You are not going to change the basic item description. The first change you want to make here is to the extended description, where you are going to add some extra text to appear on invoices.

❖ Press ▣ or ▣ (to move your cursor) until you get to the *EXT DESCRIPTION*. Enter **Y** and press ▣.

A pop up box appears. This box will contain your extended description. The description you type will appear inside the box. Do *not* press ▣ at the end of a sentence or when the words reach the box's border—just keep typing. If you want to correct a word, or change a word, press ▣ or ▣ moving the cursor along the sentence to the word you want to correct. Do *not* press the ▣ key; it takes you out of the extended description box.

Here is an example of what you can type as an extended description:

> **Advent SuperTrash Compactor. Note this Model 60JL is now serviced by Yankee Repairs. For 24-hour service, call 555-1212.**

❖ After you enter your extended description, press ▣.

The borders of the box disappear, leaving the extended description as part of the item information.

❖ Now move the cursor to *VENDOR ID*.

❖ Type **ADVENT** (the vendor in this case), then move to *VENDOR ITEM #* and type **ADT-60 JL**— Advent's stock number for this compactor. (Be sure to use all capital letters.)

This new vendor delivers the trash compactor faster than the old vendor, so W.D. Peachtree does not need to keep as many trash compactors on hand. Therefore, the reorder level can be lowered. That is, the stock of compactors can get to a lower level than with the old vendor.

When the number of units in stock gets down to the reorder level you have set, Inventory lets you know that you need to reorder this item by including it on the **Reorder Items Report**. Assume that the reorder level will be 6 and the new reorder quantity (the number of items reordered each time) will be **4**.

❖ Move the cursor to *REORDER LEVEL*. Change the reorder level to 6 by typing over the 10. Then change the *REORDER QUANTITY* to 4 by typing over the 6.

After you have made this change, every time the stock of trash compactors gets down to 6 on hand, Peachtree will order 4 from Advent.

❖ Those are all the changes you need to make in this example, so press ▣ to move to the *ACCEPT (Y/N)* prompt.

❖ Check your changes, and press ▣ to accept the screen if all the information is correct.

Inventory now asks you:

MAINTAIN YEAR-THROUGH-LAST-PERIOD INFORMATION?

❖ Answer **N** and press ▣ (since this function is normally performed only when the program is installed).

Inventory now prints a Maintain Inventory Items Control Report, and positions your cursor so that you can change another item.

❖ Read your control report. The control report should appear as follows:

```
RUN DATE:  12/02/92                          W. D. Peachtree & Company                      PAGE  1
RUN TIME:    1:06 PM                             Inventory Control
                                        Maintain Inventory Items Control Report
----------------------------------------------------------------------------------------------------
                                            ----------------------------- CHANGES ----------------------------
    ITEM ID              FIELD                 CURRENT VALUE                        INITIAL VALUE
----------------------------------------------------------------------------------------------------
PAPP10040TRA    DESCRIPTION...............:  SUPERTRASH COMPACTOR         SUPERTRASH COMPACTOR
                EXT. DESCR. FLAG .........:  Y                            N
                EXT. DESCRIPTION..........:  Advent SuperTrash Compactor.  Note
                                             this Model 60JL is now serviced by
                                             Yankee Repairs.  For 24-hour service,
                                             call 555-1212.

                PRODUCT CODE ..............:  A                            A
                PRIMARY LOCATION......:  BIN 2-2                      BIN 2-2
                RECEIVING UNIT ...........:  EACH                         EACH
                SELLING UNIT .................:  EACH                         EACH
                CONVERSION FACTOR.:           1.00                              1.00
                VENDER I.D. ...................:  ADVENT                       ACME
                VENDER ITEM # .............:  ADT-60JL                     COMP-XL
                NEGATIVE QUANTITY....:  N                            N
                COSTING TYPE ..............:  S                            S
                COMPONENT ITEM ........:  S                            S
                CURRENT COST ...........:     119.0000000                119.0000000
                LAST COST/UNIT...........:       0.0000000                  0.0000000
                SELLING PRICES
                    PRICE A ....................:             149.9500              149.9500
                    PRICE B .....................:             145.9500              145.9500
                    PRICE C .....................:             139.9500              139.9500
                ITEM TAX STATUS .........:  T                            T
                REORDER LEVEL ...........:             6.00                  10.00
                REORDER QUANTITY....:             4.00                   6.00
                ON REORDER REPORT:    /  /                           /  /
                YTLP ACTIVITY:
                    SALES .......................:             0.00                   0.00
                    COST OF SALES.......:             0.00                   0.00
                    # SOLD......................:             0.00                   0.00
                    # RECEIVED .............:             0.00                   0.00
                    # RETURNED ...........:             0.00                   0.00
                    # ADJUSTED ............:             0.00                   0.00
                    # COMPONENTS......:             0.00                   0.00

*** End of MAINTAIN INVENTORY ITEMS Control Report ***
```

Notice that the control report shows you all the changes you have made.

❖ If you made an error entering the changes in this lesson, correct your entries. Otherwise, press ⌨ to end **Maintain Inventory Items**.

❖ Press ⌨ to go to the Inventory Main Menu.

Lesson 1 Summary

You have changed vendors for an item and updated the item information. The new vendor ID appears on reports and displays, along with the new reorder level. This helps you know who to order the item from and when to order it.

You have also learned about:

• Inventory item identification.
• ⌨ and ⌨ lookups.
• Control reports.

You are now ready to receive the first order from Advent.

Lesson 2 - Receive an Item

❖ From the Inventory Main Menu, select **Processing Programs**, and then select **Enter Inventory Transactions**.

You can use **Enter Inventory Transactions** to enter inventory receipts, sales, returns and adjustments.

❖ Type **12/12/92** as the transaction date for this example.

Always use the date a transaction occurred rather then the date you are entering it. The screen will show the following:

```
================================================================================
INPROC                    Enter Inventory Transactions       COMPANY ID: WD
12/02/92                  W.D. Peachtree & Company            GENERATION #: 12
================================================================================

TRANSACTION DATE:  12/12/92

TRANSACTION ... :

ITEM TYPE .......... :
DEPARTMENT .... :
ITEM NUMBER .... :


QUANTITY.......... :
UNIT PRICE........ :                   TOTAL PRICE ..... :
UNIT COST.......... :                  TOTAL COST...... :
COMMENT.......... :




F1 - Help    F2  - Lookup                                              C
```

❖ When the prompt asks for a transaction, press ⏎ to see a pop up box that lists the valid transaction types.

❖ Select **RECEIPT**.

The next prompt is Item Type. Select **P.**

❖ Enter the item identification for the trash compactor. Use ⏎ and F2 to look up the department and item number if you don't remember them.

Hint: The department is appliances and the item number begins with 10.

After you enter the item identification, you can enter quantity received and unit cost.

❖ For this example, type **6** for the quantity received and **$119.00.** for the unit cost.

Inventory keeps track of the units in which you receive items—for instance, dozens, cases, tankloads, and the like—as well as the units in which you sell the items. It automatically converts between the two units if they are different.

You can now enter a comment. Comments can be anything you like. Many people use the shipping ticket number or invoice number (if known) for the comment.

❖ Since you do not know an actual number, type 071870.

Inventory moves you to the *ACCEPT Y/N* prompt.

❖ Check your entry and press ⌨. Inventory now prints an Enter Transactions Control Report which should appear as follows:

```
RUN DATE: 12/02/92                         W. D. Peachtree & Company                              PAGE 1
RUN TIME:   1:12 PM                              Inventory Control
                                         Enter Transactions Control Report
--------------------------------------------------------------------------------------------------------
                          P   TRANSACTION    SALES      EFFECT ON      EFFECT ON               WARNING
DATE       T/C   ITEM ID  C   QUANTITY       AMOUNT     INV. QTY.      INV. VALUE   COMMENT    MESSAGE
---------  ----- --------- --- ------------- ---------- -------------- ------------ ---------- ----------
12/12/92   REC   PAPP10040TRA  A      6.00 *     0.00        6.00          714.00      071870
```

❖ Do not go back to the menu yet—stay where you are in preparation for lesson 3.

Lesson 2 - Summary

You have now learned how to receive items. The other three inventory transactions—selling items, recording returns of items, and making adjustments to quantity—work in much the same manner.

Lesson 3 - Sell an Item

In this lesson you will learn to record a sale. Following is the scenario:

On December 12, 1992, W.D. Peachtree sold two COLORTRONIC pocket color televisions to a customer from the electronics department (ELE). You will enter this sale by:

- Entering the number sold.
- Recording the sale price.
- Commenting on the sale.

❖ If you just finished the last lesson, press ESC twice to get to *TRANSACTION DATE*. Otherwise, select **Enter Transactions** from the Processing Menu.

❖ Type **12/12/92** as the date.

❖ Type **SAL** as the transaction type (sales).

❖ Enter the item identification using the following codes.

Item Type	Dept. Code	Item Number
P	ELE	810060PTV

❖ Type **2** as the quantity sold.

Note that when you enter a sale, the program:

- Decreases the current quantities of inventory on hand by this amount.
- Increases the number of items sold.
- Decreases the inventory value.

Inventory will then prompt you for *UNIT PRICE*.

❖ Press ⌨ to look up the list of three standard selling prices for the pocket television.

You may have noticed these selling prices on the screen in lesson 1, when you changed the trash compactor information.

These three standard selling prices are preset by sales managers for each item of inventory.

❖ Assume these pocket televisions sold on a special sale for $189.99 each. Since $189.99 is neither price A, B or C, press ⌨ to remove the pop up box and then type 189.99. Do not forget the decimal point.

Inventory now gives you the opportunity to enter a unit cost for the televisions. Because these are assumed to be average cost items, it gives you the average cost of units in stock as a default.

❖ Press ⌨ for the *UNIT COST*.

Notice that Inventory shows the *TOTAL PRICE* and *TOTAL COST* for this sale. This information allows a manager's review of the reasonableness of profit on each sale.

You can now enter a comment. For sales, this is usually the sales ticket or invoice number. This is similar to the comment section used when there is a receipt of inventory (covered in Lesson 2).

❖ Type **54321**, the sales ticket number in this example, as the comment.

❖ Check your entries and accept your work if it is correct. The printer will print a summary of the transaction as follows:

| 12/12/92 | SAL | PELE810060PTV E | 2.00 | 379.98 | 2.00- | 220.00- | 54321 |

You are not going to enter any more transactions now.

❖ This is the end of Lesson 3, so you need to end the session by pressing [ESC] twice and then [F10] to end **Enter Transactions** . The printer will print the following:

```
SALE TOTALS    :    379.98         2.00-         220.00-
RETURN TOTALS  :      0.00         0.00            0.00
RECEIPT TOTALS :                   6.00          714.00
ADJUST TOTALS  :                   0.00            0.00
                    ========     ========       ========

                     379.98         4.00          494.00

        * - Quantity reflects RECEIVING units.

        *** End of Enter Transactions Control Report ***
```

Lesson 3 Summary

You have just entered the sale of an inventory item. In the normal course of a business, there are many sales each day. Therefore, a certain time each day is usually set aside to enter all sales entries at one time.

Lesson 4 - Change Inventory Item Prices

When there is a sales price change for a single item, it is easiest to make such a change through **Maintain Inventory Items**.

But, occasionally sales price changes must be made for a group of items at once, usually when a vendor raises or lowers the cost of a line of items.

Change Inventory Prices lets you make group changes such as these. In this lesson, W.D. Peachtree & Company wants to change the sales prices for all inventory items in the appliance department as a result of a two and one-half percent price increase from its vendor. The company decides to increase its sales price by two and one-half percent to maintain its present profit margin. To do this, you will select:

- What items to change.
- The kind of change, and amount.

❖ Return to the Inventory Main Menu by pressing [ESC]. Then move the cursor to Maintenance Programs and press [ENTER]. From the Maintenance Programs Menu, select **Change Inventory Item Prices**.

Inventory asks you to begin to define the inventory items for which there is a change. You can choose between *ALL ITEMS* and *RANGE OF ITEMS*.

❖ Select **Range of Items**.

Inventory next asks you to select the range. You can select it by *DEPARTMENTS* or *VENDORS.* In this example, the price increase applies only to the appliance department.

❖ Choose **Range of Departments**.

Inventory asks you to choose between changing the prices of products or changing the prices of services. Appliances are products.

❖ Select Products—item type **P**.

Inventory then asks you for the departments where you want to make a price change.

❖ Type **APP** for both the beginning and the ending department in this case.

❖ Select the option to **increase** prices.

❖ Select to increase them by a **percentage** rather than by an amount.

Inventory asks you to *ENTER THE ADJUSTMENT PERCENTAGE*.

❖ Type **2.5** to raise all sales prices by two and one-half percent.

❖ Before taking any action, check your answers.

Change Inventory Prices can let you make many changes in a very brief period of time. Be quite sure your answers are correct.

That is the last question that you must answer in this procedure. Inventory moves the cursor to the *ACCEPT Y/N* prompt.

❖ Accept the screen if you have no changes, or go back and make changes.

After you accept the screen, Inventory begins the price changes. The following Change Item Prices Control Report will be printed.

```
RUN DATE: 12/02/92                        W. D. Peachtree & Company                              Page 1
RUN TIME: 1:24 PM                              Inventory Control
                                        Change Item Prices Control Report
-----------------------------------------------------------------------------------------------------------
TYPE OF CHANGE: PERCENT      2.50
------------------ PRICE A ----------------    ----------------- PRICE B ----------------    ----------------- PRICE C ----------------
OLD          CHANGE       NEW          OLD          CHANGE       NEW          OLD          CHANGE       NEW
-----------------------------------------------------------------------------------------------------------

---------- APP ----------

0900120REF        - COMMERCIAL REFRIGER.
  779.9900     19.4997     799.4897     669.9900       16.7497     686.7397     889.0000       22.2250     911.2250

0900121REF        - COMMERCIAL REFRIGER.
  900.0000     22.5000     922.5000     999.9999       25.0000    1024.9999    1099.9999       27.5000    1127.4999

0900122REF        - COMMERCIAL REFRIGER.
 1100.0000     27.5000    1127.5000     888.8800       22.2220     911.1020    1250.5500       31.2638    1281.8138

0900210REF        - RESIDENTIAL REFRIGER.
 1100.0000     27.5000    1127.5000     888.8800       22.2220     911.1020     779.9900       19.4997     799.4897

100101OVE         - OVEN, COMMERCIAL
  700.0000     17.5000     717.5000     675.0000       16.8750     691.8750     599.9900       14.9997     614.9897

10040TRA          - SUPERTRASH COMPACTOR
  149.9500      3.7488     153.6988     145.9500        3.6488     149.5988     139.9500        3.4988     143.4488

1100101OVE        - OVEN, COMMERCIAL
  700.0000     17.5000     717.5000     675.0000       16.8750     691.8750     599.9900       14.9997     614.9897

1100102MOV        - MICROWAVE OVEN
  212.89        5.3222     218.2123     199.9900        4.9998     204.9898       0.0000        0.0000       0.0000

1200040DIS        - DISHWASHER
  599.9900     14.9997     614.9897     549.9900       13.7497     563.7397     499.9000       12.4975     512.3975

1400040TRA        - TRASH COMPACTOR
  499.9900     12.4998     512.4898     449.9900       11.2498     461.2398     399.3300        9.9832     409.3133


TOTAL NUMBER OF ITEMS CHANGED.......... : 10
TOTAL NUMBER OF ITEMS NOT CHANGED.... : 0

*** End of CHANGE INVENTORY ITEMS PRICES Control Report ***
```

When this is done, the screen displays the *ALL ITEMS/RANGE OF ITEMS* pop up box. This lets you change more item prices.

❖ Because there are no more changes in this example, press [■] to end the program.

Lesson 4 Summary

You have raised the sales prices of all appliances by two and one-half percent. The new prices take effect immediately and appear on reports and displays. You have received a control report that shows the old and new prices for each item.

Topic 2 - Monthly Tasks

A monthly task is an inventory activity that is performed once during each accounting period, usually at the end of the month.

This topic has four lessons:

1. Print a Departmental Summary.
2. Print a Period-to-Date Report.
3. Print a Transaction Register.
4. Close the Period.

Lesson 1 - Print a Departmental Summary

The **Departmental Summary** report can be printed any time during the month. It is a handy summary report during the month and is also an important end-of-period report. This report gives you a financial summary *for each department*, from the beginning of your fiscal year, to date. Here are the steps to print this useful report.

❖ From the Report Programs Menu, select **Departmental Summary**.

❖ As an example, type **12/31/92** as the *REPORT DATE*.

You could enter the date you are running the report, but it may be more useful to label it with the end of the month it summarizes.

❖ Select **P** to print the report for products only.

Most reports let you choose between products and services.

❖ Select "All Departments" to print the report.

(During the month, if you are interested in the figures for just one department you could print the report for just that department.)

After this selection, inventory prints the report.

Notice the following totals at the end of the report:

- Value of the inventory.
- Sales.
- Cost of sales.
- Margin amount—the difference between sales and cost of sales.

Lesson 1 Summary

You have just learned how to print one of the inventory reports that is used on a regular basis. This Department Summary report gives you information on sales, by department. (This is the only report in PCA that gives you this information.) Like all reports, it is very easy to print.

Lesson 2 - Period-To-Date Report

This report lists the sales and profitability for inventory items. Most businesses print it as part of their regular month-end work. If you want to do this, you must print the report before you close the period.

❖ From the Report Programs Menu, select **To Date** reports.

Inventory gives you the choice of two reports: *Period-to-Date* report or *Year-To-Date* report.

❖ Select **Period-to-Date** report to get a report at any time during the month.

❖ The inventory activity for W.D. Peachtree has occurred in December, 1992, so type the report date: **12/31/92**.

❖ Select to print only products.

❖ Select to print for departments **APP** through **ELE**.

Inventory now prints the report (5 pages). You could have printed this report for all departments.

❖ Review the report.

Look at the last report. Notice the figures for the COLORTRONIC television. You will see the transaction you entered earlier reflected in it.

❖ Press [ESC] twice and then [F10] to return to the Inventory Report Programs Menu.

Lesson 2 Summary

You can print the Period-to-Date report any time during the month. It gives you a complete picture of all activities up to that date.

After the report has been printed, it should probably be retained. It may provide information needed to make your own decisions about inventory and pricing changes.

Lesson 3 - Transaction Register

This is another report that most businesses run at the end of each month. It lists all inventory transactions and is very useful for reviewing inventory activity and for serving as an audit trail.

❖ From the Report Programs Menu, select **Transaction Register**.

❖ Type the *REPORT DATE*: **12/31/92**.

You could also have entered today's date. The date does not affect the contents of the report. It is only printed on the reports for information purposes.

Inventory now lets you choose between including products or services. You cannot include both in the same Transaction Register.

❖ Choose *PRODUCTS*.

You can now choose between a range of departments and all departments.

❖ Choose *ALL DEPARTMENTS*.

You can now choose the periods to report. Inventory uses the word "generation" to mean period and lets you choose among *CURRENT GENERATION*, a *RANGE OF GENERATIONS*, and *ALL GENERATIONS*.

❖ Select **Current Generation**.

This will give you a report for the current period only.

Inventory now prints the Transaction Register.

❖ Review the report.

Notice that the transactions you entered earlier for the receipt of the SUPERTRASH COMPACTOR and the sale of the COLORTRONIC televisions are included.

❖ Press ⌨ three times, then ⌨ to return to the Inventory Reports Menu.

Lesson 3 - Summary

The Transaction Register provides a valuable audit trail. It shows all inventory-related transactions entered into Peachtree Complete Accounting. Whenever you need to reconcile inventory levels, or try to explain inventory shortages or overages, this report can provide a great deal of help.

Lesson 4 - Close Current Period

In this lesson, you learn to close the current period. A period is usually a month, but it can also be another accounting period such as a week or a quarter.

A business will run **Close Current Period** at the end of each month, after all transactions have been entered for the period into Inventory and all the monthly reports have been run.

Among other things it does, **Close Current Period** resets to zero the period-to-date statistics for sales, receipts, and the like, for each inventory item. It also creates a new copy of the files—called a new generation—for use in the next period's processing.

You do not make any entries when you run **Close Current Period**.

❖ Press ⌨ to return to the Inventory Main Menu and then select Processing Programs. From the Inventory Processing Menu, select **Close Current Period**.

Inventory now gives you the choice of two types of closing: *END OF PERIOD* or *END OF YEAR.*

"End of year" refers to a business's fiscal year. When you select this, it resets to zero the year-through-last-period statistics as well as period-to-date statistics.

December 31, 1992 is the end of W.D. Peachtree's fiscal year.

❖ Therefore, select **Y**, to close the year.

Inventory displays the name of each file as it creates the new generation. This process will take a while.

Lesson 4 - Summary

You have now done all the tasks that would routinely be done at the end of each period.

After you run **Close Current Period**, you could begin entering transactions for the new month.

Chapter 9

End of Chapter Problem

```
                         WARNING

BEFORE CONTINUING, BE SURE THAT ALL DATA FILES HAVE BEEN RESTORED TO
THEIR ORIGINAL CONDITION.  IF YOU ARE UNSURE OF HOW TO RESTORE THESE
FILES, TURN TO THE INSTRUCTIONS FOUND ON PAGE 1-32 IN  CHAPTER 1.
```

NOTE: You may find it helpful to record the problem data on input forms before using Inventory.
Master Input Forms are included in the last section of this chapter. In some cases, you will
need to make multiple copies of a form before you begin. On the other hand, you may not
need all of the input forms provided.

Problem Set Up

The following is a list of inventory transactions during the month of December 1992 for W. D.
Peachtree & Company. For each transaction you will need to do one of the following things:

1) Make changes to an inventory item.

2) Enter a receipt, sale, return, or adjustment for goods.

3) Change the selling price of a single or group of items.

You will also run end of the period reports after entering all transactions.

Beginning from PCA Main Menu, select Inventory to see the Inventory Main Menu. You
should select one of the three menu choices (Maintenance Programs, Processing Programs, or Report
Programs) for each of the transactions listed below.

Problem Data

a.   12/01/92   The following sales were made:

Dept	Item Number	Description	Qty	Unit Price
APP	0900120REF	Commercial Refriger.	1	$799.00
APP	1200040DIS	Dishwasher	1	563.00
CLC	463487G	Girl's Print Dress	5	11.99
CLW	910535	Silk Blouse	1	44.00
CLW	910536	Silk Pants	1	49.75
SHA	514584T	Tennis Shoes	2	52.50
SPO	0100MAT	Pad	1	15.55

b.   12/01/92   W. D. Peachtree & Company has decided to change its supplier of Portable Radios (Department ELE - Item Number 810425RAD). The new Vendor ID is ELE121. The reorder level should be reduced to 10.00 and reorder quantity should be reduced to 15.00.

c.   12/05/92   The following items were received today:

Dept	Item Number	Description	Qty	Unit Cost
SHA	514582J	Jogging Sneaker	25	$22.00
SLN	0SHP-9888	Organic Shampoo	10	2.25
CLC	463444	Children's Socks	50	.59
CLC	463781	Boy's Bluejeans	10	4.49

d.   12/06/92   The following item was returned because it did not fit.

Dept	Item Number	Description	Qty	Unit Price
CLM	425308	Striped Dress Shirt	1	$21.50

Receipt No. for LIFO Costing - No. 2

e.   12/08/92   W. D. Peachtree & Company received notification from its main supplier of children's clothing of a price increase. W. D. Peachtree & Company has decided to increase its sales prices for all items in the Children's Clothing Department (CLC) by three percent (3%). (Hint: Choose "Range of Items" for the Price Change Option. Choose "Range of Departments" for the Range Option. The Starting Department is "CLC" and the Ending Department is "CLC").

f.   12/08/92   The following sales need to be posted:

Dept	Item Number	Description	Qty	Unit Price
ELE	810104SPK	Speakers	2	A
ELE	810534BAT	Batteries	12	B
ELE	810698TRN	Turntable	1	B
HDW	HDW020997	Gutter Straps	25	A
SLN	0SHP-9888	Organic Shampoo	3	C

(Hint: The price code (A, B or C) corresponds to selling prices associated with each item. To find the correct selling price for each item, you should enter the transaction in the regular way. When the computer asks for Unit Price, press ⊞ and a pop up box will appear containing all three choices. Move the cursor to the correct price and press enter.)

g.   12/15/92   W. D. Peachtree & Company has received notification that Item Number 876264 Designer Slacks (Department CLM) will no longer be available after 12/01/92. Once the inventory is exhausted, W. D. Peachtree & Company will no longer carry this item. You should make a note to this effect for this item in the Extended Description section.

h.   12/16/92   Received the following items into inventory:

Dept	Item Number	Description	Qty	Unit Cost
APP	0900220REF	Residential Refriger	2	$389.00 *
APP	1200040DIS	Dishwasher	2	267.86
CLC	463487G	Girl's Print Dress	5	5.25
SHA	514584T	Tennis Shoes	5	25.00

*   (Hint: This is a new inventory item which you will add to the inventory for APP Department. This procedure is not covered in Chapter 9, but the computer program will walk you through the process.)

The rest of the information to complete this transaction is as follows:

Item Description	:	Residential Refrigerator
Product Code	:	A
Location	:	WRHS-1
Vendor ID	:	FRIGID
Vendor Item #	:	AT9872
Costing Type	:	A
Current Cost	:	389.00
Reorder Level	:	1
Reorder Quantity	:	2

Selling Prices
Price A :   750.00
Price B :   725.00
Price   :   650.00

i.   12/20/92   W. D. Peachtree & Company received notification of a price increase effective today. The price increase covers only a range of items from a specific vendor. The Vendor is STEWRT, and you should adjust prices upward by four percent (4%). (Hint: This price increase is done for Vendors (Not Departments). The range for Vendors will be STEWRT to STEWRT.)

j.   12/22/92   The following sales should be posted:

Dept	Item Number	Description	Qty	Unit Price
APP	110010lOVE	Oven, Commercial	2	A
APP	0900220REF	Residential Refrig.	1	C
APP	1400040TRA	Trash Compactor	2	B
CLC	463487G	Girl's Print Dress	4	$10.00
CLC	463444	Children's Socks	30	1.35
ELE	810555EQU	Equalizer	2	B
ELE	810060PTV	Colortronic TV	2	A
ELE	810578CAS	Dual Cassette Deck	1	C
HAC	990001FURN	Furnace	1	1,675.00
SPO	0006BAG	Sleeping Bag	2	47.50
SPO	0400TNT	Tent	1	72.99
SPO	0500PAK	Backpack	2	A
SPO	2301DRI	Freeze Dried Food	4	B

k. 12/23/92   The supplier of the organic conditioner (Department SLN, Item Number 0CND-9887) has notified W. D. Peachtree & Company of a possible health hazard from using this product on 12/01/92. The letter was received on 12/23/92. W. D. Peachtree & Company has removed their stock of this item from the shelves. You should make the following changes to this inventory item:

1) Include the following extended description: "As of 12/23/92, none of this inventory is to be offered for sale. Any inquiries should be directed to the management."

2) Change the location to - Store Rm.

l. 12/24/92   Because of lagging sales, W. D. Peachtree & Company has decided to change the three selling prices of the Residential Refrig., Department APP, Item Number 0900210REF. The new selling prices should be:

Price A:	$1,099.99
Price B:	799.99
Price C:	599.99

m. 12/28/92   (Hint: Maintain 12/01/92 as your run date.) In a spot check of inventory items, the stock clerk discovered an error. She found that the actual number of items on hand of Color Television (Department ELE, Item Number 810340TV) was four, but the computer record shows quantity on hand as three. You should increase the quantity of this item by one. You will do this by making an adjustment. (Hint: This is similar to posting a transaction for receiving goods, except you are making an adjustment (ADJ) not a receipt (REC). Also, the serial # for this item is SP91A1028.)

n. 12/31/92   After all transactions are successfully entered into the system, you should run the end of the period reports (Product items only). You should do the following activities:

1) Print a Departmental Summary Report

2) Print a Period to Date Report

3) Print a Transaction Register (Current Generation) Report

4) Then Close the Period (End of Period not End of Year)
(You will get a series of warning messages. Answer Y at each question to complete the problem.)

INVENTORY

MASTER INPUT FORMS

Inventory Options Setup Form

General Module Options

Controller Password: __ __ __ __ __ __ __ __

Operator Password: __ __ __ __ __ __ __ __

Use Menus: Y N   (Circle one)

Allow Changes/Deletions: Y N

Force Control Reports: Y N

Keep Year-To-Date Detail: Y N

Current Inventory Generation #:   __ __

Other Module Options

Default Costing Type: S A L F U (Circle one)

Grand Totals Page: Y N

Keep Specific Unit History: Y N

Inventory Items Setup Form

Item Type (P/S):	P S (Circle one)
Department:	___ ___ ___
Item Number:	___ ___ ___ ___ ___ ___ ___ ___ ___ ___ ___ ___ ___ ___ ___
Item Description:	___ ___ ___ ___ ___ ___ ___ ___ ___ ___ ___ ___ ___ ___ ___
	___ ___ ___ ___ ___ ___ ___
Ext Description:	Y N (If Y, enter description on next page)
Product Code:	___
Location:	___ ___ ___ ___ ___ ___ ___
Receiving Unit:	___ ___ ___ ___
Selling Unit:	___ ___ ___ ___
Conversion Factor:	___ ___ ___ ___ ___ ___ . ___ ___
Vendor ID:	___ ___ ___ ___ ___ ___
Vendor Item #:	___ ___ ___ ___ ___ ___ ___ ___ ___ ___
Neg Quantity:	Y N (Circle one)
Costing Type:	S A L F U
Component Item:	S C N
Current Cost:	___ ___ ___ ___ ___ . ___ ___ ___ ___ ___ ___
Last Cost Unit:	___ ___ ___ ___ ___ . ___ ___ ___ ___ ___ ___
Item Tax Status:	T E
Reorder Level:	___ ___ ___ ___ ___ ___ ___ ___ . ___ ___
Reorder Quantity:	___ ___ ___ ___ ___ ___ ___ ___ . ___ ___
On Reorder Rpt Date:	___ ___ / ___ ___ / ___ ___
Selling Prices, A:	___ ___ ___ ___ ___ ___ . ___ ___ ___
Selling Prices, B:	___ ___ ___ ___ ___ ___ . ___ ___ ___
Selling Prices, C:	___ ___ ___ ___ ___ ___ . ___ ___ ___
Quantity-on-Hand:	___ ___ ___ ___ ___ ___ ___ . ___ ___

Year-through-Last-Period Information

Profitability

Sales: __ __ __ __ __ __ __.__ __

Cost of Sales: __ __ __ __ __ __ __.__ __

Quantity Figures

Number Sold: __ __ __ __ __ __.__ __

Number Received: __ __ __ __ __ __.__ __

Number Returned: __ __ __ __ __ __.__ __

Number Adjusted: __ __ __ __ __ __.__ __

Number as Components: __ __ __ __ __ __.__ __

Item Number: __ __ __ __ __ __ __ __ __ __ __ __ __ __

Ext Description: __ __ __ __ __ __ __ __ __ __ __ __ __ __ __

                 __ __ __ __ __ __ __ __ __ __ __ __ __ __ __

                 __ __ __ __ __ __ __ __ __ __ __ __ __ __ __

                 __ __ __ __ __ __ __ __ __ __ __ __ __ __ __

                 __ __ __ __ __ __ __ __ __ __ __ __ __ __ __

                 __ __ __ __ __ __ __ __ __ __ __ __ __ __ __

                 __ __ __ __ __ __ __ __ __ __ __ __ __ __ __

                 __ __ __ __ __ __ __ __ __ __ __ __ __ __ __

                 __ __ __ __ __ __ __ __

Serial Numbers: _____

                 _____

                 _____

                 _____

                 _____

                 _____

                 _____

                 _____

                 _____

                 _____

                 _____

Chapter 10

PAYROLL OVERVIEW

Learning Objectives:

After studying this chapter, you should be able to:

1. Describe the purposes of Payroll.

2. Describe payroll maintenance activities to change employee information such as address changes, withholding changes, raises, promotions, hirings, terminations, and transfers.

3. Describe payroll processing activities including—entering an employee's earnings and deductions each pay period, calculating the payroll, printing paychecks and reports, and closing the pay period.

4. Describe how to prepare payroll reports including—the 941 Employer's Quarterly Tax Return, the federal and state unemployment tax returns, and employees' W-2 forms.

5. Identify some of the reports printed by Payroll.

Chapter 10

Payroll Overview

A company's payroll is the amount it pays its employees as wages and salaries. In addition to regular salaries and wages, payroll includes commissions, overtime pay, tips, and bonuses earned by employees. Payroll may be the largest expense of a business.

Payroll accounts for amounts that are withheld from employees' paychecks. The employer's payroll taxes for unemployment and social security are also calculated. These amounts must be remitted to governmental (or other) agencies. Also, reports must be submitted to these agencies.

How Payroll Compares With A Manual Accounting System

In accounting textbooks, the payroll journal is sometimes contrasted with the payroll register. The payroll journal is a book of original entry from which postings are made to the general journal. A payroll register is merely a memo type record from which no postings are made to the general journal. The Peachtree Complete Accounting Payroll module functions like a payroll special journal when it is linked with General Ledger and functions like a payroll register when it is not linked with General Ledger. For each employee, Payroll calculates gross pay, payroll deductions (such as federal and state withholdings, FICA taxes, and others), net pay, and vacation and sick hours earned. Also, Payroll calculates employer payroll taxes such as state and federal unemployment taxes and the employer's portion of FICA taxes.

When the Payroll module is linked with General Ledger, the information needed for updating general ledger accounts, such as payroll expense, federal withholding tax payable, state withholding tax payable, payroll payable, and others is automatically posted in the proper general ledger accounts. When the Payroll module is not linked with General Ledger, journal entries must be made in General Ledger to record the payroll information.

Detailed payroll information must be maintained to support the issuance of payroll checks to employees and to satisfy federal and state reporting requirements regarding payroll. Often a separate payroll checking account is maintained so that reconciling of the general checking account will not involve numerous outstanding payroll checks. Peachtree Complete Accounting prints these special payroll checks. The Payroll module also prepares periodic tax reports such as the 941 report (Employer's Quarterly Tax Return filed to report federal withholdings and FICA taxes) and W-2 forms that are given to employees at the end of the year to be filed with their federal and state income tax returns.

Question Frame 1¹⁰

Indicate whether each of the following statements is true or false by writing "T" or "F" in the space provided.

_____ 1.   When Payroll is linked with General Ledger, the Payroll module functions like a manual payroll register.

_____ 2.   The Payroll module calculates gross pay, payroll deductions, and net pay, but it cannot calculate vacation and sick hours earned.

_____ 3.   Maintaining detailed payroll records is absolutely necessary.

_____ 4.   Peachtree Complete Accounting prints payroll checks.

Now turn to Answer Frame 1¹⁰ on page 10-4 to check your answers.

Answer Frame 1[10]

1. False. If Payroll is linked with General Ledger, it functions like a manual payroll journal rather than a payroll register.

2. False. Payroll also calculates vacation and sick hours earned.

3. True. Both federal and state agencies require that detailed payroll records be maintained.

4. True. The Payroll module prints payroll checks and also prepares periodic tax reports such as 941s and W-2s.

If you missed any of the above, reread Frame 1[10] before continuing.

What Payroll Does

Payroll calculates the taxes and the net pay for employees. It also keeps track of deductions, sick leave, and vacation hours for each employee. Payroll also prints paychecks and periodic tax reports. Using Payroll, you can handle the payroll for an unlimited number of employees.

Payroll supports:

- Any combination of salaried, hourly, tipped, commission, and draw employees.

- Automatic calculation of overtime rates for up to two different types of overtime.

- Automatic calculation of shift differential (amount or percent) for shifts 2 and 3.

- Any combination of weekly, monthly, semi-monthly, and bi-weekly pay periods.

- All federal, state, and local taxes, including unemployment and state industrial insurance taxes.

- Three miscellaneous income types, six miscellaneous deduction types (including printing 401K information on W-2s), and garnishments.

- Automatic accrual of vacation and sick hours earned by pay period or by hours worked.

- Complete posting of journal entries to General Ledger (optionally, by department) with the ability to divide a salaried employee's wages among three different G/L accounts and an hourly employee's wages among up to 10 accounts.

- Summary or detail posting to General Ledger.

Using Payroll

When using Payroll, you perform three different kinds of activities:

- Maintenance
- Processing
- Reports

This section gives you an overview of these types of activities.

Payroll Maintenance Activities

Maintenance activities are the tasks you perform to keep payroll information current. Maintenance includes entering or changing employee information such as address changes, # withholding changes, raises, promotions, hirings, terminations, and transfers.

You can perform Payroll maintenance activities any time **except** during payroll processing. Therefore, it is important that you take care of any maintenance activities before you begin processing the payroll. The programs you use for maintenance are:

- **Maintain Employees**
- **Maintain Tax File**
- **List Employees**
- **List Tax File**

Use **Maintain Employees** to add new employees, change information on existing employees, and change the status of terminated employees to inactive.

Use **Maintain Tax File** to enter or change federal, state, or local tax information.

Use **List Tax File** and **List Employees** to print a list of the information you entered into **Maintain Tax File** and **Maintain Employees**, respectively. Print these lists whenever you need to verify the accuracy and completeness of this information.

Question Frame 2[10]

Indicate whether each of the following statements is true or false by writing "T" or "F" in the space provided.

_____ 1. Payroll may be used for many different kinds of pay arrangements.

_____ 2. Postings to General Ledger may only be made in summary form.

_____ 3. Maintenance activities are tasks that are performed to keep payroll information current.

_____ 4. The **Maintain Employees** and **Maintain Tax File** options are used to change information, and the **List Employees** and **List Tax File** options are used to verify the accuracy and completeness of information.

Now turn to Answer Frame 2[10] on page 10-8 to check your answers.

Answer Frame 2[10]

1. True. Payroll will support any combination of salaried, hourly, tipped, commission, and draw pay arrangement. This module also calculates overtime rates for time-and-one-half or double-time. Also, the pay periods can be weekly, monthly, semi-monthly, and bi-weekly.

2. False. These entries may also be made in detail form.

3. True. Maintenance includes such activities as entering or changing employee information such as address changes, withholding changes, raises, promotions, hirings, terminations, and transfers.

4. True. The "maintain" options are used to change the information in the files, and the "list" options are used to check information in the files.

If you missed any of the above, reread Frame 2[10] before continuing.

Frame 3[10]

Payroll Processing Activities

Processing activities are the tasks performed to use Payroll in the business. They include:

- Entering an employee's earnings and deductions each pay period.
- Calculating the payroll.
- Printing paychecks and reports.
- Closing the pay period.

The programs used to complete the processing activities depend on the complexity of the company's payroll. However, no matter how simple or complex the payroll is, these programs will always be used to complete the following basic processing activities:

- **Calculate Pay** to calculate earnings, deductions, taxes, and the resulting net pay.
- **Print Checks** to print employee paychecks.
- **Print Payroll Register** to print the final record of the current period payroll.
- **Post Current Period** to update quarter-to-date and year-to-date employee totals.

Only one paycheck may be written per employee in a pay period. Therefore, any bonus check (if it is a separate check) or an advance, needs to be done in a separate pay period. PCA allows you to Enter Exceptions, Calculate Pay, and Print Checks for an employee in the same pay period after a first check, but only the final check will appear on the Payroll Register and thus only the final check will be passed on to General Ledger.

Enter Earnings and Deductions

Payroll can be set up with basic data such as standard hours and deductions. During a pay period, if there are employees with exceptions to the standard data, the following programs can be used:

- **Update from Job Cost**
- **Paymaster Worksheet**
- **Calculate Time Card Hours**
- **Enter Exceptions**

Two of the more frequently used of these programs, are **Calculate Time Card Hours** and **Enter Exceptions**.

Use **Calculate Time Card Hours** to enter time card hours for hourly employees whose hours vary from week to week. You enter the sign-in and sign-out times, and Payroll calculates the hours worked.

Use **Enter Exceptions** to enter any information unique (non-standard) to the current pay period, such as special:

- commissions
- overtime
- shift differentials
- tips
- bonuses

Enter Exceptions is primarily used to enter hours worked when they are different from the "Standard hours" in the employee file. Doing so takes less time than using Calculate Time Card Hours. It can also be used to enter deductions, such as a one-time-only stock purchase, and to update vacation and sick days taken.

Calculate Pay

Once the earnings and deductions have been entered, pay can be calculated. To accomplish this task, use the following programs:

- Calculate Pay
- Print Payroll Register

Use **Calculate Pay** to calculate the employees' earnings and deductions. This program must be used every time a payroll is processed.

Use **Print Payroll Register** to print a detailed listing of the current payroll. Checking this information is an important part of using Payroll. With the pre-check Payroll Register, payroll can be checked for accuracy before the checks are actually printed. This step is critical in processing a payroll.

Question Frame 3[10]

Indicate whether each of the following statements is true or false by writing "T" or "F" in the space provided.

_____ 1. Payroll processing activities include the bulk of the payroll effort during a pay period.

_____ 2. The **Enter Exceptions** option only is used to enter overtime information.

_____ 3. The **Calculate Pay** option is used only some of the time that a payroll is processed.

_____ 4. The **Print Payroll Register** option should be used before paychecks are written.

Now turn to Answer Frame 3[10] on page 10-10 to check your answers.

Answer Frame 3[10]

1. True. These processing activities include entering an employee's earnings and deductions each period, calculating the payroll, printing paychecks and reports, and closing the pay period.

2. False. This option is also used to enter commissions, shift differentials, tips, bonuses, stock purchases, and vacation and sick days taken.

3. False. The **Calculate Pay** option is used every time a payroll is processed.

4. True. Checking the information this report provides for accuracy is important so that paychecks will be for the correct amounts and to the correct persons.

If you missed any of the above, reread Frame 3[10] before continuing.

Frame 4[10]

Print Paychecks and Reports

Once the Payroll Register has been checked, paychecks and reports are ready to be printed. To accomplish these tasks, the following programs will be used:

- **Print Checks**
- **Hours/Earnings Report**
- **Deduction Register**
- **Print Payroll Register**

Use **Print Checks** to print the employees' paychecks. **Print Checks** prints checks only for those employees who have been included in the **Calculate Pay** program for that pay period. The **Print Checks** program is not an optional Payroll program.

Use **Hours/Earnings Report** to print a detailed report of the employees' earnings and hours for the current period. It can be printed before or after the paychecks are printed. This report is optional.

Use **Deduction Register** to print a report that lists the current period's (and, optionally, year-to-date) taxes and deductions for the employees. Again, this report is optional during processing. However, it should be printed whenever this information needs to be reviewed -- either before or after paychecks are printed.

Use **Print Payroll Register** to print the final Payroll Register. This report serves as a permanent record of the current period's payroll information. Always print this report after paychecks are printed.

Close the Period

After the pay has been calculated and all the reports needed have been printed, the payroll information can be posted. To accomplish this task, the following will be used:

- Post Current Period
- Payroll Summary
- Close Current Quarter/Year

Use **Post Current Period** to update the employees' quarter-to-date and year-to-date information. When a period is closed, Payroll adds the current period information to the quarter-to-date and year-to-date amounts. This program must be used at the end of every pay period.

Use **Payroll Summary** to print a detailed listing of the quarter-to-date and year-to-date payroll history. This report contains earnings, deductions, and hours and weeks worked. Print this report before closing the quarter and keep the report as documentation of the quarter totals.

Close Current Quarter/Year program must be used at the end of each quarter and at the end of the calendar year after running **Post Current Period**. Depending on whether it is a quarter or the year being closed, this program resets the quarter-to-date and year-to-date amounts to zero.

Note: Before the current quarter or the year can be closed, the quarterly or yearly reports must be printed as a permanent record. The next section, "Payroll Reports," discusses these reports.

Payroll Reports

At the end of the quarter and year, certain reports will be needed to help process the payroll information. Depending on the state involved, several of the following programs may be used:

- 941 Report
- California DE 3 Report
- New Jersey Reports
- Print W-2s
- Magnetic Media

As a general rule, the **941 Report** and **Print W-2s** will be used most often.

Use **941 Report** to help complete the 941 Employer's Quarterly Tax Return, the 940 Federal Unemployment Tax Return, and the state unemployment return(s).

Use **Print W-2s** to print the employees' W-2 forms. These forms can be printed at year end for all the employees or as needed for individual employees.

Question Frame 4[10]

Indicate whether each of the following statements is true or false by writing "T" or "F" in the space provided.

_____ 1. The **Print Checks** option prints checks for every employee in the company's records each pay period.

_____ 2. The Hours/Earnings Report, Deduction Register, and Print Payroll Register Report are all optional.

_____ 3. The Post Current Period, Payroll Summary, and the Close Current Quarter/Year programs must all be used each pay period.

_____ 4. The 941 Report program does more than just prepare the 941 Employer's Quarterly Tax Return.

Now turn to Answer Frame 4[10] on page 10-14 to check your answers.

Answer Frame 4[10]

1. False. The **Print Checks** option only prints checks for those employees who have been included in the Calculate Pay program during that pay period.

2. False. The first two reports are optional, but the Print Payroll Register report serves as a permanent record of the current period's payroll information and therefore is required.

3. False. The Post Current Period program must be used at the end of each pay period. The Payroll Summary should be printed before closing each quarter. The Close Current Quarter/Year program must be used at the end of each quarter and the end of each calendar year.

4. True. This program also prepares the 940 Federal Unemployment Tax Return and the state unemployment tax return.

If you missed any of the above, reread Frame 4[10] before turning to the questions at the end of the chapter.

What's Next

Now that you are familiar with the Payroll module, you are ready to practice with W. D. Peachtree's data. But first you may want to review the sample reports at the end of this chapter so that you will be familiar with the kind of reports you will generate in Chapter 11.

PAYROLL OVERVIEW

QUESTIONS

1. **What are three different kinds of activities performed by Payroll?**

   Maintanance

   Processing

   Reports

2. **Name the four Payroll maintenance programs and the function of each.**

Program Name	**Program Function**
Maintain Emp	add new or change information
Maintain Tax File	Change Tax information
List Employee	to print
List Tax File	to print

3. **When should Payroll maintenance activities be performed?**

   Before payroll period

4. **Name the four basic Payroll processing programs and the function of each.**

Program Name	**Program Function**

5. **What are two of the more frequently used programs to enter non-standard employee data?**

Name _____ ID # _____

6. Name four special earnings situations when the Enter Exceptions program could be used.

_____

_____

_____

_____

7. What is the program that must be used every time a payroll is processed?

_____

8. Why is it important to use Print Payroll Register as part of processing Payroll?

_____

_____

9. Name three programs that will be used to post payroll information at the end of a period.

_____

_____

_____

10. Of the five Payroll Report programs, which two are used most often by businesses?

_____

_____

Name _____   ID # _____

PAYROLL OVERVIEW

MATCHING

Instructions: Match each program name on the left with the proper program function on the right.

Program Name	Program Function	Answer
A. Post Current Period	1. Prints a final record of the current period's payroll.	_____
B. Maintain Employees	2. Helps prepare quarterly tax reports.	_____
C. Hours/Earnings Report	3. Changes federal tax information.	*H*
D. Print W-2s	4. Updates employee totals.	_____
E. Calculate Pay	5. Adds an employee.	B
F. Close Current Quarter/Year	6. Prints a detailed report of employees' earnings and hours for the current period.	_____
G. Print Payroll Register	7. Calculates an employee's net pay for a period.	_____
H. Maintain Tax File	8. Closes out the end of a quarter, after running Post Current Period.	_____
I. 941 Report	9. Prints employees' W-2s.	_____
J. Enter Exceptions	10. Enters a special bonus for an employee.	_____

PAYROLL
SAMPLE REPORTS

Paymaster Worksheet

```
RUN DATE: 12/31/92                    W.D. Peachtree & Company
RUN TIME: 5:58 PM                             Payroll
                                        Paymaster Worksheet
```

```
EMPLOYEE CODE 12BLAB          --------EARNINGS--------           --------DEDUCTIONS--------
                              ---RATE----  --REG. HRS.--  --OVT1 HRS.--  --OVT2 HRS.--
                              24000.000        40.00         0.00          0.00         FICA         :
Bill Blast                                                                              FEDERAL WH.  :
1912 Quail Hollow                                                                       GEORGIA   WH.:
Apt. B-6                                                                                TAX CODE 2 WH.:
Atlanta, GA      30342                                                                  TAX CODE 3 WH.:
                                                                                        TAX CODE 4 WH.:
SOC. SEC. NO. : 857-34-8172                                                             INSUR.   DED. :
PAY PERIOD   : WEEKLY                      Gross Pay Acct. Distribution                 401k     DED. :
PAY TYPE     : SALARY          Tips        ---Account---  ---Amount---                  EMP LOAN DED. :
                               MISC. #1                                                 SAVINGS  DED. :
SALARY       :    24000.000    BONUS                                                    STCK PUR DED. :
SICK HRS. TAKEN: ---------     MISC. #3                                                 SIX      DED. :
VAC. HRS. TAKEN: ---------     EIC
TAKE GROUP TERM LIFE FICA (Y/N)?: ---
```

```
EMPLOYEE CODE 50SCOB          --------EARNINGS--------           --------DEDUCTIONS--------
                              ---RATE----  --REG. HRS.--  --OVT1 HRS.--  --OVT2 HRS.--
                               11.538          40.00         0.00          0.00         FICA         :
Brad Scott                                                                              FEDERAL WH.  :
9462 Waldal Walk Circle                                                                 GEORGIA   WH.:
                                                                                        TAX CODE 2 WH.:
Atlanta, GA      30342                                                                  TAX CODE 3 WH.:
                                                                                        TAX CODE 4 WH.:
SOC. SEC. NO. : 543-54-8429                                                             INSUR.   DED. :
PAY PERIOD   : WEEKLY                      Gross Pay Acct. Distribution                 401k     DED. :
PAY TYPE     : HOURLY          Tips        ---Account---  ---Amount---                  EMP LOAN DED. :
SHIFT        : 1               MISC. #1                                                 SAVINGS  DED. :
PAY RATE     :     11.538      BONUS                                                    STCK PUR DED. :
SICK HRS. TAKEN: ---------     MISC. #3                                                 SIX      DED. :
VAC. HRS. TAKEN: ---------     EIC
TAKE GROUP TERM LIFE FICA (Y/N)?: ---
```

```
*** End of Paymaster Worksheet ***
```

Time Card Entry Report

EMPLOYEE		TIME			HOURS		
CODE	NAME	IN	OUT	TYPE	REG.	OVT. 1	OVT. 2
12CLIC	Cal Cline	9.45	14.48	R	5.03	0.00	0.00
		11.53	17.03	R	5.50	0.00	0.00
		9.52	18.12	R	8.60	0.00	0.00
		9.55	14.59	R	5.04	0.00	0.00
		17.03	22.12	R	5.09	0.00	0.00
		17.01	22.23	R	5.22	0.00	0.00
		12.05	16.33	R	4.28	0.00	0.00
					38.76	0.00	0.00

*** End of Time Card Entry Report ***

Payroll Register

W.D. Peachtree & Company
Payroll
Payroll Register

PAGE 1
PERIOD ENDING 12/31/92

DEPARTMENT 12

CODE	NAME	REGULAR EARNINGS	DISB. MISC.INC	NON-DISB MISC.INC	VOL. DEDUCT.	FED.WH.	FICA	TAX #1	TAX #2	TAX #3	TAX #4	CHECK NUMB	NET PAY
12CLIC	Cal Cline	290.70	0.00	0.00	0.00	29.90	22.24	9.40	0.00	0.00	0.00		229.16
12DELO	Oscar DeLaren	240.00	0.00	0.00	0.00	22.30	18.36	6.36	0.00	0.00	0.00		192.98
		530.70	0.00	0.00	0.00	52.20	40.60	15.76	0.00	0.00	0.00		422.14

BREAKDOWN OF MISCELLANEOUS INCOME AND TAX CODES FOR DEPARTMENT 12

DRAW	0.00	GEORGIA WH.	15.76	CURRENT DEF. DEDUCT.	0.00
COMMISSION	0.00			CURRENT ALLOC. DEDUCT.	0.00
Tips	0.00				
MISC. #1	0.00				
BONUS	0.00				
MISC. #3	0.00				

		REGULAR EARNINGS	DISB. MISC.INC	NON-DISB MISC.INC	VOL. DEDUCT.	FED.WH.	FICA	TAX #1	TAX #2	TAX #3	TAX #4		NET PAY
COMPANY TOTALS		530.70	0.00	0.00	0.00	52.20	40.60	15.76	0.00	0.00	0.00		422.14

BREAKDOWN OF MISCELLANEOUS INCOME AND TAX CODES FOR COMPANY

DRAW	0.00	GEORGIA WH.	15.76	CURRENT DEF. DEDUCT.	0.00
COMMISSION	0.00			CURRENT ALLOC. DEDUCT.	0.00
Tips	0.00				
MISC. #1	0.00				
BONUS	0.00				
MISC. #3	0.00				
EIC	0.00				

WARNING CODES LEGEND

CODE 0 = NET PAY OVER CHECK LIMIT
CODE 1 = DEDUCTIONS EQUAL OR EXCEED EARNINGS
CODE 2 = PAY MAY BE BELOW MINIMUM WAGE
CODE 3 = DRAW EXCEEDS COMMISSION

YOUR COMPANY NAME

0001436

EMP. NO.	EMPLOYEE NAME	SOCIAL SECURITY NO.	PERIOD BEG.	PERIOD END	CHECK NO.
CLIC12	Cal Cline	430-83-9320	12/25/92	12/31/92	1436

EARNINGS	HRS./UNITS	CURRENT AMOUNT	YEAR TO DATE
REGULAR	38.76	290.70	15890.70
OVERTIME 1		0.00	0.00
OVERTIME 2		0.00	0.00
SICK HOURS	0.77		40.04
VACATION HOURS	1.54		80.08

DEDUCTIONS	CURRENT AMOUNT	YEAR TO DATE
FICA	22.24	1215.64
FEDERAL WH.	29.90	1904.15
GEORGIA	9.40	527.32

PAY RATE	CURRENT EARNINGS	CURRENT DEDUCTIONS	NET PAY	YTD EARNINGS	YTD DEDUCTIONS	YTD NET PAY
7.500	290.70	61.54	229.16	15890.70	3647.11	12243.59

0001436

YOUR BANK NAME
ADDRESS
CITY, STATE ZIP CODE
00-00/000

1436

DATE 12/31/92

AMOUNT *****$229.16

SIGNATURE LINE IMPRINT

YOUR COMPANY NAME
ADDRESS
CITY, STATE ZIP CODE
PHONE AND FAX #

PAY **** TWO HUNDRED TWENTY NINE & 16 /100 DOLLARS

TO THE
ORDER
OF: Cal Cline
2301 Valley Heart Drive
Atlanta, GA   30345

⑈0001436⑈ ⑆000000000⑆ ⑈00⑈⑈000 00⑈

FORM # LC1000

PEACHTREE FORMS 1-800-553-6485

Deduction Register

```
RUN DATE: 12/31/92                                                              PAGE  1
RUN TIME: 6:14 PM
------------------------------------------------------------------------------------------
                        W.D. Peachtree & Company                         PERIOD ENDING 12/31/92
                                Payroll
                            Deduction Register


DEPARTMENT 12

EMPLOYEE CODE : 12CLIC
NAME          : Cal Cline
CHECK NUMBER  :   1436
PAY PERIOD    : WEEKLY
PAY TYPE      : HOURLY

              -CURRENT PERIOD DEDUCTIONS

FEDERAL WITH. :      29.90
FICA          :      22.24
GEORGIA   WH. :       9.40
TAX #2        :       0.00
TAX #3        :       0.00
TAX #4        :       0.00
INSUR.   DED. :       0.00
401k     DED. :       0.00
EMP LOAN DED. :       0.00
SAVINGS  DED. :       0.00
STCK PUR DED. :       0.00
SIX      DED. :       0.00

DEFER. DED.   :       0.00
  TOTAL CURR. :      61.54


*** End of Deduction Register ***
```

Hours/Earnings Report

W.D. Peachtree & Company
Payroll
Hours/Earnings Report

PAGE 1

PERIOD ENDING 12/31/92

DEPARTMENT 12

CODE NAME	CYCLE TYPE SHIFT	REGULAR EARNINGS -HOURS	OVT1. EARNINGS -HOURS	OVT2. EARNINGS -HOURS	SICK/ VAC. HOURS	TIPS	COMM. /PR.YR. DRAW	MISC. #1	BONUS	MISC. #3	EIC
12CLIC Cal Cline	W/H/1	290.70	0.00	0.00	0.00	0.00	0.00	0.00	0.00	0.00	0.00
		38.76	0.00	0.00	0.00		0.00				
12DELO Oscar DeLaren	W/H/1	240.00	0.00	0.00	0.00	0.00	0.00	0.00	0.00	0.00	0.00
		32.00	0.00	0.00	0.00		0.00				
DEPARTMENT TOTALS		530.70	0.00	0.00	0.00	0.00	0.00	0.00	0.00	0.00	0.00
		70.76	0.00	0.00	0.00		0.00				
COMPANY TOTALS		530.70	0.00	0.00	0.00	0.00	0.00	0.00			0.00
		70.76	0.00	0.00	0.00		0.00				

CODES LEGEND:

CYCLE	TYPE	SHIFT
W - WEEKLY	H - HOURLY	1 - NORMAL - NO DIFFERENTIAL
B - BI-WEEKLY	S - SALARIED	2 - TYPE 1 DIFFERENTIAL
S - SEMI-MONTHLY	D - DRAW	3 - TYPE 2 DIFFERENTIAL
M - MONTHLY	C - COMMISSION	

Payroll Summary

```
RUN DATE: 12/31/92       W.D. Peachtree & Company                      PAGE  1
RUN TIME:  6:15 PM              Payroll
                             Payroll Summary
---------------------------------------------------------------------------------
 DEPARTMENT 12

 12BLAB   Bill Blast                     857-34-8172

                             QUARTER-TO-DATE              YEAR-TO-DATE
 EARNINGS  -REGULAR      :      6000.02                      24000.08
           OVERTIME 1    :         0.00                          0.00
           OVERTIME 2    :         0.00                          0.00
           COMMISSIONS   :         0.00                          0.00
           Tips          :         0.00                          0.00
           MISC. #1      :         0.00                          0.00
           BONUS         :         0.00                          0.00
           MISC. #3      :         0.00                          0.00
           EIC           :         0.00                          0.00
                             -----------                   -----------
           GROSS PAY     :      6000.02                      24000.08

 DEDUCTIONS-FICA         :       459.00                       1836.01
            FEDERAL WH.  :       703.55                       2818.52


           TOTAL DED.    :      1390.05                       5564.53
                             ===========                   ===========
           NET PAY       :      4609.97                      18435.55

 HOURS     -REGULAR      :         0.00                          0.00
           OVERTIME 1    :         0.00                          0.00
           OVERTIME 2    :         0.00                          0.00
                             -----------                   -----------
           TOTAL HOURS   :         0.00                          0.00

 WEEKS WORKED            :        12.00                         51.00

 SICK HOURS ACCRUED      :                                      39.27
 SICK HOURS USED         :                                       0.00
 VAC. HOURS ACCRUED      :                                      78.54
 VAC. HOURS USED         :                                       0.00

*** End of Payroll Summary ***
```

Employee File List

```
EMPLOYEE CODE 16ATHA          STATUTORY : N    TAX CODE 1: GA   FILING ST.: Q   EXEM.: 0   FACTOR: 0.00%   ADDL TAX :   0.00
PROCESSING STATUS: PC         DECEASED  : N    TAX CODE 2:      FILING ST.:     EXEM.: 0   FACTOR: 0.00%   ADDL TAX :   0.00
Alma Atherton                 TIPPED    : N    TAX CODE 3:      FILING ST.:     EXEM.: 0   FACTOR: 0.00%   ADDL TAX :   0.00
3903 Butterfield Drive        LEGAL REP.: N    TAX CODE 4:      FILING ST.:     EXEM.: 0   FACTOR: 0.00%   ADDL TAX :   0.00
                              942 EMP.  : N               FEDERAL FILING ST.: M   EXEM.: 0             ADDL TAX :   0.00
Atlanta, GA        30321      DEF. COMP.: N    PENSION : N   SUTA TAXABLE: Y   INDUS.INS.: 0.00%
                              EIC STATUS: N    SICK HOURS/YEAR     :   40.00   CUR. UNCOL FICA TIP TAX:   0.00
SOC. SEC.: 999-96-4343        SHIFT     : 1    VAC. HOURS/YEAR     :   80.00   QTD. UNCOL FICA TIP TAX:   0.00
PHONE NO.: 404-555-1804       DATE EMPLOYED    : 03/16/87   SICK HOURS USED    :    0.00   YTD. UNCOL FICA TIP TAX:   0.00
COMMENT  : Children's Clothing  DATE TERMINATED  : 01/01/00   VAC. HOURS USED    :    0.00   MISC. TAX AMOUNT #1 :   0.00
PAY PER. : WEEKLY             LAST CHECK DATE  : 12/22/92   SICK HOURS ACCRUED :   39.27   MISC. TAX AMOUNT #2 :   0.00
PAY TYPE : HOURLY             LAST CHECK NO.   : 1421       VAC. HOURS ACCRUED :   78.54   MISC. TAX AMOUNT #3 :   0.00
PAY RATE : 9.250              LAST CHECK AMT.  : 278.47     CUR. DEFERRED DED. :    0.00   MISC. TAX AMOUNT #4 :   0.00
                              COMMISSION RATE  : 0.00       YTD. DEFERRED DED. :    0.00   TERM LIFE COST >50K :   0.00
                              UNION CONTRACT DATE: 01/01/00                               TERM LIFE FICA TAKEN : N
```

	LAST PAY PERIOD	QUARTER-TO-DATE	YEAR-TO-DATE
EARNINGS -REGULAR :	370.00	4810.00	19240.00
OVERTIME 1 :	0.00	0.00	0.00
OVERTIME 2 :	0.00	0.00	0.00
COMMISSIONS :	0.00	0.00	0.00
TIPS :	0.00	0.00	0.00
MISC. #1 :	0.00	0.00	0.00
BONUS :	0.00	0.00	0.00
MISC. #3 :	0.00	0.00	0.00
EIC :	0.00	0.00	0.00
GROSS PAY :	370.00	4810.00	19240.00
TOTAL DED. :	91.53	1202.08	4811.33
NET PAY :	278.47		
HOURS -REGULAR :	40.00	520.00	2080.00
OVERTIME 1 :	0.00	0.00	0.00
OVERTIME 2 :	0.00	0.00	0.00
TOTAL HOURS :	40.00	520.00	2080.00
WEEKS WORKED :	1.00	12.00	51.00

Tax File List

```
RUN DATE: 12/31/92          W.D. Peachtree & Company               PAGE  1
RUN TIME:  6:20 PM                    Payroll
                                   Tax File List
-----------------------------------------------------------------------------
VERSION NO : 9202A - W/LOCAL                        LAST UPDATED: 06/07/89
VERSION DATE: 02/03/92


CODE: US    NAME: FEDERAL

EMPLOYERS TAX ID : 123456789012
EMPLOYER FICA %  :     6.2000
EMPL. FICA LIMIT :  55500.00
FUTA PERCENT     :     6.2000
FUTA LIMIT       :   7000.00
HOURLY MIN. WAGE :      4.25

                      FIC   FICA  FUTA  EIC
TIPS TAXABLE?        :  Y    Y     Y     Y
MISC. #1 INC. TAXABLE?:  Y    Y     Y     Y
BONUS   INC. TAXABLE?:  Y    Y     Y     Y
MISC. #3 INC. TAXABLE?:  Y    Y     Y     Y

FILING STATUS
    A  single
    B  married

STARTING WITH ANNUALIZED TAXABLE WAGES

DEDUCT    2300.00 PER EXEMPTION

APPLY GRADUATED RATE TABLE BY FILING STATUS


single          PERCENT OF (WAGES - BRACKET) + AMOUNT
          bracket          percent           amount
             0.00          0.0000               0.00
          2450.00         15.0000               0.00
         22750.00         28.0000            3045.00
         47450.00         31.0000            9961.00
```

General Ledger Transaction Register

```
RUN DATE: 12/31/92                    W.D. Peachtree & Company                              PAGE  1
RUN TIME:  6:21 PM                            Payroll
                                  General Ledger Transaction Register
                                                                           PERIOD ENDING 12/31/92


ACCOUNT DP  SC   DESCRIPTION           DATE        DEBIT       CREDIT         NET
------- --  --   -----------           ----        -----       ------         ---

11000  12   P    NET PAY             12/31/92       0.00       422.14       422.14-
                                                 --------     --------      --------
                 TRANSACTIONS:  1                  0.00       422.14       422.14-


22100  12   P    FEDERAL WITHHOLDING  12/31/92      0.00        52.20        52.20-
                                                 --------     --------      --------
                 TRANSACTIONS:  1                  0.00        52.20        52.20-


22200  12   P    GEORGIA   TAX WH.    12/31/92      0.00        15.76        15.76-
                                                 --------     --------      --------
                 TRANSACTIONS:  1                  0.00        15.76        15.76-


22400  12   P    EMPLOYEE FICA        12/31/92      0.00        40.60        40.60-
22400  12   P    EMPLOYER FICA LIABILITY 12/31/92   0.00        40.60        40.60-
                                                 --------     --------      --------
                 TRANSACTIONS:  2                  0.00        81.20        81.20-


50112  12   P    GROSS PAY            12/31/92     530.70        0.00       530.70
                                                 --------     --------      --------
                 TRANSACTIONS:  1                 530.70        0.00       530.70


51400  12   P    EMPLOYER FICA EXPENSE 12/31/92     40.60        0.00        40.60
                                                 --------     --------      --------
                 TRANSACTIONS:  1                  40.60        0.00        40.60

                 TOTAL TRANSACTIONS:  7          571.30       571.30         0.00


                           *** End of General Ledger Transaction Register ***
```

941A State Wage Report

STATE NAME: GEORGIA

W.D. Peachtree & Company
3900 Peachtree Street
Atlanta, GA 30309

STATE ID: 123456789012345
UNEMPLOYMENT ID: 1234567890

		PAID THIS QUARTER			
		FICA WAGES	STATE WAGES	ST WAGES EXCESS	
857-34-8172	Bill Blast	6000.02	0.00	6000.02	12
430-83-9320	Cal Cline	4190.70	0.00	4190.70	13
542-34-4238	Oscar DeLarent	4140.00	0.00	4140.00	13
999-96-4343	Alma Atherton	4810.00	0.00	4810.00	12
543-43-3892	Buster Browne	3510.00	0.00	3510.00	12
534-22-9484	Ken Moore	9000.03	0.00	9000.03	12
407-92-8375	Amanda Range	8280.01	0.00	8280.01	12
765-34-5435	May Tagg	692.31	692.31	0.00	2
832-93-9432	Jerry Hobbs	3244.80	0.00	3244.80	12
503-82-0943	Gary Hofman	4097.60	0.00	4097.60	12
643-93-2843	Bob Katz	3494.40	0.00	3494.40	12
543-54-8429	Brad Scott	5999.76	0.00	5999.76	12
STATE TOTALS XXXXXXXXXXXXXXX		57,459.63	692.31	56,767.32	
		57,459.63			

941 Worksheet

```
RUN DATE: 12/31/92        W.D. Peachtree & Company           PAGE  1
RUN TIME:  6:21 PM               Payroll
                           941 WORKSHEET (Q-T-D)
-------------------------------------------------------------------------

DATE QUARTER ENDED.............................................    12/31/92
EMPLOYER ID. NO................................................  123456789012
01. NUMBER OF EMPLOYEES (MAR. 12 PAY PERIOD)...................
02. TOTAL WAGES & TIPS SUBJECT TO WITHHOLDING.................   $57,459.63
03. TOTAL INCOME TAX WITHHELD FROM WAGES & TIPS...............    $7,384.46
04. ADJ. OF WITHHELD INCOME TAX FROM PREV. QUARTERS..........
05. ADJUSTED TOTAL OF INCOME TAX WITHHELD.....................    $7,384.46
06.a. TAXABLE OASD WAGES PAID   $57,459.63 TIMES 12.400% =TAX     $7,124.99
06.b. TAXABLE OASD TIPS              $0.00 TIMES 12.400% =TAX         $0.00
06.c. OASD ON GROUP TERM LIFE        $0.00 TIMES 12.400% =TAX         $0.00
07.a. TAXABLE HI WAGES & TIPS   $57,459.63 TIMES  2.900% =TAX     $1,666.33
07.b. HI ON GROUP TERM LIFE          $0.00 TIMES  2.900% =TAX         $0.00
08. TOTAL FICA TAXES..........................................    $8,791.32
09. ADJUSTMENT OF FICA TAXES (FRACTION ONLY).................         $0.01
       (UNCOLLECTED FICA TAX ON TIPS)........................         $0.00
10. ADJUSTED TOTAL OF FICA TAXES..............................    $8,791.33
14. TOTAL TAXES...............................................   $16,175.79
15. ADVANCE EARNED INCOME CREDIT PAYMENTS....................         $0.00
16. NET TAXES.................................................   $16,175.79
17. TOTAL DEPOSITS FOR QUARTER FROM YOUR RECORDS.............
18. BALANCE DUE...............................................

RECORD OF FEDERAL TAX DEPOSITS   ('Next Day' Indicates One-Day Rule)
                                TAX        LAST DAY      AMOUNT
                              LIABILITY   TO DEPOSIT    TO DEPOSIT
A MONTH 1  TOTAL               $0.00       11/15/92       $0.00
B MONTH 2  TOTAL               $0.00       12/15/92       $0.00
C MONTH 3  TOTAL           $2,511.74       01/15/93   $2,511.74
D TOTAL FOR QUARTER.......  $2,511.74
E FINAL DEPOSIT MADE FOR QUARTER.............................
F TOTAL DEPOSITS MADE FOR QUARTER............................
```

Federal Unemployment Tax Report

```
RUN DATE: 12/31/92                    W.D. Peachtree & Company                              PAGE 1
RUN TIME:  6:21 PM                            Payroll
                                   Federal Unemployment Tax Report (Q-T-D)

DATE QUARTER ENDED: 12/31/92   STATE NAME: GEORGIA   STATE LIMIT:   8500.00   UNEMP. ID: 1234567890
```

SOCIAL SECURITY NO.	EMPLOYEE NAME	TOTAL WAGES	FEDERAL UNEMP. WAGES	FED. UNEMP. WAGES EXCESS	STATE UNEMP. WAGES	STATE UNEMP. WAGES EXCESS
857-34-8172	Bill Blast	6000.02	0.00	6000.02	0.00	6000.02
430-83-9320	Cal Cline	4190.70	0.00	4190.70	0.00	4190.70
542-34-4238	Oscar DeLarent	4140.00	0.00	4140.00	0.00	4140.00
999-96-4343	Alma Atherton	4810.00	0.00	4810.00	0.00	4810.00
543-43-3892	Buster Browne	3510.00	0.00	3510.00	0.00	3510.00
534-22-9484	Ken Moore	9000.03	0.00	9000.03	0.00	9000.03
407-92-8375	Amanda Range	8280.01	0.00	8280.01	0.00	8280.01
765-34-5435	May Tagg	692.31	692.31	0.00	692.31	0.00
832-93-9432	Jerry Hobbs	3244.80	0.00	3244.80	0.00	3244.80
503-82-0943	Gary Hofman	4097.60	0.00	4097.60	0.00	4097.60
643-93-2843	Bob Katz	3494.40	0.00	3494.40	0.00	3494.40
543-54-8429	Brad Scott	5999.76	0.00	5999.76	0.00	5999.76
TOTAL EMPLOYEES: 12	WAGE TOTALS:	57459.63	692.31	56767.32	692.31	56767.32

```
GEORGIA   UNEMP. TAX RATE: 3.0000% TIMES      692.31 =    20.77 STATE UNEMP. TAX

EFFECTIVE FUTA TAX RATE  :  0.8000% TIMES      692.31 =     5.54 FEDERAL UNEMP. TAX

GRAND TOTALS
TOTAL EMPLOYEES: 12       WAGE TOTALS:   57459.63    692.31    56767.32    692.31    56767.32

FEDERAL UNEMP. TAX RATE: 6.2000% TIMES      692.31 =    42.92 FEDERAL UNEMP. TAX

EFFECTIVE FUTA TAX RATE:  0.8000% TIMES      692.31 =     5.54 FEDERAL UNEMP. TAX

*** End of Federal Unemployment Tax Report (Q-T-D) ***
```

Sample W-2

1 Control number	22222	For Official Use Only ▶ OMB No. 1545-0008							Void ☐

2 Employer's name, address, and ZIP code		6 Statutory employee ☐	Deceased ☐	Pension plan ☐	Legal rep. ☐	942 emp. ☐	Subtotal ☐	Deferred compensation ☐

W. D. Peachtree & Co.
3900 Peachtree St.
Atlanta, GA   30309

7 Allocated tips	8 Advance EIC payment

3 Employer's identification number	4 Employer's state I.D. number
58-3030303	

9 Federal income tax withheld	10 Wages, tips, other compensation
1428.97	8408.15

5 Employee's social security number
284-41-4567

11 Social security tax withheld	12 Social security wages
564.77	8408.15

19a Employee's name (first, middle initial, last)
Donald D. Darlington

13 Social security tips	14 Medicare wages and tips
	8408.15

4567 Springwood Drive SE
Huntsville, AL   35803

15 Medicare tax withheld	16 Nonqualified plans
132.56	

17 See Instrs. for Form W-2	18 Other

19b Employee's address and ZIP code		
20	21	

22 Dependent care benefits	23 Benefits included in Box 10

24 State income tax	25 State wages, tips, etc.	26 Name of state
282.89	8408.15	Alabama

27 Local income tax	28 Local wages, tips, etc.	29 Name of locality

Copy A For Social Security Administration   Cat. No. 10134D   Department of the Treasury—Internal Revenue Service

Form **W-2 Wage and Tax Statement 1992**

For Paperwork Reduction Act Notice and instructions for completing this form, **see separate instructions.**

Chapter 11

PAYROLL: PRACTICING WITH A SAMPLE BUSINESS

Learning Objectives:

After studying this chapter you should be able to:

1. Perform activities to maintain employee information including—terminating an employee, adding an employee, and verifying the information you entered.

2. Perform activities to process the payroll including—gathering and entering payroll information, calculating and verifying payroll, and printing paychecks and closing the period.

Chapter 11

Payroll : Practicing with a Sample Business

This chapter guides you through lessons that give you practical experience with Payroll. You will work with the payroll of W. D. Peachtree & Company.

The lessons in this chapter are grouped into two topics:

1. Maintain Employee Information.
2. Process The Payroll.

Topic 1, Maintain Employee Information, shows you how to change employee information. These tasks are performed in a real company whenever the need arises.

Topic 2, Process The Payroll, guides you through the tasks that must be performed to pay employees and post payroll transactions. Depending on the complexity of the payroll, all these tasks probably will not be performed every pay period. However, you should complete all the lessons in this section so you know how to handle certain payroll situations when they do arise.

About the Practice Session

You do not need to complete the Payroll session in one sitting. However, if possible, you should complete all the **lessons** in a topic at the same time. Completing the lessons at one time helps you understand the relationship between the tasks in a particular topic. In addition, unless otherwise noted, complete the lessons in each topic in the order listed. Often, in Payroll, the order in which you perform tasks is important.

Payroll uses module options that control the way Payroll operates. The options for W.D. Peachtree are set to force control reports; (control reports help you verify the changes you make to Payroll). So, you can not complete many of the lessons in this practice session unless you have your printer turned on and ready to print.

About W.D. Peachtree's Data

In this session, you will work with sample data created for W.D. Peachtree & Company. Since most of Payroll revolves around employees and their payroll requirements, you should get to know the employees for whom you will be processing Payroll:

Alma A. Atherton is a W.D. Peachtree employee who has recently retired and moved to a retirement community in Alabama. For Alma, you will:

- Change her address.
- Retire her from Payroll by changing her status from Active to Inactive.

Ralph Lowren is a newly hired hourly employee. Ralph will work in the Polo Shop of the Men's Clothing department. For Ralph, you will:

- Add him to Payroll.
- Pay him a new employee bonus.
- Enter the hours he worked.

Oscar DeLarent is an hourly employee in the Men's Clothing department. Oscar usually works 40 hours a week; this week, however, he was sick one day and took one day off without pay. For Oscar, you will:

- Enter the hours he worked.
- Record 8 hours of sick leave.

Ken Moore is manager of the W.D. Peachtree Appliances department. As manager, Ken is a salaried employee. Recently, W.D. Peachtree offered all its managers the chance to purchase W.D. Peachtree stock. Ken took advantage of this opportunity. For Ken, you will:

- Enter a deduction for Ken's stock purchase.

May Tagg is a commissioned employee in the Appliances department. When W.D. Peachtree hires commissioned employees, it loans them $200 to help meet expenses. Employees must pay back all loans within three months. May has just paid back her loan. For May, you will:

- Record her commissions.
- Enter her loan repayment.

In completing the lessons of this session, you will also complete the following tasks for W.D. Peachtree:

- Pay all its employees.
- Print the reports W.D. Peachtree needs to verify its payroll.
- Close the pay period.

Beginning the Practice Session

```
                               WARNING

BEFORE CONTINUING, BE SURE THAT ALL DATA FILES HAVE BEEN RESTORED TO
THEIR ORIGINAL CONDITION.  IF YOU ARE UNSURE OF HOW TO RESTORE THESE
FILES, TURN TO THE INSTRUCTIONS FOUND ON PAGE 1-32 IN  CHAPTER 1.
```

❖ Start Peachtree Complete Accounting by changing to the directory in which you installed
Peachtree Complete and typing **PEACH**.

❖ Press ⌨.

In a few moments, PCA displays the first screen. The only information PCA provides here is
the date -- either the date you last started your computer or the date from your computer's
internal calendar.

❖ Press ⌨ to erase the date on your screen.

For this session, you should use December 29, 1992, as the date.

❖ Type **122992** for the date and press ⌨.

❖ Type **WD** for the company ID and press ⌨.

PCA displays the Main Menu. From this menu, you select which module you want to use.

❖ Use ⌨ to highlight Payroll. Then, press ⌨.

PCA displays the Payroll Main Menu.

You are now ready to begin the Payroll practice session. Start with Topic 1.

Topic 1 - Maintain Employee Information

During the year, a company often needs to change its employee information: employees move or quit; they get hired or fired. To make sure Payroll processes a company's payroll correctly, employee information must be accurate and up to date.

Unlike most Payroll tasks, the order in which you perform maintenance tasks is not crucial. Let the tasks you need to perform dictate the order you will follow.

Topic 1 has three lessons; they show you how to manage W.D. Peachtree's employee information. In this topic, you will:

1. Terminate an employee.
2. Add a new employee.
3. Verify the information you entered.

Although these lessons teach you how to change an employee's status and his or her address, the steps you follow are very similar to the steps you would follow to change any kind of employee information.

Before you can complete any of the lessons in this practice session, you will need to understand employee codes and department numbers. An employee code is a four-character code which identifies an employee for Payroll. For W.D. Peachtree, this code consists of the first three characters of an employee's last name and the first character of his or her first name. For example, SMIJ for John Smith or JONA for Ann Jones.

Employee codes are very important; Payroll tracks your employees by their codes, not by their social security numbers or names. So, throughout the practice session, pay particular attention to employee codes.

Department numbers are optional numbers that can be assigned to employees. Department numbers allow employees to be separated into smaller groups (departments). These groups can then be maintained, displayed, and printed. Department numbers can also be used to create separate payroll expense categories in the general ledger.

W.D. Peachtree uses departments because it is a large company with a lot of employees. Departments allow W.D. Peachtree to manage its payroll more efficiently. Since the W.D. Peachtree store is itself divided into departments, the department numbers used in Payroll correspond to the actual departments used in the store.

Lesson 1: Terminate an Employee

W.D. Peachtree employee Alma A. Atherton has recently retired and moved to another state. To keep your Payroll information accurate and up-to-date, you must terminate Alma in Payroll and change her address. These are the only changes necessary for Alma.

When employees leave a company, they are no longer on the payroll; they are no longer "active" employees. They should not be removed from Payroll, though, because they will still need reports about their gross pay and taxes at the end of the year (W-2 report). Additionally, the terminated employees will be included on some of the company's other year-end tax reports.

Payroll allows the termination of employees by changing their status from Active to Inactive. You will be shown how to do this is step 2 of this lesson. At the end of the year, after all the W-2s have been printed and all the yearly Payroll tasks have been completed, Payroll deletes all Inactive employees.

Step 1: Change an Employee's Address

❖ From the Payroll Main Menu, select **Maintenance Programs**.

Maintenance Programs are the programs that you use to enter and update Payroll information.

❖ From the Maintenance Programs Menu, select **Maintain Employees**.

Maintain Employees is the program you use to maintain employee information. You can add new employees, change addresses, and adjust deductions through this program.

To maintain employee information, you must always enter an employee's Department number and Employee Code. In this case, Alma's department number is 16 and her employee code is ATHA. (Be sure to use capital letters.)

❖ Enter **16** for Department.

At this point, you could simply enter Alma's employee code (ATHA), or you could look up the code using the several options illustrated in earlier chapters.

Payroll displays the following screen of information about Alma A. Atherton:

```
=======================================================================
PRMAINT                      Maintain Employees              COMPANY ID: WD
12/29/92                  W.D. Peachtree & Company            GENERATION #: 53
=======================================================================

DEPARTMENT.....: 16        EMPLOYEE CODE ........: ATHA      TITLE... : PERSONAL INFORMATION
                                                             PROCESSING STATUS ..... : PC

NAME ................................ :   Alma Atherton
ADDRESS ........................... :   3903 Butterfield Drive
ADDRESS ........................... :
CITY, STATE...................... :   Atlanta, GA
ZIP CODE........................... :   30321
SOC. SEC. NO. .................. :   999-96-4343
PHONE............................... :   404-555-1804
COMMENT ......................... :   Children's Clothing
STATUS (A/I) ..................... :   A
DATE EMPLOYED .............. :   03/16/87
DATE TERMINATED .......... :   01/01/00
LAST CHECK DATE ........... :   12/22/92
LAST CHECK NO. .............. :      1421
LAST CHECK AMOUNT ..... :       278.47

                    ACCEPT  (Y/N) : Y      (T=TERMINATE,  R=RE-ACTIVATE,
                                            D=CHANGE DEPARTMENT CODE)
                                    F8 - Undo
```

Notice the title, Personal Information, in the upper right corner of the screen. Payroll needs several screens to display employee information, so each screen has a name, a title. Pay attention to these titles; in this session, screens will be described by their titles.

Notice the prompt at the bottom of the screen, *ACCEPT (Y/N)*. Whenever this prompt appears, you can accept the information displayed on the screen by entering Y or you can change it by entering N.

❖ You need to change Alma's address, so type **N** at the *ACCEPT (Y/N)* prompt. Press .

The cursor moves to Name.

❖ Enter the following information in the proper spaces for Alma.

Address:	**1313 Mockingbird Lane**
City, State:	**Anniston, AL**
Zip Code:	**39999**
Phone:	**205-555-6662**

❖ After you finish, press 🖰.

❖ Press 🖰 at the *ACCEPT (Y/N)* prompt to accept the information you just entered.

Since Payroll uses more than one screen to display employee information, Payroll displays a second screen, the Rates & Flags screen. This screen displays information for pay rates and federal tax.

❖ For the example involving Alma Atherton, there were no changes in pay rates or tax information. You do not need to make changes to this screen, so just accept it.

Payroll continues to display the remaining employee information screens, the Tax Code and the Misc. Income screens. The Tax Code screen displays state and local tax information. The Misc. Income screen displays miscellaneous income information as well as sick pay accrual, and vacation accrual.

❖ Since you do not have any changes to make to these screens (in this case), just accept them.

After you accept the Misc. Income screen, Payroll beeps and asks, *ENTER PERIOD-TO-DATE INFORMATION (Y/N)?*

You do not need to make changes to Alma's period-to-date information.

❖ Type **N** and press 🖰.

The screen clears and the cursor returns to Department.

Step 2: Terminate an Employee

You have already changed Alma's address and phone number, but you still need to change her employee status. Whenever an employee's status is changed from Active to Inactive, the employee must first have been paid anything owed by the company. Payroll does not allow you to pay Inactive employees.

It does not matter whether you change Alma's status first or her address first, but you can not change them at the same time. So, to change her status, you will have to enter Alma's department number and employee code, again.

❖ Enter Alma's department (16) and her employee code (ATHA).

Payroll displays the first screen of information; the cursor is at the *ACCEPT (Y/N)* prompt. Your choices are:

T   to change an Active employee's status to Inactive.
R   to change an Inactive status to Active.
D   to change the employee's department code.
Y   to accept the information as displayed.
N   to change the information.

Since Alma has retired from the company, you must change her status to Inactive.

❖ Enter **T**.

Because you just changed Alma's status, Payroll asks you to confirm your choice: *TERMINATE (Y/N)*.

❖ Enter **Y**.

Payroll asks you to enter Alma's termination date.

❖ Assume Alma's last day was December 17. Enter **12/17/92**.

The screen clears and the cursor returns to Department.

❖ Press 🖭 to initiate your return to the Payroll Maintenance Menu.

Lesson 1 Summary

You have just learned how to update employee information. You will follow these same steps whenever you need to change employee information.

You have also learned how to change an employee's status. When you change that status from Active to Inactive, Payroll:

• Continues to maintain current information on the employee. You can update this information as you would update it for any Active employee.

• No longer calculates earnings and deductions for a terminated employee but still stores the year-to-date earnings and deductions information for that person. So, you should never make an employee inactive until after the employee has received the last paycheck.

• Prints W-2s for all employees -- including Inactive employees -- when you close out your fourth quarter and print W-2s.

• Deletes all Inactive employees when you close out the year.

Lesson 2: Add a New Employee

Assume W.D. Peachtree has hired a new hourly employee, Ralph Lowren. Ralph will work in the Polo Shop of the Men's Clothing department (department 12) beginning on 12/18/92. You will need to add Ralph to Payroll.

This lesson teaches you a fundamental Payroll task: adding new employees. Whenever you add a new employee, you will follow these same steps.

❖ From the Maintenance Programs Menu, select **Maintain Employees**.

❖ Enter Ralph's department number, **12**.

Since Ralph is a new employee, he does not have an assigned employee code. You will have to assign him a code. (Remember W.D. Peachtree's system for employee codes: use the first three letters of the employee's last name and then his first initial.)

❖ Enter Ralph's employee code (**LOWR**).

When entering new employees in Payroll, make sure you enter the employee codes carefully. Changing assigned employee codes is not easy in this program. (Remember, Payroll keeps employee information organized by employee code rather than by name or Social Security Number.)

Payroll does not recognize the code you just entered, so it asks, *NOT ON FILE -- ADD (Y/N)*. Payroll assumes you will add the new employee, so it automatically displays Y.

❖ Press [ENTER] to add Ralph to Payroll.

Payroll now displays the first screen of employee information, the Personal Information screen.

❖ Enter the following information for Ralph. Remember, press [ENTER] to move to each new item of information.

Name:	**Ralph Lowren**
Address:	**12 Couture Corners**
Address:	**Apt. 75A**
City, State:	**Atlanta, GA**
Zip Code:	**30303-4123**
Soc. Sec. No:	**121-34-5000**
Phone:	**404-555-1000**
Comment:	**Polo Shop**
Status:	**A**
Date Employed:	**12/18/92**

Since Ralph is a new employee, you do not need to enter anything into the remaining fields; they do not apply to new employees.

❖ After you have entered this information, check your entries, press ▣ and then accept the screen once the information appears exactly as it appears above.

Payroll displays the second screen of employee information, the Rates & Flags screen.

```
==================================================================================
PRMAINT                      Maintain Employees                    COMPANY ID: WD
12/29/92                  W.D. Peachtree & Company                  GENERATION #: 53
==================================================================================

  DEPARTMENT.....: 12      EMPLOYEE CODE ........: LOWR      TITLE...: RATES & FLAGS
                                                     PROCESSING STATUS ....: NW
  STATUTORY EMPLOYEE............:  N      CUR. DEFER. DEDUCTIONS ......:         0.00
  DECEASED.........................:  N      YTD. DEFER. DEDUCTIONS.......:         0.00
  TIPPED EMPLOYEE .................:  N      CUR. ALLOC. DEDUCTIONS ......:         0.00
  LEGAL REP........................:  N      COST OF GROUP TERM LIFE....:
  942 EMPLOYEE ....................:  N                    OVER $50000..:         0.00
  EIC STATUS ......................:  N      FICA TAKEN ON TERM LIFE.......:  N
  SHIFT CODE .......................:  1      STANDARD WORK WEEK ..........:      40.00
  PAY PERIOD.......................:  M      STANDARD OVT. 1 HOURS ......:       0.00
  PAY TYPE ..........................:  S      STANDARD OVT. 2 HOURS ......:       0.00
  PAY RATE/SALARY/DRAW ........:        0.000     PENSION........................:  N
  COMMISSION RATE % ................:      0.00      DEFERRED COMPENSATION....:  N
  MAXIMUM CHECK AMOUNT .......:        0.00      SUTA TAXABLE ....................:  Y
  FED. FILING STATUS ..................:  M      INDUSTRIAL INSURANCE % ......:         0.00
  FED. EXEMPTIONS .....................:  1
  ADDL. FED. TAX.......................:        0.00

                        ACCEPT  (Y/N) :  Y
                              F8 - Undo
```

Notice that Payroll has already made entries on this screen. Some information -- information that applies to most W.D. Peachtree employees -- was specified in another program called **Maintain Payroll Options**. (This program can be used to assign similar information for a real company's employees.)

The cursor is at the *ACCEPT (Y/N)* prompt. Not all the information displayed on this screen applies to Ralph, so you will need to make changes.

❖ Type N and press ▣.

❖ Enter the following information for Ralph:

```
Pay Period:              W          for Weekly
Pay Type:                H          for Hourly
Pay Rate/Salary/Draw:    5.00       Ralph's hourly rate
Fed. Filing Status:      S          for Single
Fed. Exemptions:         2
```

❖ After you have checked your entries, press ▣ and then accept the screen if they are correct. If you need to make corrections, do so before accepting the screen.

Payroll displays the third screen of employee information, the Tax Code screen.

```
================================================================================
PRMAINT                          Maintain Employees              COMPANY ID: WD
12/29/92                        W.D. Peachtree & Company          GENERATION #: 53
================================================================================

DEPARTMENT ....: 12       EMPLOYEE CODE........: LOWR      TITLE ...: TAX CODE
                                                          PROCESSING STATUS....: NW
   TAX        FILING                      MISC. TAX      ADDIT.        MISC.
   CODE ..........STATUS ...........EXEMPTIONS............FACTOR .............TAX .............TAX AMOUNT
1.  0                        0             0.00           0.00           0.00
2.  0                        0             0.00           0.00           0.00
3.  0                        0             0.00           0.00           0.00
4.  0                        0             0.00           0.00           0.00

                                                    TAXABLE  (Y/N)
                                            WITHHOLDING UNEMPLOYMENT
   DEDUCTIONS ...............AMOUNT...............CEILING.
   1. INSUR.     DED. A     0.00
   2. 401K       DED. A     0.00
   3. EMP LOAN   DED. A     0.00
   4. SAVINGS    DED. P     0.00
   5. STCK PUR   DED. P     0.00
   6. SIX        DED. P     0.00
                                       ACCEPT  (Y/N) : Y
                                             F8 - Undo
```

On this screen, you can enter up to four different lines of state and local tax information and up to six lines of voluntary deduction information.

Ralph is a Georgia resident, so you must enter his state tax code, GA. Georgia has specific filing statuses for its residents and allows residents to claim exemptions. Ralph has given W.D. Peachtree his filing status (Single) and exemptions (2).

❖ The cursor is at the *ACCEPT (Y/N)* Prompt. You need to make changes, so type **N** and press ⌨️.

❖ On line 1, enter the following tax information for Ralph:

Tax Code	**GA**	
Filing Status	**A**	(for Single)
Exemptions	**2**	

❖ Then press 💾 and accept the screen once you have entered the information exactly as it is above.

Payroll displays the Misc. Income screen. On this screen, you can enter miscellaneous income that occurs regularly. You can also enter accruals of vacation and sick time.

❖ You do not need to make any changes on this screen for Ralph, so just accept the screen.

Payroll asks, ENTER PERIOD-TO-DATE INFORMATION (Y/N)?

Period-to-date information includes year-to-date and quarter-to-date earnings and deductions. Since Ralph is a new employee, you do not have any period-to-date information to enter.

❖ Enter **N**.

The screen clears; the cursor returns to Department. You do not have any other employees to add, so you can return to the Payroll Main Menu.

❖ Press ▓ᴱˢᶜ▌ to return to the **Payroll Main Menu**.

Lesson 2 Summary

You learned how to enter a new employee into Payroll. You used the same program to add a new employee, **Maintain Employees**, as you did to change employee information.

Lesson 3: Verify the Information You Entered

Even though you checked your entries before you accepted them, you should still check a printed copy of those changes. Often, on a printed report, you will see mistakes that you missed on the screen. Also, many companies have a policy of retaining a printed record of all employee changes.

You can review the employee information you entered for Ralph and Alma by using **List Employees.**

❖ Select **Report Programs** from the Payroll Main Menu.

❖ Select **List Employees** from the Payroll Reports Menu.

Payroll displays Report Date and lists the current date. The date you enter for Report Date is simply the date Payroll prints on your report.

❖ Accept the displayed date.

Payroll displays a pop up box and asks you to select the report type.

❖ For now select **LIST WITHOUT PERIOD-TO-DATE INFORMATION**.

(Ralph does not have any period-to-date information and you did not make any changes to Alma's period-to-date information.)

Payroll displays another pop up box, the Select Options pop up box.

```
A - ALL DEPARTMENTS
R - RANGE OF DEPARTMENTS
M - MANUAL SELECTION
```

For Ralph and Alma you want to print information for two employees in different departments, so you will need to use Manual Selection.

❖ Select **MANUAL SELECTION**. In this option, you can request information in any order you choose. For the example involving Ralph and Alma, either one could be requested first.

❖ Enter Ralph's department number, **12**, and his employee code, **LOWR**.

Payroll prints the report; then, the cursor returns to Department.

❖ Enter Alma's department number, **16**, and her employee code, **ATHA**.

Payroll prints a report listing all the information you entered into **Maintain Employees** for Ralph Lowren and for Alma A. Atherton. The report appears as follows:

```
RUN DATE: 12/29/92                          W. D. Peachtree & Company                                  PAGE  1
RUN TIME:   3:30 PM                                   Payroll
                                                Employee File List
-----------------------------------------------------------------------------------------------------------------
EMPLOYEE CODE  12LOWR          STATUTORY  : N   TAX CODE 1: GA   FILING ST. : A  EXEM.: 2  FACTOR:  0.00% ADDL TAX :   0.00
PROCESSING STATUS:  NW         DECEASED   : N   TAX CODE 2:      FILING ST. :    EXEM.: 0  FACTOR:  0.00% ADDL TAX :   0.00
Ralph Lowren                   TIPPED     : N   TAX CODE 3:      FILING ST. :    EXEM.: 0  FACTOR:  0.00% ADDL TAX :   0.00
12 Couture Corners             LEGAL REP. : N   TAX CODE 4:      FILING ST. :    EXEM.: 0  FACTOR:  0.00% ADDL TAX :   0.00
Apt. 75A                       942 EMP.   : N         FEDERAL   FILING ST. : S  EXEM.: 2                   ADDL TAX :   0.00
Atlanta, GA        30303-4123  DEF. COMP. : N   PENSION : N  SUTA TAXABLE: Y  INDUS. INS.:   0.00%
                               EIC STATUS : N              SICK HOURS/YEAR      :   40.00   CUR. UNCOL FICA TIP TAX  :   0.00
                               SHIFT      : 1             VAC. HOURS/YEAR      :   80.00   QTD. UNCOL FICA TIP TAX  :   0.00
SOC. SEC.  : 121-34-5000       DATE EMPLOYED   :  12/18/92  SICK HOURS USED      :    0.00   YTD UNCOL FICA TIP TAX   :   0.00
PHONE NO. : 404-555-1000       DATE TERMINATED :  01/01/00  VAC. HOURS USED      :    0.00   MISC. TAX AMOUNT #1      :   0.00
COMMENT   : Polo Shop          LAST CHECK DATE :  01/01/00  SICK HOURS ACCRUED   :    0.00   MISC. TAX AMOUNT #2      :   0.00
PAY PER.  : WEEKLY             LAST CHECK NO.  :        0  VAC HOURS ACCRUED    :    0.00   MISC. TAX AMOUNT #3      :   0.00
PAY TYPE  : HOURLY             LAST CHECK AMT. :     0.00  CUR. DEFERRED DED.   :    0.00   MISC. TAX AMOUNT #4      :   0.00
PAY RATE  :        5.000       COMMISSION RATE :     0.00  YTD. DEFERRED DED.   :    0.00   TERM LIFE COST > 50K     :   0.00
                               UNION CONTRACT DATE: 01/01/00                      :          TERM LIFE FICA TAKEN      : N

EMPLOYEE CODE  16ATHA (INACTIVE)  STATUTORY  : N   TAX CODE 1: GA   FILING ST. : Q  EXEM.: 0  FACTOR:  0.00% ADDL TAX :   0.00
PROCESSING STATUS:  PC         DECEASED   : N   TAX CODE 2:      FILING ST. :    EXEM.: 0  FACTOR:  0.00% ADDL TAX :   0.00
Alma Atherton                  TIPPED     : N   TAX CODE 3:      FILING ST. :    EXEM.: 0  FACTOR:  0.00% ADDL TAX :   0.00
1313 Mockingbird Lane          LEGAL REP. : N   TAX CODE 4:      FILING ST. :    EXEM.: 0  FACTOR:  0.00% ADDL TAX :   0.00
                               942 EMP.   : N         FEDERAL   FILING ST. : M  EXEM.: 0                   ADDL TAX :   0.00
Anniston, AL          39999    DEF. COMP. : N   PENSION : N  SUTA TAXABLE: Y  INDUS. INS.:   0.00%
                               EIC STATUS : N              SICK HOURS/YEAR      :   40.00   CUR. UNCOL FICA TIP TAX  :   0.00
                               SHIFT      : 1             VAC. HOURS/YEAR      :   80.00   QTD. UNCOL FICA TIP TAX  :   0.00
SOC. SEC.  : 999-96-4343       DATE EMPLOYED   :  03/16/87  SICK HOURS USED      :    0.00   YTD UNCOL FICA TIP TAX   :   0.00
PHONE NO. : 205-555-6662       DATE TERMINATED :  12/17/92  VAC. HOURS USED      :    0.00   MISC. TAX AMOUNT #1      :   0.00
COMMENT   : Children's Clothing LAST CHECK DATE : 12/22/92  SICK HOURS ACCRUED   :   39.27   MISC. TAX AMOUNT #2      :   0.00
PAY PER.  : WEEKLY             LAST CHECK NO.  :     1421  VAC HOURS ACCRUED    :   78.54   MISC. TAX AMOUNT #3      :   0.00
PAY TYPE  : HOURLY             LAST CHECK AMT. :   278.47  CUR. DEFERRED DED.   :    0.00   MISC. TAX AMOUNT #4      :   0.00
PAY RATE  :        9.250       COMMISSION RATE :     0.00  YTD. DEFERRED DED.   :    0.00   TERM LIFE COST > 50K     :   0.00
                               UNION CONTRACT DATE: 01/01/00                      :          TERM LIFE FICA TAKEN      : N

*** End of Employee File List ***
```

Check that information; make sure you entered exactly what you should have entered. If necessary, return to **Maintain Employees** and make changes to Ralph's or Alma's information.

The cursor returns to Department. If you wanted to print employee information for more employees, you could continue entering department numbers and employee codes. Since you are finished printing both Ralph's and Alma's information, just return to the Payroll Main Menu.

❖ Press 〖ESC〗 until you see the *[F10] - MENU* prompt at the bottom of your screen.

❖ Press 〖F10〗 to return to the Payroll Reports Menu. Then, press 〖ESC〗 to return to the Payroll Main Menu.

Lesson 3 Summary

In this lesson, you learned how to check the information you entered into **Maintain Employees** by printing an Employee File List. Payroll uses the information you enter in **Maintain Employees** to process a payroll. So, you should always print an Employee File List whenever you make changes to the employee information.

Topic 2 - Process The Payroll

Every pay period a business needs to calculate its employees' earnings and taxes and to write their paychecks. The lessons in this topic guide you through all the steps you must perform to process a payroll. The topic has three lessons:

1. Gather and enter payroll information.
2. Calculate and verify payroll.
3. Print paychecks and close the period.

The order in which you perform these tasks is important, so make sure you complete all the lessons in this topic in the order listed. Depending on the complexity of a company's payroll, all the tasks described in this topic may not be performed every pay period. However, you should complete all the lessons in this section so you know how to use all the Payroll processing features.

In this topic, you will process W.D. Peachtree's payroll and pay all its Active employees. Processing payroll includes entering time card hours, sick hours used, or commissions earned. It also includes printing paychecks and closing the period. The pay period you will be processing begins 12/18/92 and ends 12/24/92. Employees receive their paychecks on 12/29/92.

To process the W.D. Peachtree payroll for this pay period, you will need to enter special earnings and deductions for four employees: Ralph Lowren and Oscar DeLarent in the Men's Clothing department and Ken Moore and May Tagg in the Appliances department. Assume these exemptions and deductions occurred only this pay period. Normally, W.D. Peachtree does not have to enter special earnings or deductions for its employees.

Lesson 1: Gather and Enter Payroll Information

W.D. Peachtree pays its employees weekly. Before you can actually print paychecks, you need to enter the time card hours for hourly employees and enter the various earnings and deductions which occur only in this pay period. You will complete these tasks in four steps:

1. Enter Time Card Hours.
2. Print and Fill Out Paymaster Worksheets.
3. Enter Non-Standard Earnings and Deductions.
4. Verify Your Entries.

Step 1. Calculate Time Card Hours

Ralph Lowren is an hourly employee whose schedule varies from week to week. **Calculate Time Card Hours** allows you to enter clock-in and clock-out times for hourly employees right from their time cards, so you will use this program to enter the hours Ralph worked.

Oscar DeLarent is an hourly employee who works a set schedule every week. Oscar does not use a time card; his manager just keeps track of any hours Oscar does not work. Although you can enter his hours worked into **Calculate Time Card Hours**, you can enter them more quickly in **Enter Exceptions**. (You complete this task in Step 3.)

For hourly employees who use time cards, you will use **Calculate Time Card Hours** to enter their clock-in and clock-out times. In addition to clock-in and out times, this program requires you to enter the type of hours worked: Regular, Overtime 1, or Overtime 2. When an employee works Overtime 1 or Overtime 2 hours, he or she is paid at some multiple of the standard hourly rate. (At W.D. Peachtree, hourly employees are paid 1-1/2 times their regular hourly rate for Overtime 1 hours and 2 times their regular hourly rate for Overtime 2 hours.)

❖ From the Payroll Main Menu, select **Processing Programs**. Then, from the Payroll Processing Menu, select **Paymaster Worksheet/Time Card**. When prompted, check your printer.

From **Select Procedure**, you can either print Paymaster Worksheets or use the **Calculate Time Card Hours** program.

❖ Select **Calculate Time Card Hours**.

Payroll asks for the report date.

❖ Accept the displayed date of **12/29/92** as the report date.

The Time Card entry screen appears. The cursor is at Department.

❖ Enter Ralph's department number **(12)** and employee code **(LOWR)**.

The cursor moves to the first line in the Time Entries section of the screen. You can enter up to 99 different lines of clock-in and clock-out times for an employee.

Notice the Time Card Hours on File section of the screen, (the upper right side, above the Total Hours section). If you had already entered time card hours for Ralph this pay period, Payroll would display those hours here and would allow you to add to those hours or to discard them completely.

To use **Calculate Time Card Hours**, you must enter the times in and out in the time formats the company uses: either 24 hour or 12 hour clock and either hours.minutes or hours.decimal hours. W.D. Peachtree uses a 24 hour clock and the hours.decimal hours format because the W.D. Peachtree time clock prints times in these formats.

❖ Enter Ralph's clock-in and clock-out times from his time card. Make sure you enter the correct pay types, R (for regular), l (for time and one-half), 2 (for double time). (The days of the week will not be entered. They are for your information only.)

Ralph Lowren 121-34-5000	Dept. 12 Men's Clothing	Type
1. (Mon) 9.45	14.48	R
2. (Tues) 11.53	17.03	R
3. (Wed) 9.52	18.12	R
4. (Thurs) 9.55	14.59	R
5. (Fri) 17.03	22.12	R
6. (Sat) 17.01	22.23	R
7. (Sun) 12.05*	16.33*	1

* Denotes Overtime (Type 1) hours

❖ When you have entered this information, check your totals for Regular and Overtime 1 hours. Regular hours should total 34.48, and Overtime 1 hours should total 4.28.

Payroll tracks this information for you on the right side of the screen, in the Total Hours section.

❖ Check your entries; if necessary, adjust them. When they are all correct, press ▣. Then, accept the screen.

Payroll prints the following Time Card Entry Report for Ralph Lowren. This report lists the clock-in and clock-out times you entered, the type of hours worked, and the total Regular, Overtime 1, and Overtime 2 hours worked.

```
RUN DATE: 12/29/92                    W. D. Peachtree & Company                       PAGE  1
RUN TIME:   3:38 PM                            Payroll
                                         Time Card Entry Report
-----------------------------------------------------------------------------------------------
              EMPLOYEE                         TIME              HOURS
 CODE          NAME                      IN      OUT    TYPE   REG.    OVT. 1    OVT. 2
            -----------------------   -------  -------  -----  -------  -------  -------

12LOWR    Ralph Lowren                  9.45    14.48    R     5.03     0.00     0.00
                                       11.53    17.03    R     5.50     0.00     0.00
                                        9.52    18.12    R     8.60     0.00     0.00
                                        9.55    14.59    R     5.04     0.00     0.00
                                       17.03    22.12    R     5.09     0.00     0.00
                                       17.01    22.23    R     5.22     0.00     0.00
                                       12.05    16.33    1     0.00     4.28     0.00
                                                              -------  -------  -------
                                                              34.48     4.28     0.00

*** End of Time Card Entry Report ***
```

The screen clears and the cursor returns to Department.

❖ Press ⌨ until the *[F10] - MENU* prompt appears at the bottom of your screen. Then, press ⌨ to return to the Payroll Processing Menu.

Step 2. Print and Fill Out Paymaster Worksheets

W.D. Peachtree has some hourly, salaried, and commissioned employees who have non-standard earnings or deductions which must be entered in Payroll. For example, this pay period, Oscar DeLarent took a paid sick day and took a day without pay, May Tagg earned commissions and paid back an employee loan, and Ken Moore made a one-time stock purchase. You will use paymaster worksheets to help you record all this information.

Each pay period, you can print worksheets for any or all of your employees. On the worksheet, you can enter:

- Sick and vacation hours taken.
- Non-standard hours worked by hourly employees.
- Sales and commissioned earnings.
- Tips and other miscellaneous income earned.
- Additional FICA, federal, and state taxes withheld.
- Additional deductions.

After you fill out the worksheets, you enter the information you recorded on them in **Enter Exceptions**.

Payroll does not require you to print paymaster worksheets to process a payroll. However, if you have hourly or commission employees, or if you have employees with non-standard earnings and deductions, paymaster worksheets can make entering this information faster and easier.

❖ From the Payroll Processing Menu, select **Paymaster Worksheet/Time Card**. When prompted, check your printer.

❖ Then, select **Print Paymaster Worksheet**.

Payroll asks you for the report date.

❖ Accept the displayed date.

The Select Options pop up box appears.

❖ Choose **All Departments** .

Payroll prints a Paymaster Worksheet for every employee in every department.

Compare the worksheets for May Tagg (a commissioned employee), Ken Moore (a salaried employee), and Ralph Lowren and Oscar DeLarent (hourly employees). The Earnings section of each worksheet lists the earnings information relevant to each employee's pay type. (The employee's pay type appears under his social security number on the left side of the worksheet.) The rest of the worksheet is the same for all employees.

Manually enter the following information for each employee on the paymaster worksheets you have just printed:

Oscar Delarent			
Category	**Line**	**Entry**	**Reason**
Employee Information	Sick Hrs. Taken	8	Paid sick day taken.
Earnings	Reg. Hrs.	32.00	Regular hours worked.*

* Note that this 32.00 total is the number of hours for which Oscar will be paid--24 hours actually worked plus 8 hours of paid sick leave.

Ralph Lowren			
Category	**Line**	**Entry**	**Reason**
Earnings	Bonus	$50.00	New Employee bonus.

Ken Moore			
Category	**Line**	**Entry**	**Reason**
Deductions	Stck Pur	$250.00	One time stock purchase.

May Tagg			
Category	**Line**	**Entry**	**Reason**
Deductions	Emp Loan	$200.00	Payment in full, Employee Loan.
Earnings	Sales	$2000.00	Total sales at 10% commission rate.
Earnings	Commission	10.0%	Commission rate for sales $1 - $2000.
Earnings	Sales	$500.00	Total sales at 12% commission rate.
Earnings	Commission	12.0%	Commission rate for sales + $2000.

For instance, the worksheet you prepare by hand for Oscar DeLarent should appear as follows:

```
EMPLOYEE CODE 12DELO          ------------------------EARNINGS------------------------------      ---------------DEDUCTIONS---------
                              ----RATE----  ----REG. HRS.----  ----OVT1 HRS.----  ----OVT2 HRS.----
Oscar DeLarent                   7.500        40.00             0.00              0.00           FICA                 : _____
666 Belmont Avenue                            32.00                                              FEDERAL WH.          : _____
                                                                                                GEORGIA WH.          : _____
Atlanta, GA  30305            _____        _____            _____            _____          TAX CODE 2 WH.       : _____
                                                                                                TAX CODE 3 WH.       : _____
SOC. SEC. NO.   : 542-34-4238 _____        _____            _____            _____          TAX CODE 4 WH.       : _____
PAY PERIOD      : WEEKLY                                                                         INSUR. DED.          : _____
PAY TYPE        : HOURLY       TIPS    :           Gross Pay Acct.  Distribution                 401K DED.            : _____
SHIFT           : 1            MISC. #1 : _____  ----Account------  ----Amount------           EMP LOAN DED.        : _____
PAY RATE        :       7.500  BONUS   :                                                         SAVINGS DED.         : _____
SICK HRS. TAKEN :          8   MISC. #3 : _____                                               STCK PUR DED.        : _____
VAC. HRS. TAKEN :  ----------  EIC     : _____                                                SIX DED.             : _____
TAKE GROUP TERM LIFE FICA (Y/N)?: -----
```

After Payroll prints the paymaster worksheets, you return to the pop up box that allows you to print paymaster worksheets or enter time card hours.

❖ Press ▣ to return to the Payroll Processing Menu.

Step 3. Enter Non-Standard Earnings and Deductions

Before you can process W.D. Peachtree's payroll, you must enter the non-standard earnings and deductions for Ralph, Oscar, Ken, and May. Now that you have manually recorded this information on paymaster worksheets, all you need to do is enter it into **Enter Exceptions**.

In the Payroll program operations, you can use **Enter Exceptions** to enter:

- Commissions.
- Overtime.
- Miscellaneous income, such as tips and bonuses.
- Deductions, such as a one-time-only stock payment.
- Vacation or sick hours taken.

You can record all this information on a paymaster worksheet and then enter it into **Enter Exceptions**, or you can enter this information directly into the program. It is a safer policy to use the worksheets.

❖ From the Payroll Processing menu, select **Enter Exceptions**.

Payroll displays a warning message:

PROCESS END OF QUARTER IF THIS PAY CYCLE HAS A CHECK DATE IN THE NEXT QUARTER

PRESS 🖳 *TO CONTINUE*

Each time you use **Enter Exceptions**, Payroll reminds you that the check date determines the quarter into which your pay period falls. The check date for the current W.D. Peachtree pay period is 12/29/92, the final pay period in the fourth quarter. Since this check date is still in the current quarter, you do not need to close the quarter before processing the pay period.

From this screen, you can choose either **Enter Exceptions** or **List Transactions File.**

❖ Select **Enter Exceptions**.

Payroll asks you to select the pay cycles and the pay types for which you will enter exceptions. You can not enter information for an employee if you do not select the appropriate pay cycle and pay type here.

❖ Since all W.D. Peachtree employees are paid weekly, select **Weekly** by entering **Y** after Weekly. Answer **N** for all the other pay cycle options.

❖ Then, select **Hourly**, **Salaried**, and **Commission** -- the pay types for Ralph, Oscar, Ken, and May. Answer **N** for any other options.

❖ Press 🖳 and then accept your selections.

Payroll asks you to enter the run date, the date you enter your exceptions.

❖ Accept the default date of **12/29/92**.

The Select Options pop up box appears.

❖ You will enter exceptions for only four employees, so choose **MANUAL SELECTION** rather than **ALL DEPARTMENTS** or **RANGE OF DEPARTMENTS.**

A. Enter Oscar DeLarent's Sick Hours and Hours Worked

You need to enter the payroll exceptions for Oscar DeLarent. This pay period, he took 8 paid sick hours and 8 hours without pay. He will be paid for 32 hours. Oscar's paymaster worksheet lists all the information you need to enter his exceptions.

❖ Enter Oscar's department number and employee code. (If you can not remember them, check Oscar's paymaster worksheet.)

Payroll displays the prompt,

ACCEPT (Y/N) ('' TO EXCLUDE FROM CURRENT PAY RUN)*

At this prompt, you can enter:

Y   to enter exceptions for the employee you selected.
N   to enter exceptions for an employee other than the one you selected.
*   to exclude the employee you just selected from the current pay period calculations.

❖ Accept Oscar **(Y).**

Payroll next displays the Enter Exceptions screen for hourly employees. This screen contains Hours and Totals sections on the right side of the screen and the entry section on the left side.

The Hours section displays the Regular, Overtime 1, and Overtime 2 hours entered for the employee in **Maintain Employees** (Standard) and in **Calculate Time Card Hours** (Time Card). If Time Card hours appear, they always override Standard hours. The Totals section displays the total Regular, Overtime 1, and Overtime 2 hours and earnings for the employee.

On the left side of the screen, you can enter hours including type of hours (Regular, Overtime 1, or Overtime 2) and shift differential (Shift 2 or Shift 3). If you enter hours on this screen, they do not add to either Standard hours or Time Card hours. Instead, they override both hours.

Note: If you need to enter a shift differential for an employee, you must use **Enter Exceptions** to enter all his or her hours.

❖ Choose not to accept the Hours screen, since Oscar has not worked his standard hours this week.

The cursor is at Hours. Generally, Oscar works 40 hours every pay period, so Payroll automatically displays 40.00 in Hours.

On this screen, you always enter the total number of hours for which the employee will be paid. Oscar worked 24 hours and took 8 paid sick hours, so he will be paid for a total of 32 hours. (If Oscar had taken 32 hours of paid sick leave, you would still enter 32 here).

❖ Enter **32** into Hours.

❖ Accept the rate, pay type, shift, actual rate, and G/L acct. Payroll displays for Oscar.

After you accept this first line of information, the cursor moves to Hours on Line 2. Payroll displays 8, the number of standard hours remaining. Since Oscar does not get paid for these eight hours, you do not want to record them.

❖ Press ▣ and accept the information you just entered.

Payroll now displays the Select Functions pop up box; you select the following different types of exceptions entries:

M   Miscellaneous Income
C   Change Deductions
V   Vacation or Sick Hours
T   Enter Taxes
L   FICA on Group Term Life
X   Employee Complete

Payroll displays this pop up box each time you accept the first Enter Exceptions screen.

❖ Because employee vacation and sick hours must be tracked, select **V** to record sick hours for Oscar.

Payroll displays the Sick - Vacation Hours screen for Oscar. Payroll displays the number of sick and vacation hours Oscar has used and the number he has accrued. (Payroll tracks this information for you; you cannot change it here, but you can change it in **Maintain Employees**.)

❖ Select not to accept the screen; you need to make a change.

The cursor is at Hours Taken.

On this screen, you enter the number of sick and vacation hours taken. The entries you make here, however, do not affect the employee's pay. For an employee to be paid for the hours entered here, you must also enter them on the **Enter Exceptions** Hours screen.

❖ Enter **8** for the number of sick hours taken.

❖ Press ▣ to accept your entries; then accept the screen by accepting the **Y** default.

❖ When the Select Functions pop up box appears, select **X** to complete Oscar's entries.

The screen clears; the cursor returns to Department.

B. Enter Ralph Lowren's Bonus

Now, you need to enter Ralph Lowren's New Employee bonus.

❖ Enter the department number and employee code for Ralph. (If you can not remember them, check Ralph's paymaster worksheet.) They happen to be the default choices for Department and Employee.

❖ Accept the screen and the **Enter Exceptions** screen appears.

❖ You already entered Ralph's hours in **Calculate Time Card Hours**, so accept the screen.

The Select Functions pop up box appears.

❖ Enter **M** to record Ralph's $50.00 New Employee bonus.

Payroll displays the Miscellaneous Income screen.

❖ Choose not to accept the screen; you need to make a change.

❖ Enter **$50.00** on the Bonus line.

❖ Press ⌨ and then accept the screen.

❖ You do not have any other exceptions for Ralph, so select **X** to complete his entries.

The screen clears; the cursor is at Department.

C. Enter Ken Moore's Stock Purchase

Next, you will enter Ken's one-time stock purchase. Remember, all the information you need to process this deduction is on Ken's paymaster worksheet.

❖ Enter Ken's department number and employee code. Look them up if you cannot remember them.

❖ Make sure you have entered the correct employee code, then accept the screen.

Notice that the screen for Ken, a salaried employee, is different than the screens for Ralph and Oscar, hourly employees. For salaried employees, you can adjust the salary, the gross pay amount, and the gross pay account.

❖ Accept the Enter Exceptions screen -- you do not need to make any changes to Ken's salary.

Payroll asks, *ENTER OVERTIME HOURS (Y/N)*.

❖ Enter **N**.

The Select Functions pop up box appears.

❖ Enter **C** to change deductions.

Payroll displays the Deductions screen for Ken.

❖ Select not to accept the screen; you need to make a change. Then, enter **250.00** for STCK PUR.

W.D. Peachtree has certain payroll deduction categories defined (Insurance, 401K, Employee Loan, Savings, and Stock Purchase). W.D. Peachtree does not need any more deductions, so it leaves the sixth deduction undefined.

❖ Press ▨ to accept your entries; then accept the screen.

❖ When the Select Functions pop up box appears, select **X** to complete Ken's entries.

The screen clears; the cursor returns to Department.

D. Enter May Tagg's Commissions and Loan Repayment

Now, you will enter W.D. Peachtree's last exceptions, those for May Tagg. Each pay period, W.D. Peachtree pays commissioned employees 10.0% on total sales between $1 and $2,000 and 12% on total sales over $2,000. (May sold $2,500 this week.) In addition, when W.D. Peachtree hires commissioned employees, it loans them $200 to meet expenses. These loans must be repaid within three months. (May has decided to repay her loan this week.)

You have already recorded May's sales for the week and her loan repayment on her paymaster worksheet. So, all the information you need to enter her exceptions are on that sheet.

❖ Enter May's department number and employee code. (Remember you can find them on the paymaster worksheet for May.)

❖ Make sure you have entered the correct employee code, then accept the screen.

Payroll displays the Enter Exceptions screen for May. Notice that this screen is different than the Enter Exceptions screen for hourly and salaried employees. You can change the gross salary and you can enter sales and commissions.

The *ACCEPT (Y/N)* prompt appears. This prompt applies only to the Salary or Draw amount (on the left side of the screen).

❖ Accept the displayed salary amount.

A second *ACCEPT Y/N* prompt appears; it applies only to the Sales Base and Commission side of the screen (the right side).

❖ Choose not to accept the screen; you need to make changes. Then, from May's paymaster worksheet, enter her sales and commissions.

❖ Press ▨ after you enter the last line of information.

Notice that Payroll has kept track of May's sales and commissions.

❖ Accept the screen.

Payroll asks, *ENTER OVERTIME HOURS (Y/N)*.

❖ Enter **N**, because May has no overtime.

❖ When the Select Functions pop up box appears; select **C** to change deductions.

You will record May's loan repayment on the Deductions screen.

❖ Choose not to accept the screen for May, so you can enter her loan repayment.

❖ For Emp Loan, enter **$200.00**.

❖ Press ⬛ and accept the screen.

❖ Select **X** to complete the entries for May.

The screen clears; the cursor returns to Department.

Step 4. Print the Transaction File List

You have entered all the non-standard earnings and deductions; now it is time to check your entries.

❖ Press ⬛ until *[F10] - MENU* appears at the bottom of your screen.

❖ Choose LIST TRANSACTION FILE.

After you enter exceptions for employees, you should always print a list of your entries. The Transaction File List shows all the non-standard earnings and deductions for employees this pay period. The information you entered in **Enter Exceptions** appears on this list.

The Select Options pop up box appears.

❖ Select **ALL DEPARTMENTS** in order to have a complete listing.

Payroll prints the Transaction File List. (The listing for May Tagg's entries is shown on the next page.) This report lists all the Payroll exceptions for each employee this pay period. It also lists shift differential and draw and commission information.

```
RUN DATE: 12/29/92                    W. D. Peachtree & Company                          PAGE 2
RUN TIME:   7:52 AM                            Payroll
                                        Transaction File List
-------------------------------------------------------------------------------------------------

EMPLOYEE: 31TAGM                         765-34-5435

REG. EARNINGS     230.77  TIPS        0.00  FICA          0.00  INSUR.   DED.    0.00  REG.HOURS        0.00
OVT1 EARNINGS       0.00  MISC. #1    0.00  FEDERAL WH    0.00  401K     DED.    0.00  OVT1 HOURS       0.00
OVT2 EARNINGS       0.00  BONUS       0.00  GEORGIA  WH.  0.00  EMP LOAN DED.  200.00  OVT2 HOURS       0.00
COMMISSIONS       260.00  MISC. #3    0.00  TAX CODE 2 WH. 0.00 SAVINGS  DED.    0.00  SICK HRS TAKEN   0.00
APPLIED TO                EIC         0.00  TAX CODE 3 WH. 0.00 STCK PUR DED.    0.00  VAC. HRS TAKEN   0.00
PRIOR YR DRAW       0.00                    TAX CODE 4 WH. 0.00 SIX      DED.    0.00  CUR. ALLOC DED   0.00


SHIFT   DIFFERENTIAL  BASE RATE  TP  COMP. RATE  HOURS  EARNINGS  GROSS PAY ACCOUNT  SALES BASE  COMM %  COMMISSION

                                                                                      2000.00    10.00     200.00
                                                                                       500.00    12.00      60.00


*** End of Transaction File List ***
```

Check your Transaction File List. Find the entries that you made and check them. If necessary, return to **Enter Exceptions** to correct any errors.

❖ Press 🖼 to return to the Payroll Processing Menu.

Lesson 1 Summary

In this lesson, you learned how to record non-standard earnings and deductions for employees and how to use the paymaster worksheet to help you enter this information into **Enter Exceptions**. You also learned how to enter time card hours for employees who use time cards and how to enter hours worked for hourly employees who do not use time cards. Finally, you learned to check the information you enter into Enter Exceptions by printing a Transaction File List.

Lesson 2: Calculate and Verify Your Payroll.

Now that you have entered the hours W.D. Peachtree employees worked as well as their non-standard earnings and deductions, you can calculate their pay. Then, after you have calculated their pay, you can verify that all pay amounts are correct.

This lesson contains the following steps:

1. Calculate Pay.
2. Print the Pre-Check Payroll Register.
3. Print the Hours/Earnings Report.
4. Print the Deduction Register.
5. If Necessary, Re-Calculate and Verify Pay.

Regardless of how simple or complex a company's payroll is, most of these steps will be completed during each pay period.

Step 1. Calculate Pay

Payroll calculates earnings, deductions, and taxes in a single step. You can calculate pay for any combination of employees types and for any combination of pay cycles. To calculate pay, you use **Calculate Pay** from the Payroll Processing Menu.

❖ From the Payroll Processing menu, select **Calculate Pay**.

Payroll displays:

PROCESS END OF QUARTER IF THIS PAY CYCLE HAS A CHECK DATE IN THE NEXT QUARTER

PRESS 🔲 *TO CONTINUE*

Since the paycheck for this pay period is in the current quarter, you do not need to worry about closing the quarter before processing this pay cycle.

Payroll asks you for the date which ends the current pay cycle (Period Ending Date).

❖ Enter **12/24/92**.

Payroll asks you to select the pay cycles and the pay types for which you will calculate pay. You can not calculate pay for an employee if you do not select the appropriate pay cycle and pay type here.

❖ Since all **W.D.** Peachtree employees are paid weekly, select **Weekly** by typing **Y** and pressing 🔲. (Answer **N** for all other pay cycle options.)

The cursor moves to Beginning (to the right of Weekly).

When you calculate pay, you must tell Payroll the beginning and ending dates for the current pay cycle. Since you entered 12/24/92 as the ending date, Payroll automatically displays 12/18/92 -- one week earlier than your ending date -- for Beginning.

❖ Accept the beginning date displayed.

❖ Select **Hourly**, **Salaried**, and **Commission** -- the pay types for Ralph, Oscar, Ken, and May. (Answer **N** for other pay type options.)

❖ Press 🔲 and then accept your selections.

The Select Options pop up box appears.

❖ Select **All Departments**.

Payroll calculates earnings, deductions, and taxes for all the employees you selected and returns you to the Payroll Processing Menu.

Step 2. Print the Pre-Check Payroll Register

Once you have calculated the employees' pay, you need to check the earnings, deductions, and taxes Payroll calculated. Payroll does not require you to check this information, however checking it before you print paychecks can save time and wasted paychecks. To check your earnings and tax amounts, next you will print the Pre-Check Payroll Register.

❖ From the Payroll Processing menu, select **Print Payroll Register**.

Payroll asks for the period ending date.

❖ Enter **12/24/92**.

You can print a Payroll Register before and after you print paychecks. If you print a register before you print paychecks, Payroll does not list check numbers. Instead, if certain pay problems occur, it lists warning codes legend.

❖ Enter **Y**. Then, from the Select Options pop up box, select **All Departments**.

Payroll prints the Pre-Check Payroll Register and returns you to the Payroll Processing Menu.

Look at the Pre-Check Payroll Register. Notice that the register prints information for each employee as well as summary information for each department. Notice the Warning Codes Legend on the last page of the register. The last page should appear as follows:

```
RUN DATE: 12/29/92                          W. D. Peachtree & Company                              PAGE 5
RUN TIME:   8:20 AM                                 Payroll
                                               Payroll Register
-------------------------------------------------------------------------------------------------------------------
            REGULAR    DISB.      NON-DISB   VOL.                                                   CHECK
CODE  NAME  EARNINGS   MISC. INC  MISC. INC  DEDUCT.   FED. WH. FICA   TAX #1  TAX #2  TAX #3  TAX #4  NUMB   NET PAY
COMPANY TOTALS 4185.01  50.00      0.00      450.00    402.77  324.00  151.53  0.00    0.00    0.00           2906.71

BREAKDOWN OF MISCELLANEOUS INCOME AND TAX CODES FOR COMPANY

DRAW           0.00            GEORGIA  WH.    151.53         CURRENT DEF. DEDUCT.      0.00
COMMISSION   260.00                                          CURRENT ALLOC. DEDUCT.    0.00
  TIPS         0.00
  MISC. #1     0.00
  BONUS       50.00
  MISC. #3     0.00
EIC            0.00


WARNING CODES LEGEND

CODE 0 = NET PAY OVER CHECK LIMIT
CODE 1 = DEDUCTIONS EQUAL OR EXCEED EARNINGS
CODE 2 = PAY MAY BE BELOW MINIMUM WAGE
CODE 3 = DRAW EXCEEDS COMMISSION
```

If any of the errors listed occur, Payroll lists the appropriate code in the Check Numb (Check Number) column. If you see any numbers listed in this column on your register, you must correct the error before continuing.

Review the Pre-Check Payroll Register. For Ralph, make sure his $50 bonus appears in the Disb. Misc. Inc. (Disburse Miscellaneous Income) column. For May and Ken, make sure their employee loan repayment ($200) and stock purchase ($250) appear in the Vol. Deduct. (Voluntary Deductions) column. If you do not see these entries, return to Enter Exceptions to correct your errors. (Refer to Lesson 1 in this topic if you need help.)

Step 3. Print the Hours/Earnings Report

The next step in verifying your payroll is printing an Hours/Earnings Report. This report lists Regular, Overtime 1, and Overtime 2 hours and earnings, sick and vacation hours taken, commissions, and miscellaneous incomes.

❖ From the Payroll Processing menu, select **Hours/Earnings Report**.

Payroll asks for the pay period ending date.

❖ Enter **12/24/92**.

❖ From the Select Options pop up box, select **All Departments**.

Payroll prints the Hours/Earnings Report and returns you to the Processing Menu. The last page of the report should appear as follows:

```
RUN DATE: 12/29/92                        W. D. Peachtree & Company                          PAGE 5
RUN TIME:  8:05 PM                                  Payroll
                                            Hours/Earnings Report
-------------------------------------------------------------------------------------------------------
                                                                                 PERIOD ENDING 12/24/92

               CYCLE   REGULAR    OVT1.     OVT2.    SICK/              COMM.
               TYPE    EARNINGS  EARNINGS  EARNINGS  VAC.               /PR. YR.
CODE   NAME    SHIFT   -HOURS    -HOURS    -HOURS    HOURS     TIPS     DRAW      MISC. #1   BONUS    MISC. #3    EIC
COMPANY TOTALS         3892.91   32.10     0.00      8.00      0.00     260.00    0.00       50.00    0.00        0.00
                       306.48    4.28      0.00      0.00               0.00

CODES LEGEND:

CYCLE                        TYPE                     SHIFT

W - WEEKLY                   H - HOURLY               1 - NORMAL -- NO DIFFERENTIAL
B - BI-WEEKLY                S - SALARIED             2 - TYPE 1 DIFFERENTIAL
S - SEMI-MONTHLY             D - DRAW                 3 - TYPE 2 DIFFERENTIAL
M - MONTHLY                  C - COMMISSION
```

Look at the entire Hours/Earnings Report. Notice that it lists hours and earnings information for each employee as well as sick and vacation hours taken. The report also summarizes this information for each department.

Review the Hours/Earnings Report. Make sure you entered the correct number of Regular and Overtime 1 hours for Ralph and that you entered his $50 bonus. Make sure you enter Regular hours for Oscar; also, make sure Sick/Vac. (Sick/Vacation) hours includes his 8 hours taken. Check May's commissions, too. If necessary, return to **Enter Exceptions** to correct any errors.

Step 4. Print the Deduction Register

The final step in verifying your payroll is printing the Deduction Register. This report lists tax and deduction information for employees. It can list just current period deductions or current period and year-to-date deductions.

Note: The year-to-date deductions do not include the current period deductions unless you print the report immediately after you close the pay period.

❖ From the Payroll Processing menu, select **Deduction Register**.

❖ Enter **12/24/92** for Period Ending Date.

You can print a Deduction Register listing only the current period information or listing both current period and year-to-date information.

❖ Enter **C** to print current information.

❖ Select **All Departments** from the Select Options pop up box.

Payroll prints the Deduction Register and returns you to the Payroll Processing Menu.

Look at the Deduction Register. Notice that the report lists only deduction and tax information for each employee. The report summarizes this information for each department as well as for the entire company. The last page of the report should appear as follows:

```
RUN DATE: 12/29/92                       W. D. Peachtree & Company                    PAGE  11
RUN TIME:   8:26 AM                                Payroll
                                             Deduction Register
-----------------------------------------------------------------------------------------------
                                                                              PERIOD ENDING 12/24/92

                    GRAND TOTALS  -  EMPLOYEES:   12

                          -- CURRENT PERIOD

FEDERAL WITH.   :           402.77
FICA            :           324.00
GEORGIA    WH.  :           151.53
INSUR.     DED. :             0.00
401k       DED. :             0.00
EMP LOAN   DED. :           200.00
SAVINGS    DED. :             0.00
STCK PUR   DED. :           250.00
SIX        DED. :             0.00
   TOTAL DED.   :          1328.30

DEFER. DED.     :             0.00
ALLOC. DED.     :             0.00

*** End of Deduction Register ***
```

Review the entire Deduction Register. Make sure the employee loan repayment for May and the stock purchase for Ken are listed. If necessary return to **Enter Exceptions** to correct any errors.

Step 5. If Necessary, Re-Calculate and Verify Pay

If you find any errors in your payroll calculations, you must correct the errors and then calculate pay again. After you calculate pay again, print the Pre-Check Payroll Register, Hours/Earnings Report, and Deduction Register. Continue to correct errors, re-calculate pay, and verify payroll until all the information is correct.

Lesson 2 Summary

In this lesson, you learned how to calculate employees' pay and how to verify the payroll calculations. You can verify these calculations with just the Pre-Check Payroll Register or just the Hours/Earnings Report. Checking these calculations before printing paychecks is not required; it can, however, prevent wasting paychecks.

Lesson 3: Print Paychecks and Close the Period

Now that you have entered all the payroll information, you can print W.D. Peachtree paychecks and close the period.

Step 1. Print Checks

After you have calculated and verified your payroll, you can print paychecks. Normally, when processing a company's real payroll, you would use company checks for this step. However, for this lesson, you should just use plain paper.

❖ From the Payroll Processing menu, select **Print Checks**.

Payroll asks, *PRINT CHECK MASK (Y/N)*.

When using actual check forms, you need to make sure that the checks are aligned properly; printing a check mask allows you to check their alignment.

❖ Enter **Y**.

Payroll prints the check mask and asks again, *PRINT CHECK MASK (Y/N)*.

❖ Enter **N**.

Payroll asks for the starting check number and displays the first available Payroll check number.

❖ Accept the check number Payroll displays.

Payroll asks for the ending date for the current pay period (Period Ending Date).

❖ Enter **12/24/92**.

Payroll asks for the paycheck date (Check Date).

❖ Accept **12/29/92** as the paycheck date.

❖ Accept the information you have entered so far.

Payroll asks you to enter the date you run **Print Checks**. (This date appears on the Print Checks Control Report.)

❖ Accept **12/29/92** as the run date.

❖ From the Select Options pop up box, select **All Departments**.

Payroll prints the W.D. Peachtree paychecks.

Then, Payroll asks you to make sure your printer is on-line and ready to print. When processing a real payroll, you would need to replace the check forms in the printer with standard paper.

❖ Since you are using standard paper already, just press [ENTER] after making sure paper is at the top of form.

Payroll prints the following Print Checks Control Report:

```
RUN DATE:  12/29/92          W. D. Peachtree & Company              PAGE 1
RUN TIME:   8:20 PM                    Payroll
-----------------------------------------------------------------------------------
CHECK DATE: 12/29/92      PERIOD ENDING DATE: 12/24/92

STARTING CHECK NUMBER: 1432    LAST CHECK NUMBER: 1443      TOTAL: 12

REPRINT: NO

TOTAL REGULAR HOURS           :          306.48
TOTAL OVERTIME 1 HOURS        :            4.28
TOTAL OVERTIME 2 HOURS        :            0.00
TOTAL EARNINGS                :        4,235.01
TOTAL NON-DISB. EARNINGS      :            0.00
TOTAL DEFERRED DEDUCTIONS     :            0.00
TOTAL ALLOCATED DEDUCTIONS    :            0.00
TOTAL DEDUCTIONS              :        1,328.30-
                                     ------------------
   TOTAL NET PAY              :        2,906.71

*** End of Print Checks Control Report ***
```

Review the paychecks. Notice that each paycheck lists both current period and year-to-date earnings, deductions, and taxes as well as sick and vacation hours accrued.

Review the control report. It lists the check date and the period ending date as well as the first and last check numbers used. This report also lists the total Regular, Overtime 1, and Overtime 2 hours worked by hourly employees as well as the total earnings and deductions for your employees.

Step 2. Print the Final Payroll Register

The next step in processing your payroll is to print the final Payroll Register. Unlike the Pre-Check Payroll Register you printed earlier, the final Payroll Register lists each employee's paycheck number. Once you print the final Payroll Register, you must close the current pay period before you can process any more payroll information.

❖ From the Payroll Processing menu, select **Print Payroll Register**.

Payroll asks you to enter the period ending date.

❖ Enter **12/24/92**.

Payroll asks, *PRE-CHECK REGISTER (Y/N).*

❖ You have already printed paychecks for W.D. Peachtree, so enter **N**.

Payroll asks, *FINAL PAYROLL REGISTER (Y/N).*

Since you have already verified the W.D. Peachtree Pre-Check Payroll Register, you can print the final Payroll Register now.

❖ Enter **Y**.

After Payroll prints the Final Payroll Register, you must close the current period. Although you can still print reports, you cannot complete any other processing for this pay period.

❖ From the Select Options pop up box, select **All Departments**.

Payroll prints the final Payroll Register and returns to the Payroll Processing Menu.

Review the final Payroll Register. Compare it to the Pre-Check Payroll Register you printed in Lesson 2. Notice that Check Numb column lists each employee's paycheck number and that warning codes do not appear.

Step 3. Close the Pay Period

The last step in processing your payroll is closing the pay period. When you close the period, Payroll:

- Adds each employee's current earnings and deductions to his quarter-to-date and year-to-date earnings and deductions.

- Updates each employee's sick and vacation hours accrued and used.

- Prepares your payroll transactions for your general ledger.

To close the W.D. Peachtree pay period, complete the following steps:

❖ From the Payroll Processing menu, select **Post Current Period**.

Payroll displays two processing messages:

VERIFYING PROCESSING STATUS

BUILDING TAX CODE WORK FILE . . .

These messages let you know Payroll is processing your payroll transactions.

Payroll asks you to enter the period ending date.

❖ Enter **12/24/92**.

Payroll asks, *IS THIS THE LAST POSTING FOR THE G/L PERIOD.*

The next pay period occurs in January, so you are posting the last pay period in December.

❖ Enter **Y**.

Payroll asks, *POST SUMMARY OR DETAIL INFORMATION.*

❖ It is safer to post all the detailed information, so Enter **D**.

Payroll displays the message, *BUILDING WORK FILE . . .*

Then, Payroll prints the General Ledger Transaction Register. This report lists all the Payroll transactions that occurred in the current pay period as well as the General Ledger account to which each transaction should be posted.

Next, Payroll asks, *RESET SICK/VACATION HOURS TO ZERO FOR UNION EMPLOYEES (Y/N).*

❖ None of the current W.D. Peachtree employees is a union member, so enter **N**.

Payroll displays the message, *BEGINNING EMPLOYEE FILE BACKUP.* Each time you run **Post Current Period**, Payroll copies its employee data file and assigns the copy a new generation number. This message lets you know Payroll is copying that file.

Payroll displays the current subdirectory path for the existing employee file and asks you to enter the path for the new employee file. Payroll assumes you will use the same path for that new file so it automatically displays the same path for the new file.

❖ Accept the displayed path. Do not change it.

Payroll prints the following Post Current Period Control Report and returns you to the Payroll Processing Menu:

```
RUN DATE: 12/29/92              W. D. Peachtree & Company                    PAGE  1
RUN TIME:   8:47 AM                       Payroll
                             Post Current Period Control Report
-----------------------------------------------------------------------------------------
                                                              PERIOD ENDING 12/24/92

TOTAL EMPLOYEES PROCESSED:   12

TOTAL HOURS              :            310.76

TOTAL EARNINGS          :          $4,235.01
TOTAL NON-DISB. EARNINGS :            $0.00
TOTAL DEFER. DEDUCTIONS  :            $0.00
TOTAL ALLOC. DEDUCTIONS  :            $0.00
TOTAL DEDUCTIONS         :          $1,328.30-
                                ------------------------
  TOTAL NET PAY          :          $2,906.71

*** End of Post Current Period Control Report ***
```

Review the control report. It lists the number of employees processed, the total hours worked by those employees, and the total earnings and deductions for those employees.

Lesson 3 Summary

In this lesson, you learned how to print paychecks and how to close the current pay period. Remember, before you begin processing a new pay period, you should change any necessary employee information and add any new employees.

Chapter 11

End of Chapter Problem

> **WARNING**
>
> **BEFORE CONTINUING, BE SURE THAT ALL DATA FILES HAVE BEEN RESTORED TO THEIR ORIGINAL CONDITION. IF YOU ARE UNSURE OF HOW TO RESTORE THESE FILES, TURN TO THE INSTRUCTIONS FOUND ON PAGE 1-32 IN CHAPTER 1.**

NOTE: You may find it helpful to record the problem data on input forms before using Payroll. Master Input Forms are included in the last section of this chapter. In some cases, you will need to make multiple copies of a form before you begin. On the other hand, you may not need all of the input forms provided.

The following problem set deals with transactions you will make using the Payroll Module. You should do each transaction in the same manner you did similar transactions while working through the Payroll Chapter. In other words, even though this problem set does not specifically tell you what to do, you can review the appropriate section in Chapter 11 to see which steps are necessary.

a.   12/11/92   A long time employee, Amanda Range, has moved. Her new address is listed below. You should make the appropriate changes in her employee file. (Hint: You should use the Maintain File program from the Payroll menu.) Her Department number is 31.

Address:	3626 Davidson Drive
City, State:	Decatur, Ga
Zip Code:	30289
Phone:	404-378-9001

b.   12/11/92   A new employee was hired today. All necessary information is listed below:

Department:	31	
Employee Code:	THOS	
Name:	Scott Thomas	
Address:	789 Toule Street	
Address:	Apt. 7	
City, State:	Atlanta, GA	
Zip Code:	30308	
Soc. Sec. No.:	555-78-9089	
Phone:	404-675-1234	
Status:	A	
Date Employed:	12/11/92	
Pay Period:	W	Weekly
Pay Type:	H	Hourly
Pay Rate:	5.00	
Fed. Filing Status:	S	Single
Fed. Exemptions:	1	

Tax Code:	GA
Filing Status	A
Exemptions:	1

c.   12/18/92   It is time to run the weekly payroll. This is for period ending 12/17/92 and period beginning 12/11/92. The pay cycle is weekly and the pay types are hourly, salaried, and commission. You will process paychecks ONLY for department 31. Since you are only processing one department, restrict ALL of your printing or processing options to a "Range of Departments" with the beginning and ending range of 31. But, print or process ALL employees within department 31. The date of the actual paycheck should be 12/22/92. All hourly employees work a standard 40 hour week except Scott Thomas. His time card report is listed below. Also, print a check mask and accept the check number as given by the computer. Other information and exceptions are listed below. Remember for this practice set it is important to follow all steps in processing this payroll. As a review, those steps are:

● Gather and Enter Payroll Information

Calculate Time Card Hours
Print and Fill Out Paymaster Worksheets
Enter Non-Standard Earnings and Deductions
Print the Transaction File List

● Calculate and Verify Your Payroll

Calculate Pay
Print the Pre-Check Payroll Register
Print the Hours/Earnings Report
Print the Deduction Register

● Print Paychecks and Close the Period

Print Checks
Print the Final Payroll Register
Close the Pay Period

Scott Thomas 555-78-9089		Dept. 31
Monday	8.00	16.00
Tuesday	9.30	12.45
Wednesday	12.00	19.50
Friday	13.30	18.45
Saturday	10.00	18.00
Sunday	13.00*	19.00*
* Denotes "Overtime 1" Hours		

May Tagg 765-34-5435	Dept. 31 Appliance Sales
Total Sales	$3,412.60
	=======
Commission @ 10%	2,000.00
Commission @ 12%	1,412.60

```
┌─────────────────────────────────────────────────────────────┐
│                                                               │
│   Amanda Range                    Dept. 31                    │
│   407-92-8375                     Appliance Sales             │
│                                                               │
├─────────────────────────────────────────────────────────────┤
│                                                               │
│   Total Sales                     $2,210.00                   │
│                                   ========                    │
│   Commission @ 10%                2,000.00                    │
│   Commission @ 12%                  210.00                    │
└─────────────────────────────────────────────────────────────┘
```

d.   12/19/92   Ken Moore received a 10% raise effective immediately. His new salary will be $39,600. Ken works in Department 31.

e.   12/24/92   It is time to run the weekly payroll. This is for period ending 12/24/92 and period beginning 12/18/92. The pay cycle is weekly and the pay types are hourly, salaried, and commission. You will process paychecks ONLY for department 31. Since you are only processing one department, restrict ALL of your printing or processing options to a "Range of Departments" with the beginning and ending range of 31. But, print or process ALL employees within department 31. The date of the actual paycheck should be 12/29/92. All hourly employees work a standard 40 hour week except Scott Thomas. His time card report is listed below. Also, print a check mask and accept the check number as given by the computer. Other information and exceptions are listed below. Remember for this practice set it is important to follow all steps in processing this payroll.

```
┌─────────────────────────────────────────────────────────────┐
│                                                               │
│   Scott Thomas                    Dept. 31                    │
│   555-78-9089                                                 │
│                                                               │
├─────────────────────────────────────────────────────────────┤
│                                                               │
│   Monday          10.00           18.00                       │
│   Tuesday                  None                               │
│   Wednesday        8.00           14.00                       │
│   Friday          13.00           21.00                       │
│   Saturday                 None                               │
│   Sunday                   None                               │
└─────────────────────────────────────────────────────────────┘
```

Employee	Department	Type of Exception	Amount	Explanation
May Tagg	31	Savings Deduction	$25.00	May wants to take an additional deduction to place into savings.
May Tagg	31	Commission Sales	$1,234.00	Remember that W.D. Peachtree & Co. pays a 10% commission on sales of $1 to $2,000, then a 12% commission on sales over $2,000.
Amanda Range	31	Commission Sales	$2,012.00	
Ken Moore	31	Vacation Pay	1 week	You should pay Ken his Regular Salary and enter 40 for his Vac. Hrs. Taken.

PAYROLL
MASTER INPUT FORMS

Module Options Setup Form

General Module Options

Controller Password:	___ ___ ___ ___ ___ ___ ___ ___
Operator Password:	___ ___ ___ ___ ___ ___ ___ ___
Use Menus:	Y N (Circle one)
Allow Changes/Deletions:	Y N
Force Control Reports:	Y N
Current G/L Period:	___ ___
Payroll Generation Number:	___ ___
Post to General Ledger:	Y N
Use Pre-Printed Checks:	Y N
Use Accounts Payable Forms:	Y N
Use 24 Hour Time Clock:	Y N
Min/Decimal Time Entry:	M D
Disburse Tips:	Y N
Departmentalize Payroll:	Y N
State/Local Tax by Dept:	Y N

Accrual Options

Automatic Sick Hours:	Y N
Automatic Vacation Hours:	Y N
Annual Sick Hours:	___ ___ ___ ___.___ ___
Annual Vacation Hours:	___ ___ ___ ___.___ ___

Overtime Rates

Rate 1:	___ ___.___ ___
Rate 2:	___ ___.___ ___

Differential Information

Amount or Percentage:	A P (Circle one)
Shift 2:	___ ___ ___ ___.___ ___
Shift 3:	___ ___ ___ ___.___ ___
Employer Depositor Status:	M S (Circle one)

Payroll G/L Account Numbers

Depts

Net Pay:	___ ___ ___ ___ ___ ___	Y N (Circle one)
Employee's FICA:	___ ___ ___ ___ ___ ___	Y N
Employer FICA Accounts		
Expense:	___ ___ ___ ___ ___ ___	Y N
Liability:	___ ___ ___ ___ ___ ___	Y N
Federal Withholding	___ ___ ___ ___ ___ ___	Y N
Misc. Deduction Accounts		
Misc. Ded. 1: _____	___ ___ ___ ___ ___ ___	Y N
Misc. Ded. 2: _____	___ ___ ___ ___ ___ ___	Y N
Misc. Ded. 3: _____	___ ___ ___ ___ ___ ___	Y N
Misc. Ded. 4: _____	___ ___ ___ ___ ___ ___	Y N
Misc. Ded. 5: _____	___ ___ ___ ___ ___ ___	Y N
Misc. Ded. 6: _____	___ ___ ___ ___ ___ ___	Y N
Earned Income Credit:	___ ___ ___ ___ ___ ___	Y N
Draw Exceeds Commission:	___ ___ ___ ___ ___ ___	Y N
Gross Pay:	___ ___ ___ ___ ___ ___	Y N
Misc. Income Accounts		
Tips:	___ ___ ___ ___ ___ ___	Y N
Misc. Inc. 1: _____	___ ___ ___ ___ ___ ___	Y N
Misc. Inc. 2: _____	___ ___ ___ ___ ___ ___	Y N
Misc. Inc. 3: _____	___ ___ ___ ___ ___ ___	Y N
Federal Unemployment Accounts		
Expense:	___ ___ ___ ___ ___ ___	Y N
Liability:	___ ___ ___ ___ ___ ___	Y N
Industrial Ins. Expense:	___ ___ ___ ___ ___ ___	Y N
Industrial Ins. Liability:	___ ___ ___ ___ ___ ___	Y N
Suspense Account:	___ ___ ___ ___ ___ ___	Y N

Miscellaneous Deductions and Income

Miscellaneous Deductions

	Name	A/P	B/A	Taxable (Y/N) FED	FICA	FUTA	Ceiling
1.	_ _ _ _ _ _ _ _ _	_	_	_	_	_	_ _ _ _ _ _ _ . _ _
2.	_ _ _ _ _ _ _ _ _	_	_	_	_	_	_ _ _ _ _ _ _ . _ _
3.	_ _ _ _ _ _ _ _ _	_	_	_	_	_	_ _ _ _ _ _ _ . _ _
4.	_ _ _ _ _ _ _ _ _	_	_	_	_	_	_ _ _ _ _ _ _ . _ _
5.	_ _ _ _ _ _ _ _ _	_	_	_	_	_	_ _ _ _ _ _ _ . _ _
6.	_ _ _ _ _ _ _ _ _	_	_	_	_	_	_ _ _ _ _ _ _ . _ _

Miscellaneous Incomes

	Name	Disburse	Amt/Pct	Ceiling
1.	_ _ _ _ _ _ _ _	_	_	_ _ _ _ _ _ _ . _ _
2.	_ _ _ _ _ _ _ _	_	_	_ _ _ _ _ _ _ . _ _
3.	_ _ _ _ _ _ _ _	_	_	_ _ _ _ _ _ _ . _

Disposable Income Calculation for Garnishments

Income

Tips:	Y N	(Circle one)
Misc. Inc. 1: _____	Y N	
Misc. Inc. 2: _____	Y N	
Misc. Inc. 3: _____	Y N	

Deductions

Misc. Ded. 1: _____	Y N
Misc. Ded. 2: _____	Y N
Misc. Ded. 3: _____	Y N
Misc. Ded. 4: _____	Y N
Misc. Ded. 5: _____	Y N
Misc. Ded. 6: _____	Y N

Federal Tax Code Setup Form

Tax Code: US

Employer's ID No: __ __ __ __ __ __ __ __ __ __ __

	FIT	FICA	FUTA	EIC
Tips Taxable (Y/N)	__	__	__	__
Misc. Inc. 1: _____ Taxable (Y/N)	__	__	__	__
Misc. Inc. 2: _____ Taxable (Y/N)	__	__	__	__
Misc. Inc. 3: _____ Taxable (Y/N)	__	__	__	__

FICA %:   __ __ __ . __ __ __ __

FICA Limit: __ __ __ __ __ __ . __ __

FUTA %:   __ __ __ . __ __ __ __

FUTA Limit: __ __ __ __ __ __ . __ __

Hourly Min. Wage: __ __ __ __ __ __ . __ __

Tax Code: SS

Withhold   __ __ . __ __ __   **Of the First:**   __ __ __ __ __ __ . __ __

Customized Tax Code Setup Form

Tax Code, State: ___ ___
Form Tax Code: ___ ___
Customized Tax Code: ___ ___
Tax Entity Name: ___ ___ ___ ___ ___ ___ ___ ___ ___

Employer ID No: ___ ___ ___ ___ ___ ___ ___ ___ ___ ___ ___ ___
___

G/L Account No: ___ ___ ___ ___ ___ ___
U/E Expense Acct: ___ ___ ___ ___ ___ ___
U/E Liability Acct: ___ ___ ___ ___ ___ ___
Unemployment ID: ___ ___ ___ ___ ___ ___ ___ ___ ___
Unemployment %:   ___ ___ ___ . ___ ___ ___ ___
Unemployment Limit: ___ ___ ___ ___ ___ ___ . ___ ___
W-2 Box: N   S   L   E   (Circle one)
941A Report (Y/N):   Y   N
FUTA Report (Y/N):   Y   N

		With.		**SUTA**		
Tips Taxable (Y/N):		Y	N	Y	N	(Circle one)
Misc. Inc. 1: _____	Taxable (Y/N):	Y	N	Y	N	
Misc. Inc. 2: _____	Taxable (Y/N):	Y	N	Y	N	
Misc. Inc. 3: _____	Taxable (Y/N):	Y	N	Y	N	

Employee Setup Form

Personal Information

Department: ___ ___

Employee Code: ___ ___ ___ ___

Name: ___ ___ ___ ___ ___ ___ ___ ___ ___ ___ ___ ___ ___ ___ ___ ___
___ ___ ___ ___ ___ ___ ___ ___

Address: ___ ___ ___ ___ ___ ___ ___ ___ ___ ___ ___ ___ ___ ___ ___ ___
___ ___ ___ ___ ___ ___ ___ ___

Address: ___ ___ ___ ___ ___ ___ ___ ___ ___ ___ ___ ___ ___ ___ ___ ___
___ ___ ___ ___ ___ ___ ___ ___

City, State: ___ ___ ___ ___ ___ ___ ___ ___ ___ ___ ___ ___ ___ ___ ___ ___
___ ___ ___ ___ ___

Zip Code: ___ ___ ___ ___ ___ ___ ___ ___ ___

Soc. Sec. No.: ___ ___ ___ ___ ___ ___ ___ ___ ___

Phone: ___ ___ ___ ___ ___ ___ ___ ___ ___ ___ ___ ___

Comment: ___ ___ ___ ___ ___ ___ ___ ___ ___ ___ ___ ___ ___ ___ ___
___ ___ ___ ___ ___

Status (A/I):   A   I   (Circle one)

Date Employed: ___ ___ / ___ ___ / ___ ___

Date Terminated: ___ ___ / ___ ___ / ___ ___

Last Check Date: ___ ___ / ___ ___ / ___ ___

Last Check No.: ___ ___ ___ ___ ___ ___ ___

Last Check Amount: ___ ___ ___ ___ ___ ___ ___ . ___ ___

Employee Setup Form

Rates & Flags

Department: ___ ___

Employee Code: ___ ___ ___ ___

Statutory Employee:	Y N	(Circle one)
Deceased:	Y N	
Tipped Employee:	Y N	
Legal Rep:	Y N	
942 Employee:	Y N	
EIC Status:	N U T	
Shift Code:	1 2 3	
Pay Period:	W B S M	
Pay Type:	H S D C	

Pay Rate/Salary/Draw: ___ ___ ___ ___ ___ . ___ ___ ___

Commision Rate %: ___ ___ . ___ ___

Maximum Check Amount: ___ ___ ___ ___ ___ . ___ ___

Fed. Filing Status: S M * ! # @ & 1 2 3 4 5 (Circle one)

Fed. Exemptions: ___ ___

Addl. Fed. Tax: ___ ___ ___ ___ ___ . ___ ___

Cur. Defer. Deductions: ___ ___ ___ ___ ___ . ___ ___

YTD Defer. Deductions: ___ ___ ___ ___ ___ . ___ ___

Cur. Alloc. Deductions: ___ ___ ___ ___ ___ . ___ ___

Cost of Group Term Life over $50000: ___ ___ ___ ___ ___ . ___ ___

FICA Taken on Term Life: Y N (Circle one)

Standard Work Week: ___ ___ ___ . ___ ___

Standard OVT. 1 Hours: ___ ___ ___ . ___ ___

Standard OVT. 2 Hours: ___ ___ ___ . ___ ___

Pension: Y N

Deferred Compensation: Y N

SUTA Taxable: Y N

Industrial Insurance %: ___ ___ ___ ___ ___ . ___ ___

Employee Setup Form

Tax Code

Department: __ __

Employee Code: __ __ __ __

Tax Code	Filing Status	Exmpt	Misc. Tax Factor	Addit. Tax	Misc. Tax Amount
__ __	__	__ __	__ __ __.__ __	__ __ __ __ __ __.__ __	__ __ __ __ __ __.__ __
__ __	__	__ __	__ __ __.__ __	__ __ __ __ __ __.__ __	__ __ __ __ __ __.__ __
__ __	__	__ __	__ __ __.__ __	__ __ __ __ __ __.__ __	__ __ __ __ __ __.__ __
__ __	__	__ __	__ __ __.__ __	__ __ __ __ __ __.__ __	__ __ __ __ __ __.__ __

			Taxable (Y/N)			
Deductions	**Amount**	**Ceiling**	**1**	**2**	**3**	**4**
Misc. Ded. 1: _____	__ __ __ __ __.__ __	__ __ __ __ __ __.__ __				
		Withholding	__	__	__	__
		Unemployment	__	__	__	__
Misc. Ded. 2: _____	__ __ __ __ __.__ __	__ __ __ __ __ __.__ __				
		Withholding	__	__	__	__
		Unemployment	__	__	__	__
Misc. Ded. 3: _____	__ __ __ __ __.__ __	__ __ __ __ __ __.__ __				
		Withholding	__	__	__	__
		Unemployment	__	__	__	__
Misc. Ded. 4: _____	__ __ __ __ __.__ __	__ __ __ __ __ __.__ __				
		Withholding	__	__	__	__
		Unemployment	__	__	__	__
Misc. Ded. 5: _____	__ __ __ __ __.__ __	__ __ __ __ __ __.__ __				
		Withholding	__	__	__	__
		Unemployment	__	__	__	__
Misc. Ded. 6: _____	__ __ __ __ __.__ __	__ __ __ __ __ __.__ __				
		Withholding	__	__	__	__
		Unemployment	__	__	__	__

Employee Setup Form

Misc. Income

Department: ___ ___

Employee Code: ___ ___ ___ ___

Misc. Income	Amount	Ceiling
Misc. Inc. 1: _____	___ ___ ___ ___ ___ ___.___ ___	___ ___ ___ ___ ___ ___ ___.___ ___
Misc. Inc. 2: _____	___ ___ ___ ___ ___ ___.___ ___	___ ___ ___ ___ ___ ___ ___.___ ___
Misc. Inc. 3: _____	___ ___ ___ ___ ___ ___.___ ___	___ ___ ___ ___ ___ ___ ___.___ ___

Accrue Sick Hours by Hours Worked: Y   N   (Circle one)

   Sick Hours per Year

Or: ___ ___ ___ ___.___ ___

   Hours Required to Accrue 1 Sick Hour

YTD Sick Hours Accrued: ___ ___ ___ ___.___ ___

YTD Sick Hours Used: ___ ___ ___ ___.___ ___

Accrue Vac. Hours by Hours Worked: Y   N   (Circle one)

   Vacation Hours per Year

Or: ___ ___ ___ ___.___ ___

   Hours Required to Accrue 1 Vac. Hour

YTD Vacation Hours Accrued: ___ ___ ___ ___.___ ___

YTD Vacation Hours Used: ___ ___ ___ ___.___ ___

Union Contract Ending Date: ___ ___/___ ___/___ ___

Employee Setup Form

Quarter-to-Date

Department: ___ ___

Employee Code: ___ ___ ___ ___

Reg. Earn/Salary/Draw: ___ ___ ___ ___ ___ ___ . ___ ___

Overtime 1 Earn: ___ ___ ___ ___ ___ ___ . ___ ___

Overtime 2 Earn: ___ ___ ___ ___ ___ ___ . ___ ___

Commissions: ___ ___ ___ ___ ___ ___ . ___ ___

Tips: ___ ___ ___ ___ ___ ___ . ___ ___

Misc. Inc. 1: _____ ___ ___ ___ ___ ___ ___ . ___ ___

Misc. Inc. 2: _____ ___ ___ ___ ___ ___ ___ . ___ ___

Misc. Inc. 3: _____ ___ ___ ___ ___ ___ ___ . ___ ___

Regular Hours: ___ ___ ___ ___ ___ ___ . ___ ___

Overtime 1 Hours: ___ ___ ___ ___ ___ . ___ ___

Overtime 2 Hours: ___ ___ ___ ___ ___ . ___ ___

Weeks Worked: ___ ___ . ___ ___

Uncol. FICA Tip Tax: ___ ___ ___ ___ ___ . ___ ___

EIC: ___ ___ ___ ___ ___ ___ . ___ ___

FICA: ___ ___ ___ ___ ___ ___ . ___ ___

Federal WH: ___ ___ ___ ___ ___ ___ . ___ ___

Tax Code 1 WH: ___ ___ ___ ___ ___ ___ . ___ ___

Tax Code 2 WH: ___ ___ ___ ___ ___ ___ . ___ ___

Tax Code 3 WH: ___ ___ ___ ___ ___ ___ . ___ ___

Tax Code 4 WH: ___ ___ ___ ___ ___ ___ . ___ ___

Misc. Ded. 1: _____ ___ ___ ___ ___ ___ ___ . ___ ___

Misc. Ded. 2: _____ ___ ___ ___ ___ ___ ___ . ___ ___

Misc. Ded. 3: _____ ___ ___ ___ ___ ___ ___ . ___ ___

Misc. Ded. 4: _____ ___ ___ ___ ___ ___ ___ . ___ ___

Misc. Ded. 5: _____ ___ ___ ___ ___ ___ ___ . ___ ___

Misc. Ded. 6: _____ ___ ___ ___ ___ ___ ___ . ___ ___

Employee Setup Form

Year-to-Date

Department: ___ ___

Employee Code: ___ ___ ___ ___

Reg. Earn/Salary/Draw: ___ ___ ___ ___ ___ ___.___ ___

Overtime 1 Earn: ___ ___ ___ ___ ___ ___.___ ___

Overtime 2 Earn: ___ ___ ___ ___ ___ ___.___ ___

Commissions: ___ ___ ___ ___ ___ ___.___ ___

Tips: ___ ___ ___ ___ ___ ___.___ ___

Misc. Inc. 1: _____ ___ ___ ___ ___ ___ ___.___ ___

Misc. Inc. 2: _____ ___ ___ ___ ___ ___ ___.___ ___

Misc. Inc. 3: _____ ___ ___ ___ ___ ___ ___.___ ___

Regular Hours: ___ ___ ___ ___ ___.___ ___

Overtime 1 Hours: ___ ___ ___ ___ ___.___ ___

Overtime 2 Hours: ___ ___ ___ ___ ___.___ ___

Weeks Worked: ___ ___.___ ___

Uncol. FICA Tip Tax: ___ ___ ___ ___ ___.___ ___

EIC: ___ ___ ___ ___ ___.___ ___

FICA: ___ ___ ___ ___ ___.___ ___

Federal WH: ___ ___ ___ ___ ___.___ ___

Tax Code 1 WH: ___ ___ ___ ___ ___.___ ___

Tax Code 2 WH: ___ ___ ___ ___ ___.___ ___

Tax Code 3 WH: ___ ___ ___ ___ ___.___ ___

Tax Code 4 WH: ___ ___ ___ ___ ___.___ ___

Misc. Ded. 1: _____ ___ ___ ___ ___ ___.___ ___

Misc. Ded. 2: _____ ___ ___ ___ ___ ___.___ ___

Misc. Ded. 3: _____ ___ ___ ___ ___ ___.___ ___

Misc. Ded. 4: _____ ___ ___ ___ ___ ___.___ ___

Misc. Ded. 5: _____ ___ ___ ___ ___ ___.___ ___

Misc. Ded. 6: _____ ___ ___ ___ ___ ___.___ ___

Chapter 12

FIXED ASSETS OVERVIEW

Learning Objectives:

After studying this chapter, you should be able to:

1. Describe the functions performed by Fixed Assets.

2. Describe setup and maintenance activities including—maintain fixed assets options and maintain assets file.

3. Describe processing entries including—depreciation inquiry, lead schedule inquiry, purge asset file, transfer to general ledger, and process end of period.

4. Describe fixed asset reports including—interim depreciation schedule, pro forma schedule, expanded depreciation schedule, asset acquisition schedule, schedule of cumulative timing differences, investment tax credit schedule, investment tax recapture schedule, property control report, individual disposition schedule, and list asset files.

5. Identify some of the reports printed by Fixed Assets.

Chapter 12

Fixed Assets Overview

Fixed assets are long life assets (also known as long-term assets, long-lived assets, or plant and equipment) that a company buys for its own operations instead of for resale (in which case it would be inventory).

This chapter describes the Fixed Assets module and gives you some practice with Fixed Assets using W. D. Peachtree & Company.

How Fixed Assets Compares to a Manual Accounting System

In a manual accounting system, acquisition and disposal of fixed assets are recorded in the general journal. Depreciation entries are adjusting entries made in the general journal. The amounts of depreciation to use for tax purposes are calculated separately at the time the tax returns are prepared. Maintaining all of this detailed information by hand can be extremely time-consuming.

The Peachtree Complete Accounting Fixed Assets module records the acquisition and disposal of fixed assets, maintains information for both accounting and tax purposes including depreciation, and prints many reports that are useful in managing and reporting on fixed assets. The fixed assets information can be transferred to the general ledger at any time (usually at the end of a month or a fiscal period). PCA generates detailed depreciation schedules quickly and accurately without pencil pushing.

Overview

Fixed Assets keeps track of the fixed assets owned by a company. A fixed asset has a useful life of over one year. Typically, fixed assets include:

- Land

- Buildings and other structures

- Machinery

- Delivery equipment

- Office equipment

- Furniture and fixtures

Assets depreciate because their usefulness is reduced through wear and tear and through obsolescence. The exception to this is land — you do not depreciate land because it does not wear out.

For financial and tax purposes, Fixed Assets calculates depreciation and keeps track of accumulated depreciation. It also produces journal entries for automatic transfer to PCA's General Ledger. In addition, Fixed Assets prints reports for use when tax returns are prepared.

Question Frame 1¹²

Indicate whether each of the following statements is true or false by writing "T" or "F" in the space provided.

_____ 1. Fixed Assets records the acquisition of fixed assets, but their disposal must be recorded initially in the general journal.

_____ 2. Fixed Assets records depreciation information for accounting purposes, but depreciation for tax purposes must be calculated manually as tax returns are prepared.

_____ 3. Not all fixed assets are subject to depreciation.

_____ 4. Fixed Assets produces journal entries for automatic transfer to General Ledger.

Now turn to Answer Frame 1¹² on page 12-7 to check your answers.

Frame 2^{12}

Managing Fixed Assets

In Fixed Assets, every asset is identified by:

- **Asset Code** — identifies each fixed asset with a unique number.

- **Class Code** — defines the General Ledger account (for example, Building, Machinery, or Furniture) to which Fixed Assets posts depreciation and disposition information. The Class Code also determines the **Property Type** of the fixed asset. The Property Type identifies the methods of depreciation to use and how long the asset can be expected to last. Every Class Code can have one of seven Property Types:

  1. **P** - Personal property.
  2. **A** - Luxury automobiles.
  3. **R** - Commercial real property.
  4. **T** - Residential real property.
  5. **L** - Land.
  6. **N** - Low income housing.
  7. **F** - Farm property.

That is, every asset must have an Asset Code and a Class Code.

Depreciating Fixed Assets

Depreciation is the portion of a fixed asset's original cost that is allocated to depreciation expense each period. In other words, an asset is depreciated each year by a percentage of its cost.

Fixed Assets provide 13 methods of depreciation:

- Method 1: Straight Line (ST-L).

- Method 2: Sum of the Years Digits (SYD).

- Method 3: Accelerated Cost Recovery System (ACRS).

- Method 4: ACRS Straight Line (AST-L).

- Method 5 through 13: Declining Balance (DB).

Methods 5 and 7 are Modified Accelerated Cost Recovery System (MACRS).

(If you would like to review these depreciation methods more thoroughly, refer to a principles of accounting textbook. For instance, see Hermanson, Edwards, and Maher, *Accounting Principles,* 5th Edition, Richard D. Irwin, Inc., pp. 479-484.)

Fixed Assets Books

Fixed Assets books are report schedules that have various uses. Fixed Assets books can be used for filing Federal and state tax returns and creating financial statements.

Fixed Assets keeps up to three sets of books. The choice of number of books and format for each is made when Fixed Assets is set up. The three books are:

1. **Tax books** for Federal tax purposes.

2. **Financial books** for a company's accounting requirements.

3. **Optional Tax books** for other tax purposes, such as state taxes.

Answer Frame 1[12]

1. False. Fixed Assets records both the acquisition and disposal of fixed assets.

2. False. Fixed Assets maintains depreciation information for both accounting and tax purposes.

3. True. Land is not subject to depreciation because it does not wear out.

4. True. This module does produce journal entries for automatic transfer to General Ledger.

If you missed any of the above, reread Frame 1[12] before continuing.

Question Frame 2[12]

Indicate whether each of the following statements is true or false by writing "T" or "F" in the space provided.

_____ l. In Fixed Assets every asset must have both an Asset Code and a Class Code.

_____ 2. Fixed Assets provides four methods of depreciation.

_____ 3. Depreciation is the amount by which the current value of a fixed asset has declined during a period.

_____ 4. Fixed Assets keeps only one set of books.

Now turn to Answer Frame 2[12] on page 12-8 to check your answers.

Answer Frame 2^{12}

1. True. Both of these codes must be identified for each fixed asset.

2. False. Thirteen methods of depreciation are provided, although methods 5-13 are really variations of the declining-balance method.

3. False. Depreciation is the portion of a fixed asset's *cost* that is allocated to expense for a period.

4. False. Fixed Assets can keep up to three sets of books—one for Federal tax purposes, another for accounting purposes, and one for state tax purposes.

If you missed any of the above, reread Frame 2^{12} before continuing.

Fixed Assets Functions Overview

Setup and Maintenance

Maintenance programs allow a company to set up module options and enter information about its fixed assets.

Maintain Fixed Assets Options lets you set up the general options, class definitions, and depreciation methods for a company. You can also assign a printer to a specific report.

Maintain Assets File lets you enter information about a company's fixed assets, like the asset code and class code. Afterward, use this program at any time to add new fixed assets or change existing information.

Processing and Transaction Entry

After fixed assets information is entered, you will use **Depreciation Inquiry** to project the depreciation expense of an asset. You can display an overview of acquisitions, dispositions, and depreciation expenses using **Lead Schedule Inquiry**.

When disposed fixed assets are ready to be removed from the records, **Purge Asset File** is used.

You can transfer fixed asset information to General Ledger using **Transfer to General Ledger** at any time. It is usually best to do this transfer at the end of a month or other fiscal period.

Fixed Asset Reporting

Fixed Assets provides several types of reports to help keep track of activity, including reports on the end-of-year process. Any report can be run as it is needed or on a schedule that has been set:

- **Interim Depreciation Schedule** lists the depreciation expense for an asset for a portion of a year or the entire fiscal year.

- **Pro Forma Schedule** provides a break down of the depreciation expense for the current year (or a future depreciation year) into weekly, monthly, quarterly, semi-annual, and annual increments.

- **Expanded Depreciation Schedule** gives the depreciation expense over the life of each asset in a given year.

- **Asset Acquisition Schedule** lists acquisitions by class code.

- **Asset Disposition Schedule** lists dispositions by class code.

- When a comparison of financial depreciation information to tax (or optional tax) depreciation information is needed, run **Schedule of Cumulative Timing Differences**.

- **Investment Tax Credit Schedule** is used for the amount of possible tax credits on recently acquired assets. (The Tax Reform Act of 1986 repealed the Investment Tax Credit. Possibly it will be reenacted some day).

- If an asset is disposed of before the expiration of its estimated life, **Investment Tax Credit Recapture Schedule** gives the amount of recaptured Investment Tax Credit for the asset.

- **Property Control Report** lists assets by their location. It also gives the property's description, vendor, and General Ledger department.

- **Individual Disposition Schedule** produces a schedule that shows the period of time an asset was held, the gain or loss upon disposition and, if applicable, any Section 1245 or 1250 recapture.

- **List Asset File gives** a complete listing of an asset, which includes its description, acquisition date, cost, and accumulation figures for each book.

At the end of the fiscal year, **Process End of Year** is used to update the last depreciation year. This also produces reports for each book that has been set up for each of the fixed assets.

Question Frame 3^{12}

Indicate whether each of the following statements is true or false by writing "T" or "F" in the space provided.

_____ 1. Setup and maintenance programs are used to set up options and enter information about a company's fixed assets.

_____ 2. Processing and transaction entry is for projection of depreciation expense, removal of disposed fixed assets from the records, transfer of fixed assets information to General Ledger, and updating of the last depreciation year.

_____ 3. The Interim Depreciation Schedule shows a comparison of financial depreciation information to either tax or optional tax depreciation information.

_____ 4. The Investment Tax Credit Schedule and Investment Tax Credit Recapture Schedule are important schedules at present.

Now turn to Answer Frame 3^{12} on page 12-12 to check your answers.

Answer Frame 3¹²

1. True. Maintain Fixed Assets Options lets you set up the general options, class definitions, and depreciation methods. Maintain Assets File lets you enter information such as asset code and class code and information concerning new fixed assets.

2. True. All of these functions are performed by processing and transaction entry.

3. False. The Interim Depreciation Schedule lists the depreciation expense for an asset for a portion of a year or the entire fiscal year. The Schedule of Cumulative Timing Differences shows the comparison described in the question.

4. False. The Investment Tax Credit was repealed in the Tax Reform Act of 1986.

If you missed any of the above, reread Frame 3¹² before turning to the questions at the end of the chapter.

What's Next

Before practicing with W. D. Peachtree's fixed asset data in Chapter 13, you may want to review the sample reports at the end of this chapter. They will give you an idea of what your reports will look like in the next chapter.

Name _____ ID # _____

FIXED ASSETS OVERVIEW
QUESTIONS

1. **What are six typical types of fixed assets?**

    _____

    _____

    _____

    _____

    _____

    _____

2. **Define depreciation:**

    _____

    _____

    _____

3. **What fixed asset is not depreciated? Why not?**

    _____

    _____

    _____

4. **Name the two ways every asset must be identified in the Fixed Assets Module.**

    _____

    _____

5. **How many depreciation methods are available in Fixed Assets?**

    _____

6. **What are Fixed Assets Books?**

    _____

Name _____ ID # _____

7. Name the three Fixed Assets books produced by this module and the function of each.

   Fixed Assets Book   **Book's Function**

   _____   _____

   _____   _____

   _____   _____

8. Identify two Fixed Assets Maintenance Programs and the function of each.

   Program Name   **Program Function**

   _____   _____

   _____   _____

9. Name the four processing programs in Fixed Assets and identify their functions.

   Program Name   **Purpose of Report**

   _____   _____

   _____   _____

   _____   _____

   _____   _____

10. List the 11 report programs in Fixed Assets and the purpose they serve.

   Program Name   **Program Function**

   _____   _____

   _____   _____

   _____   _____

   _____   _____

   _____   _____

   _____   _____

Name _____   **ID #** _____

Program Name   **Program Function**

_____   _____

_____   _____

_____   _____

_____   _____

_____   _____

Name _____   ID # _____

FIXED ASSETS OVERVIEW
MATCHING

<u>Instructions:</u>   Match each program name on the left with the proper program function on the right.

<u>Program Name</u>	<u>Program Function</u>	<u>Answer</u>
A. List Asset File	1. Add new fixed assets.	_____
B. Depreciation Inquiry	2. Lists assets by their location and gives a description, vendor, and department.	_____
C. Process End of Year	3. Removes fixed assets from the records.	_____
D. Maintain Assets File	4. Provides a breakdown of depreciation expense into periodic (weekly, monthly, quarterly, etc.) increments.	_____
E. Transfer to General Ledger	5. Lists acquisitions by class code.	_____
F. Purge Asset File	6. Updates the last depreciation year and produces reports for each Fixed Asset book.	_____
G. Pro Forma Schedule	7. Gives a complete listing of an asset, including description, acquisition date, cost and accumulation figures for each book.	_____
H. Individual Disposition Schedule	8. Transfers Fixed Asset Information to General Ledger at the end of a month.	_____
I. Asset Acquisition Schedule	9. Projects depreciation expense of an asset.	_____
J. Property Control Report	10. Shows information about disposed assets including period of time held, gain or loss, or 1245 or 1250 recapture.	_____

FIXED ASSETS

SAMPLE REPORTS

Depreciation Inquiry

```
RUN DATE: 12/31/92          W.D. Peachtree & Company              PAGE  1
RUN TIME: 11:55 AM                  Fixed Assets
--------------------------------------------------------------------------

                         DEPRECIATION INQUIRY TAX

ASSET CODE.....: EQP19   Projector System


CLASS CODE....: EQUIP                   ACQUISITION DATE: 03/06/89
CLASS DESCR...: MACHINERY & EQUIPMENT    METHOD.........: DBA
ORIGINAL COST.:       1256.50           LIFE...........:    5.0
SALVAGE VALUE.:          0.00           TEFRA BASIS ADJ.:       0.00
ORIGINAL BASIS:       1256.50           SECTION 179....:       0.00


YR ..AMOUNT...   YR ..AMOUNT...   YR ..AMOUNT...   YR ..AMOUNT...
89     251.30    90     402.08    91     241.25    92      72.37


*** END OF DEPRECIATION INQUIRY ***
```

```
RUN DATE: 12/31/92         W.D. Peachtree & Company              PAGE   1
RUN TIME: 12:01 PM                Fixed Assets
                              LEAD SCHEDULE INQUIRY
-----------------------------------------------------------------------------
                          LEAD SCHEDULE INQUIRY - FIN

FOR THE  6 MONTHS ENDING 06/30/92

   CLASS    BALANCE     -CURRENT PERIOD ACTIVITY-      BALANCE      CURRENT
   CODE     01/01/92    ACQUISITIONS DISPOSITIONS      06/30/92     EXPENSE
-----------------------------------------------------------------------------
AUTOS       22790.00        0.00        0.00          22790.00      1465.00
BUILD      104200.00        0.00        0.00         104200.00      1736.66
EQUIP       34014.50        0.00        0.00          34014.50      2821.10
FURN         5669.00        0.00        0.00           5669.00        52.21
LAND        25000.00        0.00        0.00          25000.00         0.00
TRUCKS      29303.00        0.00        0.00          29303.00      2931.24
           ---------   ---------   ---------         ---------     --------
TOTAL      220976.50        0.00        0.00         220976.50      9006.21


SECTION 179 LIMITATION.....:        10000.00
AMOUNT DEDUCTED THIS PERIOD:            0.00
```

Interim Depreciation Schedule

```
RUN DATE: 12/31/92                          W.D. Peachtree & Company                                    PAGE 1
RUN TIME: 6:31 PM                                 Fixed Assets
                                            Interim Depreciation Schedule

RECOVERY PERIOD: 5 YEAR
        PERSONAL                        Interim Depreciation Schedule - TAX        FOR THE 12 MONTHS ENDING 12/31/92

----ASSET/CLASS----    ACQ      ORIG COST/    N/  SECT 179/                          ------DEPRECIATION------
CODE    DESCRIPTION    DATE     SALVAGE VAL   U   TEFRA ADJ    LF METH  DEPR BASIS  EXPENSE   ACCUMULATED  MO

DSK10  Desk          07/29/83    668.00      N    0.00         5.0 ACRS    0.00      0.00      668.00     12
FURN   OFFICE FURNITURE            0.00           0.00

RECOVERY PERIOD: PERSONAL
TOTALS                            668.00           0.00                    0.00      0.00      668.00
                                    0.00           0.00

NUMBER OF ASSETS:  1
```

Pro Forma Depreciation Schedule

W.D. Peachtree & Company
Fixed Assets
PRO FORMA DEPRECIATION SCHEDULE

RECOVERY PERIOD: 7 YEAR
          PERSONAL   PRO FORMA DEPRECIATION SCHEDULE - TAX   FOR FISCAL YEAR ENDING 12/31/92

						--------DEPRECIATION EXPENSE BY PERIOD--------		
-------ASSET/CLASS-------	ACQ	LF/							
CODE	DESCRIPTION	DATE	METH	DEPR BASIS	WEEKLY	MONTHLY	QUARTERLY	SEMI-ANNUAL	ANNUAL	MO
DSK15	Desk	08/14/91	7.0	252.00	1.38	6.00	18.00	36.00	72.00	12
FURN	OFFICE FURNITURE		DBA96							

RECOVERY PERIOD: PERSONAL

| TOTALS | | | | 252.00 | 1.38 | 6.00 | 18.00 | 36.00 | 72.00 |
NUMBER OF ASSETS: 1

| REPORT | | | | | | | | | |
| TOTALS | | | | 252.00 | 1.38 | 6.00 | 18.00 | 36.00 | 72.00 |
NUMBER OF ASSETS: 1

*** END OF - PRO FORMA DEPRECIATION SCHEDULE ***

Expanded Depreciation Schedule

W.D. Peachtree & Company
Fixed Assets
Expanded Depreciation Schedule

PAGE 1

RECOVERY PERIOD: 7 YEAR
PERSONAL

EXPANDED DEPRECIATION SCHEDULE - TAX

FOR FISCAL YEAR ENDING 12/31/92

------ASSET/CLASS------		N/	ACQ/DIS		SALVAGE VAL/	SECTION	TEFRA BASIS	ORIGINAL	METH/
CODE	DESCRIPTION	U	DATE	ORIG COST	SALES PRICE	179	ADJUSTMENT	BASIS	LF

| DSK15 | Desk | N | 08/14/91 | 294.00 | 0.00 | 0.00 | 0.00 | 294.00 | DBA96 |
| FURN | OFFICE FURNITURE | | | | 0.00 | | | | 7.0 |

YR...AMOUNT...		YR...AMOUNT...		YR...AMOUNT...		YR...AMOUNT...		YR...AMOUNT...		YR...AMOUNT...	
91	42.00	92	72.00	93	51.43	94	36.73	95	26.24	96	26.24	97	26.24
98	13.12										

*** END OF - Expanded Depreciation Schedule ***

Asset Acquisition Schedule

```
                              W.D. Peachtree & Company                                    PAGE  1
                                    Fixed Assets
                              Asset Acquisition Schedule

CLASS: AUTOS                                                    FOR FISCAL YEAR ENDING 12/31/91
   COMPANY AUTOMOBILES

                              Asset Acquisition Schedule

--------ASSET-------- DEPT ACQ/DIS              METHOD/ LIFE/ OPT REC  ORIG COST/  SEC 179/
CODE  DESCRIPTION/SERIAL NO N/U DATE  SALES PRICE BOOK ITC RATE TEFRA SW ST-L  ACCUM DEP  TEFRA ADJ  SALVAGE VAL

VEH58  Station Wagon      0   07/31/91   0.00  TAX  DBA      5.0     13   22790.00     0.00      0.00
       HJ5096903          N                              0      0          2660.00     0.00   2280.00
                                              FIN  ST-L     7.0      0   22790.00     0.00      0.00
       VENDOR  Volvo                                    0      0          1465.00     0.00      0.00
       LOCATION                              OPT  DBA95    5.0     13   22790.00     0.00      0.00
                                                        0   1995         4558.00     0.00      0.00

CLASS:  COMPANY AUTOMOBILES
TOTALS                                         0.00
NUMBER OF ASSETS:  1                                 TAX          22790.00     0.00      0.00
                                                                   2660.00     0.00   2280.00
                                                     FIN          22790.00     0.00      0.00
                                                                   1465.00     0.00      0.00
                                                     OPT          22790.00     0.00      0.00
                                                                   4558.00     0.00      0.00

REPORT
TOTALS                                         0.00
NUMBER OF ASSETS:  1                                 TAX          22790.00     0.00      0.00
                                                                   2660.00     0.00   2280.00
                                                     FIN          22790.00     0.00      0.00
                                                                   1465.00     0.00      0.00
                                                     OPT          22790.00     0.00      0.00
                                                                   4558.00     0.00      0.00

                           *** END OF - Asset Acquisition Schedule ***
```

Asset Disposition Schedule

W.D. Peachtree & Company
Fixed Assets
Asset Disposition Schedule

FOR FISCAL YEAR ENDING 12/31/92   PAGE 1

CLASS: FURN
OFFICE FURNITURE

```
        ------ASSET------  DEPT  ACQ/DIS                         METHOD/  LIFE/  OPT REC  ORIG COST/  SEC 179/
CODE    DESCRIPTION/SERIAL NO  N/U  DATE   SALES PRICE  BOOK  ITC RATE  TEFRA RATE  SW ST-L  ACCUM DEP  TEFRA ADJ  SALVAGE VAL

DSK10   Desk                  0   07/29/83    0.00      TAX   ACRS      5.0       0       668.00     0.00       0.00
                              N   12/31/92                      0       0         668.00     0.00       0.00
                                                        FIN   DBA       5.0       0       668.00     0.00      70.00
                                                               0        0         598.00     0.00       0.00
                                                        OPT   SYD       5.0       0       668.00     0.00       0.00
                                                               0        0         668.00     0.00       0.00

        VENDOR    Furniture City
        LOCATION


CLASS:  OFFICE FURNITURE
TOTALS                                         0.00     TAX                                668.00     0.00       0.00
NUMBER OF ASSETS:  1                           ====                                        668.00     0.00       0.00
                                                        FIN                                668.00     0.00      70.00
                                                                                           598.00     0.00       0.00
                                                        OPT                                668.00     0.00       0.00
                                                                                           668.00     0.00       0.00


REPORT
TOTALS                                         0.00     TAX                                668.00     0.00       0.00
NUMBER OF ASSETS:  1                           ====                                        668.00     0.00       0.00
                                                        FIN                                668.00     0.00      70.00
                                                                                           598.00     0.00       0.00
                                                        OPT                                668.00     0.00       0.00
                                                                                           668.00     0.00       0.00
```

*** END OF - Asset Disposition Schedule ***

Cumulative Timing Differences

RUN DATE: 12/31/92
RUN TIME: 6:43 PM

W.D. Peachtree & Company
Fixed Assets
Cumulative Timing Differences

- TAX   FOR FISCAL YEAR ENDING 12/31/91

CLASS: EQUIP
MACHINERY & EQUIPMENT

Cumulative Timing Differences

CODE	ASSET DESCRIPTION	--TAX-- METH	LF	--FIN-- METH	LF	--TAX-- DEPR BASIS	--FIN-- DEPR BASIS	--TAX-- ACCUM DEP	--FIN-- ACCUM DEP	--TIMING-- DIFFERENCE
EQP19	Projector System	DBA	5.0	DBA	5.0	530.75	530.75	967.00	967.00	0.00
EQP84	Computer	DBA94	5.0	ST-L	7.0	2322.56	2701.29	2719.84	1227.85	1491.99
EQP85	Printer	DBA	5.0	ST-L	5.0	297.92	343.00	348.88	245.00	103.88
EQP92	Chainsaw	DBA95	7.0	DBA94	5.0	196.27	179.52	121.18	157.08	35.90-
EQP95	Tractor	DBA95	7.0	DBA95	7.0	19233.71	19233.71	15863.70	15863.70	0.00

CLASS: MACHINERY & EQUIPMENT

TOTALS   22581.21   22988.27   20020.60   18460.63   1559.97

NUMBER OF ASSETS: 5

REPORT
TOTALS   22581.21   22988.27   20020.60   18460.63   1559.97

NUMBER OF ASSETS: 5

*** END OF - Cumulative Timing Differences ***

Individual Disposition Schedule

```
RUN DATE: 12/31/92      W.D. Peachtree & Company                     PAGE  1
RUN TIME:  7:43 PM            Fixed Assets
                        INDIVIDUAL DISPOSITION SCHEDULE
----------------------------------------------------------------------------
                   INDIVIDUAL DISPOSITION SCHEDULE - TAX

FOR FISCAL YEAR ENDING 12/31/92

ASSET CODE: DSK10   Desk

CLASS CODE......: FURN                          SALVAGE VALUE:       0.00
CLASS DESCR.....: OFFICE FURNITURE              SALES PRICE..:      10.00
SERIAL NUMBER...:                               TEFRA BAS ADJ:       0.00
ACQUISITION DATE: 07/29/83                      SECTION 179..:       0.00
DISPOSITION DATE: 12/31/92                      PROPERTY TYPE: PERSONAL
HELD  9 YEARS  5 MONTHS                         SECTION......: 1245

METHOD..................:       ACRS
ESTIMATED LIFE..........:        5.0
ACTUAL LIFE.............:        9.0

UNADJUSTED BASIS........:     668.00
ACCUMULATED DEPRECIATION:     668.00
NET BASIS ADJUSTMENT....:       0.00
                               -------
NET BOOK VALUE..........:       0.00

SALES PRICE.............:      10.00
NET BOOK VALUE..........:       0.00
                               =======
GAIN/(LOSS).............:      10.00

ACCUMULATED DEPRECIATION:     668.00
NET BASIS ADJUSTMENT....:       0.00
                               =======
TOTAL DEP ALLOWED - 1245:     668.00

ORDINARY INCOME.........:      10.00
POTENTIAL CAPITAL GAINS.:       0.00
```

Individual Disposition Schedule Summary

```
RUN DATE: 12/31/92                                                                                PAGE  1
RUN TIME: 7:43 PM                          W.D. Peachtree & Company
                                                Fixed Assets
                                    INDIVIDUAL DISPOSITION SCHEDULE SUMMARY

CLASS: FURN
   OFFICE FURNITURE         INDIVIDUAL DISPOSITION SCHEDULE SUMMARY SUMMARY - TAX    FOR FISCAL YEAR ENDING 12/31/92

-----ASSET------   ACQ        DIS    --LIFE--  UNADJUSTED  NET BASIS   ACCUMULATED   NET BOOK   SALES    GAIN/
  CODE/DESCRIPTION  DATE       DATE   EST ACT   BASIS       ADJUSTMENT  DEPRECIATION  VALUE      PRICE    (LOSS)

DSK10           07/29/83  12/31/92 5.0  9.0    668.00       0.00        668.00        0.00      10.00    10.00
  Desk

CLASS: OFFICE FURNITURE
   TOTALS                                       668.00       0.00        668.00        0.00      10.00    10.00

                                               ==========  ==========  ============  =========  =======  =======
REPORT
  TOTALS                                        668.00       0.00        668.00        0.00      10.00    10.00

NOTE: AN ASSET HAS BEEN DISPOSED.
Entries for Depreciation and the Gain/Loss on the sale will be transferred to General Ledger.
You will need to make the remaining entries to record the sale and remove the asset(s)
and its accompanying Accumulated Depreciation from the General Ledger Books.

                  *** END OF INDIVIDUAL DISPOSITION SCHEDULE SUMMARY ***
```

```
RUN DATE: 12/31/92                        W.D. Peachtree & Company                                    PAGE  1
RUN TIME: 6:52 PM                              Fixed Assets
                                              LIST ASSET FILE

CLASS: TRUCKS                                                            CLASS RANGE TRUCKS TO TRUCKS
       TRUCKS                                                            ASSET RANGE ALL

* MIDQUARTER CONVENTION APPLIES

-----ASSET----- DEPT ACQ/DIS                  METHOD/  LIFE/ OPT REC  ORIG COST/  SEC 179/
CODE  DESCRIPTION/SERIAL NO N/U DATE   SALES PRICE BOOK ITC RATE TEFRA SW ST-L  ACCUM DEP  TEFRA ADJ  SALVAGE VAL
----  -------------------- --- ----   ----------- ---- -------- ----- -------  ---------  ---------  -----------

VEH51 Truck                  0  03/19/90  0.00  TAX  DBA94  5.0        0   15489.00    0.00       0.00
      F569409V4             N   / /                        0  1994      11028.17    0.00
      VENDOR   Ford                          FIN  DBA    3.0        0   15489.00    0.00    2000.00
                                                          0          13489.00    0.00
      LOCATION                               OPT  DBA    5.0        0   15489.00    0.00       0.00
                                                          0          11028.17    0.00

VEH55 Truck                  0  06/05/91  0.00  TAX  DBA95  5.0        0   13814.00    0.00       0.00
      SJ400AA593            N   / /                        0  1995       7183.28    0.00
      VENDOR   Dodge                         FIN  DBA    5.0        0   13814.00    0.00    1380.00
                                                          0           7183.28    0.00
      LOCATION                               OPT  DBA95  5.0        0   13814.00    0.00       0.00
                                                          0           7183.28    0.00

CLASS: TRUCKS                            -----------                  ----------
       TOTALS                               0.00        TAX           29303.00    0.00       0.00
                                                                      18211.45    0.00
       NUMBER OF ASSETS:  2                              FIN           29303.00    0.00    3380.00
                                                                      20672.28    0.00
                                                        OPT           29303.00    0.00       0.00
                                                                      18211.45    0.00

REPORT                                   ===========                  ==========
       TOTALS                               0.00        TAX           29303.00    0.00       0.00
                                                                      18211.45    0.00
       NUMBER OF ASSETS:  2                              FIN           29303.00    0.00    3380.00
                                                                      20672.28    0.00
                                                        OPT           29303.00    0.00       0.00
                                                                      18211.45    0.00

                              *** END OF - LIST ASSET FILE ***
```

Transfer to General Ledger Control Report

```
RUN DATE: 12/31/92                    W.D. Peachtree & Company                                    PAGE 1
RUN TIME: 4:59 PM                          Fixed Assets
                                     TRANSFER TO GENERAL LEDGER

CLASS: AUTOS                      GENERAL LEDGER TRANSFER CONTROL REPORT      FROM 12/01/92 TO 12/31/92
       COMPANY AUTOMOBILES

ASSET   -------DEPRECIATION-------          --------DEBIT DISTRIBUTION--------     CREDIT DISTRIBUTION
CODE    BEG OF PER  ACCUMULATED  CURRENT EXP  ACCT 100% AMOUNT  ACCT 0% AMOUNT   ACCT    AMOUNT

VEH58    1705.16    4395.00      2689.84      55500   2689.84   0    0.00       16000   2689.84

CLASS
TOTALS   1705.16    4395.00      2689.84              2689.84        0.00               2689.84
```

```
ASSET   -------DEPRECIATION-------          --------DEBIT DISTRIBUTION--------     CREDIT DISTRIBUTION
CODE    BEG OF PER  ACCUMULATED  CURRENT EXP  ACCT 100% AMOUNT  ACCT 0% AMOUNT   ACCT    AMOUNT

VEH51   12165.20   13489.00      1323.80      55500   1323.80   0    0.00       16000   1323.80
VEH55    3125.13    7183.28      4058.15      55500   4058.15   0    0.00       16000   4058.15

CLASS
TOTALS  15290.33   20672.28      5381.95              5381.95        0.00               5381.95

REPORT  =========  ===========  ==========           =========  ==========           ===========
TOTALS  46583.69   63459.28     16875.59             16875.59        0.00              16875.59
```

NOTE: AN ASSET HAS BEEN DISPOSED.
Entries for Depreciation and the Gain/Loss on the sale will be transferred to General Ledger.
You will need to make the remaining entries to record the sale and remove the asset(s)
and its accompanying Accumulated Depreciation from the General Ledger Books.

*** END OF - TRANSFER TO GENERAL LEDGER ***

Property Control Report

RUN DATE: 12/31/92
RUN TIME: 6:49 PM

W.D. Peachtree & Company
Fixed Assets
PROPERTY CONTROL REPORT

Property Control Report

PAGE 1

| LOCATION | ------ASSET------ | | SERIAL | VENDOR | LOCATION RANGE HEADQ | | |
	CODE	DESCRIPTION	NUMBER	NAME	GL DEPT	HEADQ TO HEADQ	ACQ DATE
HEADQ	CHR01	10 Chairs		Furniture City	0		01/15/83
HEADQ	DSK05	Walnut Desk		Mitchell Bros.	0		01/15/83
HEADQ	DSK07	Walnut Credenza		Mitchell Bros.	0		01/15/83
HEADQ	DSK15	Desk		Ross & Lane	0		08/14/91
HEADQ	EQP84	Computer	9327476	IBM	0		04/30/90
HEADQ	EQP85	Printer	E657890X	Epson	0		04/30/90

Chapter 13

FIXED ASSETS: PRACTICING WITH A SAMPLE BUSINESS

Learning Objectives:

After studying this chapter, you should be able to:

1. Add and dispose of assets.

2. Print reports relating to fixed assets.

3. Transfer fixed asset information to General Ledger.

4. Close out the year.

Chapter 13

Fixed Assets: Practicing With A Sample Business

This chapter guides you through lessons that give you practical experience in working with Fixed Assets. You work with the fixed assets of W. D. Peachtree & Company.

The lessons in this chapter are grouped under these topics:

Topic 1: Adding and Disposing of Assets.

Topic 2: Printing Reports.

Topic 3: Transfer to General Ledger.

Topic 4: Close Out the Year.

Topic 1, Adding and Disposing of Assets, lets you add an asset to Fixed Assets and dispose of an asset.

Topic 2, Print Reports, gives you reports on disposition gains and losses, and accumulated depreciation and depreciation expense.

Topic 3, Transfer to General Ledger, updates your accumulated depreciation for the period and gets this information ready to send to General Ledger.

Topic 4, Close Out the Year, closes your books for the year and creates information for posting to General Ledger.

W. D. Peachtree groups its assets into six Class Codes. Here is a list of each Class Code, followed by its description and Property type:

1. EQUIP—Machinery and equipment (P).

2. FURN—Office furniture (P).

3. AUTOS—Company automobiles (A).

4. LAND—Land (L).

5. BUILD—Buildings (R).

6. TRUCKS—Trucks (P).

The lessons in this chapter guide you through typical Fixed Assets operations. You can complete the lessons in one session or you can do them in several sessions. The choice is yours.

Beginning the Practice Session

```
                              WARNING

BEFORE CONTINUING, BE SURE THAT ALL DATA FILES HAVE BEEN RESTORED TO
THEIR ORIGINAL CONDITION. IF YOU ARE UNSURE OF HOW TO RESTORE THESE
FILES, TURN TO THE INSTRUCTIONS FOUND ON PAGE 1-32 IN  CHAPTER 1.
```

❖ Start Peachtree Complete Accounting by changing to the directory in which Peachtree Complete is installed and typing **PEACH**. Then press ⌨.

❖ Press ⌨ to erase the date shown on your screen.

❖ Type **123192** and press ⌨.

❖ Type **WD** and press ⌨.

PCA displays the **Main Menu**.

❖ Select Fixed Assets.

This starts PCA's Fixed Assets. PCA displays the **Fixed Assets Main Menu**.

You are now ready to begin the practice session.

Topic 1 - Adding and Disposing of Assets

You add fixed assets to a business when they are acquired and dispose of them when they are sold. There are also times when you have to change information about fixed assets. For example, you may have to move an asset from one place to another. You will need to record the new location in Fixed Assets.

The lessons in this topic help you become familiar with the functions that update the information about the assets a company owns. Topic 1 has two lessons:

1. Adding an Asset.

2. Disposing of an Asset.

Lesson 1 - Adding an Asset

When a company purchases an asset, it must be added to the Fixed Assets' information. This lesson shows you how to add a fixed asset.

W. D. Peachtree & Company has purchased a conference table for use in their board room. You are going to add the conference table to Fixed Assets.

❖ Select **Maintenance Programs** from the Fixed Assets Main Menu.

❖ From the Maintenance Programs menu, select **Maintain Asset File**.

Fixed Assets displays the following screen:

```
==============================================================================
FAMAINT                           Maintain Asset File              COMPANY ID: WD
12/31/92                        W.D. Peachtree & Company
==============================================================================

     ASSET CODE ................:
     CLASS CODE ................:

     ASSET DESCRIPTION ...:
     SERIAL NUMBER ...........:
     ACQUISITION DATE ......:              ITC RATE ................................:
     NEW OR USED. (N/U) ...:              TEFRA CODE  (0 - 3) ................:
     GL DEPARTMENT .........:              SECTION 179 ...........................:
     LOCATION ......................:              ORIGINAL COST .......................:
     VENDOR NAME ..............:              SALVAGE VALUE ......................:
     DISPOSITION DATE ......:              TEFRA BASIS ADJUSTMENT ....:
     SALES PRICE ................:              METHOD  (1 - 13) .......................:
                                          LIFE ...........................................:
                                          ACCUM DEPRECIATION ...........:
                                          OPT RECOVERY PERIOD .........:
                                          AUTO SW TO ST-L  (Y/N) ..........:
                                          YEAR OF SW TO ST-L ..................:
                                          MID-QUARTER CONV.  (Y/N) ....:
     F1-Help        F2 - Lockup                   F10 - Menu        Shft F10 - Home
```

❖ Enter **TBL01** as the Asset Code and press 〔ENTER〕. (Be sure to use all capital letters.)

Fixed Assets tells you that this Asset Code is not found and asks if you want to add it. Do so.

❖ Accept the **Y** default by pressing 〔ENTER〕 to add the new Asset Code.

❖ Press 〔F2〕 at the *CLASS CODE* prompt.

Fixed Assets displays a "pop up box" that has the Class Codes for all W. D. Peachtree's fixed assets.

❖ Move the highlight bar to **FURN** (using the arrow keys) and then press 〔ENTER〕.

❖ Enter **Conference Table 72 X 216** as the asset's description and press 〔ENTER〕.

❖ Enter **51A** as the Serial Number and press 〔ENTER〕.

Fixed Assets displays 12/31/92 as the acquisition date.

❖ Accept this date by pressing 〔ENTER〕.

An asset is either new or used. W. D. Peachtree & Company bought a new conference table.

❖ Press 〔ENTER〕 to accept **N** for New Asset.

If you interface with General Ledger, Fixed Assets allows you to enter a two digit department code in the G/L Department field. The asset is then charged to that department when you run Transfer to G/L. For example, if the conference table was purchased by Human Resources for use by that department alone, you would enter the Human Resources Department Code in the G/L Department field. In this case, however, the table is for the entire company so leave the G/L Department field as 0.

❖ Press 〔ENTER〕 to accept 0 for GL Department.

❖ Enter **HEADQ** for the asset's location.

❖ Enter **Roundtables Co.** as the vendor name.

Fixed Assets does not let you make an entry in *DISPOSITION DATE* or *SALES PRICE*. You enter information here only when you dispose of an asset.

W. D. Peachtree & Company uses three sets of books: Tax, Financial, and Optional Tax. You may enter different values and methods for each book.

Notice that the title *TAX* is at the top of the right-hand column on your screen. This means that Fixed Assets is ready to take your entries for the Tax Book.

This is the information to enter for the Tax Book:

	Tax
ITC RATE	0
TEFRA CODE (0 - 3)	0
SECTION 179	500
ORIGINAL COST	7500
SALVAGE VALUE	0
TEFRA BASIS ADJ.	0
METHOD (1 - 13)	5
LIFE	10
ACCUM DEPRECIATION	0
OPT RECOVERY PERIOD	0
AUTO SW TO ST-L (Y/N)	N
YEAR OF SWITCH TO ST-L	0
MID-QUARTER CONV.	N

❖ Enter the Tax Book information.

❖ When you make the last entry for your Tax Book information, press ⌨.

❖ Press ⌨ to accept the screen.

After you press ⌨ to accept the screen, Fixed Assets displays the *Financial Book screen followed by the Optional Tax Book screen*. You enter information for these screens just as you did for the Tax Book.

When you finish entering Financial Book information, press ⌨ after you make your last entry. Accept the screen at the *ACCEPT Y/N* prompt. Fixed Assets then presents you with the third and last screen—*OPTIONAL TAX*. Type the information for the Optional Tax Book.

This is the information to enter for the Financial Book and Optional Tax Book:

	Fin.	Optional
ITC RATE	0	0
TEFRA CODE (0 - 3)	0	0
SECTION 179	0	500
ORIGINAL COST	7500	7500
SALVAGE VALUE	500	0
TEFRA BASIS ADJ.	0	0
METHOD (1 - 13)	1	5
LIFE	10	10
ACCUM DEPRECIATION	0	0
OPT RECOVERY PERIOD	0	0
AUTO SW TO ST-L (Y/N)	N	N
YEAR OF SWITCH TO ST-L	0	0
MID-QUARTER CONV.	N	N

Fixed Assets lets you browse through the information in the fixed asset file.

❖ At the Asset Code prompt, type **TBL01** and press ⌨. (Be sure to use all capital letters.)

Fixed Assets displays the information for that asset and places your cursor on the *ACCEPT Y/N* prompt.

❖ Enter **B** (for "browse") at the *ACCEPT Y/N* prompt, and press ⌨.

Fixed Assets takes you to the next asset in the file. You can browse through the tax information for each asset by pressing ⌨.

❖ Press ⌨ to review the fixed asset information in Fixed Assets until you return to the asset you just entered.

❖ Press ⌨ to clear the screen.

❖ Press ⌨ to go to the Fixed Assets Maintenance Menu.

❖ Press ⌨ to return to the Fixed Assets Main Menu.

Lesson 1 Summary

You have just added an asset to Fixed Assets' information.

You have also learned about:

- Entering book information.
- Browsing through the assets.

Lesson 2 - Disposing of an Asset

❖ From the Fixed Assets Main Menu, select **Maintenance Programs**, then select **Maintain Asset File**.

W. D. Peachtree & Company is renovating its board room. One of the items it no longer uses is a movie-projection system and screen, since it is purchasing a new video system.

W. D. Peachtree sells the projection system.

EQP19 is the asset code for the projection system. When you enter this number, Fixed Assets displays the asset's information.

❖ Enter **EQP19** as the Asset Code and press ⌨.

Fixed Assets places the cursor at the *ACCEPT Y/N* prompt. You want to remove the asset from Fixed Assets.

❖ Enter **D** at the *ACCEPT Y/N* prompt and press [ENTER].

Fixed Assets asks if you want to dispose of the asset.

❖ Enter **Y** to dispose of the asset and press [ENTER].

The cursor moves to *DISPOSITION DATE*. This is the date the asset is removed from Fixed Assets.

❖ Enter **120892** as the disposition date, and press [ENTER].

You need to enter a sales price for the disposed asset.

❖ Enter **100.00** as the sales price and press [ENTER].

❖ Press [F10] to return to the *ACCEPT Y/N* prompt.

Fixed Assets returns you to the *ACCEPT Y/N* prompt. This lets you confirm your entries.

When you enter Y at this prompt, you can no longer make changes to any information for this asset. It remains on your list of fixed assets as a disposed fixed asset for two years from the beginning of the next fiscal year.

After that time, you can run **Purge Asset File** to remove it (and any other assets disposed of in this year) from Fixed Assets.

When you browse through your assets, this asset's information appears with other assets' information. You can tell by the disposition date that the asset is disposed.

❖ Accept the **Y** default by pressing [ENTER].

❖ Press [F10] to return to the Fixed Assets Maintenance Menu.

❖ Press [ESC] to return to the Fixed Assets Main Menu.

Lesson 2 Summary

You have disposed of a fixed asset and entered the asset's disposition date and sales price.

Fixed Assets keeps the asset information available as a disposed asset, but it no longer calculates any depreciation past the disposition date for this asset.

Topic 2 - Printing Reports

You can print reports that show accumulated depreciation, depreciation expense, gains or losses on disposition and other information about your assets.

This topic covers five reports commonly used.

1. List Asset File.
2. Depreciation Inquiry.
3. Lead Schedule Inquiry.
4. Interim Depreciation.
5. Property Control Report.

Lesson 1 - List Asset File

List Asset File shows information on your assets. You can print the entire listing of all assets your company owns or you can print the reports by Class Codes or Asset Codes.

Use this program any time, but particularly when you add assets or change asset information. Use it to verify that you entered correct information.

❖ From the Fixed Assets Main Menu, select **Report Programs**, and then select **List Asset File**.

❖ For this report, the default option to print has been selected, so make sure that your printer is turned on and press ⏎ to continue.

You can print the report by Class Code or Asset Code.

❖ Press ⏎ to print the report by Class.

Fixed Assets displays a pop-up box with the report options. You can either print for all classes or a range of classes. We are going to print the report for all office furniture W. D. Peachtree & Company owns and lists as fixed assets.

❖ Select **Range of Classes**.

To tell Fixed Assets that you want to print this report for only one class of assets, enter the same class code as the beginning and ending class code.

❖ Enter **FURN** for the Starting Class Code and press ⏎.

Fixed Assets suggests FURN as the ending Class Code.

❖ Press ⏎ to accept the Ending Class Code.

Fixed Assets displays another pop up box. You can print this report for specific assets or for every asset.

❖ Press ⏎ to print for all assets in the Class Code you selected.

Fixed Assets prints the following report:

```
RUN DATE: 12/31/92                          W. D. Peachtree & Company                              PAGE 1
RUN TIME:  11:48 AM                              Fixed Assets
                                                 List Asset File
-----------------------------------------------------------------------------------------------------------------
CLASS: FURN
       OFFICE FURNITURE                                                         CLASS RANGE FURN  TO FURN
                                                                               ASSET RANGE ALL
   *  MID QUARTER CONVENTION APPLIES
   ------- ASSET --------     DEPT  ACQ/DIS                    METHOD/  LIFE/   OPT REC  ORIG COST/   SEC 179/
   CODE   DESCRIPTION/SERIAL NO  N/U  DATE    SALES PRICE  BOOK ITC RATE TEFRA  SW ST-L  ACCUM DEP    TEFRA ADJ   SALVAGE VALUE
```

CODE	DESCRIPTION/SERIAL NO	DEPT N/U	ACQ/DIS DATE	SALES PRICE	BOOK	METHOD/ ITC RATE	LIFE/ TEFRA	OPT REC SW ST-L	ORIG COST/ ACCUM DEP	SEC 179/ TEFRA ADJ	SALVAGE VALUE
CHR01	10 Chairs	0 N	01/15/83 / /	0.00	TAX	ACRS 0	5.0 0	0 0	3870.00 3870.00	0.00 0.00	0.00
					FIN	DBA 0	5.0 0	0 0	3870.00 3463.00	0.00 0.00	387.00
	VENDOR Furniture City				OPT	SYD 0	5.0 0	0 0	3870.00 3483.00	0.00 0.00	387.00
	LOCATION HEADQ										
DSK05	Walnut Desk	0 N	01/15/83 / /	0.00	TAX	ACRS 0	5.0 0	0 0	495.00 495.00	0.00 0.00	0.00
					FIN	DBA88 0	7.0 0	1988 0	495.00 428.74	0.00 0.00	0.00
	VENDOR Mitchell Bros.				OPT	SYD 0	5.0 0	0 0	495.00 495.00	0.00 0.00	0.00
	LOCATION HEADQ										
DSK07	Walnut Credenza	0 N	01/15/83 / /	0.00	TAX	ACRS 0	5.0 0	0 0	342.00 342.00	0.00 0.00	0.00
					FIN	DBA 0	10.0 0	0 0	342.00 291.21	0.00 0.00	0.00
	VENDOR Mitchell Bros.				OPT	ACRS 0	5.0 0	0 0	342.00 342.00	0.00 0.00	0.00
	LOCATION HEADQ										
DSK10	Desk	0 N	07/29/83 / /	0.00	TAX	ACRS 0	5.0 0	0 0	668.00 668.00	0.00 0.00	0.00
					FIN	DBA 0	5.0 0	0 0	668.00 598.00	0.00 0.00	70.00
	VENDOR Furniture City				OPT	SYD 0	5.0 0	0 0	668.00 668.00	0.00 0.00	0.00
	LOCATION										
DSK15	Desk	0 N	08/14/91 / /	0.00	TAX	DBA96 0	7.0 0	0 1996	294.00 47.90	0.00 0.00	0.00
					FIN	DBA 0	5.0 0	0 0	294.00 66.51	0.00 0.00	0.00
	VENDOR Ross & Lane				OPT	DBA95 0	5.0 0	0 1995	294.00 66.51	0.00 0.00	0.00
	LOCATION HEADQ										
TBL01	Conference Table 72 x 216 51A	0 N	12/31/92 / /	0.00	TAX	DBA 0	10.0 0	0 0	7500.00 0.00	500.00 0.00	0.00
					FIN	ST-L 0	10.0 0	0 0	7500.00 0.00	0.00 0.00	500.00
	VENDOR Roundtables Co.				OPT	DBA 0	10.0 0	0 0	7500.00 0.00	500.00 0.00	0.00
	LOCATION HEADQ										

```
CLASS:  OFFICE FURNITURE              ================                    ===========  ==========  ================
TOTALS                                    0.00                      TAX    13169.00     500.00          0.00
NUMBER OF ASSETS:  6                                                        5422.90       0.00
                                                                    FIN    13169.00       0.00        957.00
                                                                            4867.46       0.00
                                                                    OPT    13169.00     500.00        387.00
                                                                            5054.51       0.00
```

```
RUN DATE: 12/31/92                          W. D. Peachtree & Company                              PAGE 2
RUN TIME:  11:48 AM                              Fixed Assets
                                                 List Asset File
-----------------------------------------------------------------------------------------------------------------
   *  MID QUARTER CONVENTION APPLIES
   ------- ASSET --------     DEPT  ACQ/DIS                    METHOD/  LIFE/   OPT REC  ORIG COST/   SEC 179/
   CODE   DESCRIPTION/SERIAL NO  N/U  DATE    SALES PRICE  BOOK ITC RATE TEFRA  SW ST-L  ACCUM DEP    TEFRA ADJ   SALVAGE VALUE
REPORT                               ================                    ===========  ==========  ================
TOTALS                                    0.00                      TAX    13169.00     500.00          0.00
NUMBER OF ASSETS:  6                                                        5422.90       0.00
                                                                    FIN    13169.00       0.00        957.00
                                                                            4867.46       0.00
                                                                    OPT    13169.00     500.00        387.00
                                                                            5054.51       0.00

                            *** END OF - LIST ASSET FILE ***
```

❖ Notice the following totals at the end of the report:

- Number of assets.
- The original cost of each asset.
- Any Section 179 amounts taken on each asset in the year of acquisition and the TEFRA adjustment.
- Salvage value.

After printing, Fixed Assets returns you to the Range of Classes prompt in case you want to run this report again for another range of classes. Do not run this report again at this time.

❖ Press **ESC** until you return to the *PRINT BY CLASS or ASSET CODE (C/A)* prompt.

❖ Press **F10** to return to the Fixed Assets Reports Menu.

❖ Press **ESC** to return to the Fixed Assets Main Menu.

Lesson 1 Summary

You have just learned how to print one of the reports used regularly in businesses. Like all reports, it is very easy to print.

This report shows information on all assets with a Class Code of FURN.

Notice that the asset you added in Lesson 1 shows on this report.

Lesson 2 - Depreciation Inquiry

Depreciation Inquiry lets you know the depreciation expense over the life of an asset, that is, the amount of depreciation you can take in each year of the asset's life.

You now will examine the Tax Book depreciation information for the recently disposed of projection system.

❖ From the Fixed Assets Main Menu, select **Processing Programs** and then select **Depreciation Inquiry**.

You want to check the depreciation expense incurred over the life of the projection system disposed of in Lesson 2 of Topic 1, "Adding and Disposing of Assets. "

❖ Enter **EQP19** as the asset's code. (Be sure to use all capital letters.)

❖ Select **T** for the Tax Book.

You can display the information on your terminal or send it to your printer.

❖ Select **T** to display the information on your terminal.

Fixed Assets displays this screen:

```
================================================================================
                            DEPRECIATION INQUIRY TAX
================================================================================


ASSET CODE .........:   EQP 19   Projector System


CLASS CODE .........:   EQUIP                        ACQUISITION DATE .. :  03/06/89
CLASS DESCR........:   MACHINERY & EQUIPMENT         METHOD ...................:  DBA
ORIGINAL COST .....:       1256.50                   LIFE...........................:      5.0
SALVAGE VALUE....:          0.00                     TEFRA BASIS ADJ.....:         0.00
ORIGINAL BASIS .....:      1256.50                   SECTION 179 .............:         0.00


YR ...AMOUNT ....    YR ... AMOUNT ....    YR ....AMOUNT .....    YR ....AMOUNT.....    YR ....AMOUNT ....
89      251.30       90        402.08      91      241.25        92        72.37
```

Now that you have seen it on the screen, print a copy of this report.

❖ Press ▣ to return to the previous screen.

❖ Enter **EQP19** as the asset's code.

❖ Select **T** for Tax Book.

❖ Select **P** to print the information.

❖ Make sure your printer is turned on and press ▣ to print.

Fixed Assets prints the report.

❖ Review the report.

Look at the information at the bottom of this report. It lists the depreciation expenses for each fiscal year.

After printing the report, Fixed Assets returns you to the *Asset Code* prompt in case you want to check another asset. You are through for now.

❖ Press ▣ to return to the Fixed Assets Processing Menu.

❖ Press ▣ to return to the Fixed Assets Main Menu.

Lesson 2 Summary

You can print a depreciation inquiry report any time. It gives you a complete picture of the asset's depreciation.

Lesson 3 - Lead Schedule Inquiry

Lead Schedule Inquiry reports acquisitions and dispositions and the depreciation expense caused by such activity. This schedule does not change any information.

❖ From the Fixed Assets Main Menu, select **Processing Programs** and then **Lead Schedule Inquiry**.

Print the report for the Financial Book.

❖ Type **F** for Financial Book and press [ENTER].

You can print the report for 1 month and up to 12 months.

❖ Enter **6** to print the schedule for the first six months of the year.

❖ Press [ENTER] to accept the current fiscal year as the depreciation year for the schedule.

❖ Select **P** to print and press [ENTER].

❖ Make sure your printer is turned on and press [ENTER].

Fixed Assets prints the following report:

```
RUN DATE: 12/31/92                 W. D. Peachtree & Company                    PAGE  1
RUN TIME:   12:01 PM                      Fixed Assets
                                     LEAD SCHEDULE INQUIRY
----------------------------------------------------------------------------------------
                             LEAD SCHEDULE INQUIRY  --  FIN

FOR THE 6 MONTHS ENDING 06/30/92

    CLASS        BALANCE      --------CURRENT PERIOD ACTIVITY----------    BALANCE      CURRENT
    CODE         01/01/92     ACQUISITIONS          DISPOSITIONS          06/30/92      EXPENSE
-----------    -----------    ---------------     ----------------      -----------    ----------
AUTOS           22790.00            0.00                0.00             22790.00       1465.00
BUILD          104200.00            0.00                0.00            104200.00       1736.66
EQUIP           34014.50            0.00                0.00             34014.50       2821.10
FURN             5669.00            0.00                0.00              5669.00         52.21
LAND            25000.00            0.00                0.00             25000.00          0.00
TRUCKS          29303.00            0.00                0.00             29303.00       2931.24
               -----------    ---------------     ----------------      -----------    ----------
TOTAL          220976.50            0.00                0.00            220976.50       9006.21


SECTION 179 LIMITATION....................:      10000.00
AMOUNT DEDUCTED THIS PERIOD....:                     0.00
```

❖ Review the schedule.

Notice the following totals at the end of the report. For each Class Code there is the:

- Beginning fiscal year balance.
- Current acquisitions and dispositions.
- Current balance.
- Current expense.

Once the printing has been completed, Fixed Assets returns to the Lead Schedule Inquiry screen.

❖ Press [F9] to return to the Fixed Assets Processing Menu.

❖ Press [ESC] to return to the Fixed Assets Main Menu.

Lesson 3 Summary

You can print this Lead Schedule Inquiry report at any time. When you run **Process End of Year**, Fixed Assets prints this report for you.

When you print this report at the end of the year, it is a good idea to keep a copy of it.

Lesson 4 - Interim Depreciation Schedule

Interim Depreciation Schedule reports how much depreciation expense your assets generate.

❖ From the Fixed Assets Main Menu, select **Report Programs**.

❖ Then select **Depreciation Schedules** from the Fixed Assets Report Menu.

❖ Enter **122992** as the run date and press [ENTER].

Fixed Assets offers a choice of three schedules.

❖ Select **1** to print the Interim Depreciation Schedule.

❖ Make sure your printer is turned on and press [ENTER].

❖ Select **F** to print Financial Book information.

You can print the schedule for 1 month or up to 12 months.

❖ Press [ENTER] to accept **12** and print the schedule for one year.

Fixed Assets asks you to enter the year for which you want to print this schedule.

❖ Accept the default, **92**, the last two digits of the year for which you want to print this schedule.

Fixed Assets displays a pop-up box with the options for this report. You can print for all Asset Classes or a Range of Classes.

❖ Select **R** to print for a range of classes.

We are going to print this report for all assets in the FURN class.

❖ Enter **FURN** as the Starting Class Code and as the Ending Class Code.

Fixed Assets displays another pop-up box. This one lets you choose whether to print the report for all the assets in this Class Code or for selected assets in this Class Code.

❖ Select to print all fixed assets in this class.

Fixed Assets displays the final prompt to ask whether to print all assets (including fully depreciated assets still on the books) or only those assets with a current expense.

❖ Accept the default, **A,** to print for all assets and press .

Fixed Assets prints the following report:

```
RUN DATE:  12/31/92                        W. D. Peachtree & Company                              PAGE  1
RUN TIME:    12:05 PM                              Fixed Assets
                                           Interim Depreciation Schedule
------------------------------------------------------------------------------------------------------------

CLASS: FURN
       OFFICE FURNITURE              Interim Depreciation Schedule -- FIN             FOR THE 12 MONTHS ENDING 12/31/92

------------ASSET------------     ACQ      ORIG COST/   N/   SECT 179/     ----------------DEPRECIATION----------------
CODE        DESCRIPTION           DATE     SALVAGE VAL  U    TEFRA ADJ     LF   METH    DEPR BASIS    EXPENSE    ACCUMULATED   MO

CHR01       10 Chairs             01/15/83    3870.00   N      0.00        5.0  DBA        387.00       0.00       3483.00     12
FURN        OFFICE FURNITURE                   387.00          0.00

DSK05       Walnut Desk           01/15/83     495.00   N      0.00        7.0  DBA88        0.00       0.00        495.00     12
FURN        OFFICE FURNITURE                     0.00          0.00

DSK07       Walnut Credenza       01/15/83     342.00   N      0.00       10.0  DBA         51.64      10.33        300.69     12
FURN        OFFICE FURNITURE                     0.00          0.00

DSK10       Desk                  07/29/83     668.00   N      0.00        5.0  DBA         70.00       0.00        598.00     12
FURN        OFFICE FURNITURE                    70.00          0.00

DSK15       Desk                  08/14/91     294.00   N      0.00        5.0  DBA        235.20      94.08        152.88     12
FURN        OFFICE FURNITURE                     0.00          0.00

TBL01       Conference Table 72 x 216  12/31/92  7500.00  N    0.00       10.0  ST-L      7000.00     350.00        350.00      1
FURN        OFFICE FURNITURE                   500.00          0.00

CLASS: OFFICE FURNITURE                     ----------     ----------                ----------   ----------     ----------
TOTALS                                       13169.00         0.00                      7743.84     454.41       5379.57
NUMBER OF ASSETS:      6                       957.00         0.00
```

```
RUN DATE:  12/31/92                        W. D. Peachtree & Company                              PAGE  2
RUN TIME:    12:05 PM                              Fixed Assets
                                           Interim Depreciation Schedule
------------------------------------------------------------------------------------------------------------

CLASS: FURN
       OFFICE FURNITURE              Interim Depreciation Schedule -- FIN             FOR THE 12 MONTHS ENDING 12/31/92

------------ASSET------------     ACQ      ORIG COST/   N/   SECT 179/     ----------------DEPRECIATION----------------
CODE        DESCRIPTION           DATE     SALVAGE VAL  U    TEFRA ADJ     LF   METH    DEPR BASIS    EXPENSE    ACCUMULATED   MO

REPORT                                      ----------     ----------                ----------   ----------     ----------
TOTALS                                       13169.00         0.00                      7743.84     454.41       5379.57
NUMBER OF ASSETS:      6                       957.00         0.00

                               *** END OF - Interim Depreciation Schedule ***
```

❖ Review the report.

Notice the following totals at the end of the report. It gives you the:

• Number of assets in the report.

• Original cost and salvage value.

• Depreciation amounts by month and accumulated depreciation.

After the report prints, Fixed Assets returns to all or range of classes.

❖ Press ▓▓ six times, then press ▓▓ to return to the Fixed Assets Reports Menu.

Lesson 4 Summary

Use this report to see depreciation for a class of fixed assets for a year. Fixed Assets prints this report automatically when you run **Process End Of Year**.

Lesson 5 - Property Control Report

The **Property Control Report** lists your assets by their physical location. You can print this report for all locations or a specific location.

❖ From the Fixed Assets Reports Menu, select **Supporting Schedules**.

❖ Enter **122992** as the date and press ▓▓.

Fixed Assets displays a pop-up box containing 6 schedules.

❖ Select Schedule 6, **Property Control Report**.

This report can be printed for all locations or for a range of locations.

❖ Make sure your printer is turned on and press ▓▓ to continue.

❖ Press ▓▓ to print the report for all locations.

Fixed Assets prints the following report:

```
RUN DATE: 12/31/92                    W. D. Peachtree & Company                         PAGE 1
RUN TIME:   12:43 PM                          Fixed Assets
                                       PROPERTY CONTROL REPORT
-------------------------------------------------------------------------------------------------
                                    Property Control Report              LOCATION RANGE ALL

                      -----------------ASSET------------------    SERIAL       VENDOR    GL    ACQ
LOCATION              CODE         DESCRIPTION                    NUMBER        NAME      DEPT  DATE
--------              ----         -----------                    ------        ------    ----  ----
```

LOCATION	CODE	DESCRIPTION	SERIAL NUMBER	VENDOR NAME	GL DEPT	ACQ DATE
	BLD01	Headquarters Building			0	05/01/87
	DSK10	Desk		Furniture City	0	07/29/83
	EQP92	Chainsaw		Ed's Lawn/Tract	0	08/10/90
	EQP95	Tractor	FF435736	Ed's Lawn/Tract	0	11/28/90
	LND01	Land			0	05/01/87
	VEH51	Truck	F569409V4	Ford	0	03/19/90
	VEH55	Truck	SJ400AA593	Dodge	0	06/05/91
	VEH58	Station Wagon	HJ5096903	Volvo	0	07/31/91
HEADQ	CHR01	10 Chairs		Furniture City	0	01/15/83
HEADQ	DSK05	Walnut Desk		Mitchell Bros.	0	01/15/83
HEADQ	DSK07	Walnut Credenza		Mitchell Bros.	0	01/15/83
HEADQ	DSK15	Desk		Ross & Lane	0	08/14/91
HEADQ	EQP84	Computer	9327476	IBM	0	04/30/90
HEADQ	EQP85	Printer	E657890X	Epson	0	04/30/90
HEADQ	TBL01	Conference Table 72 x 216	51A	Roundtables Co.	0	12/31/92

*** END OF -- PROPERTY CONTROL REPORT

❖ Review the report.

Notice that this report contains the:

- Location of each asset.
- Description.
- Asset's serial number.
- Vendor's name.
- Acquisition date.

After printing, Fixed Assets returns you to the **Select Schedule** pop-up box.

❖ Press [ESC], then [↵] to return to the Fixed Assets Reports Menu.

❖ Press [ESC] to return to the Fixed Assets Main Menu.

Lesson 5 Summary

This Property Control Report is a good report to print and keep for easy reference.

Topic 3 - Transfer to General Ledger

Transfer to General Ledger updates the G/L Transfer Ending Date (in the company information) and the Accumulated Depreciation amounts (in the asset information) for each of the books.

Transfer to General Ledger prepares Fixed Assets information for transfer to PCA General Ledger and prints a report of this information. You can also just print the report and use it to transfer depreciation expenses to a manual General Ledger.

In this lesson you will run **Transfer to General Ledger** for the period ending 12/31/92.

❖ From the Fixed Assets Main Menu, select **Processing Programs**.

❖ From the Fixed Assets Processing Menu, select **Transfer to General Ledger**.

❖ Make sure your printer is turned on and press [ENTER] to print the control report.

The beginning date is pre-set. This is the General Ledger Transfer Ending Date plus one day. You cannot enter anything here. After you transfer to G/L, this date updates to the date of this transfer, plus one day.

You must enter an ending date.

❖ Accept **123192** as the transfer ending date.

The Fixed Assets options for the sample company has been pre-set to report to Peachtree Complete Accounting General Ledger.

Fixed Assets asks you if you want to build a transfer file. If you select Y, Fixed Assets processes and updates all information. If you answer N, Fixed Assets will *only* print the Transfer to General Ledger Control Report, which (at this point) is just a trial run for your G/L transfer information.

❖ Accept **Y** by pressing [ENTER].

Fixed Assets asks if this is the last transfer of the period. Since this is December, accept the default.

❖ Accept **Y** by pressing [ENTER].

Fixed Assets prints the Transfer to General Ledger report.

❖ Review the control report.

This process builds a transfer file containing:

- Depreciation amounts.
- Debit and credit distributions.

After the report prints, PCA returns you to the Fixed Assets Processing Menu.

❖ Press 【ESC】 to return to Fixed Assets Main Menu.

Lesson Summary

You just transferred fixed assets information to General Ledger and printed a control report.

Topic 4 - Process End of Year

Process End of Year closes the Fixed Assets books for the year. It updates depreciation information and prepares information for posting to General Ledger.

Process End of Year prints these reports:

- End of Year Depreciation Schedule.
- Individual Disposition Schedule.
- Lead Schedule Inquiry.
- Investment Tax Credit Schedule.
- Investment Tax Credit Recapture Schedule.

Process End of Year also runs **Transfer to General Ledger**.

❖ From the Fixed Assets Main Menu, select **Report Programs**.

WARNING

If you continue with the remainder of the procedures described, you will print between 40 and 50 pages of reports. If you do not want to print these reports, exit the program now by pressing [ESC] twice to return to the PCA Main Menu. If you decide you want to print the reports, please continue with the following steps. If you escape now, you will not be able to close out the year.

❖ From the Fixed Assets Reports Menu, select **Process End of Year**.

Fixed Assets gives you a warning that your fixed assets information is about to be updated and that you should make a backup before you run this program. A backup is important because running this program has far-ranging effects on your fixed assets information.

Make sure your printer is at the top of the form. Fixed Assets prints the following five reports automatically:

1. End of Year Depreciation Schedule.
2. Individual Disposition Schedule.
3. Lead Schedule Inquiry.
4. Investment Tax Credit Schedule.
5. Investment Tax Credit Recapture Schedule.

It prints each of these reports for each asset book.

After the reports finish printing, you close the "End of Year." "End of Year" refers to your fiscal year. When you run this, Fixed Assets calculates year-end depreciation for all assets during the current fiscal year.

❖ Fixed Assets prints the reports. Your printer will run for a long time (about 15-20 minutes).

❖ After reports are printed, you are again prompted to make sure your printer is turned on. Press [ENTER] to continue.

❖ When asked if you are ready to begin End of Year Update, accept the **Y** default and press [ENTER].

After the report has printed, you are through and can return to the Main Menu.

Lesson Summary

In this lesson you have closed out the company's books for the year and created information for transfer to PCA General Ledger.

You have now done all the tasks that you will routinely do at the end of the year.

Chapter 13

End of Chapter Problem

> **WARNING**
>
> **BEFORE CONTINUING, BE SURE THAT ALL DATA FILES HAVE BEEN RESTORED TO THEIR ORIGINAL CONDITION. IF YOU ARE UNSURE OF HOW TO RESTORE THESE FILES, TURN TO THE INSTRUCTIONS FOUND ON PAGE 1-32 IN CHAPTER 1.**

NOTE: You may find it helpful to record the problem data on input forms before using Fixed Assets. Master Input Forms are included in the last section of this chapter. In some cases, you will need to make multiple copies of a form before you begin. On the other hand, you may not need all of the input forms provided.

Problem Data

During the end of December 1992, W. D. Peachtree & Company made a few changes in its assets. The warehouse manager finally received approval to purchase a new delivery truck. The President of the company decided that his walnut desk was not large enough for his spacious office, so he sold it and purchased a new desk. Also, the maintenance supervisor decided to get rid of the bulky tractor and purchase a top of the line riding lawn mower to keep the grounds cut. These changes need to be reflected in the company's Fixed Asset accounts. You will find attached separate data for each transaction described above. Enter each transaction as indicated, after which you will run end of the month reports.

1:    Delivery Truck (VEH012)

- Serial No. GMC0987653
- Acquired for $12,567.00 on 12-31-92 from General Trucks
- Will be depreciated over 5 years using the declining balance method (#5) and will switch to straight-line in 1995
- For Section 179 information, enter $1,256.00
- Enter 0 for any other data fields
- Warehouse location

2:    President's New Desk (DSK99)

- Serial No. WAL1034
- Acquired for $1269.00 on 12-31-92 from Ethan Woods
- Headquarters (HDQTRS) location
- Depreciation facts

  •• Tax books - declining balance (Method 5); 5 year life; switch to straight-line in 1995; mid-quarter convention used; $126.90 for Section 179.

  •• Financial books - straight-line method (Method 1); 10 year life; $100 salvage value; no mid-quarter convention; no Section 179 application.

  •• Optional tax books - declining balance (Method 7); 5 year life; switch to straight-line in 1994; no mid-quarter convention; $126.90 for Section 179.

3:    Disposed Walnut Desk (DSK05)
- Sold for $75.00 on 12-31-92

4: Riding Lawn Mower (EQ74)
    • Serial No. SNA67809
    • Acquired for $758.36 on 12-31-92 from Snap-It Mowers
    • Office location
    • Depreciation facts

    •• Tax books (both) - declining balance (Method 5); 5 year life; switch to straight-line in 1995; no mid-quarter convention used; $75.84 for Section 179.

    •• Financial books - straight-line method (Method 1); 8 year life; no mid-quarter convention; $75.84 for Section 179.

5: Tractor (EQP95)

    • Sold for $18,500 on 12-31-92

a. Now that all changes have been made to the Fixed Asset accounts, a list of all assets should be run. From the Report Program choose the List Asset File option and print the report by class for ALL classes of assets. The run date should be 12/31/92.

b. Next, run an Interim Depreciation Schedule. Follow the steps as outlined in the chapter. The Run Date is 12/31/92. Select the "T" option to print the report for tax purposes. Print the report for the full 12 months for year 1992. You need only print a Range of assets, so enter "EQUIP" as the beginning range and "TRUCKS" as the ending range. Print ALL assets in this range.

c. Print a Property Control Report. Use 12/31/92 as the report date and select option 6 from the Supporting Schedules report option. Print the report for all locations.

d. Finally, transfer the data from the Fixed Assets module to the General Ledger module. Follow the example as outlined in the chapter.

FIXED ASSETS

MASTER INPUT FORMS

Fixed Assets Module Options Setup Form

General Options

Controller Password: ___ ___ ___ ___ ___ ___ ___ ___

Operator Password: ___ ___ ___ ___ ___ ___ ___ ___

Use Menus: Y   N   (Circle one)

Allow Changes/Deletions: Y   N

Report to G/L: Y   N

Current G/L Period: ___ ___

Use Dept Code in G/L: Y   N

Tax/Financial the Same: Y   N

Transfer Tax: Y   N

Last Month of Fiscal Year: ___ ___

Section 179 - Financial: Y   N

Use Optional Tax: Y   N

Depreciation Convention: 1   2   3

First Business Month: ___ ___

First Accounting Year: ___ ___

Last Depreciation Year: ___ ___

Incorporated: Y   N

GL Transfer Ending Date: ___ ___ / ___ ___ / ___ ___

Use Optional Book for Amount: Y   N

Fixed Assets Module Options Setup Form

Fixed Assets Class Definitions

CLASS CODE	DESCRIPTION	PROPERTY TYPE
——————	————————————— ————————————	——
——————	————————————— ————————————	——
——————	————————————— ————————————	——
——————	————————————— ————————————	——
——————	————————————— ————————————	——
——————	————————————— ————————————	——
——————	————————————— ————————————	——
——————	————————————— ————————————	——

Fixed Assets Module Options Setup Form

General Ledger Interface

CLASS CODE 1   **Class Code:**   __ __ __ __ __ __

                                    G/L Expense Acct. Distr:

                                         %:   __ __ __

                                         Account: __ __ __ __ __ __

                                         %:   __ __ __

                                         Account: __ __ __ __ __ __

                                         %:   __ __ __

                                         Account: __ __ __ __ __ __

                                     G/L Credit Accounts:

                                         Accum: __ __ __ __ __ __

                                         Loss: __ __ __ __ __ __

                                         Gain: __ __ __ __ __ __

CLASS CODE 2   **Class Code:**   __ __ __ __ __ __

                                    G/L Expense Acct. Distr:

                                         %:   __ __ __

                                         Account: __ __ __ __ __ __

                                         %:   __ __ __

                                         Account: __ __ __ __ __ __

                                         %:   __ __ __

                                         Account: __ __ __ __ __ __

                                     G/L Credit Accounts:

                                         Accum: __ __ __ __ __ __

                                         Loss: __ __ __ __ __ __

                                         Gain: __ __ __ __ __ __

Fixed Assets Module Options Setup Form

Fixed Assets Depreciation Methods

METHOD	DESCRIPTION		DB%
1	STRAIGHT LINE (ST-L)		
2	SUM-OF-THE-YEARS-DIGITS (SYD)		
3	ACCELERATED COST RECOVERY SYSTEM (ACRS)		
4	ACRS STRAIGHT LINE (AST-L)		
5	DECLINING BALANCE	(DBA)	200
6	DECLINING BALANCE	(DBB)	175
7	DECLINING BALANCE	(DBC)	150
8	DECLINING BALANCE	(DBD)	125
9	DECLINING BALANCE	(DBE)	___ ___ ___
10	DECLINING BALANCE	(DBF)	___ ___ ___
11	DECLINING BALANCE	(DBG)	___ ___ ___
12	DECLINING BALANCE	(DBH)	___ ___ ___
13	DECLINING BALANCE	(DBI)	___ ___ ___

Fixed Assets Setup Form

Asset Information

ASSET CODE __ __ __ __ __ __

CLASS CODE __ __ __ __ __ __

ASSET DESCRIPTION __ __ __ __ __ __ __ __ __ __ __

__ __ __ __ __ __ __ __ __ __

SERIAL NUMBER __ __ __ __ __ __ __ __

ACQUISITION DATE __ __ / __ __ / __ __

NEW OR USED (N/U) **N   U**   (Circle one)

GL DEPARTMENT __ __

LOCATION __ __ __ __ __ __

VENDOR NAME __ __ __ __ __ __ __ __ __ __ __ __

Fixed Assets Setup Form

Tax Book Information

ITC RATE: ___ ___ ___

TEFRA CODE: 0   1   2   3   (Circle one)

SECTION 179: $ ___ ___,___ ___ ___,___ ___ ___.___ ___

ORIGINAL COST: $ ___ ___,___ ___ ___,___ ___ ___.___ ___

SALVAGE VALUE: $ ___ ___,___ ___ ___,___ ___ ___.___ ___

TEFRA BASIS: $ ___ ___,___ ___ ___,___ ___ ___.___ ___

METHOD (1-13):   ___ ___

LIFE: ___ ___.___ ___

ACCUM DEPRECIATION: $ ___ ___,___ ___ ___,___ ___ ___.___ ___

OPT RECOVERY PERIOD: ___ ___

AUTO SW TO ST-L (Y/N): Y   N   (Circle one)

YEAR OF SW TO ST-L: ___ ___ ___ ___

MID-QUARTER CONV. (Y/N): Y   N   (Circle one)

Fixed Assets Setup Form

Financial Book Information

ITC RATE: ___ ___ ___

TEFRA CODE: 0   1   2   3   (Circle one)

SECTION 179: $ ___ ___,___ ___ ___,___ ___ ___.___ ___

ORIGINAL COST: $ ___ ___,___ ___ ___,___ ___ ___.___ ___

SALVAGE VALUE: $ ___ ___,___ ___ ___,___ ___ ___.___ ___

TEFRA BASIS: $ ___ ___,___ ___ ___,___ ___ ___.___ ___

METHOD (1-13):   ___ ___

LIFE: ___ ___.___ ___

ACCUM DEPRECIATION: $ ___ ___,___ ___ ___,___ ___ ___.___ ___

OPT RECOVERY PERIOD: ___ ___

AUTO SW TO ST-L (Y/N):   Y   N   (Circle one)

YEAR OF SW TO ST-L: ___ ___ ___ ___

MID-QUARTER CONV. (Y/N):   Y   N   (Circle one)

Fixed Assets Setup Form

Optional Tax Book Information

ITC RATE: ___ ___ ___

TEFRA CODE: 0 1 2 3 (Circle one)

SECTION 179: $ ___ ___,___ ___ ___,___ ___ ___.___ ___

ORIGINAL COST: $ ___ ___,___ ___ ___,___ ___ ___.___ ___

SALVAGE VALUE: $ ___ ___,___ ___ ___,___ ___ ___.___ ___

TEFRA BASIS: $ ___ ___,___ ___ ___,___ ___ ___.___ ___

METHOD (1-13): ___ ___

LIFE: ___ ___.___ ___

ACCUM DEPRECIATION: $ ___ ___,___ ___ ___,___ ___ ___.___ ___

OPT RECOVERY PERIOD: ___ ___

AUTO SW TO ST-L (Y/N): Y N (Circle one)

YEAR OF SW TO ST-L: ___ ___ ___ ___

MID-QUARTER CONV. (Y/N): Y N (Circle one)

Chapter 14

FINANCIAL STATEMENT ANALYSIS

Learning Objectives:

After studying this chapter, you should be able to:

1. Identify the three major financial statements used for analysis.

2. Describe how horizontal analysis, vertical analysis, and ratio analysis differ.

3. Describe the purpose and format of the Statement of Cash Flows.

4. Calculate ratios including the—current ratio, quick ratio, accounts receivable turnover, inventory turnover, stockholders' equity ratio, rate of return on operating assets, and rate of return on average stockholders' equity.

Chapter 14

Financial Statement Analysis

Introduction to Analyzing Financial Statements

Up to this point in this book, you have concentrated on the recording, summarizing, and reporting of financial information. This chapter will give you an idea of how the reports you have learned to generate can be used to make decisions.

Financial reports are used internally by managers and externally by investors and creditors to make decisions. In general, managers use detailed reports about parts of a business (like departments), while investors and creditors usually evaluate the business from an overall perspective.

There are three major financial statements used as a basis for analysis. You have learned about two of them already in Chapter 3: the Balance Sheet and the Income Statement. The third is a Statement of Cash Flows, and it will be explained in this chapter.

There are many ways to analyze financial statements, and only a few of them will be presented here. However, for the most part, all analysis can be described as having two general objectives: assessing a company's **past performance** and its **current financial position**. Information relating to these two objectives gives all interested parties an impression of the results of management's decision and forms a foundation for making future predictions.

Horizontal, Vertical, and Ratio Analysis of Financial Statements

Comparative financial statements present two (or more) of a business's financial statements in side-by-side columns so that they can be compared. The comparisons can be between two periods or between actual and budgeted figures. Comparing figures *horizontally* helps detect changes in a company's performance and highlights trends.

Information about a company can also be gained by *vertical* analysis, which consists of studying a single financial statement where each item is expressed as a percentage of a significant total.

Ratios are expressions of logical relationships between certain items in the financial statements. A ratio can show a relationship between two items on the same financial statement (like the Income Statement) or between two items on different financial statements (like the Balance Sheet and the Income Statement).

To show you how a business can be evaluated using its reports, this chapter has four main sections: analyzing the Balance Sheet, analyzing the Income Statement, a discussion of the cash flow statement, and a review of some key financial ratios.

Question Frame 1[14]

Indicate whether each of the following statements is true of false by writing "T" or "F" in the space provided.

_____ 1. Managers, investors, and creditors generally use financial reports to evaluate the overall performance of the company.

_____ 2. There are only two financial statements of a company that are used by investors and creditors.

_____ 3. When a company's financial statements are shown side by side for the current year and either last year or budgeted amounts, the comparison is called horizontal analysis.

_____ 4. Ratios only show significant relationships between two items on the same financial statement.

Now turn to Answer Frame 1[14] on page 14-4 to check your answers.

Answer Frame 1[14]

1. False. While investors and creditors use financial statements to evaluate the overall performance of the company, managers generally use detailed financial reports to make decisions about a part of a company.

2. False. There are three financial statements that are used by creditors and investors—the Balance Sheet, Income Statement, and Statement of Cash Flows.

3. True. And the other method is called vertical analysis—where each item in a single financial statement is expressed as a percentage of a significant total, such as net sales.

4. False. Ratios can show significant relationships between items on the same financial statement or between two items on different financial statements.

If you missed any of the above, reread Frame 1[14] before continuing.

Some Common Peachtree Report Features

You will recall that both the Balance Sheet and the Income Statement are generated by General Ledger (Chapter 3). The more up-to-date a General Ledger is, the more effective the reports will be. Before using any reports for analysis, all relevant transactions should have been entered.

The Statement of Cash Flows is not generated by PCA. But the information needed to prepare this statement is generated. Some detailed analysis is required to produce this statement, and it is usually done manually using working papers. An illustration of a Statement of Cash Flows is presented in this chapter.

How Long G/L Can Maintain Information

General Ledger's financial statements allow the production of reports for:

- The current period.
- A prior period.

Whenever you run a financial statement, **General Ledger** asks if you want to print Zero Balance accounts. This lets you select whether accounts without a balance are printed on the statement. The default option is set for "N."

Comparative Financial Statements

Comparative financial statements can be generated by PCA's General Ledger where the following items can be compared:

- Figures for any period in the current fiscal year with the amounts budgeted for the period.
- Figures for any of the last 12 periods (including the current period) with the figures for the same period in the previous year.

Department Level Information

When reports allow the examination of information at a department level, the following choices are available:

- A single department, including any summary department.
- All departments.

Question Frame 2^{14}

Indicate whether each of the following statements is true or false by writing "T" or "F" in the space provided.

_____ 1. In PCA, financial statements are generated by using the General Ledger module.

_____ 2. General Ledger can maintain information only for the current period and one prior period.

_____ 3. The Statement of Cash Flows is generated by PCA.

_____ 4. Whenever you print a financial statement, you must print accounts with zero balances.

Now turn to Answer Frame 2^{14} on page 14-8 to check your answers.

Balance Sheet

Purpose

This financial statement summarizes the condition of a company by reporting the ending balances of all Asset and Liability & Owners' Equity accounts at the close of an accounting period.

As with all financial statements, a Balance Sheet might list only one period or it might list comparative information.

Comparative Balance Sheets let you compare balances for a specified period either with budgeted figures for that period or with balances one year ago.

When to Run This Report

Balance Sheet should be run only after General Ledger has been confirmed to be in balance and before closing the current period. A Balance Sheet can not be run until everything balances.

Variations

A Balance Sheet can be listed for the current period or for any prior period up to two years ago.

You can list comparative information based on comparing balances for the period in question to:

- Balances one year ago.
- Figures budgeted for the period in question.

Sort, Subtotals, and Totals

General Ledger lists accounts in numerical order on this report and reflects Balance Sheet subtotals and totals as established in the Chart of Accounts.

G/L subtotals any subsidiary posting accounts into their Master Control account balances. It also subtotals any department posting accounts into their Department Control account balances.

Answer Frame 2¹⁴

1. True. Two of the financial statements, the Balance Sheet and the Income Statement, are generated by PCA. The third statement, the Statement of Cash Flows, can be prepared from information taken from the Balance Sheet and Income Statement.

2. False.   PCA can maintain information for up to 24 periods. Each period's information is referred to as a separate generation of information. Information from any of these periods can be used in a horizontal analysis of a business.

3. False. But the information for preparing the Statement of Cash Flows is provided.

4. False. General Ledger provides you with an option to exclude accounts with zero balances.

If you missed any of the above, reread Frame 2¹⁴ before continuing.

Frame 3¹⁴ (Continued)

Income Statement
Departmental Income Statement

Purpose

Income Statements are also called Profit and Loss statements or Operating Statements. These statements show the current and ending balance of all Income (Revenue) and Expense accounts (including Other Income and Other Expense) for an accounting period.

An Income Statement can be run for a specified period, or a Comparative Income Statement can be created. On the Comparative Income Statement, G/L compares balances (both current and year-to-date) for a specified period either with budgeted figures for that period or with the balances one year ago.

General Ledger permits the entering of a figure—called the Income Ratio—that it compares to the ending balance of each account. It then computes the ratio between the two figures. If 0 is entered for this ratio, G/L prints a column on the report showing the ratio of each line—income or expense—to net sales. This feature is explained in greater detail later.

Departmental Income Statement

All the information in this section also applies to the **Departmental Income Statement.** This version of the report gives the option to obtain an Income Statement for either:

- A single department, including any summary department.
- All departments.

When to Run this Report

In order for General Ledger to produce an Income Statement for the current period, General Ledger must be in balance. *General Ledger will not allow you to generate an Income Statement if G/L is out of balance.*

Variations

If a manager wanted to examine income and operating expenses for another period or obtain comparative financial information for a period other than the current one, **(Departmental) Income Statement** could be run and the period for which the report was wanted could be specified.

Comparative information can be listed and based on comparing balances for the period in question to either:

- Balances one year ago.
- Figures budgeted for the period in question.

When comparing budget figures, the Income Statement includes a year-to-date variance column. This column shows the amount each account is above or below budget. A dash (-) beside an amount indicates that the account is below budget.

Sort, Subtotals, and Totals

General Ledger lists all accounts in numerical order and reflects Income Statement subtotals and totals as established in the Chart of Accounts.

Income Ratio

General Ledger compares the balance of each Income Statement account to a given amount. This determines the *income ratio* of that account. G/L always includes income ratio columns on your statement. If 0 is entered for this ratio, G/L prints columns showing the ratio of each line to net sales.

Question Frame 3^{14}

Indicate whether each of the following statements is true or false by writing "T" or "F" in the space provided.

_____ 1. A Balance Sheet should be run only after closing the current period.

_____ 2. If you try to run Balance Sheet before entering all transactions for a period, PCA will print the Balance Sheet.

_____ 3. On comparative Income Statements, the current period can only be compared with budgeted amounts for that same period.

_____ 4. When Departmental Income Statement is selected, the Income Statement for all departments must be printed.

_____ 5. If you select an income ratio of 0, General Ledger will show the ratio of each line in the Income Statement to net sales.

Now turn to Answer Frame 3^{14} on page 14-12 to check your answers.

Statement of Cash Flows

Analyzing the Balance Sheet and Income Statement does not answer some important questions about the company—questions concerning how much cash the company received; where it got the cash; how much cash was spent; and, what the cash was used for. Questions such as these may be answered by a Statement of Cash Flows, the main purpose of which is to report on the cash receipts and disbursements of a business for a period.

Both managers within the company and external creditors and investors are interested in the Statement of Cash Flows. To help their analysis, the statement is divided into three main sections that group similar activities affecting cash. The three sections are cash flows from operating activities, investing activities, and financing activities.

The preparation of a Statement of Cash Flows requires a detailed analysis of both the Balance Sheet (account by account) and the Income Statement. An experienced PCA user could use the external report program, PDQ, to prepare a Statement of Cash Flows. However, because it is rather complex in its production, it will only be discussed and summarized here. An example is provided for your review. [For a complete discussion of the Statement of Cash Flows, see Hermanson, Edwards, and Maher, *Accounting Principles* (5th Edition, Richard D. Irwin, Inc. pp. 873-895) or some other principles of accounting text.]

Operating Activities

Operating activities generally include the cash effects of doing business, or generating net income. Sources of cash in this category include cash from sales of goods or services, interest and dividend income received, or other sources of cash that cannot be classified as either investing or financing. In this respect, the operating activity category is somewhat of a catch-all category.

Uses of cash in the operating section include cash paid out for inventory and raw material purchases, salaries, rent, and other operating expenses, taxes, interest, and any other expense item that cannot be considered a investing or financing activity.

Cash flows from operating activities can be computed using either the *direct* or the *indirect* method. The direct method converts each item on the Income Statement to the cash basis. The indirect method, on the other hand, begins with net income and adjusts it for items that did not affect cash. Although standard-making bodies encourage the use of the direct method, the indirect method has been used more frequently in statements of cash flows, perhaps because it is somewhat easier to produce.

Investing Activities

Investing activities generally relate to the acquisition or disposal of noncurrent assets. In other words, this section includes cash received or paid for the sale or purchase of long-term investments or for the sale or purchase of property, plant, and equipment. Any other cash effect relating to other long-term assets, such as a long-term note receivable or an intangible asset, is considered an investing activity.

Answer Frame 3¹⁴

1. False. A Balance Sheet should be run *before* closing the current period and only after the general ledger is in balance.

2. True. A Balance Sheet will be printed, but it will be incorrect. To prepare a correct Balance Sheet, make sure that all transactions for the period have been entered.

3. False. The current period amounts can also be compared with amounts of the preceding year.

4. False. You have a choice of printing the Income Statement for a single department or for all departments.

5. True. And it is often very meaningful to know what percentage an amount is of net sales. For instance, if cost of goods sold was 30% of net sales one year and 40% of net sales the next year, it could mean that employees or customers are stealing inventory from the company.

If you missed any of the above, reread Frame 3¹⁴ before continuing.

Frame 4¹⁴ (Continued)

Financing Activities

Financing activities relate to transactions with creditors and owners and involve noncurrent liabilities and owners' equity accounts. For example, cash received from issuing bonds, acquiring a mortgage or long-term note, or issuing stock are considered cash generated from financing activities. Similarly, cash paid out to repay long-term debt, to pay dividends, or to purchase treasury stock are uses of cash for financing activities.

The following pages show financial statements for W. D. Peachtree at 12-31-92, its year-end. There are two Balance Sheets: one at the end of the current year and one at the end of the prior year. There is also an Income Statement for the twelve month period ended 12-31-92. These financial statements were used to prepare the Statement of Cash Flows for the year ended 12-31-92, shown on page 14-15. The Statement of Cash Flows explains a net increase of $75,012.17 in W. D. Peachtree's cash for the year 1992.

These financial statements will also be used in the next section, **Ratio Analysis.**

W. D. PEACHTREE & COMPANY
Balance Sheets
As of 12/31/92 and 12/31/91

CURRENT ASSETS

Cash	184,396.73		109,384.56	
Accounts Receivable	204,809.18		135,938.52	
Allowance for Bad Debts	(7,500.00)		(5000.00)	
Inventory	173,753.88		304,543.19	
Total Current Assets		555,459.79		544,866.27

FIXED ASSETS

Furniture & Fixtures	4,999.00		4,999.00	
Machinery & Equipment	45,724.57		37,054.00	
Buildings	104,200.00		104,200.00	
Land	25,000.00		25,000.00	
Vehicles	56,934.00		22,570.32	
Accumulated Depreciation	(56,351.89)		(43,953.23)	
Total Fixed Assets		180,505.68		149,870.09

OTHER ASSETS

Deposits	1,000.00		0.00	
Total Other Assets		1,000.00		0.00
Total Assets		736,965.47		694,736.36

CURRENT LIABILITIES

Accounts Payable	216,432.93		298,405.13	
Accrued Payroll	3,700.00		5,200.00	
Notes Payable-Bank	2,356.87		2,356.87	
Payroll Taxes Payable	21,345.09		28,403.66	
Sales Tax Payable	34,529.66		33,493.94	
Total Current Liabilities		278,364.55		367,859.60

LONG TERM LIABILITIES

Notes Payable-Bank	15,000.00		35,000.00	
Total Long Term Liab.		15,000.00		35,000.00
Total Liabilities		293,364.55		402,859.60

STOCKHOLDERS EQUITY

Common Stock	75,000.00		75,000.00	
Retained Earnings	221,876.76		122,842.12	
Current Earnings	146,724.16		99,034.64	
Total Equity		443,600.92		291,876.76
Total Liab. & Equity		736,965.47		694,736.36

W. D. Peachtree & Company
Income Statement
For the 12 Months Ended 12/31/92

INCOME

Sales	4,892,034.53
Service	149,304.00
Returns & Allowances	(150,435.34)
Sales Discount	(23,045.05)
Finance Charge Income	19,853.23
Tailoring	14,329.43
Delivery Fee Income	36,053.43
Miscellaneous Income	2,340.43
Net Sales	4,940,434.66

COST OF GOODS SOLD

Cost of Sales	2,519,621.68
Freight	3,458.30
Purchase Discounts	(241,587.25)
Total Cost of Goods Sold	2,281,492.73
Gross Profit	2,658,941.93

EXPENSES

Salaries	1,738,489.55
Payroll Taxes	409,800.29
Advertising	162,540.30
Auto Expense	18,934.54
Bad Debts	2,500.00
Commissions	4,940.43
Depreciation	20,083.51
Employee Benefits	8,539.45
Insurance	6,503.50
Interest Expense	2,300.89
Miscellaneous Expense	1,234.34
Office Expense	5,704.24
Professional Fees	6,500.00
Rent	30,000.00
Repairs & Maintenance	15,940.34
Taxes-Property	1,595.09
Utilities	45,964.64
Total Expenses	2,481,571.11
Net Operating Income	177,370.82

OTHER INCOME

Gain on Sale of Asset	3,745.75
Total Other Income	3,745.75

OTHER EXPENSES

Loss on Sale of Asset	(1,294.52)
Total Other Expenses	(1,294.52)
Income Before Taxes	179,822.05
Income Taxes	(33,097.89)
Net Income	146,724.16

W. D. Peachtree & Company
Statement of Cash Flows
For the Year Ended 12/31/92

Cash Flows from Operating Activities

Net Income		146,724.16
Add (Deduct) Items Not Affecting Cash:		
Increase in Accounts Receivable (net)	(66,370.66)	
Decrease in Inventory	130,789.31	
Decrease in Accounts Payable	(81,972.20)	
Decrease in Accrued Payroll and Taxes	(8,558.57)	
Increase in Sales Tax Payable	1,035.72	
Depreciation Expense	20,083.51	
Loss on Sale of Asset	1,294.52	
Gain on Sale of Asset	(3,745.75)	(7,444.12)
Net Cash Flows from Operating Activities		139,280.04

Cash Flows from Investing Activities:

Sale of Machinery & Equipment	13,500.00	
Purchase of Machinery & Equipment	(29,404.19)	
Purchase of Vehicles	(34,363.68)	
Increase in Deposits	1,000.00	
Net Cash Used by Investing Activities		(49,267.87)

Cash Flows from Financing Activities

Payment of Note	(20,000.00)	
Issuance of Common Stock	5,000.00	
Net Cash Used by Financing Activities		(15,000.00)
Net Increase in Cash		75,012.17

Question Frame 4¹⁴

Indicate whether each of the following statements is true or false by writing "T" or "F" in the space provided.

_____ 1.   The Statement of Cash Flows shows where cash inflows came from and the causes of cash outflows.

_____ 2.   The three sections on a cash flow statement are cash flows from operating activities, investing activities, and borrowing activities.

_____ 3.   The Statement of Cash Flows can be prepared by carefully analyzing both the Balance Sheet and the Income Statement.

_____ 4.   Investing activities relate to transactions with creditors and owners.

Now turn to Answer Frame 4¹⁴ on page 14-21 to check your answers.

Frame 5¹⁴

Ratio Analysis

Many different ratios can be used to give an indication of a business's performance. A few of the major ones will be presented here. You should use the Balance Sheet and Income Statement for W. D. Peachtree at 12-31-92 to find the amounts needed for the following ratios.

Liquidity ratios

Liquidity ratios give interested analysts an idea of the company's ability to pay its current debts. The most well-known liquidity ratio is the *current ratio* (also known as the working capital ratio). The current ratio is computed by dividing current assets by current liabilities. Both of these subtotals can be found on the Balance Sheet.

$$\text{CURRENT RATIO} = \frac{\text{Current Assets}}{\text{Current Liabilities}}$$

The current ratio for W. D. Peachtree as of 12-31-92 is:

$$\frac{\$555,459.79}{\$278,364.55} = 2.0:1$$

A "rule of thumb" is that the ratio should be at least 2:1. If the ratio is less than 1:1, the company may have difficulty paying its current liabilities. On the other hand, a very high current ratio is not necessarily good. It may indicate that the company has cash that should be invested or customers that are slow in paying (resulting in excessively high accounts receivable).

A variation of the current ratio is the quick (or acid-test) ratio. Quick assets are those current assets that can be quickly converted into cash—cash, short-term investments in stocks, and accounts receivable. Inventories, although current, are excluded from this ratio because they might not be quickly convertible. The quick ratio, then, is computed by dividing quick assets by current liabilities.

$$\text{QUICK RATIO} = \frac{\text{Quick Assets}}{\text{Current Liabilities}}$$

The quick ratio for W. D. Peachtree at 12-31-92 is the total of Cash and Accounts Receivable (less Allowance for Bad debts) divided by Current Liabilities:

$$\frac{\$381,705.91}{\$278,364.55} = 1.4:1$$

A "rule of thumb" for this ratio is that it should be at least 1:1. But determination of the "ideal" level of the ratio depends on the industry in which a company operates and the rate at which the company generates cash.

Accounts Receivable Turnover

Accounts Receivable Turnover is the number of times per year that the average amount of accounts receivables is collected. There are several ways that this ratio can be computed, but an easy and acceptable computation is to divide Net Sales by Average Accounts Receivable.

$$\text{ACCOUNTS RECEIVABLE TURNOVER} = \frac{\text{Net Sales}}{\text{Average Accounts Receivable}}$$

At the beginning of the year W. D. Peachtree's Net Accounts Receivable (Accounts Receivable less Allowance for Bad Debts) was $130,938.52 ($135,938.52 - $5,000.00). Since this year's net accounts receivable is $197,309.18, the average accounts receivable can be said to be:

$$\text{Average Accounts Receivable} = \frac{\$130,938.52 + \$197,309.18}{2} = \$164,123.85.$$

Accounts Receivable Turnover for W. D. Peachtree can then be computed as follows:

$$\frac{\$4,940,434.66}{\$164,123.85} = 30.1 \text{ times.}$$

The average number of days' sales can then be found by dividing the accounts receivable turnover into 365 days:

$$\text{Average Number of Days' Sales in Accounts Receivable} = \frac{365}{\text{Accounts Receivable Turnover}}$$

$$= \frac{365}{30.1} = 12 \text{ days.}$$

Inventory Turnover

Another turnover ratio is Inventory Turnover. This ratio shows the number of times per period that a company's average inventory is sold. As with all ratios, there may be slight variations in the way it is calculated, but inventory turnover is usually calculated by dividing Cost of Goods Sold by Average Inventory.

$$\text{INVENTORY TURNOVER} = \frac{\text{Cost of Goods Sold}}{\text{Average Inventory}}$$

W. D. Peachtree's Inventory at the beginning of the year was $304,543.19, and the inventory balance at 12-31-92 was $173,753.88. The average inventory for the period would be computed as follows:

$$\text{Average Inventory} = \frac{\$304,543.19 + \$173,753.88}{2}, \text{ or } \$239,148.54.$$

Inventory turnover can then be computed for W. D. Peachtree as of 12-31-92:

$$\frac{\$2,281,492.73}{\$239,148.54} = 9.5 \text{ times or every 38.3 days (365 divided by 9.5).}$$

Stockholders' Equity Ratio

The Stockholders' Equity ratio is one way to assess the relationship of a company's debt position. It is computed by dividing Stockholders' Equity by Total Assets.

$$\text{STOCKHOLDERS' EQUITY RATIO} = \frac{\text{Stockholders' Equity}}{\text{Total Assets}}$$

The lower this ratio is, the higher is the company's debt. Internally, managers may desire a high debt position, since interest on the debt is tax deductible. However, external creditors probably prefer to see a high ratio, since it would indicate better protection for creditors in the event of a company loss. For W. D. Peachtree, the stockholders' equity ratio is:

$$\frac{\$443,600.92}{\$736,965.47} = .60 \text{ or } 60\%$$

Profitability Ratios

There are many ways to assess a company's profitability—its ability to recover costs and expenses or its ability to earn income on its assets. Two of the most frequently used ratios are *Rate of Return on Operating Assets* and *Rate of Return on Average Stockholders' Equity*.

Rate of Return on Operating Assets

Rate of Return on Operating Assets is an indication of the earning power of the business based on its operating assets. This ratio is a measure of how efficiently management has used a company's assets to generate profits.

Operating assets are those assets that are used in carrying out business and not those that may be held for investment or other purposes. Likewise, net income is modified to include only the income generated from doing business, and therefore excludes Income Statement elements such as extraordinary items, and interest income and expense. The ratio is computed by dividing Net Operating Income by Operating Assets.

$$\textbf{RATE OF RETURN ON OPERATING ASSETS} = \frac{\textbf{Net Operating Income}}{\textbf{Operating Assets}}$$

Assume that all of W. D. Peachtree's assets are operating assets except for those included in the "OTHER ASSETS" category (i.e., Total Assets of $736,965.47 minus $1,000.00 or $735,965.47. Net Operating Income is shown as a subtotal on the Income Statement—$177,370.82. This amount should be adjusted for interest expense of $2,300.89, making Adjusted Net Operating Income $179,671.70. The rate of return on operating assets for W. D. Peachtree at 12-31-92 is:

$$\frac{\$179,671.70}{\$735,965.47} = .244 \text{ or } 24.4\%$$

Rate of Return on Average Stockholders' Equity

Rate of Return on Average Stockholders' Equity is a ratio of Net Income to Average Stockholders' Equity. This is an important ratio to investors, since it is a measure of the return a company earns on each dollar of stockholders' equity.

$$\textbf{RATE OF RETURN ON AVERAGE STOCKHOLDERS' EQUITY} = \frac{\textbf{Net Income}}{\textbf{Average Stockholders' Equity}}$$

W. D. Peachtree's Stockholders' Equity at the beginning of the year was $291,876.76. Since stockholders' equity at the end of the year was $443,600.92, the average is then:

$$\text{Average Stockholder's Equity} = \frac{\$291,876.76 + \$443,600.92}{2}$$

or $367,738.84.

Then the return on stockholders' equity can be calculated:

$$\frac{\$146,724.16}{\$367,738.84} = .399 \text{ or } 39.9\%.$$

Summary

This chapter has presented a brief description of how the financial statements generated by Peachtree Complete Accounting can be used to prepare a Statement of Cash Flows and various ratios. The purpose of generating financial statements is to report the results of operations to both management and those outside the company. All parties can use this information to make informed decisions regarding the company.

Answer Frame 4^{14}

1.   True. The Statement of Cash Flows shows the sources of inflows of cash and the causes of cash outflows. Because the accrual basis of accounting should be used, revenues (as shown on the Income Statement) usually differ from inflows of cash, and expenses usually differ from cash outflows. For example, depreciation expense does not cause a cash outflow during the current period.

2.   False. The third category is *financing* activities rather than borrowing activities.

3.   True. For a detailed discussion of the process of preparing the Statement of Cash Flows you should consult a principles of accounting text.

4.   False. Investing activities generally relate to the acquisition or disposal of noncurrent assets. Financing activities relate to transactions with creditors and owners.

If you missed any of the above, reread Frame 4^{14} before continuing.

Question Frame 5^{14}

Indicate whether each of the following statements is true of false by writing "T" or "F" in the space provided.

_____ 1.   The current ratio is found by dividing quick assets by current liabilities.

_____ 2.   The accounts receivable turnover is found by dividing net sales by average accounts receivable.

_____ 3.   If costs of goods sold is $1,000,000 and the average inventory is $100,000, then the inventory turnover is 10 times.

_____ 4.   The stockholders' equity ratio could be computed by dividing stockholders' equity by total liabilities plus stockholders' equity.

_____ 5.   The rate of return on operating assets is likely to be larger than the rate of return on stockholders' equity.

Now turn to Answer Frame 5^{14} on page 14-22 to check your answers.

Answer Frame 5[14]

1. False. The current ratio is found by dividing <u>current</u> assets by current liabilities. The quick (or acid-test) ratio is found by dividing quick assets by current liabilities.

2. True. And then this ratio can be divided into 365 to find the average number of days' sales in accounts receivable. If this ratio is too low, credit terms may be too lenient, collection efforts may be ineffective, and too much cash may be tied up in accounts receivable. If the ratio is too high, credit terms may be too strict, collection efforts may be too harsh, and sales may suffer.

3. True. Cost of goods sold ($1,000,000) divided by average inventory ($100,000) is 10 times. If this ratio is too low, too much cash is tied up in inventory, and storage and insurance costs may be excessive. If the ratio is too high, the company may lose sales and incur excessive ordering costs because not enough inventory is on hand.

4. True. The formula is stockholders' equity divided by total assets. But, since total assets are equal to total liabilities plus stockholders' equity, the method described will work.

5. False. Net operating income is not likely to be much different than net income (usually only interest income and interest expense are excluded). But operating assets are likely to be much larger than stockholders' equity, since almost all assets are operating assets. Thus, the numerators of the two ratios are likely to be almost alike, while the denominator of the rate of return on operating assets is likely to be much larger than the denominator of the other ratio. Therefore the rate of return on operating assets is likely to be smaller than the rate of return on stockholders' equity.

If you missed any of the above, reread Frame 5[14]. You have now completed this text on Peachtree Complete Accounting. The skills you have learned should be very valuable to you in the future. You also may be asked to work the comprehensive problem at the end of this chapter.

Chapter 14

Comprehensive Problem

<table>
<tr><td>

WARNING

BEFORE CONTINUING, BE SURE THAT ALL DATA FILES HAVE BEEN RESTORED TO THEIR ORIGINAL CONDITION. IF YOU ARE UNSURE OF HOW TO RESTORE THESE FILES, TURN TO THE INSTRUCTIONS FOUND ON PAGE 1-32 IN CHAPTER 1.
</td></tr>
</table>

NOTE: You may find it helpful to record the problem data on input forms before working the Comprehensive Problem. Master Input Forms are included in the last section of this chapter. In some cases, you will need to make multiple copies of a form before you begin. On the other hand, you may not need all of the input forms provided.

This is a comprehensive problem which involves using all modules covered in this text. Therefore, you should not attempt this Comprehensive Problem until you have successfully completed all other requirements.

The data provided below are selected items from December's activity. When you begin the session, use 12-31-92 as your initial date, and you can change your transaction date throughout the problem as you need to.

This problem is just a sample of what a month's activity involves, and the following data do not include everything that would normally occur in a large retail business at the end of the year. The selected data, though, will give you the opportunity to use all the modules together. However, the financial statements you will print at the end of the problem will have November 30 as the report date. This is because you will not have closed out November, nor will you have entered a whole month's business activity. Yet, the financial statements at the end are better to use for ratio analysis since they are more representative of an actual retail business.

Problem Data

a.   12/01/92   Before making any entries, print a copy of the (Detailed) Trial Balance found in the General Ledger Module. This will be your starting point and should be used if you need to trace any individual transactions.

b.   12/01/92   W. D. Peachtree & Co. decided to sell two of its Fixed Assets. Use the following information to record the sale of these assets.

(1) A Chainsaw (EQP92), originally purchased from Ed's Lawn & Tractor on 8-10-90, was sold on 12-1-92 for $125.00.

(2) A projection system in the boardroom (EQP19) was sold on 12-1-92 for $500.00.

c.   12/02/92   The company hired a new employee today. Use the following information to add this employee to the Payroll file.

Scott Reynolds (SSN 255-99-8000) was hired in department 50 on December 2, 1992. His address is:

> **4567 North Street**
> **Apt. #78**
> **Atlanta, GA 30034**
> **(404) 895-8765**

He will be paid weekly, earning $6.50 per hour for a standard 40 hour work week. He is single and claims one exemption (for federal and state filing purposes). (Accept all other default information.)

d.   12/02/92   The Purchasing Department has notified you that three _new_ vendors have been approved. These three new vendors need to be processed. Use the following information to help you put these new vendors into the system. (All three will involve G/L Account 13500.)

(1) BUTCHER BLOCKS OF AMERICA (BUTCHB)
P. O. Box 768
3400 Nettles Street
Chicago, IL 99807
(675) 909-4531
Contact: Bill Settles
Fed ID# 76-908765

(2) S. BEAR'S OUTDOOR EQUIP. (SBEAR)
P. O. Box 876
9909 South Main Street
San Francisco, CA 98765
(415) 734-6289
Contact: "Guppy" MacDougal
Fed ID# 45-768342

(3) CUNIP'S APPLIANCES (CUNIP)
567 Mitchell Road
Atlanta, GA 30389
(404) 569-4900
Contact: Bill Mitchell
Fed ID# 11-00876

e.   12/03/92   Two customers have notified you of changes that need to be made in their account information. Jonathan S. Fields has changed his address and wants a Shipping Address added. James R. Holloway has negotiated new terms with the credit department and wants to make sure the terms code in his account has been changed properly.

(1) Jonathan S. Fields' new address is:

106 Bull Street
Norcross, GA
30092
404/263-8486

Also, his new shipping address is:

Shipping ID	1200MW
Name	Jonathan S. Fields
Address	1200 Mexico Way
Address	Job Sites 2-9
City, ST	Marietta, GA
Zip Code	34098
Telephone	404-892-8700

(2) James R. Holloway's new Terms Code is:

Terms Code   3

f.   12/03/92   Two Vendors have notified you of changes in their accounts. You should make the following changes in the Accounts Payable Module.

(1) Vendor ID   :   CANNON
    Address   :   P. O. Box 87623
    Address   :   425 Westwood Circle
    Address   :   Springfield, GA
    Postal Code   :   38387

(2) Vendor ID   :   ELE006
    Remit To   :   P. O. Box 8900
                             Chicago, IL
    Postal Code   :   67054

g.   12/05/92   The Receiving Department has notified you of a new shipment of merchandise received today. Use the following data to record this information.

(1) 24 pair of designer slacks at $22.98 each (Dept CLM).

(2) 5 colortronic TVs at $110.00 each (Dept ELE).

(3) 12 portable radios (810425 RAD) at $10.59 each (Dept ELE).

(4) 100 aluminum gutters at $1.88 each (Dept HDW).

(5) 1 furnace at $800.88 (Dept HAC).

h. 12/10/92 Having reconciled the bank statement, you now need to make Miscellaneous Journal Entries in the General Ledger Module. Use the following information to make your entries:

Source Code: 3

LN	REF	DATE	DESCRIPTION	ACCOUNT	AMOUNT
1	BKRECON	12/10/92	Bank Service Chrg.	54000	32.50
2	BKRECON	12/10/92	Bank Loan Repayment	21500	2,000.00
3	BKRECON	12/10/92	Cash Deducted by Bank	11000	2,032.50-

Note: At the beginning screen you should input the following variables:

Number of Transactions: 3
Hash Total   86500

i. 12/12/92 Some of W. D. Peachtree & Co.'s customers paid on their accounts today. Use the following information and the "Apply Payments" program to record these payments.

(1) Gloria Cooper paid $410.00 toward invoice no. 023105 (CK# 4956).

(2) Gloria Cooper also paid $61.40 toward invoice no. 023490 and $284.60 toward invoice no. 023519 (CK# 4957 for $346.00).

(3) Charles Gray paid $463.04 toward invoice no. 022969, $1,166.00 toward invoice no. 023488, and $1.00 toward invoice no. 023514 (CK# 6958 for $1630.04).

(4) Kathy Henderson paid $1,249.69 toward invoice no. 023500 (CK# 426).

(5) James Holloway paid $912.32 toward invoice no. 023493 (CK# 983).

(6) Michael Johnson paid $515.75 toward invoice no. 022887 and $1,812.60 toward invoice no. 023495 (CK# 7095 for $2328.35).

j. 12/12/92 You need to record sales made on this day. Use the "Invoicing" module to record the following data. You will also need the following information:

(1) At the initial screen you should input the following variables:

Process Repeating Invoices   "N"
Invoice Option   "C"
Print Invoice Alignment   "N"

At the prompt to transact Invoices or Credit Memos, choose Invoices for all of the following activity.

(2) Be sure to print each invoice so you will have an audit trail.

<u>Customer Invoice Information</u> (all 12-12-92 invoices and all are taxable)

   (A) Mrs. Fremont Duncan should be billed for 1 dishwasher - $549.99 (Dept APP).

   (B) Send Dorothy Durant a (credit) invoice showing her return of 1 silk blouse - $44.00 (Dept CLW). Use transaction type of RE and unit cost of $10.00.

   (C) Kathy Henderson should be billed for the purchase of a trash compactor at $415.20 (Dept APP). Do <u>not</u> allow her usual 10% discount.

   (D) Thomas Mitchell bought 12 furnace air filters for $9.50 each (Dept HAC). Do <u>not</u> allow his usual 5% discount.

(3) Also, be sure to post these invoices before you leave the Invoicing module. Answer "P" to the Program Option to post the current invoices and then "A" to post all invoices. Ignore the warning, since you will not need to edit these invoices.

(4) Remember to print a Transaction Register Report through the Accounts Receivable Report programs. Select "all transactions" and "current generation." <u>Note</u>: The transaction report will contain invoices from the month of November which you did not enter. This is OK for this problem. In real life this usually would not happen.

k. 12/12/92   You need to record a receipt of inventory for department HAC (Item No. 9900201FURN): 48 items at $5.50 each.

l. 12/12/92   It is time to run W. D. Peachtree's payroll. In order to save time and paper, you will restrict this payroll run to Department 50. You will do this by entering a Beginning and Ending Range of 50 <u>anytime</u> the program allows you to choose a range. Only one employee in Department 50 needs special treatment. Scott Reynolds (ID# REYS) is a part-time employee. You should enter the following hours in the Calculate Time Card Hours Program for Scott:

Time		
<u>In</u>	<u>Out</u>	<u>Type</u>
8.00	17.00	R
8.00	13.00	R
10.00	18.00	R
18.00	20.00	1
12.00	18.00	R

You will <u>not</u> need to print a Paymaster Worksheet, so next you should calculate pay. Use the following options when doing this:

Pay Cycles
       Weekly   Beg. Period 12/6/92
                                               Ending Period 12/12/92

       Monthly   Beg. Period 11/13/92
                                             Ending Period 12/12/92

Pay Types
       Hourly
       Salaried
       Commission

*<u>Remember</u> - <u>Only</u> Calculate Pay for employees in Department 50.

Finally, follow these remaining steps to complete the payroll:

—Print the Pre-check Payroll Register
—Print the Hours/Earnings Report
—Print the Deductions Register
    Note: Only for the <u>Current</u> period
—Print Checks
    Note: Check Date is 12/16/92, no check mask is required, accept
    starting check number
—Print Final Payroll Register

m.   12/20/92   Invoices received from outside vendors need to be posted.

Note: At the initial screen input these variables:

Beg. Balances   "N"
Auto. Invoices   "N"
Beg. Month/Day/Year for Auto. Inv.   12/20/92
Default Invoice Date 12/20/92

You can accept all other default options after entering the following information.

(1) Invoice no. 56790, dated 12-15-92, was received from Butcher Blocks of America for \$2,315.00. A \$46.30 discount was offered if payment is made before 12-25-92. Otherwise the whole amount is due on 1-14-93.

(2) Received an invoice numbered 312NP from S. Bear's Outdoor Equipment dated 12-10-92. The invoice, which offers no terms, is due on 1-9-93 in the amount of \$678.32.

(3) Cunip's Appliances sent invoice no. APP890765 dated 12-12-92. \$6,754.56 is due on 1-11-93, but if the bill is paid by 12-22-92, a \$202.64 discount is offered.

n.   12/20/92   You need to pay invoices that are due. In order to save time and paper, you should only select certain vendors. Do this by first going into the Select Invoices for Payment Program from the Processing Menu. At the initial screen you should accept the following variables:

Cash Account Code   :   1

Cash Account Code	:	1
Auto Select	:	"N"
Beginning Discount Date	:	12/20/92
Ending Discount Date	:	12/27/92
Due Date	:	12/20/92

At the next screen enter "S" to let the computer know you want to select invoices by vendor. Then select only the following vendors and invoices for payment:

Vendor ID	Invoice Number
BLASS	9453BB08
	9687BB08
BRATCH	BB42530807
	BB46378999
	BB46399765
CANNON	810987B50
CURTIS	10060P10
	10287P11
DIOR	D91013222
ELE001	810534B100
	810765B100
ELE010	JVP9385433
	JVP9386532
ELE022	810945R20
	811965R20

After you have selected all the proper vendors and invoices, your cash requirement total should equal $25,180.63. If it does not, then print a pre-check register to see where you might have gone wrong.

Once your cash requirement equals $25,180.63, you should follow these steps:

—Print the Pre-check Register
—Print Accounts Payable Checks, starting check #100. Do not print a check mask. Do not print the control report on blank paper.
—Print Check Register
—Update Accounts Payable Checks

o.   12/31/92   End of the Month Routines

(1) For Accounts Payable, you should:

(a) Print a Transaction Register Report.

—Select Generation "C" for Current Generation
—Select Vendor "R" for Range Beginning AUTFNC Ending ELE022

(b) Create G/L Journal Entries. Remember to select all three options.

(2) For Accounts Receivable, you should:

   (a) Apply Service Charges
       Ending Date: 12/31/92, Starting Date: 12/01/92, Final Run.

       <u>Do</u> <u>Not</u> Create Invoices
       <u>Do</u> <u>Not</u> Review Customers

   (b) Print the following Reports:

      —Transaction Register

Select Report Type	"R"
Select Transactions	"A"
Select Generation	"C"

      —Customer Statements

Statement Date	12/31/92
Statement Ageing Date	12/31/92
Statement Message	"N"
Print Dunning Message	"N"
Print Zero Balance Statements	"N"
Sort by	"I"
Select Customers	"R"
Beginning COOPEG Ending MITCHT	
Print Alignment Guide	"N"

      —Aged Receivables

Report Date	12/31/92
Customer Type Option	"A"
Update Bal. Fwd. Ageing	"N"
Ageing Date	12/31/92
Select Ageing Option	"S"
Select Customers	"R"
Beginning COOPEG Ending MITCHT	

   (c) Create G/L Journal Entries. (Select transfer option "T" only which will list and create G/L transfers).

(3) For Inventory, you should print the Transaction Register for product items only. Also, be sure to only print a Range, with the beginning range of APP and the ending range of HDW. Select "C" for the current generation.

(4) For Payroll you should Post the Current Period then Close the Current Quarter found in the Processing Menu. This is the last posting for the G/L period and a detail report should be run. Accept "Y" at all warning prompts.

(5) For Fixed Assets you should Transfer to the General Ledger. Answer "Y" to Build the Transfer File. This is the last transfer of the period.

(6) After you have successfully completed all of the above, you should go to the General Ledger module and perform the following steps:

    (a) Transfer the Summary Journals for Accounts Payable and Accounts Receivable (answer "N" for Payroll and Fixed Assets).

    (b) Print a Summary Trial Balance.

    (c) Print a Balance Sheet, Current Period, Standard.

    (d) Print an Income Statement, Current Period, Standard.

Financial Statement Analysis

Now that you have printed a Balance Sheet and Income Statement, use the information contained in these financial statements to compute the following:

a. Current Ratio

b. Quick Ratio

c. Accounts Receivable Turnover

    (Use the Net Accounts Receivable balance at 11/30/92 as the average Net Accounts Receivable amount).

d. Inventory Turnover

    (Use the Inventory balance at 11/30/92 as the average Inventory amount).

e. Stockholders' Equity Ratio

f. Rate of Return on Average Stockholders' Equity

    (Use the Stockholders' Equity balance at 11/30/92 as the average Stockholders' Equity amount).

COMPREHENSIVE PROBLEM

MASTER INPUT FORMS

Employee Setup Form

Personal Information

Department: __ __

Employee Code: __ __ __ __

Name: __ __ __ __ __ __ __ __ __ __ __ __ __ __ __ __
__ __ __ __ __ __ __ __

Address: __ __ __ __ __ __ __ __ __ __ __ __ __ __ __ __
__ __ __ __ __ __ __ __

Address: __ __ __ __ __ __ __ __ __ __ __ __ __ __ __ __
__ __ __ __ __ __ __ __

City, State: __ __ __ __ __ __ __ __ __ __ __ __ __ __ __ __
__ __ __ __ __

Zip Code: __ __ __ __ __ __ __ __ __

Soc. Sec. No.: __ __ __ __ __ __ __ __ __ __ __

Phone: __ __ __ __ __ __ __ __ __ __ __

Comment: __ __ __ __ __ __ __ __ __ __ __ __ __ __ __ __
__ __ __ __ __

Status (A/I): **A I** (Circle one)

Date Employed: __ __/__ __/__ __

Date Terminated: __ __/__ __/__ __

Last Check Date: __ __/__ __/__ __

Last Check No.: __ __ __ __ __ __

Last Check Amount: __ __ __ __ __ __ __.__ __

Employee Setup Form

Rates & Flags

Department: __ __

Employee Code: __ __ __ __

Statutory Employee:	Y N (Circle one)
Deceased:	Y N
Tipped Employee:	Y N
Legal Rep:	Y N
942 Employee:	Y N
EIC Status:	N U T
Shift Code:	1 2 3
Pay Period:	W B S M
Pay Type:	H S D C
Pay Rate/Salary/Draw:	__ __ __ __ . __ __ __
Commision Rate %:	__ __ . __ __
Maximum Check Amount:	__ __ __ __ __ . __ __
Fed. Filing Status:	S M * ! # @ & 1 2 3 4 5 (Circle one)
Fed. Exemptions:	__ __
Addl. Fed. Tax:	__ __ __ __ . __ __
Cur. Defer. Deductions:	__ __ __ __ . __ __
YTD Defer. Deductions:	__ __ __ __ . __ __
Cur. Alloc. Deductions:	__ __ __ __ . __ __
Cost of Group Term Life over $50000:	__ __ __ __ __ . __ __
FICA Taken on Term Life:	Y N (Circle one)
Standard Work Week:	__ __ __ . __
Standard OVT. 1 Hours:	__ __ __ . __
Standard OVT. 2 Hours:	__ __ __ . __
Pension:	Y N
Deferred Compensation:	Y N
SUTA Taxable:	Y N
Industrial Insurance %:	__ __ __ __ __ . __ __

Employee Setup Form

Tax Code

Department: ___ ___

Employee Code: ___ ___ ___ ___

Tax Code	Filing Status	Exmpt	Misc. Tax Factor	Addit. Tax	Misc. Tax Amount
__ __	__ __	__ __	___ __.__	_____ __.__	_____ __.__
__ __	__ __	__ __	___ __.__	_____ __.__	_____ __.__
__ __	__ __	__ __	___ __.__	_____ __.__	_____ __.__
__ __	__ __	__ __	___ __.__	_____ __.__	_____ __.__

Deductions	Amount	Ceiling	Taxable (Y/N) 1	2	3	4
Misc. Ded. 1: _____	_____.__	_____.__	__	__	__	__
Withholding			__	__	__	__
Unemployment			__	__	__	__
Misc. Ded. 2: _____	_____.__	_____.__	__	__	__	__
Withholding			__	__	__	__
Unemployment			__	__	__	__
Misc. Ded. 3: _____	_____.__	_____.__	__	__	__	__
Withholding			__	__	__	__
Unemployment			__	__	__	__
Misc. Ded. 4: _____	_____.__	_____.__	__	__	__	__
Withholding			__	__	__	__
Unemployment			__	__	__	__
Misc. Ded. 5: _____	_____.__	_____.__	__	__	__	__
Withholding			__	__	__	__
Unemployment			__	__	__	__
Misc. Ded. 6: _____	_____.__	_____.__	__	__	__	__
Withholding			__	__	__	__
Unemployment			__	__	__	__

Maintain Vendors Setup Form

Vendor ID   ___ ___ ___ ___ ___

Vendor Name   ___ ___ ___ ___ ___ ___ ___ ___ ___ ___ ___ ___

                       ___ ___ ___ ___ ___ ___ ___ ___ ___ ___

Address   ___ ___ ___ ___ ___ ___ ___ ___ ___ ___ ___ ___

                       ___ ___ ___ ___ ___ ___ ___ ___ ___ ___

Address   ___ ___ ___ ___ ___ ___ ___ ___ ___ ___ ___ ___

                       ___ ___ ___ ___ ___ ___ ___ ___ ___ ___

Address   ___ ___ ___ ___ ___ ___ ___ ___ ___ ___ ___ ___

                       ___ ___ ___ ___ ___ ___ ___ ___ ___ ___

Postal Code   ___ ___ ___ ___ ___ ___ ___ ___ ___ ___

Telephone   ___ ___ ___ ___ ___ ___ ___ ___ ___ ___ ___

Contact   ___ ___ ___ ___ ___ ___ ___ ___ ___ ___ ___ ___

                       ___ ___ ___ ___ ___ ___ ___ ___ ___ ___

G/L Account Number ___ ___ ___ ___ ___ ___

Temporary Vendor   Y   N   (Circle one)

1099 Vendor   Y   N

1099 Type   A B D G I M O P R

1099 Misc Box   1 2 3 5 6 7 8

Federal ID Number ___ ___ ___ ___ ___ ___ ___ ___ ___ ___

YTD Purchases

   Calendar   ___ ___ ___ , ___ ___ ___ , ___ ___ ___ . ___ ___

   Fiscal   ___ ___ ___ , ___ ___ ___ , ___ ___ ___ . ___ ___

YTD Payments

   Calendar   ___ ___ ___ , ___ ___ ___ , ___ ___ ___ . ___ ___

   Fiscal   ___ ___ ___ , ___ ___ ___ , ___ ___ ___ . ___ ___

**Change Vendor Remit
To Address Line 1:** __ __ __ __ __ __ __ __ __ __ __ __ __

__ __ __ __ __ __ __ __ __ __

Line 2: __ __ __ __ __ __ __ __ __ __ __ __ __

__ __ __ __ __ __ __ __ __ __

Line 3: __ __ __ __ __ __ __ __ __ __ __ __ __

__ __ __ __ __ __ __ __ __ __

Postal Code: __ __ __ __ __ __ __ __ __

Customer Information Setup Form

Customer ID: __ __ __ __ __ __

Customer Name: __ __ __ __ __ __ __ __ __ __ __ __

__ __ __ __ __ __ __ __ __ __ __ __

Address: __ __ __ __ __ __ __ __ __ __ __ __

__ __ __ __ __ __ __ __ __ __ __ __

Address: __ __ __ __ __ __ __ __ __ __ __ __

__ __ __ __ __ __ __ __ __ __ __ __

City, ST: __ __ __ __ __ __ __ __ __ __ __ __

__ __ __ __ __ __ __ __ __ __ __ __

ZIP Code: __ __ __ __ __ __ __ __ __

Telephone: __ __ __ __ __ __ __ __ __ __

Contact: __ __ __ __ __ __ __ __ __ __ __ __

__ __ __ __ __ __ __ __ __ __ __ __

Salesperson: __ __ __ __ __ __ __ __

Customer Class: __

Account Type: R   B   T   (Circle one)

Terms Code: 1   2   3   4   5

Sales Tax Code: __ __ __

Discount Percent: __ __ . __ __

Ship Addresses: Y   N

Dunning Notices: Y   N

Credit Limit: __ __ __ __ __ __ __ . __ __

Service Chg Code: 1   2   3   4

Print Statements: Y   N

Print Invoices: Y   N

Balance Forward Ageing (Only for Balance Forward Customers)

Current: __ __ __ __ __ __ __ __ __ . __ __

1 - 30 Days: __ __ __ __ __ __ __ __ __ . __ __

31 - 60 Days: __ __ __ __ __ __ __ __ __ . __ __

Over 60 Days: __ __ __ __ __ __ __ __ __ . __ __

Debit_____

Last Date: ___ ___/ ___ ___/ ___ ___

Last Amt: ___ ___ ___ ___ ___ ___ ___ ___ .___ ___

YTD Amt: ___ ___ ___ ___ ___ ___ ___ ___ .___ ___

Credit_____

Last Date: ___ ___/ ___ ___/ ___ ___

Last Amt: ___ ___ ___ ___ ___ ___ ___ .___ ___

YTD Amt: ___ ___ ___ ___ ___ ___ ___ .___ ___

Payments_____

Last Date: ___ ___/ ___ ___/ ___ ___

Last Amt: ___ ___ ___ ___ ___ ___ ___ .___ ___

YTD Amt: ___ ___ ___ ___ ___ ___ ___ .___ ___

Service Charges_____

Last Date: ___ ___/ ___ ___/ ___ ___

Last Amt: ___ ___ ___ ___ ___ ___ ___ ___ .___ ___

YTD Amt: ___ ___ ___ ___ ___ ___ ___ ___ .___ ___

Customer Shipping Addresses Setup Form

Customer ID: __ __ __ __ __ __

Shipping ID: __ __ __ __ __ __

Customer Name: __ __ __ __ __ __ __ __ __ __ __ __ __ __

__ __ __ __ __ __ __ __ __ __ __

Address: __ __ __ __ __ __ __ __ __ __ __ __ __

__ __ __ __ __ __ __ __ __ __ __

Address: __ __ __ __ __ __ __ __ __ __ __ __ __

__ __ __ __ __ __ __ __ __ __ __

City, ST: __ __ __ __ __ __ __ __ __ __ __ __ __

__ __ __ __ __ __ __ __ __ __ __

ZIP Code: __ __ __ __ __ __ __ __ __ __

Telephone: __ __ __ __ __ __ __ __ __ __ __ __

Shipping ID: __ __ __ __ __ __

Customer Name: __ __ __ __ __ __ __ __ __ __ __ __ __ __

__ __ __ __ __ __ __ __ __ __ __

Address: __ __ __ __ __ __ __ __ __ __ __ __ __

__ __ __ __ __ __ __ __ __ __ __

Address: __ __ __ __ __ __ __ __ __ __ __ __ __

__ __ __ __ __ __ __ __ __ __ __

City, ST: __ __ __ __ __ __ __ __ __ __ __ __ __

__ __ __ __ __ __ __ __ __ __ __

ZIP Code: __ __ __ __ __ __ __ __ __ __

Telephone: __ __ __ __ __ __ __ __ __ __ __ __

Customer Transactions Setup Form

Customer ID: __ __ __ __ __ __

Trans. Type: __ __

Product Code: __

Invoice Number: __ __ __ __ __ __

Terms Code: __

Trans. Date: __ __/ __ __/ __ __

Due Date: __ __/ __ __/ __ __

Discount Date: __ __/ __ __/ __ __

Trans. Amount: __ __ __ __ __ __ __.__ __

Comment: __ __ __ __ __ __ __ __ __ __

T/E: T   E   (Circle one)

State Tax: __ __ __ __ __ __ __.__ __

County Tax: __ __ __ __ __ __ __.__ __

City Tax: __ __ __ __ __ __ __.__ __

G/L Transactions Setup Form

Source Code: ___

Reference: __ __ __ __ __ __ __ __

Date: __ __ / __ __ / __ __

Description: __ __ __ __ __ __ __ __ __ __ __ __ __ __ __ __ __ __
__ __ __ __ __ __ __ __ __

Account: __ __ __ __ __ __

Amount: __ __ __ __ __ __ __ __ . __ __

Source Code: ___

Reference: __ __ __ __ __ __ __ __

Date: __ __ / __ __ / __ __

Description: __ __ __ __ __ __ __ __ __ __ __ __ __ __ __ __ __ __
__ __ __ __ __ __ __ __ __

Account: __ __ __ __ __ __

Amount: __ __ __ __ __ __ __ __ . __ __

Source Code: ___

Reference: __ __ __ __ __ __ __ __

Date: __ __ / __ __ / __ __

Description: __ __ __ __ __ __ __ __ __ __ __ __ __ __ __ __ __ __
__ __ __ __ __ __ __ __ __

Account: __ __ __ __ __ __

Amount: __ __ __ __ __ __ __ __ . __ __

Appendix A

Job Cost Overview

Jobs are projects your business completes for a customer. They are completed over a period of time and can usually be broken down into several distinct tasks. Job costs consist of money you spend while completing a project. These might include the purchase of items like materials, labor, subcontractors, and equipment used, as well as overhead.

This overview describes the Job Cost module and how it interacts with other Peachtree Accounting modules.

What Job Cost Does for You

Peachtree Accounting Job Cost allows you to track expenses, revenues, and the allocation of your resources -- including employees and equipment -- for each project your company undertakes.

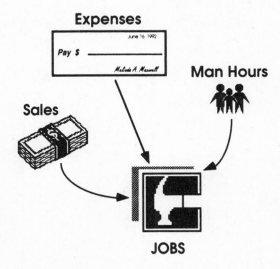

Job Cost lets you enter and change estimates and actual cost information. It also

- keeps track of customer billings and payments received from a customer for each job, and the net due for each job

- maintains job starting and completion dates, and percentage of completion

- prints comparisons of estimated and actual costs

- provides reports on total job costs broken down by phases, or cost code

- lets you add and track change orders

- tracks costs associated with transactions entered in Accounts Payable

Setting Up

You can activate Job Cost at anytime of the year. It does not have to be at the beginning of an accounting period or year. You can also enter jobs that have already been started.

Using Job Cost for Your Business

Job Cost maintains the jobs that your company does by tracking expenses and revenues. Job Cost also lets you create estimates for new jobs as well as use an existing estimate to create a new one.

Definitions

Certain definitions are fundamental to Job Cost. Here are some terms we use:

Job -- A job is a specific project for one customer, done for pay. Generally, a job lasts for a period of time, can be broken down into specific tasks, and involves various types of costs.

Cost -- A cost is an expenditure which takes place on or for a job. Job costing is based on the tracking of costs, and their reporting, either in detail or summary form. There are two types of cost:

- **Actual Cost** -- An actual cost is one that actually exists and has been paid. Actual costs generally come from transactions in Accounts Payable, time card entries, or manual entries in **Enter Miscellaneous Costs**.

- **Estimated Cost** -- An estimated cost is your approximate calculation of a cost.

Phase -- A phase is a logical division, or stage, of a job. A phase can be an entire job, or division of a job. Whenever you enter costs, you tell Job Cost to what phase the cost belongs.

For example, if you're constructing a building you may have individual phases for site preparation, foundations, framing, etc.

Phase Code -- A phase code is used to identify each phase or major step of a project. You assign phases to jobs using this code.

Cost Code -- A cost code represents a specific type of cost expenditure within a phase of your job.

Whenever you enter estimated units and dollars or actual costs, you usually assign them to a cost code as well as a phase. This helps you understand your costs and profitability on a job.

Cost Type -- A cost type is a sub-category used to break down costs into related types.

Job Cost groups costs into five cost types: Labor, Materials, Equipment, Subcontractors and Other. As you enter costs for a job, Job Cost records the cost type. Later, it can sort (and summarize) costs by cost type.

Note: When reading about Job Cost, distinguish "cost code" from "cost type." These words are very similar and may confuse you unless you are careful.

Allocations -- Additional costs that are added to a specific phase/cost code combination.

How Job Cost Works with Other Modules

If you plan to use Job Cost with Payroll, Accounts Payable, Accounts Receivable, and Invoicing, we suggest that you activate those four modules before you install Job Cost. This will save you from entering Job Cost information more than once.

How Job Cost Information Flows

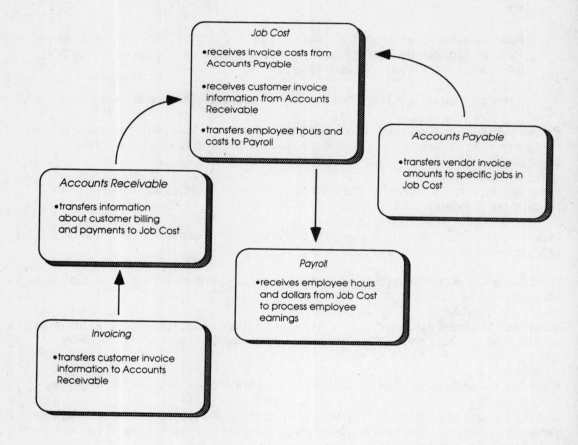

Appendix B

Purchase Order Overview

What Purchase Order Does for You

A purchase order is a written order for merchandise. Purchase Order prints orders to your suppliers for the non-stock and inventory products and services you need to run your business.

A non-stock item is an item you don't enter into Inventory. It's usually for the maintenance and running of your business, such as light bulbs or a janitorial service. These non-stock maintenance items are frequently called "general supplies" or "operational supplies." Additionally,

- A non-stock item can also be something you special order.

- Inventory items are products and services you stock and sell.

In addition to the number of items ordered and unit cost, a purchase order provides valuable information to your vendor, such as your purchaser's name, shipping information, and standard payment terms. You can also add miscellaneous costs, such as shipping charges or special taxes.

You can use Purchase Order to add a new vendor to Accounts Payable. Also, if you're ordering an item that hasn't been entered into Inventory, you can use Purchase Order to assign the item an inventory item identification and add the item to Inventory.

You can easily make changes to a purchase order if you find out you incorrectly entered information. Purchase Order also prints Change Order Notices and Cancellation Notices.

Use Purchase Order to receive your non-stock and inventory items. You can receive

- full or partial shipments

- more items than you ordered

- items you didn't order, but want to keep

- items set for specific unit costing

Purchase Order records your partial shipments and keeps track of back orders. You can use Purchase Order to transfer receipts to Inventory and to update Accounts Payable so that your vendor can be paid.

How Purchase Order Works with Other Modules

You *must* use Purchase Order with Peachtree Accounting Accounts Payable. Purchase Order won't work unless you install Accounts Payable first.

You can also use Purchase Order with Peachtree Accounting Inventory. If you plan to use Purchase Order with Inventory, it's best to install Inventory before you install Purchase Order so you can look up inventory item numbers and add items when you place orders. You will also be able to update Inventory through Purchase Order when an order is received. Also, when you decide to use Purchase Order with Inventory, you must close or cancel all existing purchase orders before you activate Inventory.

Purchase Order is a bridge between Accounts Payable and Inventory. When used together, these three modules provide a complete ordering, receiving, and invoicing management system.

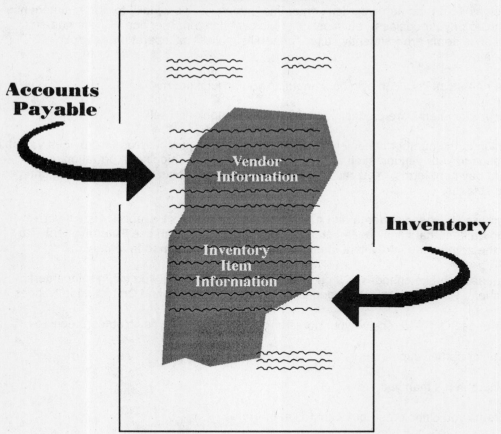

Purchase Order allows you to use the same vendor IDs that you use in Accounts Payable or to add new vendors to Accounts Payable when you enter a purchase order. After you enter receipts, Purchase Order allows you to enter information from the vendor invoice into Accounts Payable so you can pay your vendors.

Purchase Order orders any inventory item you stock, whether it is a product or service. It lets you look up Inventory item numbers when you order or receive items, and lets you add new items to Inventory. You can easily order all inventory items that are at or below their reorder level. Purchase Order updates the units on-order when orders are entered and updates the quantity-on-hand when items are received in Inventory.

Purchase Order has no direct connection to Job Cost. However, use Purchase Order to order materials, equipment, or subcontractor services you use on your jobs. Purchase Order has no connection, direct, or indirect, to any other Peachtree Accounting module.

Appendix C

PDQ Overview

PDQ is different in purpose and concept from Peachtree Complete Accounting. Each Peachtree Complete Accounting software module has one set of related jobs to do. To make it do those jobs, you follow the same steps each day, each week, or each month. In return, Peachtree Complete Accounting does similar processing and gives you similar output each time you use it. Software modules like those which compose Peachtree Complete Accounting are applications -- software packages designed to be applied to one job. PDQ is different because it is a tool. You can use it for almost any job involving the accounting data stored in Peachtree Complete Accounting. PDQ can do so many jobs for you because it is really a tool kit, not just a single tool.

Because PDQ doesn't have any one set job, there is no set of instructions for using it. Rather, there is a group of skills involved in using PDQ, just as there is in using a hammer or a sewing machine. As you learn to use PDQ, you will learn to use this group of skills. It is up to your imagination to devise jobs for the PDQ tool kit, and to tailor your use of PDQ for the jobs you devise. As with other tools, start by using a small set of PDQ skills. Later, expand that set.

Each of the jobs you devise for PDQ is called a **procedure**. A procedure is a set of steps. In learning PDQ, you learn about the different steps that can make up a procedure. PDQ lets you store procedures on your disk and run them at a later time.

How PDQ Works

Like most software packages, PDQ's functions can be divided into three areas:

1. It **reads** Peachtree Complete Accounting's data from your disk.

2. It **processes** the data.

3. It **presents** the data to you as lists, displays, graphs, and reports.

You control what data PDQ reads, how much data it reads, how it filters and sorts the data, how it creates totals and comparisons, and how it presents the information to you. You **cannot** use PDQ to enter new Peachtree Complete Accounting data, or to change Peachtree Complete Accounting data.

PDQ was designed to be easy to use. For instance, PDQ always lists your choices on the screen. To select a choice, just move the highlighted bar to your choice and press [ENTER]. We call this method of selection "point and shoot." PDQ always displays an instruction box at the bottom of the screen, and you can get on-screen help at almost any time by pressing [F1]. For instance, here is the PDQ Main Menu:

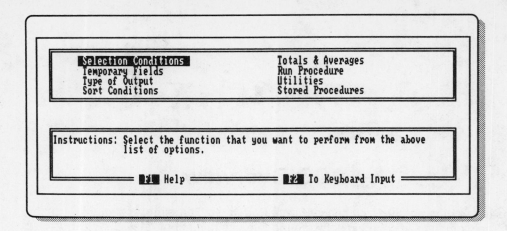

```
┌─────────────────────────────────────────────────────────┐
│  Selection Conditions          Totals & Averages        │
│  Temporary Fields              Run Procedure             │
│  Type of Output                Utilities                 │
│  Sort Conditions               Stored Procedures         │
│                                                           │
│                                                           │
│  Instructions: Select the function that you want to      │
│                perform from the above list of options.   │
│                                                           │
│        ▓█▓ Help              ▓█▓ To Keyboard Input        │
└─────────────────────────────────────────────────────────┘
```

PDQ Input: Peachtree Accounting Data

This section tells you how PDQ gets information from the Peachtree Complete Accounting modules and how you select the information it gets.

How Peachtree Accounting Stores Information

PDQ is designed to read data from Peachtree Complete Accounting. This data is stored in **files** on your disk. Each file is a collection of information about a single topic within a Peachtree Complete Accounting module. PDQ can read information from any of Peachtree Complete Accounting's modules.

Each file is compose of records; each record is composed of fields:

- A **field** is a piece of information, such as John Doe's zip code or the part number for a 6-foot length of 1/4" copper pipe. As you use PDQ, you tell it what fields to display or print for you.

- A **record** is a group of fields that describe a given employee, account, part, invoice, customer, or other person or thing. Optionally, you can tell PDQ to pick only certain records, based on the contents of a particular field (for instance, customers whose ACCOUNT-TYPE = 'R').

- A **file** contains the records for **all** of your employees, **all** of your accounts, or for **all** of any other type of related thing or person.

Many Peachtree Complete Accounting modules store data in more than one file. For instance, the Accounts Receivable module uses eight files. Most of the fields in each file are different: each file contains a different type of information about your customers and your accounts receivable. For instance, there is one file that has fields containing information about customers and another that contains information about transactions. Some fields, such as customer number, appear in many files.

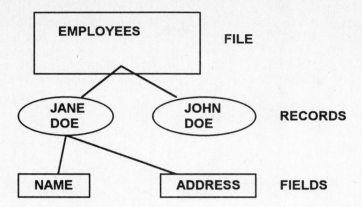

Generally, Peachtree Complete Accounting has one screen that you use to enter most of the data that eventually goes into each file. For instance, the **Maintain Customers** screen builds the Customer Master file. Several screens build the Accounts Receivable Transaction file.

How PDQ Lets You View Data

The files used by your Peachtree Complete Accounting modules, taken collectively, have several thousand fields. To make handling that data easier for you and for PDQ, we have divided the Peachtree Complete data into different **groups** of fields. Each group of fields focuses on a specific area. For instance, in Payroll, the views we provide are:

EMPLOYEE HISTORY
EMPLOYEE PERIOD TO DATE DATA
EMPLOYEE PERSONAL DATA
EMPLOYEE QUARTERLY 941
EMPLOYEE TAX CODES & DEDUCTIONS
EMPLOYEE TRANSACTIONS

Each of these groups is a pre-defined view of **some** of your employee data. Each view gives you access to fields that you are likely to use for a specific type of report. For instance, the EMPLOYEE PERSONAL DATA view gives you access to fields that you might use to build a report about your employee's hire dates and pay rates.

To help explain what a view is, we are going to use the image of a person peering into the window of a house. Let's say that:

- The house is your Peachtree Complete Accounting data.

- Each room is a file.

- Each piece of furniture is a field.

One room might be the file that contains Customer Information, another your Company File, another the Accounts Receivable Transaction File, and so on.

When someone looks into a window, he or she can see most of the furniture in one room, and some of the furniture in other rooms, but not all of it. A view is a window that lets you see data inside your "house." Just as our peering person can see most of one room and/or parts of several rooms, each view lets you see parts of several files. Similar to a window, each view gives you access to most of the fields in one file and some of the fields in one or more other files.

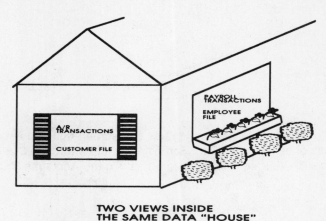

**TWO VIEWS INSIDE
THE SAME DATA "HOUSE"**

It is important to be able to "see" fields from more than one file at a time because the fields from just one file may not have all the information you need to produce a comprehensive report. For instance, the A/R Transaction File does not contain the customer's name. It only contains the customer ID. In order to produce a report that has the customer name **and** has transaction information, you must use fields from two files: the A/R Transaction File and the Customer File. Views we provide let you do just that, painlessly. By using a view, you are able to view into more than one file -- and produce a report that includes all the information you need.

Whenever you use PDQ, you **must** tell it which view has the fields you want to use. PDQ then lets you use the fields that compose that view. You can only use one view at a time, but common fields are contained in several different views. For instance, all views include the COMPANY-NAME field, a field in the Company file. Several views include CUSTOMER-NAME.

PDQ makes selecting a view fairly simple: it shows you a list of available views and lets you select one from the list.

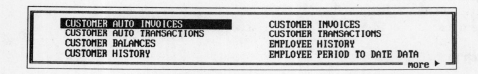

Note the word **more** in the lower right hand corner. That means you can use the ⬚ key, the ⬚⬚ keys, or the ⬚ key to see more views.

The views we include as part of PDQ are based both on our experience and on requests users have made. Each is arbitrary, but carefully considered.

Note: Other software packages sometimes use **view** with different meanings. This reflects the richness of the English language -- and a sometimes confusing lack of precision in the vocabulary of data processing. Our definition is common in discussions of data query software and data bases.

Deciding What View to Use

Most of the time, you can decide what view to use by simply reading the list that PDQ displays. If you press [F1] (the help key) when you see the list of views, PDQ displays a brief explanation of each view.

Views that Present Information from More than One Generation

Even if you do not choose to keep Year-to-Date detail in the Peachtree Accounting modules that allow you to do so, PDQ can provide reports that include several months' information. **History views** let you use information from more than one month (or accounting data file generation) at a time.

PDQ's history views are:

> CUSTOMER HISTORY
> EMPLOYEE HISTORY
> GENERAL LEDGER HISTORY
> INVENTORY HISTORY
> VENDOR HISTORY

Peachtree Accounting stores each accounting generation as a separate set of data files. These files contain a snapshot of your business at the end of each month (or accounting period or pay period). When you use multiple generations, PDQ treats the files for the selected generations as if they were one large file. PDQ lets you distinguish between generations if you want to. It also lets you choose not to show open accounts receivable or accounts payable transactions carried over from one month to the next.

When you select a history view, PDQ shows you a list of the data file generations available on your disk. You can then use point and shoot to select those generations you want to include. (If you select a history view and you only have one generation of information available, PDQ does not ask you to select generations.)

When you select to use a view other than a history view, PDQ asks you to enter a single generation number. This is the data PDQ will use.

Usually, you will enter the current generation for the module whose data you want to work with. Enter a previous generation number to use older data. This can be useful if you forget to run a Peachtree Accounting report before closing your month.

Note: You can always get previous month's general ledger account and budget totals from the General Ledger Accounts view. If you use the option, available in several Peachtree Accounting modules, to keep transaction detail, you can prepare reports that include several months' worth of information without using (and you should not use) history views.

Selecting Fields

As you use PDQ, it asks you which fields to use for several different purposes. These include:

- To print or display as part of your output.

- To use as the basis for record selection.

- To use to sort your output.

Whenever you must select fields, PDQ shows you the field selection box. This is the field selection box you will see when you work with General Ledger Accounts view:

```
┌─────────────────────────────────────────────────────────────────────┐
│  ACCOUNT-TYPE          PD-BAL-NONCUR/TRANS      PD-BAL-LASTYR-1-13     │
│  MASTER-DEPT           PRIOR-PD-ADJ             BUDGET-ANNUAL          │
│  BEGINNING-BALANCE     ACCOUNT-BAL-YTD          BUDGET-CURYR-1-13      │
│  PD-BAL-CUR/TRANS      PD-BAL-CURYR-1-13        BUDGET-NXTYR-1-13      │
│                                                            more ▶      │
└─────────────────────────────────────────────────────────────────────┘
```

Note the word **more** in the lower right hand corner. That means you can use the ▶ key, the CTRL ▶ keys, or the PGDN key to see more fields from the view.

Different Ways PDQ Can Present Your Data

With PDQ you can:

- DISPLAY automatically formatted reports on your screen.

- LIST automatically formatted reports on your printer.

- Display or print two-dimensional BAR GRAPHs and HISTOGRAMs.

- Design your own custom-formatted REPORTs.

- TRANSFER your information to Lotus 1-2-3™, Symphony™, MultiPlan™, VisiCalc® and dBase™, and to word processors and other packages that accept ASCII or DIF® files.

The Type of Output option on the PDQ Main Menu allows you to select the type of output PDQ presents to you.

Appendix D

DOS Fundamentals

Peachtree Complete Accounting insulates you from the ins and outs of DOS as much as possible. Still, it is helpful to have some knowledge of DOS. The more you know, the more control you have over your computer and the easier it is to solve any problems that may come up.

Only the Basics   *DOS Fundamentals* covers only the basic DOS commands that help you work with Peachtree Complete Accounting (PCA). It does not attempt to cover all DOS commands, nor does it teach all the variations and short cuts available for the commands discussed. After reading this appendix, you should understand basic DOS concepts and be able to take care of some of the more common DOS tasks with confidence.

Learning More   If you want to learn more about DOS and how to use it, read the DOS manual that came with your computer. You may find your DOS manual easier to understand after reading this *appendix*. Many DOS tutorial books are also available, and people often find these easier to understand than DOS manuals.

What Is In This Appendix   This appendix presents some of the fundamentals you need to work confidently with DOS.

If you are already familiar with DOS, its files, directories, and so on, feel free to skip over or skim through this appendix.

You will encounter some new terms as you read this appendix. DOS has its own jargon but the explanations are in plain English.

What You Need to Know About DOS

What is DOS

DOS is an acronym for **D**isk **O**perating **S**ystem. An operating system is a set of special programs that tell your computer what other programs -- such as Peachtree Complete Accounting -- want it to do.

Most programs do not communicate directly with your computer hardware (keyboard, disks, printer, monitor); nor does your hardware talk directly with most programs. Instead, most communication takes place through DOS. Like all operating systems, DOS acts as a mediator or translator, between your hardware and your programs.

Handling Information

One of the main DOS tasks is to handle the information on your disks: DOS stores the information, keeps track of it, retrieves it, and -- when you tell it to -- removes it. Most of what this chapter teaches you about DOS relates to your disks, and their directories and files.

How DOS Stores Information

This section explains how DOS stores information on your disk and retrieves it from your disk. You will learn some basics about disk drives, directories, and files here.

The Big Picture

DOS stores its information in files. A **file** is a collection of related information, similar to what you might find in a file folder. DOS keeps its files in a kind of file drawer called a **directory** that usually contains file folders -- that is, files.

Both files and directories are stored by disk drives. **Disk drives** comprise a computer's storage space and are the actual media on which information is written.

That is it in a nutshell: files contain information, reside in directories, and are stored by disk drives. Next these ideas will be discussed more completely.

How DOS Uses Disk Drives

Your computer probably has at least two disk drives: one diskette drive and one hard disk drive. You must have at least one diskette drive and one hard disk drive to use PCA. Unlike hard disk drives, **Diskette drives** use diskettes that can be inserted and removed. **Hard disk drives** have a much greater storage capacity than diskettes, though. They also let DOS read and write information much faster than diskettes.

Disk Drive Letters

DOS uses separate letters to indicate each disk drive. Set-ups for disk drives can vary from computer to computer, but typically:

A: indicates your first diskette drive.
B: indicates your second diskette drive, if you have one.
C: indicates your hard disk drive.

You need to know how the disk drives are set-up for the computer you will be using for this course. If you do not know already, ask your instructor.

The Current Drive

The **current drive** is the disk drive that DOS uses unless you tell it otherwise. If you give DOS a command without specifying a disk drive, DOS applies the command to the current drive. Most computers with a hard disk usually specify C: as the current drive.

Changing the Current Drive

DOS sets the current drive when your computer starts up, but you can change it whenever you like. For example, typing:

A: [ENTER] makes A: the current drive. Because A: is a diskette drive, insert a diskette in this drive before entering this command.

C: [ENTER] makes C: the current drive. Because C: is usually a hard disk drive, you do not have to worry about diskettes here.

If you enter only the drive letter but leave off the colon, DOS will not understand you, so make sure you enter both.

DOS Prompt

Usually, the current drive is shown by the first letter of your DOS prompt. DOS displays the **DOS prompt** on your screen whenever it is ready for your commands. A simple DOS prompt looks like this:
C>

All About Directories

DOS stores its information in files -- collections of related information -- on your disk drives or diskettes. Different types of files contain, naturally enough, different types of information. For now, just think of a file as containing either a program or data needed for a program.

Directories Contain Files

DOS keeps its files in directories that act like file drawers. Directories let you group related files so you can put similar files in one place. For example, you can put all your accounting programs in a directory called **pca** (for Peachtree Complete Accounting).

Besides helping you keep things straight, using different directories for your files reduces the time it takes DOS to find the files. This is a good reason to keep all your DOS commands and programs in a directory of their own.

Directories Contain Directories Too

Just as a file drawer may also contain dividers that separate groups of related files, directories may also contain other directories. In turn, these directories can contain files and even directories of their own. *Any directory can contain files, other directories, or a combination of both.* It is up to you.

Subdirectories

When a directory is contained inside another directory, it is called a **subdirectory**. You need not worry about the distinction between a directory and a subdirectory; you can call a directory whatever you like as long as you know how it works. DOS uses a backwards slash, the "backslash" character (\), as shorthand for the root directory. (Locate the character on your computer's keyboard.)

Peachtree Complete Accounting uses directories to keep track of your PCA information. For example, unless you tell it otherwise, PCA:

- Puts all the PCA programs in a directory called **PCA**.
- Puts all the General Ledger data in the **xxGLDATA** subdirectory (where xx is the company ID) inside the **PCA** directory.
- Puts all the Accounts Receivable data in the **xxARDATA** subdirectory inside the **PCA** directory.
- Puts all Accounts Payable data in the **xxAPDATA** subdirectory inside the **PCA** directory.
- Puts all the Inventory data in the **xxINDATA** subdirectory inside the **PCA** directory.
- Puts all the Payroll data in the **xxPRDATA** subdirectory inside the **PCA** directory.
- Puts all the Fixed Assets data in the **xxFADATA** subdirectory inside the **PCA** directory.

The DOS Directory Structure

DOS connects directories together in a particular way. The DOS directory structure looks something like this:

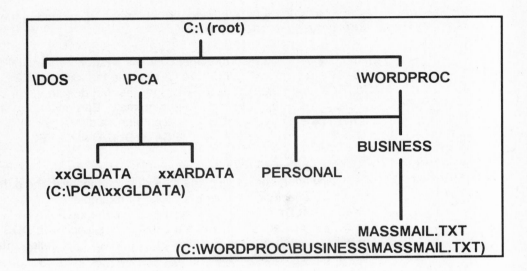

Like so many other things in DOS, the name for this directory structure depends on what book or computer manual you read. Common names for this layout include: **tree-structured directory, multi-leveled structure,** or **hierarchical structure**.

An Upside-down Tree

Imagine the directory structure as an upside-down tree.

- At the top of the structure is the root directory -- **C:** -- the root of the tree. The **root directory** is the main directory on any hard disk or diskette. You never create this directory; it appears when you first prepare the disk for use by DOS.

- Moving down the structure, we see directories in the root directory -- such as **\DOS, \PCA,** and **\WORDPROC** -- the main branches of the tree. (Remember that the backslash is used for directories.)

- In turn, these directories contain other directories -- such as **xxGLDATA** and **xxARDATA** which are offshoots from the main branch **\PCA**.

Any directory may contain files -- such as **MASSMAIL.TXT** -- the twigs or leaves on the tree.

Using Paths to Tell DOS Where to Look

You can tell DOS where a given file or directory is by telling it what branches to follow from the root (top) of the tree. When you do this, you're using a **path** to give DOS directions. It is as if you are telling DOS to "go down this street three blocks, take a left at the stoplight, and turn into the big parking lot on your right."

Some Examples

For example, if the **PCA** directory is a directory contained in the root directory, you refer to it as **\PCA**.

In the diagram, the **PCA** directory contains a (sub)directory called **xxGLDATA**. The **\PCA\xxGLDATA** refers to the **xxGLDATA** directory. The first backslash stands for the root directory; the second backslash separates directory names. Carrying it one step further: if the directory **xxGLDATA** contained a directory called **NOTES**, you would refer to it as **\PCA\xxGLDATA\NOTES**.

Being Explicit with DOS

The foregoing examples presume the directories are on the current drive. However, you can include a disk drive along with the path to completely specify a location to DOS. For example, **C:\PCA\xxGLDATA** tells DOS exactly where the **xxGLDATA** directory is located. Here, you are being very explicit with DOS: you are telling it to start at the root directory (\) of drive **C:**, follow it to the **PCA** directory, and then look for the **xxGLDATA** directory.

Specifying a File

Telling DOS about a file merely extends this idea. From the diagram you can see that the complete path to the **MASSMAIL.TXT** file is **C:\WORDPROC\BUSINESS\MASSMAIL.TXT**. As always, the first backslash represents the root directory and the remaining ones serve as separators. In this case, the last backslash separates a directory name from a file name.

In some computer manuals, you will see this way of completely specifying a file represented as:

DRIVE: PATH FILE.EXT

The useful thing about drive names and paths is that they let you tell DOS to perform commands on specific disk drives, directories, and files regardless of your location.

The Current Directory

Just as DOS has a current drive it uses if you do not tell it what drive to use, DOS also has a current directory. In a way, the current drive and current directory are just two aspects of the same thing: DOS's current location. The **current directory** is the directory DOS uses when you do not tell it which directory to use. You can think of this as the directory in which you're located. Some people call this directory the **default directory** or the **working directory**. All three names mean the same thing.

What happens if you tell DOS to do something but do not tell it which drive or directory to use? DOS applies the operation to the current drive and the current directory.

Changing the Current Directory

You can change the current directory whenever you want. To change the current directory, type **CD** (for Change Directory) and a directory name. Then press . For example, typing:

CD\DOS

changes the current directory to a directory called **DOS** in the root (\) directory.

Seeing the Current Directory

You can also use the CD command to find out the current directory. To have DOS display the current directory, type:

CD

Viewing a Directory's Contents

The DOS command DIR lets you see what files and/or directories are contained in a directory. If you type:

DIR

DOS displays the contents of your current directory. You can think of a directory as a location, that is, "a place where files and other directories reside." Or, you can think of a directory as "a listing of files and directories." You will probably encounter both of these meanings. Both are valid.

Directory Names

Directory names can be up to eight characters long and can contain letters, numbers, and some punctuation characters. You should use meaningful names and restrict yourself to using only letters and numbers; avoiding punctuation and other special characters keeps things simple. DOS lets you enter directory names in uppercase letters, lowercase letters, or a mixture of both.

DOS File Names

Like directories, files have names too. DOS files have first names and last names. The first name is usually called the **file name**. The last name, called the **extension** or **suffix**, is optional. If you use an extension, it is always separated from the first name by a period (.) character. An example is **RESULTS.RPT**. File names and extensions never have spaces in them.

File Extensions
File extensions help identify the type of file. For example, DOS knows the **.EXE** and **.COM** extensions indicate program files that can be run directly by DOS and the extension **.BAT** indicates a batch file.

A file extension typically reflects the type of data a file contains. Peachtree Complete Accounting's data files, for example, have extensions that start with **.D** or **.K** and end with the company ID. This book uses a sample business called W. D. Peachtree & Company, whose ID is **WD**. PCA uses **.DWD** and **.KWD** as the extension for this company's data files. As another example of an extension, most of PCA's program files use the **.RTM** extension (for "run time module").

Meaningful Names
Whenever you create or name a file, try to use meaningful file names and extensions. Ask yourself this question: "If I see this file eight months from now, will I know what's in the file from the file name and extension?"

The Bottom Line
Taken together, directory names, file names, and extensions can provide a lot of useful information about your files. Since files tend to accumulate over time, this can really help you in your day-to-day work.

Some Useful DOS Commands

This section shows you how to use some DOS commands you may find particularly useful.

Through examples, you will see common usage for these DOS commands. All possible variations are not covered. See your DOS manual for an in-depth discussion of these commands and for other commands not addressed here.

Four Types Four types of commands are discussed in this section:

1. **System commands** are a group of miscellaneous commands, such as DATE and TIME, that do not affect your files or disk.

2. **Directory commands** let you see, create, move among, and delete directories.

3. **File commands** let you list, copy, delete, and rename files.

4. **Disk commands** let you prepare new disks, copy the contents of entire diskettes, and verify a disk's integrity.

First, some odds and ends about using DOS commands need to be mentioned.

Tips for Using DOS Commands

**Remember Your
Current Drive
and Directory**

As you know, DOS applies its commands to the current drive and directory unless told otherwise. Do not lose track of your current drive and current directory. If you are not where you think you are, DOS may surprise you when you give it commands based on your current drive and directory.

PROMPT is a System Command that sets your DOS prompt to always show your location. For more explanation of how to use PROMPT, consult your DOS manual.

**Telling DOS
What You Need**

Depending on the circumstances, you may need to tell DOS about a drive, directory, file and extension name, or all of these. Include whatever it takes to make things clear to DOS. See the DOS Directory Structure section of your DOS manual for details on how to do this.

DOS Search Path

Make sure your DOS search path is set correctly. If it isn't, DOS may have trouble finding and running your executable (program, command, and batch) files. (See PATH, a system command, in your DOS manual for details.)

**Uppercase and
Lowercase**

DOS doesn't care if you use uppercase letters, lowercase letters, or a mixture of both. This applies to the names of commands, programs, batch files, disk drives, files, and directories.

System Commands

The commands we describe in this section let you define and customize your DOS working environment:

- DATE -- Sets the date on your system.

- TIME -- Sets the time on your system.

- PATH -- Defines the DOS search path DOS uses to find programs and commands when it can't find them in the current directory.

- PROMPT -- Tells DOS what information to include in your DOS prompt.

- SET -- Shows you the current setting for the DOS search path and for your DOS prompt.

To some extent, these commands all affect the way your system works but they do not do anything significant to your disk drives, directories, or files. If you want to learn more about these system commands, consult your DOS manual.

Directory Commands

The five commands described here let you work with directories:

- DIR -- lets you see the contents of a directory.
- TREE -- shows you the names of all the directories on your system.
- MKDIR or MD -- lets you make (create) a directory.
- CHDIR or CD -- lets you change your current directory.
- RMDIR or RD -- lets you remove (delete) a directory.

DIR

What it does This command lets you examine the contents of a directory. It also tells you how much disk space is available for storage.

What DIR Shows You For each file or directory, the DIR command shows:

- The name of the file or directory.
- For files, any extension is shown. DOS does not display the period that separates the file name from the extension name. Instead, it leaves a space for the period in the directory listing.
- For directories, <DIR> follows the directory's name.
- For files, the size of the file, in bytes, follows the file name. It takes approximately one byte of memory to store one character.
- For directories, the date and time indicate when the directory was created.
- For files, the date and time indicate when the file was created or last modified.

Finally, DIR tells you how many files are listed (it counts directories as files) and tells you how many bytes are available on the disk being examined.

How It Works To look at a listing of the current directory's contents, type:

dir [ENTER]

To look at the contents of a directory other than the current one, follow **dir** with a directory name and press [ENTER]. You can also include a drive name when specifying a directory if the directory you want is not on the current drive.

Here are some examples:

dir \ ⌨

tells DOS to report on the root directory of the current drive.

dir A: ⌨

tells DOS to report on the current directory of drive A:

dir \PCA\xxGLDATA ⌨

tells DOS to report on the **xxGLDATA** directory contained in the **PCA** directory on the current drive where xx is the company ID.

Long and Wide Directory Listings

There are two useful variations on the DIR command. The first one helps out when you have a lot of files in the directory by preventing the file names from scrolling off the screen. If you type:

dir C: /P ⌨

it tells DOS to report on the current directory of drive C: and to pause (/P) between each screen's worth of information. When it pauses, DOS asks you to:

Strike a key when ready . . .

Press any handy key (such as the space bar) and DOS displays more of the directory listing.

If you have a lot of files in a directory and just want to examine the names of the files, you can type:

dir C: /W ⌨

Here, DOS reports on the current directory of drive C: but only displays file and extension names. It also uses a wide (**/W**) format -- five columns -- to display these names.

TREE

What it does   The TREE command lets you look at your directory "tree". Remember the diagram of the tree-structured directory in the first part of this chapter. The TREE command shows you all the directories that make up your directory tree.

How It Works   Look at your directory tree by typing **tree** and pressing ⏎.

tree ⏎

DOS displays the directory tree of the current drive.

MKDIR (MD)

What It Does   The MKDIR command (for MaKe DIRectory) lets you make or create a new directory. You can abbreviate this command as MD if you like.

How It Works   Create a new directory by typing **mkdir** (or **md**) followed by the name of the directory you want to create and pressing ⎆. For example, typing:

mkdir batch ⎆

creates a directory called **batch** in the current directory of the current drive.

DOS lets you create directories anywhere in its directory structure (not just in the current directory) and on any of your drives (not just the current drive). For example:

md B:\letters\acme ⎆

creates a directory called **acme** in the **\letters** directory of the **B:** drive. Notice that we used **md** -- the shorter form of MKDIR.

A Few Tips   Directory names can be up to eight characters long and contain letters, numbers, and some punctuation characters. Keep things simple by avoiding punctuation and other special characters.

Select meaningful names when you create directories. For example, create a directory called **budget** for your budget files. Resist using directory names like **dir2** and **dir3** since they don't indicate a directories contents.

CHDIR (CD)

What it does The CHDIR command (for CHange DIRectory) lets you change your current directory or have DOS display the name of your current directory. You can abbreviate CHDIR as CD if you like.

How It Works To change your current directory, type **chdir** (or **CD**) followed by a directory name, and press [ENTER]. For example:

> **chdir ** [ENTER]

changes your current directory to the root directory of the current drive and:

> **cd \PCA\xxARDATA** [ENTER]

changes your current directory to **xxARDATA** in **\PCA** on the current drive where xx is your company ID.

You can include a drive name if you want to change the current directory for a drive other than the current one. For example:

> **chdir C:\PCA** [ENTER]

changes the current directory to **\PCA** on the **C:** drive. If the current drive is C:, the above command is fine; it just is not necessary to enter the drive if it is the current drive.

To find out what your current directory is, type:

> **cd** [ENTER]

You can also ask DOS what the current directory is on another drive. For example, if you are on drive **A:** and can not remember your current directory on C:, type:

> **cd C:** [ENTER]

DOS responds with the current directory of drive C:.

RMDIR (RD)

What It Does   The RMDIR command (for ReMove DIRectory) removes a directory from your disk. You can abbreviate RMDIR as RD if you want. Deleting directories is serious business. Treat this command accordingly.

First Things First   Before removing a directory, you have to remove all the files and/or directories it contains. The directory *must* be empty before DOS lets you remove it. Make sure that you either have backups of these files or do not need them anymore. When you are ready to remove all the files from the directory -- perhaps after saving them on a diskette -- use the DEL (for DELete) command to remove the files. You should also know that DOS will not let you remove the current directory.

> **Warning:** Use extreme care when using this command. Unless you are thoroughly familiar with DOS, you probably should not use this command at all.

File Commands

These commands let you work with files on your disk:

- **TYPE** -- displays the contents of a file on your screen.
- **COPY** -- lets you make copies of one or more files.
- **DEL** or **ERASE** -- lets you delete or erase one or more files.
- **RENAME** or **REN** -- lets you rename a file.

You can also effectively "move" one or more files by copying them somewhere and then deleting the originals.

File names and wildcards will be discussed next before getting to the command descriptions.

File Names and Wildcards

Telling DOS about Files

Whenever you use the DOS file commands, you need to tell DOS with which files to work. You can tell DOS about files in directories other than the current directory or on drives other than the current drive by including drive and/or directory names along with file names.

When you specify files to DOS, you must provide complete file and extension names. One way to fill this requirement is by using DOS wildcards.

DOS Wildcards

Wildcards give you a shorthand way to tell DOS to perform some action on an entire group of files. DOS provides two "wildcards" to let you specify groups of files -- the asterisk (*) and the question mark (?). These wildcards let you easily copy, delete, or get statistics (with DIR) on a set of files.

DOS wildcards replace characters in file names. This works with both file names and extension names as the following examples illustrate.

Assume you have the following files:

> budget92.rpt
> budget93.rpt
> budget92.act
> budget93.act
> buddy
> current.rpt
> update.act

The * Wildcard   Given these files:

- The file name **bud*.*** matches all files starting with **bud** and ending with anything (with or without an extension). This matches the first five files (**budget92.rpt** through **buddy**).

- The file name ***.rpt** matches all files that have **.rpt** as an extension. This includes **budget92.rpt**, **budget93.rpt**, and **current.rpt**.

- The file name **budg*.act** matches all files that begin with **budg** and have the **.act** extension. This includes **budget92.act** and **budget93.act**.

- The file name ***.*** matches all files in the current directory of the current drive. Because ***.*** may affect a large number of files, you should be *very careful when you use it.*

Thus, the asterisk replaces any **number** of characters from its location to the end of the file name or extension name. It is wild for any set of related characters.

The ? Wildcard   Using the same files as examples, here are some illustrations of the **?** wildcard:

- The file name **budget9?.rpt** matches all files starting with **budget9**, followed by any single character and ending with **.rpt**. This matches **budget92.rpt** and **budget93.rpt**.

- The file name **budget?3.???** matches all files that start with **budget**, followed by any single character, followed by a **3**, followed by any three-character extension. This matches **budget93.rpt** and **budget93.act**.

Thus, the question mark replaces any **single** character that is in the same position in the file or extension name. It is wild for any single character.

Using * and ?
Together

You can use these wildcard characters together. Using the same list of files:

- The file name budget?3.* matches all files starting with budget, followed by any single character, followed by a 3, followed by any extension. This matches budget93.rpt and budget93.act. Notice the similarity to the budget?3.??? file name used earlier. The previous example matched only three-character extensions but this file name matches any size extensions and even matches files without an extension.

Where Wildcards are Useful

Using Wildcards
to Copy Files

One common use for wildcards is to copy a set of files. If, in the sample files listed above, you want to copy all the report (**.rpt**) files to a diskette in drive A:, just tell DOS to:

copy *.rpt A: ⌨ENTER

DOS obediently looks in the current directory on the current drive, finds all files with the **.rpt** extension, and copies them to the specified diskette.

Using Wildcards
to List Files

You will also find wildcards useful when you want to get a directory listing of selected files. For example, typing:

dir *.?WD ⌨ENTER

tells DOS to list all the files in the current directory that use the company ID **WD** as the last two characters of the extension. If your current directory is **\PCA\PCDATA**, this command lists all the sample files for the imaginary company, W. D. Peachtree & Company.

As always, DOS looks for all files specified by wildcards in the current directory of the current drive unless you tell it otherwise. Now, on to the file commands.

COPY

What it Does   The COPY command lets you copy your files from place to place: from one directory to another or from one disk drive to another.

How it Works   When you use the COPY command, you copy files from a source to a destination. Generally, it looks something like this:

        COPY *source destination*

Let's look at some examples before we get into other details.

- To copy a single file, called **alpha.txt** from the current directory of the current drive to the current directory of the diskette in drive A:, type:

    copy alpha.txt A: ⏎

- To copy all the files with the **.txt** extension from the current directory of the current drive to the current directory of the diskette in drive A:, type:

    copy *.txt A: ⏎

- To copy the file **beta.txt** from the **\DOCU** directory of drive B: (not the current drive) to the root directory of the diskette in drive A:, type:

    copy B:\DOCU\beta.txt A: ⏎

- To copy the same file as above to the same place, but to rename the copy on A: to **alpha.txt**, type:

    copy B:\DOCU\beta.txt A:\alpha.txt ⏎

- To copy all the files in the current directory of the diskette in drive A: to the directory **TOYS** located in the root directory of the current drive, type:

    copy A:*.* \TOYS ⏎

Some Details   You can see from these examples that COPY is a flexible command. For both the **source** and **destination** parts of the COPY command, you can completely specify a file using:

drive: path file.ext

but it makes more sense and saves typing to give DOS only as much information as it needs.

Remember that the *source* part of the command specifies one or more files to be copied and the *destination* part of the command generally specifies a location. If you're copying only one file, you can include a file and extension name in the **destination** part to give the copy of the file a different name.

Whenever you copy a group of files using wildcards, DOS displays the name of each file it copies as it performs the operation.

Watch Out for   As with so many DOS commands, it is important to keep track of
This   your current drive and current directory. If you forget "where" you are, DOS may surprise you when you tell it to copy files based on your current drive and directory.

To sidestep problems like this, avoid using *.* with COPY unless you are in the directory and on the drive from which you want to copy the files.

DEL or Erase

What it Does   The DEL (for DELete) or ERASE command deletes (removes) files from your disk. You may want to use this command to delete certain PCA files that are no longer needed such as old report files and old "generations" of Payroll.

Always take a moment to consider the consequences before you delete files and then enter the command carefully. Although you can buy software that helps you recover deleted files, DOS doesn't provide any commands to do so. Generally, once you delete a file, it is gone forever.

How it Works   Delete a file by typing **del** (or **erase**) followed by a file and extension name and pressing ⏎. For example, typing:

> **del oldnotes.txt** ⏎

deletes the **oldnotes.txt** file from the current directory of the current drive and:

> **erase B:\LETTERS\oldnotes.txt** ⏎

removes a file of the same name from the **\LETTERS** directory of the **B:** drive.

Using Wildcards   You can specify files using wildcards with the DEL (ERASE) command. For example:

> **del C:\LETTERS*.txt** ⏎

deletes all the files in the **\LETTERS** directory of the **C:** drive that contain the **.txt** extension. DOS does not ask you to confirm the operation before deleting the files.

Note: *Take care when using wildcards with the DEL (ERASE) command;* it can quickly erase a large number of files. A simple typing mistake here can ruin your entire day.

Check the
Directory First

Before using DEL (ERASE) with a wildcard, you should first enter a DIR command using the same wildcard pattern. This step will allow you to look at the files you will delete in the next step. This is a safety procedure that you can use to make sure you delete only those files you mean to delete.

The files (but not directories) listed by that DIR command will be deleted next by a DEL command that uses the same wildcard pattern. For example, you should enter:

dir C:\LETTERS*.txt ⏎

to look at all the files that will be deleted by the command:

del C:\LETTERS*.txt ⏎

before you enter the DEL command. This technique protects you *only* if you type in exactly the same location and wildcard pattern in both cases.

A Lethal
Example

A more lethal use of wildcards is *.* since it matches *every* file in a directory. For example, if you type:

del *.* ⏎

DOS prompts you:

Are you sure (Y/N)?

to make sure you really want to do this. If you confirm by typing **Y** and pressing ⏎, DOS deletes *all* the files from the current directory of the current drive *regardless of their file or extension name.* (If you answer **N** to the DOS prompt, DOS does not do anything.)

You will find this wildcard combination useful when you want to delete all the files in a directory, perhaps when you are intending to remove the directory.

Warning: Because *.* affects *all* the files in a given directory, it should be used with the utmost care. Unless you are thoroughly familiar with DOS, you should probably avoid typing *.* with the DEL command.

Giving DEL a
Directory Name

Another way to use the DEL (ERASE) command to remove all the files in a directory is to specify a directory along with the command. For example, to remove all the files from a directory called **OLDSTUFF** in the root directory of your current drive, type:

del \OLDSTUFF ⏎

As before, DOS prompts you to confirm the operation before it actually removes the files.

RENAME (REN)

What it Does The RENAME command lets you change the name of a file. You can abbreviate this command as REN if you like.

How it Works Rename a file by typing **rename** (or **ren**), followed by the original name and new name of the file and pressing [ENTER]. For example, typing:

rename oldnotes.txt newnotes.txt [ENTER]

changes the name of the **oldnotes.txt** file in the current directory of the current drive to **newnotes.txt**.

As always, you can specify a drive and directory. For example, typing:

ren C:\config.sav config.sys [ENTER]

renames **config.sav** (the saved version of your configuration file) in the root directory of **C:** to **config.sys**. Notice in this example:

- If a file named config.sys exists before you run this command, you must delete or rename that file before you can use its name for another file. If you are intending to replace the file anyway, this is just as well.

- For the new name, you need only supply the file and extension name, not the drive or directory. You do not need to specify a location for the new name because DOS does not use it.

If the File Already Exists As we mentioned above, DOS does not let you rename a file to a name already being used. If you tell DOS to use a name that's already assigned, it says:

Duplicate file name or File not found

to remind you that you can not use the same name twice.

"Moving" Files

DOS does not provide an explicit "move" command. However, you can effectively move files by copying them to a different location and then deleting them from the original location.

Disk Commands

The commands we cover here let you work with disk drives and diskettes:

- FORMAT -- lets you prepare disks for use by DOS.
- DISKCOPY -- lets you make copies of disks.
- CHKDSK -- lets you check the integrity of a disk and find out how much storage space is used and available.

For ease of discussion, both hard disks and diskettes are referred to as "disks" in this section. More precise terms will be used when needed.

FORMAT

What it Does

The FORMAT command prepares a hard disk or diskette so that DOS can use it for files and directories. When FORMAT runs, it also looks for defective areas and, if it finds any, marks them as unusable.

Note: You should know that the FORMAT command *destroys any existing data on the disk* being formatted. You should never use this command with any disk that has data you want to use.

Sizes and Densities

Because the FORMAT command lets you prepare a wide assortment of disks for use with DOS, all the possibilities are not covered here. Consult your DOS manual for details on formatting disks and diskettes that are not discussed here.

Diskettes come in different sizes (like 5 1/4" and 3 1/2") and in different densities, measured in kilobytes or megabytes.

A **kilobyte** is 1024 bytes (though some people use the term loosely to refer to 1000 bytes) and is often abbreviated as "K" or "Kb." A "360K" diskette holds 360 kilobytes -- over 360,000 characters.

A **megabyte** is roughly one million (actually 1,048,576) bytes and is often abbreviated as "Mb" or "M." A "1.44Mb" diskette holds about one and a half million bytes.

DOS knows what density is standard for a diskette in any given disk drive. If you tell DOS to FORMAT a 5 1/4" diskette in a 360K drive by only specifying the drive, DOS tries to FORMAT that diskette as a 360K diskette. If your diskette drive uses 3 1/2" diskettes with a density of 720K, then DOS tries to FORMAT a diskette in that drive as a 720K diskette. You should find out what type of diskette you will be using in this course.

How it Works   Format a diskette by placing the diskette in your disk drive, typing **format** followed by the drive name, and pressing ![ENTER]. For example, typing:

> **format A:** ![ENTER]

formats the diskette in drive A: to the default density and

> **format B:** ![ENTER]

does the same thing according to the density of the B: drive.

Warning: Be extremely careful when typing in the command to format a disk. If, when entering a FORMAT command, you accidentally enter the drive name for your hard disk, all of the information on that disk will be destroyed. This is the most dangerous of all the DOS commands.

Formatting for Different Densities   If you have a high-density disk drive, read the next few paragraphs; if you don't, skip to the next section.

We consider a **high-density disk** drive to be one which uses:

- 5 1/4" diskettes (1.2Mb diskettes).
- 3 1/2" diskettes (1.44 Mb diskettes).

If you have one of these high-density drives, you may encounter the need to format lower-density diskettes on it. Also, DISKCOPY only lets you copy between diskettes of the same density, which means that you must format lower-density diskettes before you can make working copies of the distribution diskettes.

These commands let you format lower-density diskettes on high-density drives.

5 1/4" Diskettes

To format a 5 1/4" diskette that holds 360K on drive A:, type:

- **FORMAT A: /4** ![ENTER].
  or
- for DOS 4.0 or later: **FORMAT A: /F:360** ![ENTER]

3 1/2" Diskettes

To format a 3 1/2" diskette that holds 720K on drive B:, type:

- **FORMAT B: /N:9 /T:80** ![ENTER].
  or
- for DOS 4.0 or later: **FORMAT B: /F:720** ![ENTER]

DISKCOPY

What it Does
The DISKCOPY command lets you make a copy of an entire diskette. This command only works on diskettes, not on hard disks. DISKCOPY also will automatically format a disk that has not already been formatted.

Note: DISKCOPY *destroys all* information on the diskette to which you are copying. Make sure you don't need the information on this diskette before making the copy.

How it Works
To copy the contents of an entire diskette from drive A: to a diskette in drive B:, type:

diskcopy A: B:

If the diskette in drive B: is not formatted, DOS formats the diskette before attempting to copy information to it. By the way, typing:

diskcopy

is equivalent to the above command except that DOS asks you to insert the diskettes to copy to and from instead of expecting them to be there.

With a Single Diskette Drive
If you only have one diskette drive, DOS sometimes treats it as drive A: and sometimes treats it as drive B:. This allows you to copy files between diskettes with only one diskette drive.

When you tell DOS to perform a DISKCOPY from A: to B:, it prompts you to insert diskette A: in the diskette drive. DOS then reads information from A: into memory and asks you to remove A: (the original diskette) and:

Insert diskette for drive B: and strike any key when ready

When you replace diskette A: with B: (the diskette to which you are copying) and press a key, DOS writes the information from memory onto the second diskette (B:).

CHKDSK

What it Does   The CHKDSK command (for CHeck DiSK) inspects the integrity of a disk (or diskette) and provides useful statistics about it, including:

- The total amount of space on the disk.
- The number of files present.
- The number of any bad sectors found on the disk.
- The amount of available space on the disk.
- The total amount of memory and available amount of memory on your computer.

We find CHKDSK particularly useful for finding out how much available memory you have to run programs.

How it Works   To use this command, type **chkdsk** followed by a drive name and press ⏎. For example:

> **chkdsk C:** ⏎

checks and tells you about drive C: and:

> **chkdsk A:** ⏎

does the same thing for the diskette in drive A:. If you enter:

> **chkdsk** ⏎

without providing a drive name, DOS performs the disk check on the current drive.

Bad Sectors   If the CHKDSK command indicates more than a few bad sectors on your disk, it may indicate damage to your files as well as potentially serious hardware problems. We can't help you here with problems of this nature; please contact your hardware vendor or your local PC expert for help.
